MEN SPEAK OUT

Men Speak Out: Views on Gender, Sex, and Power, Second Edition highlights new essays on pornography, pop culture, queer identity, Muslim masculinity, and the war on women. With personal candor and political insight, this collection of diverse authors explores sex work, digital activism, incarceration, domestic violence, surviving incest, and standing firmly as male allies facing the backlash against women's reproductive rights.

Featuring eleven new essays and six revised thematic sections, this second edition of a favorite anthology continues to encourage robust discussion and vibrant debate about masculinity and the possibilities for progressive change. The contemporary, compelling essays in *Men Speak Out* appeal to students, scholars, activists, and everyday readers.

Shira Tarrant is an Associate Professor in the Department of Women's, Gender, and Sexuality Studies at California State University, Long Beach. Her earlier successful book, *When Sex Became Gender*, was published by Routledge in 2006.

MEN SPEAK OUT

Views on Gender, Sex, and Power

Second Edition

Shira Tarrant

Routledge
Taylor & Francis Group

NEW YORK AND LONDON

Second edition published 2013
by Routledge
711 Third Avenue, New York, NY 10017

Simultaneously published in the UK
by Routledge
2 Park Square, Milton Park, Abingdon, Oxon OX14 4RN

Routledge is an imprint of the Taylor & Francis Group, an informa business

First edition published by Routledge 2008

Library of Congress Cataloging in Publication Data
Men speak out: views on gender, sex and power/edited by Shira
Tarrant;
foreword by Jackson Katz.
      p. cm.
  1. Sex role—Philosophy. 2. Feminist theory—History.
  3. Sex differences (Psychology) I. Tarrant, Shira, 1963–
  II. Katz, Jackson.
  HQ1075.M46 2007
  305.42081—dc22   2007018015

ISBN: 978–0–415–52107–9 (hbk)
ISBN: 978–0–415–52108–6 (pbk)
ISBN: 978–0–203–07678–1 (ebk)

Typeset in Abode Caslon
by Keystroke, Station Road, Codsall, Wolverhampton

CONTENTS

List of Contributors		ix
Editor's Acknowledgments		xix
Foreword		xxi
Jackson Katz		

Introduction		1
Shira Tarrant		

PART I: MASCULINITY AND IDENTITY — 9

Introduction — 11

1 Daytona Beach: Beyond Beats and Rhymes — 21
Byron Hurt

2 The Enemy Within: On Becoming a Straight White Guy — 28
Jacob Anderson-Minshall

3 The Bullying Demands of Masculinity: A Genderqueer Escape — 34
River Willow Fagan.

4 Redefining Manhood: Resisting Sexism — 39
Ewuare X. Osayande

5 Stepping Out of Bounds — 43
Nathan Einschlag

6 Grooming Masculinity: Cleans Your Balls, Yes. But What
   Else Does It Do?   47
   Michael J. Murphy

7 Searching for the Colorful Faces of Muslim Men   53
   Amanullah De Sondy

8 *Hombres y Machos*   58
   Alfredo Mirandé

PART II: THE POLITICS OF SEX AND LOVE   67

   Introduction   69

9 Just a John? Pornography and Men's Choices   74
   Robert Jensen

10 Male and Queer in the Porn Industry   80
   Ned Mayhem

11 Bye-Bye Bi? Bailey, Biphobia, and Girlie-Men   87
   Marcus C. Tye

12 Darker Shades of Queer: Race and Sexuality at the Margins   94
   C. Winter Han

13 Let Us Be Seen: Gay Visibility in Homophobic Poland   102
   Tomek Kitlinski and Pawel Leszkowicz

14 The Real Slim Shady   106
   Ryan Heryford

PART III: DEALING WITH VIOLENCE AND ABUSE   113

   Introduction   115

15 How We Enter: Men, Gender, and Sexual Assault   123
   B. Loewe

16 An Abused State of Mind   128
   Anonymous

17 Prison Breakthrough   135
   A. Razor

18 Men's Manifesto 2012   144
    Ben Atherton-Zeman

19 Violation   148
    Eli Hastings

20 Breaking the Silence One Mile at a Time   153
    Grantlin Schafer

21 Being a Social Justice Ally: A Feminist's Perspective on
    Preventing Male Violence   156
    Jonathan Ravarino

PART IV: MASCULINITY AT WORK AND HOME   165

    Introduction   167

22 Rebuilding Houses and Rethinking Gender: Construction
    Volunteer Work in Post-Katrina New Orleans   175
    Ian Breckenridge-Jackson

23 Exposed in Iraq: Sexual Harassment and Hidden Rank
    Structure of the U.S. Army   181
    Marshall Thompson

24 Gender in Jakarta: Lessons on Discourse and Disparity   188
    Bryan Talbot Morris

25 Listening, Learning, Speaking Up   193
    Daniel Simon

26 A Tribute to My Father   197
    Chris Dixon

27 Playground Vertigo   203
    Jeremy Adam Smith

28 Judging Fathers: The Case for Gender-Neutral Standards   207
    Donald N.S. Unger

29 What's Wrong with Fathers' Rights?   213
    Michael Flood

PART V: MEN AND FEMINISM   221

    Introduction   223

30 It's Just Common Sense   232
    Brandon Arber

31 Why I Am Not a Feminist   234
    Haji Shearer

32 The Starbucks Intervention   239
    Greg Bortnichak

33 From Oppressor to Activist: Reflections of a Feminist Journey 243
    Amit Taneja

34 Abandoning the Barricades: or How I Became a Feminist   252
    Michael S. Kimmel

35 Confessions of a Premature Pro-Feminist   263
    Rob Okun

PART VI: TAKING ACTION, MAKING CHANGE   271

    Introduction   273

36 Men for Women's Choice   277

37 Living Online   280
    Jeff Pollet

38 Steel-Toed Boots   288
    Tal Peretz

39 Good Ol' Boy: A Tale of Transformation in the Rural South   295
    Jay Poole

40 Breaking Down the Bro Code   299
    Thomas Keith

41 How Can I Be Sexist? I'm an Anarchist!   305
    Chris Crass

    Bibliography   315
    Index   323

CONTRIBUTORS

Jacob Anderson-Minshall has been many things in his life, including carny, farm boy, park ranger, magazine founder, and a woman. After eighteen years as a butch-identified lesbian, he transitioned to male, but hasn't quite resolved his issues about becoming the enemy: the "straight," white guy. Jacob authored the syndicated column "TransNation" that ran in queer publications from San Francisco to Boston. With his wife Diane, he co-authors the Blind Eye Detectives mystery series that premiered with *Blind Curves* (Bold Strokes Books).

Anonymous had a happy, normal childhood with a whole lotta weirdness thrown in. Due to his traumatic experiences he has blocked out a lot of his childhood. His therapist said that was self-protection kicking in, shielding him from bad things so he could cope and deal with the reality of his growing up. Now, still growing up, for the first time he has written about this experience and begun the work of retelling his life's stories over and over, until he can remember it all and be free.

Brandon Arber is an attorney practicing in Boston, Massachusetts. He graduated from Boston College Law School. In college, Brandon was captain of the men's swim team. He majored in political science and graduated with honors.

Ben Atherton-Zeman is a spokesperson for the National Organization for Men Against Sexism and the author of "Voices of Men" (www.voicesofmen. org), an educational comedy about men's violence against women. His email is benazeman@hotmail.com.

Greg Bortnichak resides in Sarasota, Florida, with his partner Erin Murphy. Together they run Finch House records and tour the world playing music. When he is not working with pro-feminist, queer-positive bands such as Bard and Mustache, Sparta Philharmonic, Richard Cortez, and Circa Survive, Greg enjoys searching for gators in nearby retention ponds and comparison-shopping for sweet deals on cello bows.

Ian Breckenridge-Jackson is completing his PhD in sociology at the University of California, Riverside. He specializes in race, gender, and class inequality with an emphasis on social movements. Ian was awarded a National Science Foundation Graduate Fellowship and a grant from the University of California Center for New Racial Studies for his work studying activism and volunteerism in post-Katrina New Orleans. He is a co-founder of the Lower Ninth Ward Living Museum in New Orleans.

Chris Crass is a longtime organizer working to build powerful working-class-based, feminist, multiracial movements for collective liberation. Throughout the 1990s he was an organizer with Food Not Bombs, an economic justice, anti-poverty group, strengthening the direct-action, anti-capitalist political left. As part of the global justice movement, he helped start the Catalyst Project in 2000, and was a member of the leadership collective for eleven years. He is a stay-at-home dad, contributing to the power of the Occupy movement of the 99%. Chris is excited about his new book *Towards Collective Liberation: Anti-racist Organizing, Feminist Praxis, and Movement Building Strategy* (PM Press). He lives in Knoxville, Tennessee, with his partner and their son, River.

Amanullah De Sondy is Assistant Professor of Islamic Studies in the Department of Religious Studies at the University of Miami. Born and raised in Scotland to Pakistani parents, he holds a PhD in theology and religious studies from the University of Glasgow, Scotland. His main academic interest is gender and sexuality in classical/modern Islam, specifically Islamic masculinities. Aman has studied Arabic and Islamic Studies in France, Jordan, and Syria, and is proficient in the Urdu and Punjabi languages.

Chris Dixon, originally from Alaska, is a longtime activist, writer, and educator with a PhD from the University of California at Santa Cruz. His writing has appeared in five book collections and numerous periodicals, and he is currently completing a book based on interviews with anti-authoritarian organizers involved in broader-based movements. Dixon serves on the board of the Institute for Anarchist Studies and the advisory board for the activist journal, *Upping the Anti*. He lives in Sudbury, Ontario, Canada, where he is involved with the Sudbury Coalition Against Poverty. Contact him at chrisd@resist.ca.

Nathan Einschlag was born and raised in Jackson Heights, Queens, and graduated from a liberal arts college in Baltimore, Maryland, where he majored in elementary education and minored in theater. After living for two years in Shanghai, he now lives in New York City where he is completing a Masters Degree in Teaching English as a Second Language. Despite what happened on the basketball team, Nathan wants people to know that he appreciated his college experience and never once regretted choosing the school he did. Through college, he has met some truly inspiring people that have changed the course of his life for the better.

River Willow Fagan lives in Portland, Oregon. Their non-fiction appears in the anthology *Why Are Faggots So Afraid of Faggots?: Flaming Challenges to Masculinity, Objectification and the Desire to Conform* (AK Press); their fiction can be found in *The Year's Best Science Fiction and Fantasy 2011* (Prime Books). Fagan is also the author of several essays addressing queer sexual violence. They enjoy dancing, making vegetable stock, and carving the raw stuff of life into stories that can be used as tools to dismantle kyriarchy. You can find out more at willowfagan.livejournal.com.

Michael Flood is a researcher, educator, and activist. He is a Senior Lecturer in Sociology at the University of Wollongong, Australia, and his research addresses men's violence against women and its prevention, heterosexual men's sexualities, fathering, and pornography. Michael has had a long involvement in men's antiviolence work and profeminist activism more generally. He has worked with sporting organizations, community services, and governments, participated in international expert meetings, and contributed to social change campaigns. Michael is a co-editor of the *Routledge International Encyclopedia of Men and Masculinities* and he maintains the comprehensive online resource site on masculinities, http://xyonline.net.

C. Winter Han is an Assistant Professor of Sociology at Middlebury College where he teaches classes on race and ethnicity, sexuality and gender, and social psychology. A former journalist, his writings have appeared in over two dozen different publications.

Eli Hastings works in social services and the arts in Seattle where he is also pursuing an MA in psychology/family therapy. He holds an MFA from the University of North Carolina at Wilmington. His books include *Falling Room*, published in the American Lives Series at University of Nebraska Press, *Clearly Now, the Rain: A Friendship*, an elegy/memoir (ECW Press), and his agent is pushing a Young Adult thriller. He wins contests sometimes, has twice been nominated for a Pushcart, and has published in many anthologies and journals including *Cimarron Review*, *Third Coast*, and *YES! Magazine*. Eli is a nonfiction editor at *Cedars Literary* (www.cedarsmag.com) and he blogs (www.elihastings.com).

Ryan Heryford is completing his PhD in literature at the University of California, San Diego, where he focuses on varying forms of containment and spaces of alienation in early-twentieth-century American culture. When not working at the university, he can be found on tour with the experimental folk band, The Wild Geese.

Byron Hurt is an award-winning documentary filmmaker, published writer, anti-sexist activist, and lecturer. Byron is also the former host of the Emmy-nominated series, "Reel Works with Byron Hurt." *The Independent* named him one of the Top 10 Filmmakers to Watch in 2011. His most popular documentary, *Hip-Hop: Beyond Beats and Rhymes* (BBR) premiered at the Sundance Film Festival and was later broadcast on the PBS series *Independent Lens*. In 2010, MSNBC's *TheGrio.com* named BBR one of the Top 10 Most Important African-American Themed Films of the Decade. Byron's writing has been published in several anthologies and his work has been covered by the *New York Times, O Magazine, AllHipHop.com,* NPR, CNN, *Access Hollywood,* MTV, BET, *ABC News World Tonight, Black Enterprise,* C-Span, and many other outlets. Byron's latest film, *Soul Food Junkies,* airs nationally on PBS' Emmy award-winning series, *Independent Lens.* Learn more at www.bhurt.com. You can friend Byron on Facebook and you can also follow him on Twitter.

Robert Jensen, a journalism professor at the University of Texas at Austin, is the author of *Getting Off: Pornography and the End of Masculinity* (South End Press), and co-author of *Pornography: The Production and Consumption of Inequality* (Routledge). He can be reached at rjensen@uts.cc.utexas.edu.

Jackson Katz, PhD, is an educator, author, filmmaker and cultural theorist who is internationally recognized for his groundbreaking work in the fields of gender violence prevention education and critical media literacy. He has conducted hundreds of lectures and professional trainings in the United States, Canada, Europe, and Australia. He is the co-founder of the Mentors in Violence Prevention (MVP) program, the leading gender violence initiative in college and professional athletics, and is a key architect of the popular bystander approach to gender violence prevention. He founded the first worldwide domestic and sexual violence prevention program in the United States Marine Corps and has helped to develop and implement system-wide prevention programs in all the U.S. military services. Katz is also the creator and co-creator of educational videos including *Tough Guise, Wrestling with Manhood,* and *Spin the Bottle.* He is the author of *The Macho Paradox: Why Some Men Hurt Women and How All Men Can Help* (Sourcebooks) and *Leading Men: Presidential Campaigns and the Politics of Manhood* (Interlink).

Thomas Keith teaches philosophy at California State University, Long Beach and California Polytechnic University, Pomona. He specializes in American philosophy and pragmatism with an emphasis on issues of race, class, and gender. He directed and produced the bestselling film, *Generation M: Misogyny in Media & Culture*, which is used in classrooms around the world. Keith also directed and produced the film *The Bro Code: How Contemporary Culture Creates Sexist Men*. The author of a number of articles, Thomas Keith screens his films and facilitates discussions about issues of sexism to audiences around the United States.

Michael S. Kimmel, after completing his PhD in sociology at the University of California, Berkeley, taught at Rutgers, University of California at Santa Cruz, Berkeley, and State University of New York, Stony Brook, where he is currently Professor of Sociology. He has worked for the past two decades to build the subfield of masculinity studies—through teaching innovative courses, writing and editing books and articles, and founding and editing the scholarly journal *Men and Masculinities*. One of the founders of the National Organization for Men Against Sexism (NOMAS), he remains a spokesperson for the organization and lectures around the world encouraging men to support gender equality.

Tomek Kitlinski and **Pawel Leszkowicz** are partners in life and in artistic, academic, and activist projects in Poland. They lecture at the Universities of Lublin and Poznan, Poland. Kitlinski studied at Lublin's Curie University and with Julia Kristeva at the University of Paris 7. Leszkowicz studied at the University of Poznan and at the Courtauld Institute of Art in London. They have coordinated numerous queer and feminist projects and performance art events across Eastern Europe, including curating an international queer exhibition *Ars Homo Erotica* at Warsaw's National Museum. They were Fulbright Scholars at the New School for Social Research in New York. Currently, Leszkowicz is Marie Curie Fellow at the Centre for Sexual Dissidence at the University of Sussex. He curated *Love Is Love: Art as LGBTQ Activism* at Lublin's Labirynt Gallery and co-curated *Civil Partnerships: Queer & Feminist Art & Activism* at the University of Brighton. Their publications include *Love and Democracy: Reflections on the Homosexual Question in Poland* (Aureus) and a book on the male nude, *The Naked Man* (Poznan). Their multi-authored essay "Monica Dreyfus" appears in *Our Monica, Ourselves: The Clinton Affair and the National Interest* (New York University Press).

B. Loewe, over the past 15 years, has served as a high school student organizer in the Maryland suburbs where he grew up, worked for police accountability in Cincinnati, as a farmer in Maine, an anti-war organizer in Oakland, and most proudly, as a participant in the migrant rights movement in Chicago, Arizona, and nationally. B. was taught from early on that those who set out to transform the world will surely be transformed themselves. His essay in this book is evidence of that. His essay is also the product of three years of writing that wouldn't have been possible without the loving support, patient pushing, and thoughtful edits of lovers and friends. Read more of B.'s writing at bstandsforb.wordpress.com and follow B. on twitter @bstandsforb.

Ned Mayhem is a kinky queer porn performer and adult web developer. Ned's performances have won awards at AVN, Cinekink, and the Feminist Porn Awards, and his first self-produced feature "Trespass," co-directed with Bianca Stone, was recognized at the 2012 Feminist Porn Awards. When he isn't behind the camera, Ned uses his background in experimental physics to reprogram the porn industry, working to give independent performers the tools to monetize their sexuality on their own terms. With his partner Maggie Mayhem, Ned has built and maintains the couple's porn site MeetThe Mayhems.com, and he has also built such progressive adult sites as QueerlySF. com, Femifist.com, KittyStryker.com, and others.

Men for Women's Choice is not an organization, but rather one expression of the opinion of many men around the world. It is written by Michael Kaufman, Harry Brod, Michael Kimmel, and Gary Barker, and named after a campaign initiated in Canada by Michael Kaufman and Gord Cleveland in 1989. Readers are invited to circulate the statement to express that they too are a man in support of women's reproductive rights. Harry Brod teaches philosophy at University of Northern Iowa, Michael Kimmel teaches sociology at State University of New York, Stony Brook, Gary Barker is the International Director of Promundo, and Michael Kaufman is a writer and co-founder of the White Ribbon Campaign. All have been long-time activists in the pro-feminist men's movement.

Alfredo Mirandé is Professor of Sociology and Ethnic Studies at the University of California, Riverside. He is the author of *The Stanford Law Chronicles: Doin' Time on the Farm* (University of Notre Dame Press), *Hombres y Machos: Masculinity and Latino Culture* (Westview Press), *The Age of Crisis* (Harper & Row), *La Chicana: The Mexican-American Woman* (University of Chicago Press), *The Chicano Experience* (University of Notre Dame Press), and *Gringo Justice* (University of Notre Dame Press). He is a Stanford Law graduate and a practicing attorney. His book *Rascuache Lawyer* was recently published by the University of Arizona Press.

Bryan Talbot Morris wrote his essay based on his experiences as a Fulbright Scholar to Indonesia. He has an MA in international development from Ohio University and a BA in communications from Mercer University. He works in the field of global health and development and has worked for the United Nations Development Programme, UNAIDS, and The Global Fund to Fight AIDS, Tuberculosis, and Malaria.

Michael J. Murphy is Assistant Professor of Women and Gender Studies at the University of Illinois Springfield, where he teaches courses in critical men's/masculinity studies, lesbian, gay, bisexual, transgender, and queer (LGBTQ)/sexuality studies, and visual and popular culture. He holds a master's and doctorate in the history of American art and visual culture from Washington University in St. Louis. His essay is the product of conversations over several years with students in his Sex, Gender and Popular Culture class and he thanks them for their patience and suggestions as he developed his thoughts on recent advertisements for men's grooming products.

Rob Okun is editor and publisher of *Voice Male*, a profeminist, antiviolence magazine (www.voicemalemagazine.org). His commentaries on men and masculinity have been broadcast on public radio and published in print publications and online at *Ms.* and *Women's eNews*. The father of four adult children, he is a psychotherapist practicing in Amherst, Massachusetts, where he lives with his wife.

Ewuare X. Osayande is an activist, educator, author, and nationally recognized lecturer on race, class, gender, and social justice. Osayande is the author of several books including a collection of essays titled *Misogyny and the Emcee: Sex, Race and Hip Hop* and a collection of poems titled *Whose America?* For more information on his work, visit www.osayande.org.

Tal Peretz is a doctoral candidate in sociology and gender studies at the University of Southern California. His dissertation looks at how different socially marginalized groups of men organize to oppose sexism in their communities. His topics of interest include masculinities, men's feminist and antisexist engagements, and intersectionality, and especially how privileged individuals learn to recognize their status and reject or redirect it for positive social change.

Jeff Pollet is a technical writer living and working in Oakland, California. He still writes from time to time about feminism on feministallies.blogspot.com.

Jay Poole, PhD, grew up in rural North Carolina and despite his destiny to become a good ol' boy, he is now a social worker and educator who constantly poses the challenge to his clients and students as well as himself to call all things into question. Jay holds a master's degree in social work, he is a licensed clinical social worker, and he is Assistant Professor in the Department of Social Work at the University of North Carolina at Greensboro where he teaches and learns from undergraduate and graduate students. His recent work can be found in *Sexualities in Education: A Reader* (Peter Lang).

Jonathan Ravarino is dually licensed as a Counseling Psychologist and Clinical Social Worker and practices psychotherapy in Salt Lake City, Utah. Jonathan holds adjunct teaching positions at the University of Utah College of Social Work and Department of Educational Psychology. Jonathan works primarily with men and boys in therapy and uses a mindfulness-based therapy approach that is informed by a feminist/multicultural lens. Jonathan is married and has two children.

A. Razor is a writer, activist, ex-convict, filmmaker, photographer, artist, editor, publisher, and a case manager for a nonprofit that delivers treatment, housing, and services to homeless persons with co-occurring disorders.

Grantlin Schafer is a social worker in Loudoun County, Virginia. He is an alumnus of the One in Four tour and continues to educate and promote healthy relationships for teens and adults. More information can be found at www.oneinfourusa.org.

Haji Shearer is director of a statewide fatherhood initiative in Massachusetts and a frequent contributor to *Voice Male* magazine. He founded the fathers program at the Family Nurturing Center, which serves men in Boston's urban communities. He is a Licensed Social Worker who spent many years doing crisis intervention with families. He frequently presents at conferences across Massachusetts on father involvement, male intimacy, and co-parenting. Haji promotes gender awareness through facilitating Men's Healing Circles, Boys to Men Rites of Passages, and Couples Workshops. He is especially interested in seeing African-American and Latino men heal the twin traumas of racism and patriarchy. Haji and his wife are proud parents of two young adults. He is a long-time student of meditation who believes in the power of love.

Daniel Simon is completing his American Studies PhD at the University of Hawaii. He specializes in race, health, and memory. Simon writes a column for *Random Lengths News* in San Pedro, California, titled "Random Profiles," which focuses on the lives of overlooked and interesting people. He is allergic to walnuts, pecans, and hazelnuts.

Jeremy Adam Smith is Web Editor of the University of California, Berkeley, Greater Good Science Center, and author or coeditor of four books, including *The Daddy Shift: How Stay-at-Home Dads, Breadwinning Moms, and Shared Parenting are Transforming the American Family* (Beacon Press) and *Rad Dad: Dispatches from the Frontiers of Fatherhood* (PM Press). He has received many honors for his journalism, including a 2010–11 John S. Knight fellowship at Stanford University and a 2011 PASS Award from the National Council on Crime and Delinquency.

Amit Taneja currently serves as the Director of the Days-Massolo Cultural Education Center at Hamilton College. His dissertation focuses on the intersection of race, class, gender, and sexual orientation for lesbian, gay, bisexual, and transgender (LGBT) students of color on historically white college campuses. He served on the Consortium of Higher Education LGBT Resource Professionals executive board for five years, serving as co-chair from 2007 to 2010. He serves as a consultant and speaker on a range of issues including LGBT inclusion and campus climate, challenges faced by LGBT students of color, Facebook use and implications for higher education professionals, and practicing affirmative action in higher education settings.

Marshall Thompson, a Sergeant Army reservist, spent a year in Iraq working as a military journalist. He served in the same capacity in Kosovo, Macedonia, and South Korea. In November 2006, Thompson completed a 500-mile walk across his home state of Utah to protest the war and call for withdrawal of U.S. troops. Thompson and his wife Kristen have a daughter, Eliza, who was born during Thompson's tour in Iraq.

Marcus C. Tye, PhD, is Professor of Psychology at Dowling College in Oakdale, New York. A clinical psychologist, his scholarly work is in the field of law and psychology, and also gender and sexuality. He is author of a textbook, *Sexuality & Our Diversity: Integrating Culture with the Biopsychosocial* (Nova).

Donald N.S. Unger, MFA, PhD, is a lecturer in the Program in Writing and Humanistic Studies at the Massachusetts Institute of Technology. His scholarly interests include tracking changes in the representation of men, masculinity, and fatherhood in both language use and in popular culture. He has been writing about fatherhood—as well as doing occasional commentary for local National Public Radio (NPR) affiliates on the topic—since before the birth of his daughter Rebecca, in 1995. Unger is the author of *Men Can: The Changing Image and Reality of Fatherhood in America* (Temple University Press). Further information is at www.donunger.com.

EDITOR'S ACKNOWLEDGMENTS

I am incredibly glad to write new acknowledgments for this revised edition of *Men Speak Out*. All things are changeable in politics and love, and this is particularly true since the first edition of this book came out. Rewriting my Thank-You's is like hitting the cosmic refresh button and it's a welcome opportunity to signify the personal transformations that underscore my journey as a writer, friend, and scholar.

One thing doesn't change, though: I send all of love to my daughter, Emilie Tarrant. Your intelligent insight improves this book; your dry wit adds to all else. Roma Rozenblyum: Thank you for softening the edges of my world. Family, friends, and colleagues have been generous with their intellectual and moral support, offering much food for thought and sustenance for the soul. I extend much love especially to my Feingold, Pollak, Rosen, Cohen, Simon, and Arons family.

Discussions with students and faculty at Ohio University during my campus stay as the Glidden Endowed Professor were particularly timely.

Samantha Barbaro, Leah Babb-Rosenfeld, Steve Rutter, Dave Jurman, and the editorial team and production staff at Routledge have seen this project through with aplomb.

Pickle was a wonderful best friend who took me on regular walks, greeted me at the door with unparalleled enthusiasm, and expressed so much character, affection, and amusing aloofness; he is deeply missed.

Chad Sniffen, Cassie Comley, Milton Sanabria, and Johnny Felix provided feedback that improved this book. I would also like to thank the following reviewers for their constructive feedback: Sandra Godwin, Brenda Weber, Wade Edwards, Susan Peppers-Bates, Simona Sharoni, Leandra Preston-Sidler, Elisa Garza-Leal, Linda Van Ingen, and Jessica J. Eckstein.

My students, past and present, have been a source of inspiration, insight, and lively conversation. My appreciation remains for everyone who provided helpful comments on the first edition of this book.

Finally, here's to all the feminists, profeminists, and allies out there, past, present, and future, who have the imagination to picture a different kind of world and the dedication to make it happen.

FOREWORD

Jackson Katz

At first glance, a book titled *Men Speak Out* might strike some as oddly redundant, if not downright satirical. After all, haven't men—especially privileged white men—had ample opportunity to vocally express their opinions and narrate their own lives? Just what are these (presumably) formerly muzzled men going to speak out about? In fact, as I was writing the Foreword to the first edition of *Men Speak Out*, radio "shock jock" Don Imus had just been fired by CBS because, like countless arrogant men in the past and present, he abused his license to speak one too many times by mocking and denigrating people—in this case young African American women—with much less social power. Since then, right-wing talk radio host Rush Limbaugh has accused Georgetown University law student Sandra Fluke of being a slut and a prostitute—simply because she testified before Congress about the importance of insurance coverage for birth control. When it comes to questions of gender, sex, and power, there is clearly no shortage of men speaking out.

The rationale for this book is not that men have been silenced and need to reclaim our voice. That, of course, is a powerful feminist narrative about *women's* voices and *women's* lives. What makes this book special is that it features the stories of twenty-first-century American *men* whose lives have been shaped in unprecedented ways by the social changes catalyzed by modern multicultural women's movements. As some fascinating essays in this volume attest, feminism inspired a number of self-critical reflections from men. When I was in college in the early 1980s, I read and was moved by a groundbreaking anthology titled *For Men Against Sexism*, edited by Jon Snodgrass, which was published in 1977. It helped me, and some of my fellow student activists, to envision a number of ways that we as men could contribute to the enormous transformations in the gender and sexual order that were taking place all around us— as well as within us.

Men Speak Out is in its own way a kind of cultural milestone. But it is a book of essays by men that could not have been written a generation ago, because while it was possible in the 1970s to speculate about how men's lives would change in the wake of feminism, there is now an entire generation of men who have lived through, indeed, pioneered those changes.

Notably, the authors in this book are men from diverse backgrounds who have learned to see men's lives—their lives—from the standpoint of women's experience. Along with their own conventional and countercultural experiences as straight, gay or bisexual men, many of the authors have had the opportunity to receive a formal women's, gender, or masculinities' studies education or have been mentored by feminist women. Many are well-read in intersectional feminist and womanist literature. Some have had close relationships with women that have enabled them to "walk a mile in her shoes."

Contrary to those who would dismissively assert that this has feminized or emasculated them, women's input has not in any way diluted the power of these men's insights into their's or other men's lives. Rather, it has strengthened it. As the eminent feminist philosopher Sandra Harding maintains, the "view from women's lives" can illuminate men's lives by creating "a broader context and contrasting perspective from which to examine their own beliefs and behaviors, social relations and institutions."[1]

Harding argues that it is important for men (and whites, heterosexuals, citizens of wealthy Western countries) to learn about themselves through the lens of the experiences of subordinated groups. But she also acknowledges that men must struggle for a kind of self-awareness, a process that is painful for men who find themselves "abandoning cherished beliefs about themselves and their worlds, and choosing new behaviors and life projects."[2]

In the spirit of this struggle, it is altogether fitting that the editor of *Men Speak Out* is . . . a woman. One of the many ironies of contemporary history—both in the U.S. and around the world—is that women's leadership has made possible a more open and meaningful conversation *among men* about a wide range of issues that profoundly affect us. I know that I only started to think critically about men and masculinities—and my own gendered experiences as a (white, Jewish) boy and man—when as a young college student I was first introduced to feminist ideas by women, inside and outside the classroom.

To be sure, the essays contained in this collection advance the project of men thinking openly and meaningfully about our everyday lives as well as our generational location in the grand sweep of history. But this openness is not without its costs, because introspection can be unsettling. Taking a good hard look in the mirror requires a questioning nature and an adventurous spirit, even a certain kind of courage. Consider some of the challenging and provocative questions the authors grapple with: Is it possible to play out conventional heterosexual scripts between consenting adults and still be a committed anti-sexist man? Can men of color identify as feminists? Where do struggles against heterosexism fit into movements against sexism and racism? Is men's attraction to pornography about desire or power? Can those two concepts ever be separated? When a man has been sexually abused by another man—or by a woman—to what extent does it affect his masculine identity? Are stay-home dads at the leading edge of a cultural revolution? Why haven't more progressive men recognized that working to end men's violence against women is a social justice imperative? How does the destabilization of traditional masculine/feminine categories prompted by the transgender revolution challenge our assumptions about the kinds of folk wisdom embodied in the phrase "boys will be boys?"

These kinds of questions can be quite discomfiting, at least in part because the answers are often complicated, or unsatisfying. There is much more reassurance in simplistic clichés like "men are from Mars" than in the idea that what is considered masculine or "manly" is ever-shifting and contingent on a constellation of economic, social, political, and historical forces. When you factor in the responsibility that members of privileged groups have not only to be aware of their unearned advantages but to work against them, you can see why there is built-in reluctance to set the entire process in motion. Perhaps that explains why many of my academic colleagues who teach college courses on men and masculinity report that it is common for them to have only three or four male students in a classroom of thirty.

In the face of this kind of resistance to introspection, it is tempting to try to reassure men that their lives—including their relationships with women and other men—might actually improve if they have the will to critique and challenge the precepts of traditional masculinity. In fact, many more men would likely be drawn to feminist ideas if they understood that a commitment to gender justice entails deep concern for the wounds of boys and men—wounds that are inflicted by the same oppressive, sexist system that does such harm to women.

Just the same, I believe there are certain privileges men will have to forego if we are ever to be more than rhetorically committed to equality between the sexes. One of those privileges is the ability not to think about our privilege.

During the Clarence Thomas–Anita Hill hearings in 1991, when the mainstream media turned its full attention to the topic of sexual harassment for the first time, many men reacted defensively as the spotlight shifted toward our attitudes and behaviors toward women. Newspaper stories and cable TV programs featured interviews with countless men who hyperbolically asserted that, "It's gotten so bad I'm scared to say anything to a woman anymore." But was it really such a bad thing that men were being asked merely to stop and think about the effects on women of their words and actions? For years now, this type of introspection has been derided as political correctness. But far from being a debilitating burden, self-reflexivity should be seen as an indispensable character trait for members of any dominant group who want to be better, more compassionate people.

In the 1960s and 1970s, women formed consciousness-raising groups in part to help each other draw connections between personal issues in their own family and work lives and those in the broader movement for women's equality. Today, as the number of men who do profeminist work proliferates, there is a need for men to do consciousness-raising of a different sort: *self-consciousness-raising*. Of course, in our culture we generally use the term "self-conscious" to mean someone who is nervous and insecure. But that is a rather narrow definition. The great nineteenth-century German philosopher G.W.F. Hegel equated being self-conscious with being self-aware. In our time, when there is so much violence perpetrated by narcissistic, angry men—acting as lone school shooters, rapists, or as agents of state authority at the highest levels of power—encouraging men to be more self-aware would seem to be a task of the utmost urgency.

Fortunately we are in the midst of what the sociologist Raewynn Connell calls the "ethnographic moment" in writing about men's lives. In many cultures around the world, growing numbers of men are publicly discussing their personal and political struggles—as well as their joys and triumphs—around issues related to masculinity, violence, sex, and feminism. The willingness of men like the contributors to *Men Speak Out* to engage in what the writer John Stoltenberg calls acts of "revolutionary honesty" is a gift to anyone who yearns and works not only for equality and justice for women—but for men, too, as well as for human rights, non-violence, and an end to so much of the unnecessary suffering in the world.

1 Sandra Harding, *Whose Science? Whose Knowledge?: Thinking from Women's Lives.* Ithaca, NY: Cornell University Press, 1991, p. 286.
2 Ibid., p. 287.

INTRODUCTION

Shira Tarrant

Feminism is a dirty word. It conjures images of whiny, bitchy women with sanctimonious complaints about men. And the men who call themselves "feminist"? If they aren't simply whipped, then it's a cheap ploy at getting laid. Or so the story goes. But that's an old version of the story. Hopefully, we're in the midst of change.

A few years ago, I was teaching in the women's studies program at an East Coast liberal arts college outside of Baltimore. At first, there were only one or two young men among the women enrolled in my classes. Soon there were more. They trickled in from the soccer team, the basketball team, the swim team, and the arts. They majored in physics, political science, mathematics, and dance. *Who were these guys?*, I wondered. *And how could I find more of them?*

Some answers came from conversations that I had with these same young men after class, sitting on the campus lawn. What they asked for was a book of essays written by men who had stories to tell about challenging the concepts of gender. They wanted to know if there were other men out there who were also trying to make sense of their experiences in today's culture, finding some past assumptions about both men and women no longer serve them. They wanted to know that they weren't alone in their thinking, and that it was possible to make a change. They wanted to know that they—and these other men—weren't wimps.

This anthology is a fresh look at gender, sex, and power—and feminism. It is a collection of essays about modern men making their way in a world that is struggling to rethink how it understands manhood and masculinity, just as it is struggling with changing ideas about women and femininity. This is a collection about men—written by men—who are willing to stare down these issues head on. Their attention to the interconnection and impact of gender, race, class, and sexuality is contemporary and vital. Our assumptions about men, women, and gender are shifting. We're not always sure where we're heading or where we want to end up. This book helps navigate the course.[1]

I set out to collect a series of essays that are direct and expressive in their interrogation of masculinity and power. I posted my request for essays to a number of relevant websites, blogs, and listservs. I wanted to compile as diverse a selection as possible. Queries came from activist men, university men, men who used to be women, men from the South, men from the North, and men from places in between. I heard from queer men, straight men, and bi men; from young men, older men, Black, Latino, Jewish, and white men. Emails of interest and support poured in from New Zealand, South Africa, England, Australia, Poland, Uruguay, Vietnam, Lapland—you get the picture. Many sent notes just to say thanks in advance for a book they've been waiting for. This response—awesome and humbling—was good news. There are many good men out there actively working to end male pattern domination and the abuse and misuse of power over others. There are so many creating new answers to old problems.

Encouraged by the response, I hatched a plan while preparing for a cross-country move back to California. Armed with over 2,000 photocopied announcements explaining the book and inviting men to send in their written thoughts, I planned to leave fliers behind at every college town and coffee house, truck stop and Bob Evans restaurant, coast to coast. This ambitious idea petered out somewhere around Indiana, where the road ahead looked longer and longer and the days and nights joined together as I drove across the country. I did get the chance, though, to leave fliers at many places: at a corner bar in Athens, Ohio; a Starbucks in Cleveland; the Presbyterian Manor Senior Retirement Home in Salina, Kansas; at a down-on-its-luck casino outside of Reno, Nevada. I papered the National Women's Studies Association Conference in Oakland before heading south to Los Angeles, and stuck my head into the kitchen at a Mexican restaurant along the way to share some fliers. To my utter surprise and delight, the cook there said he'd already seen the call for submissions online. The word was out and the response was tremendous.

With this second edition of *Men Speak Out* a few things have changed and many have stayed the same. In a short time, social media shifted how we mobilize in a digital world; global SlutWalk movements were launched; controversies ensued. The "It Gets Better" video campaign went viral to support youthful targets of homophobic, hateful bullying. The Occupy Movement brought attention and pushback to economic abuses perpetrated by those 1 percent of people holding vastly disproportionate power and wealth. The conservative right in the United States launched a systematic backlash against equality in their War on Women.[2] Despite laments about "the end of men" or claims that women are the new economic victors in an allegedly post-recession economy, the fact is most men continue to out-earn women and some men continue to face barriers to success, exacerbated by race, class, ethnicity, and geographic location. Men fill our prisons and jails. With the conviction of former Penn State assistant football coach Jerry Sandusky, public conversation is breaking some of the silence surrounding the sexual abuse of boys. Interpersonal violence and sexual assault continue to be perpetrated disproportionately by men, whether aimed toward children, women, queer or transgender individuals—or other men. In other words, there are still compelling reasons to keep talking critically and bravely about masculinity, identity, politics, and progressive social change.

Some men in this book recount their personal challenges with living up to the demands of so-called traditional masculinity. Others are quintessential guys' guys who love sports and beer. But one thing brings these men together on these pages if not in their day-to-day lives: Each of them struggles, in his own way, with the personal and political limits that conventional masculinity imposes. Their unflinchingly honest prose tackles the politics of domination and strategies for change. They reflect, with kaleidoscope effect, on the issues of men, masculinity, identity, sexism, and feminism from different angles, revealing new insights and shifting patterns. The essays in this book deal not only with the difficulties of being a man, but also with the challenges of being a man who is grappling with sexism.

What becomes immediately clear is that there is no monolithic meaning of masculinity shared by all the authors. There is, instead, what Josephine Peyton Young describes as the "existence of multiple masculinities."[3] There is tension and interaction between gender, class, race, ethnicity, and sexuality. Age and youth lend additional viewpoints to these issues. There is also an encouraging theme: that we have tremendous potential for personal and political change. Grantlin Schafer describes getting on the road with a group of guys on a cross-country RV tour to speak out against sexual violence. Tal Peretz, a recent college graduate from Pittsburgh, Pennsylvania, describes the radical transformation of his friend Cliff from a racist skinhead to feminist ally. For other men, complacency was never an option. C. Winter Han calls out the gay community for its racism and white privilege while simultaneously attempting to stake a claim as oppressed sexual minorities. Nathan Einschlag takes on his college coach and basketball team for their upside-down expectations that place hooking up above personal ethics. Greg Bortnichak wonders out loud how he can remain true to his nonsexist ideals without falling into the trap of paternalistic protection when a much older man wants to hit on his girlfriend. Jacob Anderson-Minshall questions the expectations of straight men who assume he's one of them, and lesbian women who assume he's not. For all these men, asking soul-searching questions is a moral imperative, even if doing so leads to danger, rage, distress, or initial alienation from their peers.

Ryan Heryford, Robert Jensen, and Ned Mayhem grapple with masculinity and gender politics through the lens of personal struggle in relationships, the problems of pornography, and perspectives from a queer man working within the independent porn industry. We learn from Tomek Kitlinski and Pawel Leszkowicz that being out and gay in Poland is a risk far greater than we in the United States might imagine, with members of the far-right youth militia hurling stones and threatening their lives. Essays by Byron Hurt, Haji Shearer, Ewuare X. Osayande, and Amit Taneja teach us that there are multiple ways of understanding the intersections of race, nation, identity, and change. On fatherhood, we begin to imagine a world in which men are actively engaged parents, and to consider why some versions of fathers' rights groups do not work in the best interest of women, children, or men. Michael Kimmel and Rob Okun remind us where we came from so we can better see where we're going.

These essays, and the others in this collection, bring personal insight and critical awareness to our ideas about masculinity and feminism. Each is written through the unique lens of individual experience. There may be points of discomfort, and there are certainly questions raised but left unanswered, or only partially answered. There will be women who distrust men writing about feminism, and doubtless there will be men who are suspicious about a woman editing the voices of men. But as I see it, this discomfort can be productive. This anthology is part of a process of discovering the personal and political meanings of progressive manhood and feminist men. This process of discovery is certainly not a destination but it is a solid beginning.

There is a serious and growing movement of men who are committed to addressing problems we live with every day: domestic violence, rape and sexual assault, racism, homophobia, unequal pay, objectification, and standards of gender that are impossible to live up to. It's all part of the same package. There are men out there who stand beside women in feminist struggle, and this book is intended to give voice to those men and to provide role models for others coming up behind them. This book is intended to provide ideas and encouragement for the process of ongoing change.

In feminist theory and practice there is a tradition of coming to voice, of taking personal experience seriously, and of commitment to acknowledging that personal experience is political. We have heard plenty from men over the years, but to date we haven't heard enough from feminist allies about issues of identity, politics, and the potential for change.

Men Speak Out draws on feminist foundations and the work of feminist scholars who identify the ways in which we experience power, domination, freedom, and liberation. Kimberlé Crenshaw writes that people live multiple identities.[4] Because it is possible that we are simultaneously members of more than one community, we can experience both privilege and oppression at the same time. For example, a black man may enjoy gender privilege yet also experience racism. A gay white man may experience skin privilege but suffer the effects of homophobia. Building on this theoretical paradigm enables us to think about the feminist understandings of masculinity. We must take into account, as these essays do, broad differences such as immigrant standing, nation of origin, religion, race, sexual orientation, and trans-status. The potential is here for taking feminist scholarship in new directions, further extending conversations into areas such as research on transnational masculinities or on the efficacy of men as strategic political allies in achieving feminist goals. To this end, *Men Speak Out* adds in a hopefully significant way.

THE ESSAYS

The authors write about men and feminism, growing up male, recognizing masculine privilege, taking action to change the imbalance of power and privilege, and the constraints that men experience in confronting sexism. The essays describe individual authors' successes and challenges in confronting patriarchal systems in a culture that can be unsupportive of, if not downright hostile to, this perspective. Some of these stories reflect on growing up, whereas others are vignettes of a day in the writer's life. Several authors draw from their academic expertise or political experience, while others ask tough questions about being a feminist ally who is living, working, thinking, and learning in a sexist society.

The essays in this collection are thematically organized into six parts beginning with Part I, "Masculinity and Identity." In this first part are a variety of perspectives: an athlete writes about the pressures of hooking up; a man who used to be a woman describes his transition; a Muslim man asks us to consider the dangers of stereotyping; a scholar calls out advertisements depicting limited—and limiting—ideas about men. These authors explore issues of experience and agency, and they raise questions of race and masculinity, while suggesting answers to the puzzle of living as a man in a highly gendered world. The essays in Part II, "The Politics of Sex and Love," are about sexual desire, sexual politics, and sexual orientation. These forthright discussions look at men's use of pornography, what happens when lust from the waist down interferes with politics from the neck up, the media's assumptions about bisexuality, and racism in the gay community.

In Part III, "Dealing with Violence and Abuse," the authors address urgent and wrenching issues of abuse and violence from the perspectives of men working to prevent it, those who have perpetrated it, and from those who have been victims and survived it. Part IV, "Masculinity at Work and Home," presents reflections on fatherhood, academia, construction sites, and the military.

In Part V, "Men and Feminism," the reader will explore dynamic views on men, masculinity, and political engagement. The writers here do not agree on what feminism means, or even if it is a title they want to claim. What they do share, however, is an interest in gender equality and healthy masculinity, and a dedication to figuring out what this means. The essays include authors' recollections of the early women's liberation and anti-war movements, and the necessity of integrating public and private beliefs in equality. The title of the final section is "Taking Action, Making Change." Some of these authors have chosen very public forms of activism that we readily associate with political action while, for other men, progressive change takes the form of deeply personal transformation.

HOW TO USE THIS BOOK

Men Speak Out is strategically positioned at the intersection of feminist literature and masculinity studies. This book is designed to appeal to curious readers, students and professors, activists and organizers alike. Admittedly, this is a tall order, but the essays are written in first-person, accessible prose. These are not disembodied perspectives but voices coming from real people. The brief introduction to each part is intended to satisfy readers wanting an overview of the theoretical issues and to present supporting resources that can be used for further investigation. I hope that readers will select from this combined material as each sees fit.

Taken as a collective whole, the essays in this anthology highlight the personal struggles, changing viewpoints, and learning that the authors have undergone in negotiating a wide variety of experiences of masculinity and ethical concern. These are forthright accounts that I think will enable the reader to better understand these personal and political issues. I hope that this book provokes discussion and that readers will relate to, argue about, agree and disagree with, expand on, and improve upon the ideas presented here.

1. Websites, blogs, and media coverage about men and masculinity have notably increased in number over recent years. *Voice Male* magazine has been among the vanguard since 1983. Described as unabashedly profeminist and male positive, this national magazine supports radical and progressive views about men's role in a host of debates including fatherhood, masculinity, pop culture, reproductive rights, and domestic violence. For more information, see http://voicemalemagazine.org/. The academic field of masculinities studies is rapidly growing. For examples of representative work, see the collected essays in Rachel Adams and David Savran, eds., *The Masculinity Studies Reader*, Malden, MA: Blackwell Publishing, 2002; R.W. Connell, *Masculinities*, second edition, Los Angeles: University of California Press, 2005; and Judith Kegan Gardiner, *Masculinity Studies and Feminist Theory*, New York: Columbia University Press, 2002. In contrast to these theoretical accounts, *Men Speak Out* explores masculine identity and feminist politics primarily through narrative and personal experience.
2. For information on state legislative measures to limit or eradicate women's access to family planning, see the Guttmacher Institute, "States Enact Record Number of

Abortion Restrictions in 2011," January 5, 2012. Available at: http://guttmacher institute.com/media/inthenews/2012/01/05/endofyear.html (accessed June 25, 2012).

3. Josephine Peyton Young, "Review. *Masculinities, Gender Relations, and Sport*," *Gender and Society*, vol. 15, no. 5 (Oct. 2001): 779.

4. Kimberlé Crenshaw, "Demarginalizing the Intersection of Race and Sex: A Black Feminist Critique of Antidiscrimination Doctrine, Feminist Theory, and Antiracist Politics," in Katharine T. Bartlett and Rosanne Kennedy, eds., *Feminist Legal Theory: Readings in Law and Gender*, Boulder, CO: Westview Press, 1991. For discussion on structural and political intersectionality in policy-making, see Mieke Verloo, "Multiple Inequalities, Intersectionality and the European Union," *European Journal of Women's Studies*, vol. 13, no. 3 (2006): 211–228.

Part I

Masculinity and Identity

INTRODUCTION

When it comes to gender, we are living in interesting times. Warrior masculinity is reinscribed and reinforced through military conflicts around the globe.[1] At the same time, the term "metrosexual" rolls easily off our tongues and we're no strangers to the gender-policing phrase, *Dude, you're a fag*.[2] Violent video games and combat sports like mixed martial arts encourage an aggressive kind of masculinity, while TV commercials are full of grown men acting like developmentally arrested twelve-year-olds, and pop culture foists lad lit on us, replete with bumbling male incompetence and failures to launch.[3] There is serious, ongoing male-on-male gang violence at the same time as more American men are contentedly doing domestic work.[4] Advances in medical technology make it easier to sync up our bodies with our genders, and we know that masculinity is not only for men, but music videos like Nelly's "Tip Drill" remain infamous, and a credit-card swipe down a woman's backside is still not an unusual video move. Then there is Eminem's depiction of interpersonal violence in "Love the Way You Lie." The chart-topper glamorizes and normalizes men's violence toward women while, in real life, patterns of sexualized and gendered violence are stubbornly resistant to change.[5] The first national study on eating disorders reveals that 25 percent of all anorexic, bulimic, and binge-eating adults are now male.[6] So what, exactly, does it mean to be a man in the twenty-first century?

The essays in this section are written by men from many walks of life who explore the issues of power and masculinity. They dispel homogenous stereotypes about what it means to be a man.

These essays are timely since there is growing interest in the subject of masculinity. There is increasing curiosity about how it might be possible for men to "do" masculinity differently; that is to say, in ways that are not limiting or harmful to any of us. Susan Faludi's book, *Stiffed: The Betrayal of the American Man*,[7] drew mainstream attention to the subject. *Bitch*,[8] a magazine of feminist response to pop culture, devoted an entire issue to masculinity. Rebecca Walker's book, *What Makes a Man: 22 Writers Imagine the Future* and Daniel Jones's *The Bastard on the Couch: 27 Men Try Really Hard to Explain Their Feelings About Love, Loss, Fatherhood, and Freedom*[9] explore questions of manhood and masculine identity. Feature film rights for Michael Kimmel's book, *Guyland: The Perilous World Where Boys Become Men*, have been optioned to Dreamworks. With a shaky economy and shifting labor patterns at work and home, there is much emerging debate about what it means to be a man in the twenty-first century—and whether our boys and men are somehow failing. Morgan Spurlock's documentary film, *Mansome*, insists that men are bewildered about their current condition and unsure about their masculinity. Hanna Rosin's book, *The End of Men*,[10] proposes that dominant manhood, as we know it, has come to a screeching halt. I'm not convinced.

That said, there is good reason to continue critical investigation into the meanings of masculinity and the social rewards or penalties that come with it. In academic circles, critical gender studies, masculinities studies, queer theory, and post-queer theory are dissecting the assumptions of biological essentialism. Genetics may explain a lot, and biological arguments about how men and women's behaviors and traits are "hardwired" are in vogue. But we also know that culture has deep effects on the social construction of gender and masculinity.[11] In *Manhood in America: A Cultural History*, Michael Kimmel makes the case that manhood is a constantly shifting cultural construction. Cordelia Fine's *Delusions of Gender* debunks pseudo-scientific myths about hardwired differences between men's and women's brains to explain, instead, how our minds, society, and neurosexism work together in creating sexual distinctions.[12] Raewynn Connell's *Masculinities* complements the recent stream of publications, offering suggestions on how we might study masculinity in the interest of progressive gender politics.[13]

Connell proposes that there is not *one* true version of masculine identity. Rather, there are many aspects of, and multiple ways of performing, *masculinities*.[14] But there are also tenacious mainstream assumptions about what it means to be a man. Conventional manhood—and its close cousin, hegemonic masculinity—can be summed up in three short words: no sissy stuff.[15] This imperative for masculine leadership dominates our collective imagination by invoking unrealistic expectations that men are by nature stoic, unemotional, aggressive, and interpersonally detached. In keeping with these stereotypes, physical contact is never okay unless it takes place on the wrestling mat, on the football field, or in a fight.

This picture of masculinity is restrictive to men and oppressive to all. Moreover, it is just plain inaccurate. Conventional masculinity is a style of manhood that many men (and women) are complicit in upholding, although few actually embody. There is nothing traditional, universal, or eternal about our current conventions of masculine gender. The more pertinent issue is, rather, "how particular groups of men inhabit positions of power and wealth, and how they legitimate and reproduce the social relationships that generate their dominance."[16]

The default setting for a masculinity defined by male dominance and aggression also makes the invalid assumption that all men are white, heterosexual, American, able-bodied, and middle class. Yet masculinity comes in many forms and packages and these multiple masculinities are informed, limited, and modified by race, ethnicity, class background, sexual orientation, and personal predilections. As Kimmel points out, hegemonic masculinity not only involves men dominating women, but men exerting power over other men, as well.[17] This particular version of manhood *may* use force or violence to uphold itself, but force is not necessarily required. Iris Marion Young explains how oppression or submission of the target group requires only the threat of violence to be effective.[18] By the same token, men—as members of the dominant group—can also be harmed by hegemonic masculinity. Experiencing harm is different, though, from being oppressed or subjugated because although "sexist notions of masculinity prevent men from showing emotion, for instance . . . failure to cry does not routinely cause men to lose out on the best jobs or receive lower pay."[19]

Dominator versions of masculinity continue to exist by recreating situations where men can exert power over women in general and various subordinated groups of men: immigrant, gay, or effeminate men, for example. The interplay between the powerful and less-powerful "is an important part of how a patriarchal social order works,"[20] but this isn't the end of the story. The dominance of any group of men is open to challenge and to change.[21]

Standards of masculinity are a cultural ideal, not a reality. The images of "real men" that public media show us do not correspond to the actual personalities of most men. Let's face it: How many guys are John Wayne, Rambo, James Bond, Barry Bonds—or even want to be? Yet many of us are complicit in upholding the masculine mystique. Doing so results in perceived gratification or the promise of a positive reward such as camaraderie, or vicarious aggression, or a passive sense of accomplishment. Going along to get along can also help guys avoid such negative sanctions as ostracism, ridicule, violence, and discrimination.

There is also the possibility that hegemonic masculinity, which is usually defined with fixed, negative connotations, might be transformed into a positive force. "It is quite conceivable," writes Connell, "that a certain hegemony could be constructed for masculinities that are less toxic, more cooperative and peaceable, than the current editions."[22] Scholars such as Demetrakis Z. Demetriou disagree, however, cautioning against prematurely celebrating the improved forms of masculinity that Connell claims are possible at new historical junctures. Patriarchal masculinity has a long history and is more persistent and sly, he claims. The hegemonic bloc may appear to change but in very deceptive ways through negotiation and appropriation, and "through the transformation of what appears counter-hegemonic and progressive into an instrument of backwardness and patriarchal reproduction." In other words, Demetriou explains, we ought to "avoid falling into the trap of believing that patriarchy has disappeared simply because heterosexual men have worn earrings."[23]

bell hooks's theories indirectly modify these arguments. She highlights the politics and patterns of domination—not of men or masculinity, *per se*—as the core area of concern for liberation struggle. The sociopolitical dynamics of exploitation and subjugation describe a broader abuse of power that is not necessarily limited to individual practitioners, although there are certainly individuals whom we can hold accountable for bad behavior. For hooks, social, political, economic, and cultural domination is predicated on what she calls white, supremacist, capitalist patriarchy.[24] This model of masculinist power is played out by dominating groups on the backs of subjugated peoples.

The presence of multilayered patterns of subjugation is why some people prefer the term "kyriarchy" instead of "patriarchy" to describe sociopolitical structures of domination and the abuse of power. Patriarchy refers literally to "rule of the father," but all men do not have the same access to power and privilege. *All* men do not dominate *all* women equally, in the same way. Theologian Elisabeth Schüssler Fiorenza coined the term "kyriarchy," which comes from *kyrios*, the Greek term for "lord" or "master," and *archein*, meaning "to rule or dominate," explaining that kyriarchy points to how the structures of domination are intersecting and "multiplicative." It is a system "of ruling and oppression," explains Schüssler Fiorenza. It is not the case that men *always* have privilege even if they are at the center of power structures in various instances. It is possible for men to simultaneously inhabit many worlds with different degrees of privilege and powerlessness. Some men experience masculine privilege within a family setting or on the job, yet they may also experience disadvantage as, say, a black man in white-dominated settings or as a Muslim man in white, Christian communities.[25]

While we continue to question the assumptions that accompany privilege and subjugation, we do well, however, to remain concerned about the effects of hegemonic masculinity. It harms women—and all people—because it is the strategic institutionalization of men's dominance over others. Maintaining this more complex political and social definition of power and subjugation is important in creating a more accurate understanding of identity and what it means to be a man.

The men writing here about masculinity build on popular trends and academic groundwork. But they are also creating an invigorating history of their own by speaking out about how gender ideals can operate in constricting ways, and the limitless possibilities for change. This section on masculinity and identity explores the myths and realities, and the doubts and certainties, of men's lives. The voices are those of real men reflecting on their own experiences. These essays put an active face on what Rachel Adams and David Savran describe as the process of unsettling assumptions "that govern dominant understandings of masculinity."[26]

Men Speak Out opens with Byron Hurt—hip-hop head, former college football quarterback, and creator of the acclaimed film *Hip Hop: Beyond Beats and Rhymes*. Hurt explains that as he learned more about sexism, violence, and homophobia in hip hop, he became more conflicted about the music that he loved. This conflict led Hurt to turn on the camera and create his documentary about masculinity in mainstream hip-hop culture. In his essay, "Daytona Beach: Beyond Beats and Rhymes," Hurt chronicles the hypermasculine behavior, the crude objectification of women, some women's complicity in the game, and the complicated issues of race, gender, violence, and sex that he sees played out while filming in Florida during BET's Spring Bling celebration. The limitations of hypermasculinity and the violent crime and homicide rates affecting young black men are serious issues. Yet the corporate media continues to record and distribute monolithic images of masculinity, providing limited models for becoming a man. Perceiving few options, many continue to go along with it. While the rap-star images we see on TV are slick and well edited, Hurt reveals the more complex gender politics behind the scene. Back from filming the crowds and interviewing fans at the Spring Bling in Daytona, Hurt got eight hours of footage in the can and a story to tell.[27]

In "The Enemy Within: On Becoming a Straight White Guy," Jacob Anderson-Minshall writes about his transformation from a young girl growing up in rural Idaho, to an adult lesbian woman, to becoming a straight white man living in the Bay area. Anderson-Minshall's sexual trajectory has taken him deep undercover: He's had intimate access to the worlds of both heterosexual men and lesbian women. Since for Jacob, sex and gender have been transitional states—not biological givens—Anderson-Minshall is able to raise provocative questions about both masculine and feminine identity.

In their essay, "The Bullying Demands of Masculinity: A Genderqueer Escape," River Willow Fagan extends the topic of sexuality and gender, honing in specifically on queer identity. Although "queer" may have once been a term of insult, this is no longer the case. Queer theory breaks down binary categories that presume there are two sexes (female and male), two genders (feminine and masculine), and two sexualities (homosexual and heterosexual). Fagan, who grew up in a fundamentalist Christian family, was a kid who loved reading, drawing, comic books, and creepy-crawly bugs. Over time, Fagan began to realize that social demands about being a boy and liking girls were not features that fit them well. Fagan faced bullying by peers and other forms of pressure to conform to The Man Box (and The Heterosexual Box), and they began a process of sorting out their gender identity and their sexual orientation in searching for a genuine sexual and gendered self. As Fagan so aptly demonstrates from their personal life, to be queer means seeking the freedom of authenticity and self-creation, independent from the limitations or expectations of society.

In "Redefining Manhood: Resisting Sexism," Ewuare X. Osayande also tells a profoundly personal story: Osayande's father was murdered in January 2000. The killer was the abusive ex-boyfriend of a woman who was dating Osayande's father. Osayande details how the murderer "resorted to the most violent expression of male domination. In his sexist mind, the woman was his property. She had no agency or capacity to create a life outside of his desires." When she started dating Osayande's father, this violent man struck out at both of them in the most extreme manifestation of sexism and hegemonic masculinity. An activist and writer from Philadelphia, Osayande ties together male entitlement and domination, feminism, and the black liberation struggle. Complicating efforts to resolve sexism, Osayande explains, has been the racism of some feminist white women. Osayande points to this as limiting the radicalizing potential of feminism within the black community in part because "sexist black men" have successfully used racism within feminism "to trump any real discussion of sexism within the black community."[28] Osayande's commentary draws from his personal observations of sexism and racism in the black community, and speaks directly to the need and possibilities for improving feminism.

On a different note, Nathan Einschlag recounts his life-changing and heartbreaking experience playing college basketball at a school filled with privileged—and in many ways protected—young students. Growing up in the immigrant neighborhood of Jackson Heights in Queens, New York, Einschlag saw things that the guys on his team "only read about in magazines, or saw on TV." During high school, playing ball kept Einschlag off the streets and out of trouble. Now in college, Einschlag finds himself surrounded by teammates who think that excessive drinking and sexual conquest are equated with their ability to be a guy and play the game. Einschlag faces a difficult choice: to play college basketball and go along with the expected standards of masculine behavior, or stay true to himself and possibly leave the team behind.

Shifting attention from the basketball court to the pop culture landscape, Michael J. Murphy addresses advertising efforts that pressure boys and men to conform to dangerously limited ideas about manhood. "Grooming Masculinity: Cleans Your Balls, Yes. But What Else Does It Do?" explains how marketers exploit consumers by hawking sexism and orthodox masculinity along with the brands and products on their rosters. Advertisements that objectify men through sexual innuendo resist easy feminist analysis, but it is crucial that we "sharpen our cultural criticism skills, read more widely, and think a bit differently about how sexism rears its ugly head." To understand "what sexist media looks like at the dawn of the twenty-first century," Murphy explains, means that we must closely consider the conservative and reactionary lessons about masculinity that are conveyed through ads for men's health and body products.

Amanullah De Sondy also picks up the issue of media, turning his focus to the question *What does a Muslim man look like?* "Just as there are no two

Christians or Jews alike, no two Muslims are the same," De Sondy writes. "Yet we are bombarded by media with a fairly monolithic picture of Muslim men." In this post-9/11 political climate rife with stereotypes about Muslim masculinity, De Sondy provides alternative examples of Muslim men that go beyond xenophobic imagery of violent, bearded extremists. "Searching for the Colorful Faces of Muslim Men" explores meanings of Muslim masculinity and how we might broaden our conceptualizations beyond prejudice and stereotypes that are at odds with the actual diversity and variety of Muslim men globally.

Also addressing the political harm of stereotypes, Alfredo Mirandé focuses on machismo and Chicano/Latino masculinity in his essay, *"Hombres y Machos."* Mirandé recalls his experiences growing up in an extended family in Mexico, and reflects on how stereotypes of machismo are at odds with his memories of boyhood. This disjuncture led Mirandé to conduct empirical research investigating issues of machismo and masculinity in Chicano and Latino culture. Mirandé launched this project because although patriarchy, machismo, and "excessive masculinity" are assumed to be prevalent among Latino and Chicano men, there has been little research to establish this. Until recently, Mirandé writes, these generalizations about machismo "were based on meager, nonexistent, and misinterpreted evidence."[29] With *Hombres y Machos* Mirandé corrects the record. This project is of particular importance because of the ways in which images of machismo are used to perpetuate negative conceptions, and legitimize the economic and political subordination, of Mexican and Latino men.

1. While both women and men are involved in war, there are gendered aspects of global violence that are worth attention. The Summer 2007 special issue of the journal *Signs* titled *War and Terror: Raced-Gendered Logics and Effects* cites, for example, the gendered logic of masculine warrior ethic by which "peace is commonly associated with 'feminine virtues' and war with regimes of masculinity . . . Depending on the definition of war there are between sixty-five and two thousand sustained wars ongoing in the twenty-first century." Recent feminist scholarship suggesting that "deep-seated cultural, racial, and gender stereotypes" intensify during wartime thus becomes particularly relevant. See "Call for Papers," *Signs: Journal of Women in Culture and Society*, vol. 31, no. 1 (Autumn 2005): ix. For discussion about gendered discourse and thinking about war (as distinct from gendered participation in war), see Carol Cohn, "Wars, Wimps, and Women: Talking Gender and Thinking War," in Michael S. Kimmel and Michael A. Messner, eds., *Men's Lives*, seventh edition. San Francisco: Pearson, 2007. For further discussion about militarism, war, and contemporary gender politics, see, for example, Cynthia Enloe, *Bananas, Beaches and Bases: Making Feminist Sense of International Politics*. Berkeley: University of California Press, 2001; Bonnie Mann, "How America Justifies Its War: A Modern/Postmodern Aesthetics of Masculinity and Sovereignty," *Hypatia*,

vol. 21, no. 4 (Fall 2006): 147–163; Francis Shor, "Hypermasculine Warfare: From 9/11 to the War on Iraq," available at: http://bad.eserver.org/reviews/2005/shor.html (accessed April 29, 2012); Shira Tarrant, "Who's Accountable for the Abuse at Abu Ghraib?" *off our backs*, September–October 2004.

2. C.J. Pascoe, *Dude, You're a Fag: Masculinity and Sexuality in High School*. Los Angeles: University of California Press, 2011.

3. Shira Tarrant, "Guy Trouble: Are Young Men Really in Crisis, or Are These Boys Done Just Being Boys?" *Bitch Magazine: Feminist Response to Popular Culture*, Issue 43 (Spring 2009).

4. Lakshmi Chaudhry, "Growing Up to Be Boys," *AlterNet*, available at: http://www.alternet.org/story/33801 (accessed April 29, 2012).

5. Rachel Alicia Griffin and Joshua Daniel Phillips, "Eminem's *Love the Way You Lie* and the Normalization of Men's Violence Against Women," in Rebecca Ann Lind, ed., *Race/Gender/Class/Media 3.0: Considering Diversity Across Content, Audiences, and Production*. New York: Pearson, 2013.

6. Denise Gellene, "Men Found to Be Anorexic, Bulimic Also," *Los Angeles Times*, February 1, 2007, A12.

7. Susan Faludi, *Stiffed: The Betrayal of the American Man*. New York: Harper Perennial, 2000.

8. *Bitch: Feminist Response to Pop Culture*, Issue 28 (Spring 2005).

9. Rebecca Walker, ed., *What Makes a Man: 22 Writers Imagine the Future*. New York: Riverhead Books, 2005; Daniel Jones, ed., *The Bastard on the Couch: 27 Men Try Really Hard to Explain Their Feelings About Love, Loss, Fatherhood, and Freedom*. New York: Harper Paperbacks, 2005.

10. Michael Kimmel, *Guyland: The Perilous World Where Boys Become Men*. New York: Harper, 2008; Morgan Spurlock, dir., *Mansome*. Paladin, 2012; Hanna Rosin, *The End of Men: And the Rise of Women*. New York: Riverhead, 2012.

11. For discussions about how biological explanations came in and out of fashion as the dominant paradigm for explaining gender during the twentieth century, see Shira Tarrant, *When Sex Became Gender*. New York: Routledge, 2006. See also Martha McCaughey, *The Caveman Mystique: Pop-Darwinism and the Debates Over Sex, Violence, and Science*. New York: Routledge, 2007.

12. Michael Kimmel, *Manhood in America: A Cultural History*. New York: Oxford University Press, 2011; Cordelia Fine, *Delusions of Gender: How Our Minds, Society, and Neurosexism Create Difference*. New York: W.W. Norton, 2011.

13. This list is, of course, only partial, but it is evidence of the burgeoning critical interest in men, masculinity, and contemporary society.

14. R.W. Connell, *Masculinities*. Los Angeles: University of California Press, 1995; reprinted 2005.

15. Deborah S. David and Robert Brannon, eds., *The Forty-Nine Percent Majority: The Male Sex Role*. Reading, MA: Addison-Wesley, 1976.

16. Tim Carrigan, Bob Connell and John Lee, "Toward a New Sociology of Masculinity," in Rachel Adams and David Savran, eds., *The Masculinity Studies Reader*. Malden, MA: Blackwell, 2002, p. 112.

17. Michael S. Kimmel, *The History of Men: Essays on the History of American and British Masculinities*. Albany: SUNY Press, 2005. For resources on global masculinities, see the Global Masculinities Series (series editor, Michael S. Kimmel) published by Zed Books. Titles include, for example, Victor J. Seidler, ed., *Young Men & Masculinities*. London: Zed Books, 2006; Lahoucine Ouzgane, ed., *Islamic Masculinities*. London: Zed Books, 2006; Adam Jones, ed., *Men of the Global South*. London: Zed Books, 2006.

18. Iris Marion Young, *Justice and the Politics of Difference*. Princeton, NJ: Princeton University Press, 1990.

19. Kelly Rae Kraemer, "Solidarity in Action: Exploring the Work of Allies in Social Movements," *Peace & Change*, vol. 32, no. 1 (January 2007): 24.

20. R.W. Connell, *Gender and Power: Society, the Person and Sexual Politics*. Stanford: Stanford University Press, 1987, p. 183.

21. R.W. Connell, *Masculinities*. Los Angeles: University of California Press, 1995, p. 77. Challenging this domination is a central aspect of the essays included in Part V of *Men Speak Out* titled "Men and Feminism."

22. R.W. Connell, "Reply," *Gender & Society*, vol. 12, no. 4 (August 1998): 475.

23. Demetrakis Z. Demetriou, "Connell's Concept of Hegemonic Masculinity: A Critique," *Theory and Society*, vol. 30, no. 3 (June 2001): 355.

24. Sut Jhally, dir., *bell hooks: Cultural Criticism and Transformation*. Northampton, MA: Media Education Foundation, 1997.

25. Shira Tarrant, *Men and Feminism*. Berkeley, CA: Seal Press, 2009, pp 108–109; Elisabeth Schüssler Fiorenza, *Wisdom Ways*. New York: Orbis Books, 2001. Also see Lisa Factora-Borchers' discussion about kyriarchy at http://myecdysis.blogspot.com/2008/04/accepting-kyriarchy-not-apologies.html.

26. Rachel Adams and David Savran, eds., *The Masculinity Studies Reader*. Malden, MA: Blackwell, 2002, p. 337.

27. The Black Youth Project, led by Dr. Cathy J. Cohen, Professor of Political Science at the University of Chicago, collected empirical data to answer questions about black youth and empowerment, including a content analysis of rap music. The project conducted in-depth interviews about (among other things) political efficacy, gender and politics, and hip hop and politics. See http://blackyouthproject.uchicago.edu/ for further information.

28. See Winifred Breines, *The Trouble between Us: An Uneasy History of White and Black Women in the Feminist Movement*. New York: Oxford University Press, 2006. Despite efforts in the 1960s to embrace antiracist politics and build interracial political movements, Breines argues that white women's "staunch commitment to universal feminism revealed insensitivity to the differences between Black women and themselves." Although black and white feminists have achieved some success working together, "legacies of racial divisions and racism linger in contemporary social movements." Verta Taylor, "Review. *The Trouble between Us*," *Gender & Society*. vol. 21, no. 1 (February 2007): 137–138. For writings by women on contemporary issues of racial identity and feminist movement, see Lisa Weiner-Mahfuz, "Organizing 101: A Mixed-Race Feminist in Movements for Social Justice," and Rebecca Hurdis, "Heartbroken: Women of Color Feminism and the Third Wave," in Daisy Hernández

and Bushra Rehman, eds., *Colonize This! Young Women of Color on Today's Feminism*. Emeryville, CA: Seal Press, 2002; and Susan Muaddi Darrraj, "Third World, Third Wave Feminism(s): The Evolution of Arab American Feminism," in Rory Dicker and Alison Piepmeier, eds., *Catching a Wave: Reclaiming Feminism for the 21st Century*. Boston: Northeastern University Press, 2003.

29. Alredo Mirandé, *Hombres y Machos: Masculinity and Latino Culture*. Boulder, CO: Westview Press, 1997, p. 5. For a discussion about machismo and Puerto Rican men, see José B. Torres, "Masculinity and Gender Roles among Puerto Rican Men: Machismo on the U.S. Mainland," in Michael S. Kimmel and Michael A. Messner, eds., *Men's Lives*, seventh edition. San Francisco: Pearson, 2007.

DAYTONA BEACH: BEYOND BEATS AND RHYMES

Byron Hurt

Daytona Beach, Florida. I'm at BET's annual Spring Bling, an event fashioned after MTV's Spring Break, a yearly-televised weeklong party and hedonistic mating ritual. Like the MTV version, BET's Spring Bling looks like mad fun on television, and is well attended. One big distinction between the two music television shows (both are under the corporate banner of Viacom): MTV's Spring Break is largely white with some faces of color sprinkled throughout the crowd; BET's Spring Bling is clearly black space. White folks here are mostly cultural tourists.

I am here to shoot footage for my film *Hip-Hop: Beyond Beats and Rhymes*, a documentary about manhood in rap music and hip-hop culture. I am hoping to interview rap artists and fans about their thoughts and feelings about sexism and misogyny in mainstream hip-hop music.

There is a lot of energy here, and it is shaping up to be the type of event I've been to many times before—from the annual Greek Fest on Long Island's Jones Beach, to July Fourth weekend at Martha's Vineyard, to Atlanta's Freaknic, to the Grand Conclave of my fraternity, Omega Psi Phi. At thirty-five years old, this kind of thing ain't new to me. I've seen it all when it comes to social events for young black folks like this one. I'm older, and it's been a while, but amazingly, I still feel comfortable in this crowd.

The morning starts out mildly, with young black men and women from all walks of life congregating in hotel lobbies, chilling on the popular strip, and out on Daytona Beach. Hip-hop music thumps in the background. Before lunchtime there are hundreds of hip-hop heads on the scene, doing what has become typically hip-hop—promoting parties, shamelessly plugging and passing out CD demos and mix tapes, igniting impromptu freestyle battles, and, of course, lots and lots of flossin'. The party at Daytona Beach has officially begun. And everyone, including myself, loves a good hip-hop party.

Just before my trip, BET denied my request for press credentials and backstage access—a last minute curveball. But I am here anyway, hoping to somehow bullshit my way behind the scenes to score interviews with A-List rappers. Once here though, I find BET's on-location headquarters to be well organized. Security is extra tight. At the press check-in table, I politic for an "elite access" badge, claiming I never received a declination of my credentials request, which I have with me, hard copy in hand. The polite but firm BET event coordinators recognize my name and the name of my film production. They assure me that my request had been seriously considered, but tell me that unfortunately, the powers that be at BET denied my request.

They turn my crew and me away, and ask me to step aside so they can help the next production crew in line. Malik, my production assistant, Caleb, my soundman, and Bill, my director of photography, are all here with me. As the film's director, I must come up with a Plan B.

We head back through the hotel lobby, which is now a spectacle. Dudes are freestyling and waging MC battles ten feet from the hotel's concierge. A street team comprised mostly of black men dressed in black and white short-sleeved tees holds placards on wooden sticks high above their heads. Bold white letters on the black laminated poster boards read "Let's Get Free," promoting rapper Freeway's upcoming new album. Men fully dressed in summer gear ogle scantily dressed women who pass by. How hotel security manages all of this traffic, I don't know.

Throngs of men, donning du-rags underneath carefully placed baseball caps, slightly tilted, and barely touching the scalp, perform a brand of hip-hop masculinity reserved only for true thugs, pimps, and playas. A few folks, some older and black, some white and un-hip-hop, are clearly not associated with the event and look uncomfortably out of place.

With all of the video cameras, throwback jerseys, tricked-out rides and bling, I am starting to feel like I am in a real live hip-hop music video. Everyone comes, it seems, to play a role. The men behind their cameras (and it is mostly men with video cameras) shoot black female bodies at camera angles intended for the male gaze. Men in hip-hop drag do their best G-Unit impersonations on camera. Instead of throwing up the Roc (Rocafella Record's world famous hand gesture in the shape of a diamond), they throw up homemade hand signals repping their hood or fledgling record companies. And the women, well, some of the women at least (save the ones disinterested in serving as props), play the role of the sex kitten—the object of the men's desire.

The main drag now is a car show. 50 Cent's *P.I.M.P.* is ubiquitous on the strip and blares out of tricked out cars with brilliant color combinations. One car, a refurbished '74 Chevy Impala, is money green with burnt orange trim. Twenty-two inch rims spin, even as the car stands still in bumper-to-bumper traffic. As the car slowly passes a large crowd, the passenger, clearly a showman, opens his door revealing a bucket seat with a fuzzy wool seat cover. He spins the seat 360 degrees. The crowd is awed, and in unison, everyone screams "Oooohhhh!" By today's conventions, this is all so hip-hop.

As the day grows longer, the energy increases, and all of the elements for this live hip-hop video are in place. Everyone is ready on set. Lights, camera, action.

As I stand on the busy sidewalk with my Angela Davis T-shirt and blue New York Yankees fisherman's hat pulled down just above my eyes, it does not take long to find Plan B. The story reveals itself. What my crew and I catch on camera next is far more important, alarming, and compelling than backstage access or any interview with an A-list rapper could provide.

A BET performance lets out, and now there are thousands of hip-hop fans on the strip. It is hot. Very hot. Men drape their shoulders with white hand towels and occasionally wipe away their sweat. Some let their towels hang long from their back pockets, a hip-hop fashion statement. They all swagger. I quickly realize that this is not just black space—this is black *male* space. The masculine energy is palpable. Women in small groups stick close together as they walk to their next destination. Suddenly, as if a tacit agreement among the men had been reached, the men begin to make life difficult for the women. As women in skimpy bathing suits exit the beach area to cross the crowded Daytona strip, men with video cameras follow. One unfortunate threesome (one white, one black, and one Latina), get stuck at a crosswalk and wait for their turn to cross the street. The men with video cameras descend. A man with audacious gumption lifts the white women's blue and white sundress, and records her bare ass. As he tilts his camera upward, she swipes at his hands and spins. Simultaneously, the light turns red, as if to save her from further distress. She begins to cross the street. Her two friends try to prevent themselves from being recorded, but to no avail. The men capture their bodies on camera, without their approval. Who knows where these women's likenesses will end up?

On the same sidewalk, about twenty yards ahead, a man in a red, white, and blue T-shirt hustles homemade DVDs from last year's Spring Bling. Titled *Dirty South*, an image of a black woman's behind graces the cover. You do not see her face, just her buttocks and legs. I tell my cameraman to get a shot of him. Realizing he is on camera, he hams it up. Holding one DVD close to the lens, he endorses his product like a hip-hop Donald Trump. He knows his target audience—young, male, with hip-hop sensibilities. He looks directly into the camera when he speaks, and then to me when he is done. He has no clue I am an anti-sexist activist. No one here does.

I blend right in the crowd because I am a man. Not even my Angela Davis T-shirt gives me away.

I head up the street with my crew behind me. I tell Bill to stay close to me as we move through the thick crowd. The men form lines on both sides of the sidewalk as the women walk through the center. It is clearly a set-up. One by one, as women with various shapes, skin complexions, and hairstyles walk through, the men—showing no restraint— grab at body parts. Arms, shoulders, hands, chests, and asses, nothing is off limits. Some women yell, "Stop! Quit! And "Get off of me!" Others helplessly ask, "What are you doing?" Most remain silent; one out of maybe ten of the women swings violently at a male offender. They are the courageous ones. Resistors this brave are rare. The others seem to endure it.

Then, out of nowhere, I hear a roar. I turn around and see a young man, probably in his mid-twenties, pulling down a heavy-set woman's bikini top. She stands there, smiling. She is complicit, but doesn't seem well. She looks mentally challenged. I watch as he and his boy stand around the woman, smiling, pointing at her bare breasts. Video cameras, including mine, roll. As an anti-sexist activist, my first instinct is to intervene. But I remember I am here to document this event, not to be a proactive bystander. My inaction fills my body with inner-conflict. I feel tense, uncomfortable, nervous. I am vexed at what I see, but I remain focused on capturing the moment on film for the greater good of revealing the prevalence of misogyny in hip-hop culture, and how normalized it has become. No one challenges the two men at all. In fact, men cheer from the sidelines, rewarding the duo's sexual violence. In an instant, I muster the courage to approach the two men. I walk closer to the scene. Bill and Caleb are in tow. "What makes you feel like it is okay to pull this woman's top off like this in public?" I ask. The one caught in the act sheepishly grins, revealing braces on his teeth. He tries to be coy. "Nah, see what happened was, I was walking past her, right, and she grabbed my ass, so I grabbed her tits," he says. I look him straight in the eye as if to say, *Yeah, right, man. Don't try to play me.* I repeat my question. His husky friend, apparently his road dog for the weekend, jumps in. He begins to break down the situation on behalf of all black men in America. "Look here," he says. "The white boys got their *Girls Gone Wild*, now this is our *Girls Gone Wild*, you see? Why should the white boys have all the fun? They have their MTV Spring Break, now this is our Spring Break. The white boys do it. Why can't we? We're not trying to hurt no one; we're just trying to have a good time."

Unmoved, I reframe my question. "What if someone did something like that to your daughter or your sister?" He becomes defensive. "Aw, man, why you trying to play me out like that, brother?" He then motions to Bill to turn the camera off. I give Bill a quick, sharp look—nonverbal communication for *Don't you even think about turning off that camera!* The guy, realizing now that I was dead serious about challenging their behavior, tries to shift the conversation, and questions my racial loyalty. "Yo man, how you gonna play the black man out like that, man? Don't make us look bad on camera like that, man." Then he says, "Look, we're brothers, right? Why would you play us out like the white man? The white man always plays us out like we're bad people, man. Don't be like the white man."

Admittedly, this taps into my concern about revealing negative black male behavior to a largely white PBS audience. I am fearful about reinforcing stereotypes of black men as oversexed to an audience of unsophisticated, conservative white people. I almost retreat. But just before I do, I come up with a comeback line that I think might work. "But she's a black woman, though," I say. "How could I be against the race if I am supporting a black woman? It's not like she's white, or green, or an alien," I say, growing more confident in my position. "This is a black woman you are disrespecting and you're challenging my blackness?"

Stumped, he tries to deflect by pointing at my shirt. "Who is this?" he asks, looking down at the iconic photo of the Afro-wearing woman on my chest. "She's a Black Panther, right?"

"Yeah," I say. "This is Angela Davis."

"My daddy was a Black Panther," he says. "I got mad respect for the Panthers."

"Well, not only was she a Black Panther," I tell him, "but she is also a black feminist."

"Oh, word?" He seems to lose interest.

"Word," I say. "And she would never approve of you treating black women this way."

Moving closer to me he as if to share a well-kept secret, he says, "Dawg, I know it's wrong, but if the women let us treat them this way, then we're going to treat them this way, *you-know-what-I'm-sayin*? It's just how it is."

I smell alcohol on his breath and realize this conversation is only going to go so far. I tell him that it doesn't matter if women allow us to mistreat them, it's still not cool. Just as I was making my point, a tricked-out car passes by, which catches everyone's attention. Suddenly, the interview is over.

I looked away for a second, and the two men were gone.

At dusk, the scene at Daytona worsens. The men here are completely out of control. Check that. The men here are completely *in control*. They are benefiting from the type of male privilege that transcends race. Even the police officers, who are white, remain silent. If the women were white, I wonder if they would be so nonchalant about enforcing the law. The women, save but a few resistive voices, are too complacent, too accepting of sexist behavior without resistance. My crew and I grow tired of shooting scene after scene of sexual assaults, and take a break. We find a place on the strip that is not as crowded, and sit down on the curb. My soundman, Caleb, asks if we can go home. "I knew it was going to be wild down here, but I didn't expect this," he says. Stunned by the enormity of the situation, I sit with my head cradled in my hands. My young production assistant, Malik, seems less disturbed than the rest of us. "I'm going to get some pizza. Do y'all want anything?" he asks. There is a long silence. No one answers. Then Bill, who is white, says softly, as if he's unsure if it is cool to say aloud, "This is exactly what white people think of black people. You know that, right, Byron?" I sigh. His question is genuine, honest, and perfectly timed. I am thinking the same thing, but don't want to admit to Bill. To outsiders we look really bad to people who do not understand our complex history and culture. Shit, we look bad, period, no matter the spectator. There's no comeback for Bill's sad-but-true admission. I feel disappointed in my people, both male and female. I sit thinking about my work as an anti-sexist activist—a man who speaks to groups of men about rape and sexual assault—and how much work there is to be done before this kind of male behavior becomes socially unacceptable. I think also about women who, just like men, internalize sexism, and how so many participate in their own degradation. I feel sad and overwhelmed.

Later in the evening during another break, I run into a woman who sticks out like a sore thumb. She wears a natural hairstyle, locked, and reminds me of some of the gender-conscious women I know back home. Unlike many of the women here who seem aloof—even validated by the negative attention some men give them—she seems like she is studying her environment. She is here with a group of friends from New York. She looks pensive, and is deep in thought. I strike up a conversation, and we talk about the Daytona scene. This is her first time at BET's Spring Bling. She says she is working on her PhD, and is here on Spring Break. She "needed to get away," she tells me. Her university is predominantly white, and she wanted to be around black people and have a good time this weekend. She, too, is disappointed. I have lots of questions for her. I am thinking about interviewing her for the film, but right now, the camera is off. I ask her why women come to events like this, and why women put up with this kind of behavior by men? Her answer hits me over the head like a club.

"I don't know," she tells me. "I think most women put up with this kind of treatment because we live most of our lives dealing with men who are assholes," she explains. "We expect ya'll to act like this. It's almost a fact of life, so we grin and bear it and try to have a good time despite trifling brothers who act like they've never seen a woman before."

Wow. What a powerful statement. What strikes me most about her comments is the fact that when describing men's behavior, she uses the word "y'all" to describe all men. Without knowing my feminist sensibilities, this woman sees no difference between me, and the "typical" man on the strip. Who could blame her?

Still, something about her not distinguishing me from the rest of the men stings. Like the men on the strip, she doesn't know I am an anti-sexist activist. I flash back to my own past, before I became a gender-conscious male, before I learned about sexism, before I understood the reality of women who live in a rape culture. Back then, I was just as typical as some of the men here today in Daytona: male privileged, selfish, unconcerned about women's issues, guarded about the image of black men, defensive, and insecure about my masculinity. Fortunately for me, I had the opportunity to learn about gender issues in ways many of these men have not. That's the only thing that separates me from them. Other than that, we are all the same. We are men who learn sexism from myriad places in the culture. Hip-hop is just one place that informs us about how to treat women.

A month later I'm home watching BET on a Saturday afternoon. Spring Bling is on television and it looks like nothing but fun for all who attended. The final package is slick, well edited, and entertaining. You see concerts, hip-hop executives, celebrities, star-struck fans, tons of bling, and interviews with A-List rappers—all of the footage I would have shot had BET given me the backstage pass I requested. But what you will never see on BET is what happens away from all the glitz and the glamour at this particular Spring Bling—men gone wild, and women who came here for a party, but who go home as sexual assault survivors.

With eight hours of footage in the can, I have a story to tell.

THE ENEMY WITHIN: ON BECOMING A STRAIGHT WHITE GUY

Jacob Anderson-Minshall

I've seen the enemy, and he is me. But it hasn't always been that way.
From the time I was in preschool, I've been agitating for social change. I accompanied my mother to women's rights rallies, and door-to-door campaigns for ratification of the Equal Rights Amendment. In high school, I joined anti-nuclear protests. In college, I worked against apartheid and marched in support of women's reproductive rights. After graduating, I canvassed for the anti-nuclear group SANE/FREEZE and made phone calls on behalf of NARAL Pro-Choice America before turning my attention to gay and lesbian rights, then joining the environmental fight against the destruction of the natural world. The demographic of most protests leaned heavily toward the female gender, while those being protested almost always shared their own set of characteristics: They were primarily straight white men. At the time, I was a white lesbian woman.

Today, when I look in the mirror, I find a man looking back and I wonder if, in the coming years, I will lose my feminist sensibilities. I recently read *The Testosterone Files*, the memoir of Max Wolf Valerio, a man who, like me, is a former lesbian feminist. A writer featured in the influential work by feminists of color, *This Bridge Called My Back*, Max's hormones have now engulfed him and he can't remember these days what it felt like to be a woman. Max now gets accused of being sexist—a charge he *never* thought would be leveled at him. In a lot of ways I am just beginning my own journey, and I wonder if I will follow in Max's footsteps or blaze my own trail.

My own struggles with gender identity and expression, my discomfort with my physical body, and my attempts to come to term with the labels assigned me, started early and continued for decades. I was born a girl, but I like to say that I was raised a boy. My parents didn't seem to care that I was a tomboy and they allowed me to wear boys' clothes, roughhouse freely, and play with action figures and cars instead of dolls. At home, especially after we moved to a small farm in rural Idaho, I was allowed to be pretty much as masculine as I wanted to be.

The same could not be said about my experience at school. Our move to the farm dropped us into a conservative religious community to which we didn't naturally belong and to which we failed to assimilate. We were uninvited to most social functions and children were directed by their parents to avoid us. But there was also an incredible increase in the communal pressure for me to conform to gender expectations. When I was ten years old, for example, I was called into the school's administrative office where the district psychologist proceeded to interrogate me. He demanded to know why I only hung out with a group of boys and suggested that I would be much happier if I had female friends. I experienced the confrontation as an implicit threat: Stop hanging out with the boys or start seeing the shrink more often. I quickly became a loner.

Influenced by my mother's spirit of social justice, I chose to attend a small Quaker college. I took women's studies classes and majored in Peace and Global Studies. I adored Audre Lorde, the writings of Barbara Smith, and Adrienne Rich's theory about compulsory heterosexuality. I learned to recognize the oppressive patriarchal system, to acknowledge my own privileges, and to view straight white men as the oppressive enemy.

Although I came out as a lesbian in college I wasn't comfortable with this identity until I blended my college's compulsory academic-feminist-androgynous-lesbian look with dive-bar, old-school, blue-collar dyke and found solace in the guise of a butch-identified lesbian. Dating women and dressing in men's attire, I finally felt at home until I'd pass a mirror and notice that my reflection didn't reveal the physical person I felt I was.

In graduate school, I co-founded a student LGBT organization, ran for homecoming king, met my wife, and continued to inform my studies with a feminist perspective. I wrote my master's thesis, "Lesbianism as Confrontational Rhetoric," in which I argued that it was not just the words lesbian women used or the political actions they took, but lesbianism itself that was confrontational. In the study of social movement rhetoric, the level of institutional response can be a fair indicator of the threat that is perceived in a group's confrontational actions. Now I recognize that it's not merely sexual orientation, but gender variance, that provokes discomfort in individuals and institutions. This discomfort and perceived threat result in violence and ❡ discrimination against gender non-conformists.

The Combahee River Collective's "A Black Feminist Statement" could have been written about transgender people rather than black women. To paraphrase their argument, cataloging the cruel, often murderous treatment black women and transgendered people receive indicates how little value and how much fear has been projected on our lives.

Gender variance doesn't just threaten patriarchal gender/sex roles; it seems to intimidate some feminists as well. Transgender people might undermine the argument that gender is socially constructed. Transpeople, along with intersex people, threaten conservative assumptions that there are two, and only two classes of human beings—men and women—and radical assumptions that gender classes are entirely socially created, rather than having some biological roots. Although studies of transgender individuals are sparse, findings seem to indicate that hormone-disrupting environmental pollutants may impact the development of a fetus's brain and their gender identities by producing, for example, male-brained persons with female genitalia.

Anecdotal accounts of transmen also seem to indicate that biology can out-maneuver socialization. Despite being raised female, years on hormonal treatment seem to produce men as diverse as the rest of the world's guys including those who are sexist jerks.

In order to transition from one sex to another, you first spend a great deal of time speaking with a psychiatrist about your gender issues. The first time I verbalized my feelings about my gender to a shrink, I said, "I'd hate to be the woman that proves Freud right." It's hard to admit to penis envy when women, especially lesbians, have been struggling against that misconception for over a century. I was worried about being seen as a gender traitor and losing a twenty-year relationship I had with the lesbian community—a community to which I still feel a great deal of allegiance.

When I was younger, I spent many years with little or no interaction with straight men. My friends were women and gay men. I worked in women-only businesses. My mother used to worry that I'd never meet a nice guy by hanging out in all-lesbian venues. She was right. When I was a woman, I didn't meet a lot of so-called nice guys hanging out with straight people either. Every time I thought I was making a friend, guys apparently thought I'd just given them permission to hit on me.

For me, men's advances were as unwanted and unappreciated as they would be to a homophobic man. I found their sexual gaze offensive. I didn't understand why they didn't see the man inside of me. Now that I live as a man, I don't mind at all when the gay boys think I'm hot. I know they're seeing me as a *man*, and that makes all the difference in the world.

I didn't decide to transition because I was thrilled by the men I met. I accepted my masculinity despite the bad examples. After thirty years trying to convince myself that I was just a different kind of woman, I've found comfort in defining myself as a different kind of guy.

As a transman I still see myself as a little queer, but now my queerness, my *other*ness, isn't readily visible. Straight men assume I'm one of them and suddenly treat me as a member of a special club, swapping inside jokes and slapping me heartily on the back. In the lesbian community that has been my home for twenty years, some now view me as a straight white man and reject me as such. I am no longer a welcome contributor to certain publications. My trans status threatens to give my lesbian wife a bad name and could even cost her her career. Now that the woman she married is a man, my wife hears upfront doubt that she's still a lesbian and vocal criticism about the fact that she edits a lesbian magazine. Like an estranged family member, I find myself defending my personal sense of allegiance to the lesbian community. Other transmen have accused me of discounting my own masculinity by repudiating my alignment with straight America, and some lesbians doubt my ability to be an ally in this new man's body.

Masculine transpeople are assumed to be renouncing femininity by their transition; they are often accused of gender treachery. Gender theorist Judith "Jack" Halberstam argues that even for female-to-male transpeople, misogyny goes hand-in-hand with masculinity.

I don't *think* I'm a misogynist. So far, even under the influence of testosterone I continue to believe that institutions of patriarchy and the minutiae of male indoctrination are in place to deny women's power. I believe that women have natural power that comes not only from their sexuality, but also from their ability to make life. Men, on the other hand, have institutional power that comes from controlling the governmental, medical, religious, and educational institutions. Indoctrinating socialization distracts women from recognizing their own power and keeps them at the mercy of men. And it disguises its real purpose from men, so most men have no idea that their actions promote the current patriarchal regime. They're just being men.

As a white person I've always had racial privilege and I know my life and options would have been entirely different if I hadn't. Although the trips to thrift stores and the reliance on our homegrown food might have confused me as a child, my family was first generation middle class. I haven't always lived up to my economic heritage—I've been a carny making less than a dollar an hour, I've lived out of our vehicle, I've worked as a day laborer—but I do have resources unavailable to the working poor and outright destitute.

As a transperson who appears male and straight I now have even greater privilege. It doesn't evaporate just because you don't want it. And I do want it. After twenty years, I am tired of being a starving lesbian writer. I want to be well paid and make the full dollar instead of eighty cents. Don't we all want that? I want that for all of us. But what's the appropriate, feminist response to this added privilege? What are my responsibilities? What should I do if I'm offered more for a job now than I was as a woman? And will I stop noticing these differences at some point?

As soon as I changed my name from Susannah to Jacob, I started to be treated differently. It started even before I began hormone treatment; commencing in cyberspace and slowly rippling out into the real world until now I pass in almost every arena. Men grant me greater respect and are willing to see me as an authority. Women and men alike stopped being courteous. Women no longer appreciate me expressing my opinion. Traits like being outspoken that were formerly lauded as feminist, are now seen as just another guy's propensity for interrupting and valuing their own opinions over women's. I wonder how long it will take before being treated differently will make me a different person. I have more questions than answers and I'm not exactly sure how to bridge my feminist past with my male future. Coming to terms with my place in this oppressive patriarchal system means learning how to balance being a feminist with being a man. Maybe that means constantly evaluating the manner in which I'm expressing my masculinity.

Recognizing the inherent privilege in my situation doesn't mean that privilege can't be taken away because of my trans status. I'm always at risk for my biological beginning being discovered and held against me. My place in the power hierarchy can always be reiterated through rape or other violence. In most locales in America it is still legal to discriminate against trans people. Like women, a lot of transpeople are being shafted—just differently. In fact, as the authors of the 2006 anthology *Transgender Rights* explain, the same institutionalized, sexist assumptions that keep women down are used in legal settings to deny transpeople their rights. For example, in determining which binary sex to ascribe a transsexual defendant, some modern-day courts have relied on antiquated notions of femaleness like defining female sex as the ability to be sexually penetrated within the confines of "normal" heterosexual intercourse.

Becoming a man has opened my eyes and I no longer see all men—even straight, white, natal men—as inherent enemies to women or peace or the environment. That's not to say that it isn't mostly men who are controlling the political and economic power in this country. They are. Those holding the axe over our collective heads are more likely to be men. That said, there are a great number of men who are suffering intensely from our current economic woes: men who are imprisoned by their masculine roles; men who are sent to their death in the name of freedom; men who long for women to take on more responsibility.

A patriarchal system keeps our country in the control of men, and that male domination clearly denigrates all things feminine. But the male-centric nature of our society doesn't—by itself—explain America's racial and economic stratification. If patriarchy is not the sole cause of men's oppression (be these men minorities in race, religion, class, sexuality, gender identity and expression, or ability, etc.), then there is certainly something else going on here as well. This deserves our attention especially since the difficulties that some men face these days don't seem like signs of patriarchy crumbling. (If patriarchy was the only source of oppression, and if it was collapsing, there would presumably be a leveling out of privilege, wealth, and power. And I don't think we can argue this has happened.)

There are a lot of awful problems in the world today, and to solve them we need to make allies and build bridges to other movements seeking change. We need to accept the problems of others as our own. Until we understand that the unbelievably high rate of African-American incarceration is an American tragedy not just a black one, we won't be addressing racial inequities. Until we see that rape, domestic violence, and childcare are not women's issues but our issues, we won't improve women's status or win their respect. Until we truly accept same-sex marriage we are not honestly striving for sexual equality. Until we demand universal healthcare we will continue to allow people just like us to die on the streets.

To start, here's what I have to say to all my brothers: Until being called pussy, girl, fag, and pansy isn't the worst thing in the world, we won't eliminate misogyny. We do have different expectations for women and men, although there is some leeway for women to be masculine because our society values masculinity. But the fact that men can't be feminine without being punished by our society is proof that we still don't value femininity: It's treated as reprehensible—at least when it appears in men and boys.

One day when I was walking my dogs in the local park, I passed a group of Little League boys running sprints while their coach yelled motivational phrases. "*What are you? Pussies? Is that all you can do, girls?*" This shit stuns me. I can't believe that we're still teaching our boys to push themselves harder by threatening that if they don't, they'll be girls and that being a girl is a terrible thing. If we really believed that the sexes are equal, this wouldn't happen.

When we respond violently to those who question our (hetero)sexuality— say with taunts of "sissy" or "pansy"—isn't that just another example of fearing our own femininity? Homophobes fear nothing more than being feminized by another man's sexual gaze. To avoid being seen as woman-like, they are willing to deprive fellow citizens of their civil rights and even, in some cases, their lives. This again begs the question: What's so awful about being women?

I have one advantage in this arena: I'm a man who was called a girl, not occasionally, but every day, for decades. Even when I excelled at sports or academics. Sure, it felt wrong, because it wasn't accurate, but it wasn't a put down. Not then, not now. I'm comfortable enough in my masculinity to not have to prove it. When someone calls me a pussy I don't get offended. I've had one. I've been one. Being a girl wasn't right for me, but it sure as hell wasn't the worst thing in the world.

THE BULLYING DEMANDS OF MASCULINITY: A GENDERQUEER ESCAPE

River Willow Fagan

Growing up as a boy in a fundamentalist Christian family I was reminded again and again that I was failing to be masculine enough. I was clumsy and timid when I played baseball or soccer. I much preferred to spend my time reading or writing or drawing instead of helping my dad fix cars in the garage. But most importantly, I failed at the most primal commandment of American masculinity: I failed to be aggressive enough to fight back against the older boys who bullied me.

Whether they were taunting me with names or knocking me to the ground—attacking my sense of self emotionally or physically—I froze up. I knew that I was expected to man up and defend myself, but something deep inside of me just couldn't do it.

Despite my inability to be physically aggressive, in other ways I fit the standard ideas of boyhood. I loved monsters and wizards, comic books and dinosaurs and UFOs. In the muddy days of spring, I would run around my backyard, turning over rocks and watching with fascination all the creepy-crawly bugs scurrying for cover. Most of my other friends were nerdy boys, and we would have sleepovers and play complicated board games with names like Tower of the Wizard King.

Perhaps because of these attributes, I never really questioned whether I actually *was* a boy or not, whether that identity truly fit the shape of my soul. There was no one—not in the sunlit world of the suburbs and not in the hazy dream worlds of novels and video games in which I increasingly immersed myself—who questioned the gender that had been assigned to them. And I certainly didn't know anybody who lived outside the assumptions that everyone was either a boy or a girl.

This binary view of gender was presented to me as both Divine order and a clear biological fact. The power imbalance between men and women, which was present in my parents' house and their church and the fundamentalist Christian school they sent me to, was part of God's plan.

I have a vivid memory of sitting in the bathtub as a twelve-year-old, wishing that I could be a girl. I thought maybe if I was a girl, then my personality—my creativity, my intense emotional responses, my compassion, my desire to approach conversations as a dance of equal partners—might make more sense. Then maybe everyone wouldn't think I was weird and push me away. And beneath these concerns, was the hazy sense that if I was a girl, my attraction to other boys would be okay.

It wasn't until I was sixteen that I could fully admit that my world would light up when a cute boy smiled at me. Knowing this, I could no longer accept what I had been taught, what I had accepted as true for my whole life. I could no longer believe in a religion which taught that my desire, my love, my *self* was sinful. Rejecting Christianity was a major step in my personal liberation, my journey towards embracing my genderqueerness and my sexual queerness.

The problem was, I still had not figured out a way to end the bullying. Andy, an older boy who sat behind me in my first-hour social studies class, spent almost every morning poking me in the back or quietly kicking the leg of my desk. Boys in my gym class frequently said things like, "What would you do if I pushed you through that window right now?" or "You're a faggot, aren't you?"

I survived this time in my life largely through reading. Fiction offered an escape from painful realities; non-fiction, including feminist books, equipped me with powerful new lenses through which to interpret my experiences. Understanding the underlying dynamics of subjugation and silencing gave me some sense of power. Ascribing the cause of this violence to a deeper social pattern also lessened my feeling that something was wrong with me; perhaps I wasn't failing masculinity. Perhaps masculinity was failing me. Connecting my personal story to the broader story of feminism also opened up the possibility that I, too, might find some kind of liberation.

As a gay teenager in a suburban world in which everyone appeared to be straight, I felt a deep hunger for queer stories. What I craved most was a sense of queer history and a connection to others. I needed to disprove the wounding, still-aching claim that people like me were some kind of unnatural aberration. I wanted to point to a timeline, a diagram of roots that showed that we had been here for a long time, that we had a rightful place in the world.

The books that most fulfilled this need drew from many indigenous cultures. I read *Queer Spirits: A Gay Men's Myth Book* by Will Roscoe and *Coming Out Spiritually* by Christian de la Huerta, and books about the spiritual and social roles that gay men have played in various cultural and historical contexts. The books helped in some ways but they ignored a lot of context and twisted original histories into shapes more easily comprehended by (or less threatening to) white Americans. What really struck me, though, was the idea that there can be a third gender. This deeply resonated with me and affirmed my sense that I had never been like other boys. I started sorting out my gender identity and my sexual orientation.

In college, the straight boys in my dorm would talk about girls, how attractive and mysterious they were, and the strategies one might use to get dates with them. I felt like a visiting anthropologist in disguise. The boys thought I was one of them and treated me accordingly. But I wasn't.

Living away from home for the first time, and in a social environment where I was no longer continually bombarded with bullying, I began slowly to relax and unfold. I began to explore expressing my internal sense of androgyny through my appearance. I let my hair grow long. I nervously, self-consciously, bought a long brown hippie skirt. I wore it first as part of a Halloween costume or to a costume party. Then I began to wear it more often, until I was wearing skirts to every party with a theme.

I was acutely aware of how I communicated and the way I moved through the world. I paid attention to social space and I was careful not to take up too much of it. I was interrupted much more frequently than I interrupted anyone. My feminist and LGBTQ friends (of all genders) confirmed that I didn't really seem like a man. But I also didn't feel like a woman. I felt like some mix, some new and unnamed blend of masculine and feminine, boy and girl.

One of my friends, who was active as a drag king, playfully asked me one day what *my* drag name would be. I came up with some quick answer, but the question inspired some deep introspection. What if I could choose a new name, a name that would reflect my queerness, my androgyny? I found one that felt right, both in terms of gender and in terms of my personality. And that is how I became River.

Around this time I came across the word "genderqueer" and felt a profound sense of relief and expanded possibility. There were other people like me. It was possible to walk through the world as something other than a man or a woman, and to still be seen and understood.

As a genderqueer person who was assigned male at birth, and who is frequently read as a cisgendered man, navigating the landscape of privilege and accountability is often quite tricky. Ironically, I didn't really confront this issue in any of my college Women's Studies classes. Mostly, I think, because they were designed for and focused on the issues of women; they weren't meant to educate people who experience male privilege.

In my senior year in college, I took a course on multicultural psychology. This class involved a lot of personal reflection and group dialogue, and the professor brought the very useful perspective that almost everyone experiences privilege in some aspects of their identities and oppression in others.

I felt a deep resistance to accepting my own male privilege. How could I benefit from being a man when I didn't experience myself as a man? I also had trouble with some of the ways in which male privilege was described; for example, the idea that the ability to rape people could be considered a privilege. Framing things in such a way made it seem like committing acts of sexual violence with impunity was a good thing, a benefit, the way that being paid well for your work was.

The idea that privilege comes about not from your internal experience or identity, but from other people's perceptions of you helped me somewhat. But what has helped most for me is a phrase that I heard a transwoman use once: "nonconsensual male privilege." For me, this phrase highlights a fundamental wrinkle in all experiences I have of male privilege. If someone treats me favorably because they perceive me to be a man—and a straight man— they are simultaneously ignoring and erasing my gender queerness and my sexual queerness, as well.

In light of these insights and as my healing journey progressed, I began to wonder if it would be beneficial for me to reclaim masculinity in some way, to try to discover or create some kind of positive male identity. I grew out my facial hair until I had a thick dark beard and I embarked on another odyssey of reading, a quest to discover the spiritual essence of masculinity.

I read many of the books popular in the men's movement, in particular, depth psychology explorations of mythic and sacred masculinity. But none of them felt like true alternatives to me. Either they rang hollow or they were the same old patriarchal lies dressed up in new clothing, paying lip service to feminism but still ultimately based on domination and disconnection. The most vivid example in my memory is a book that attempted to use "The King" as an archetype of healthy masculinity. But the description of the archetype used the same logic as the medieval concept of the Divine Right of Kings.

I could find no definition or description of masculinity that resonated for me or seemed to be a healthy model. bell hooks came close in her book *The Will to Change: Men, Masculinity and Love*, in which she differentiated patri-archal masculinity and feminist masculinity. But her description of feminist masculinity, which focused on being aware of one's emotions and cultivating relationships and community, seemed to be simply a description of a healthy person not a healthy man; nothing in it felt specific to manhood or masculinity.

And there my quest ended. I realized there was no spiritual essence to masculinity, no primal untouched core to recover from the chains of patriarchy. Masculinity was simply something we had made up, a game we had invented and then, forgetting its invention, taken deadly seriously.

My invented androgynous gender was just as real, just as authentic and natural as anyone's manhood or womanhood.

Feminism is central to my ability to understand and speak the story of my life. That story is deeply intertwined with the devastating impacts that patriarchy has on everyone, including those labeled men and boys. In order to breathe, in order to draw air into my lungs and sing and speak, it has been necessary for me to step outside the walls of manhood, to tear the image of my father's face inked over my skin. Feminism gave me the tools to do so: wire-cutters to break through the hard lines of compulsory gender; a new island to stand on and overlook, from a fresh vantage point, my history; a mirror in which my own image, bearded and long-haired, wearing a skirt and a suit jacket, could slowly surface.

REDEFINING MANHOOD: RESISTING SEXISM

Ewuare X. Osayande

"**D**on't you grow up to be a black man!" The words would echo in my young and impressionable mind for years. They belonged to my mother. The source of her message was the combination of internalized oppression as a black woman living in a white supremacist society, and her pain and frustration with the men in her life who abused and misused her. I came to understand my mother's outcry as a desperate plea for her son not to grow up and be like the men she knew.

I saw the worst of patriarchal abuse in the tragic murder of my father, caught in the path of a jealous man who thought that women were his property. Despite these traumatic experiences, I am today a proud, self-loving, heterosexual black man. I have decided to respond to my mother's lament by working to redefine what manhood means to me and to the men I come in contact with. This means confronting racism, sexism, and masculine violence when and where I see it.

I did not have many men to look up to during my childhood. Soon after I was born, my father joined the Army and eventually ended up stationed in Germany. My mother's first marriage was to a man who was hardly ever around. When he was, he never showed any real interest in my life. As I became a teenager, I promised myself that I would never be like either of my fathers. Although I did not know what to do, I certainly knew what not to do. But it wasn't until I got married that I came face to face with my own issues of manhood.

The marriage lasted less than three years. I quickly realized that I was not able to fulfill the socially ascribed role of being the "man of the house," even though I tried to the best of my ability. The pressure of providing for a growing family and finding affirming work became overwhelming. The marriage quickly dissolved even as my self-criticism and awareness were beginning to evolve. There is nothing about masculinity in that period of my life that makes me happy or proud. I am ashamed of the man I was, and I remain ever-vigilant to prevent the man I was from becoming the man I am. But my early confusion led me to a process of political self-awareness that has rooted me ever since.

I do not remember how I came across the work of feminist writer bell hooks, but I do know that I read her book, *Sisters of the Yam*, in one sitting. Although written for black women, this book helped me make sense of the problems I experienced in my marriage and it helped me make sense of myself. I had heard about feminism before, but never paid it much mind. I dismissed it as "that white women's stuff."

I had long been involved in black liberation struggle. I went from being a staunch black student activist in college to being a respected community activist in Philadelphia. Like many black men, I believed that racism was the only oppression that required our community's attention. Reading bell hooks helped correct my vision and revise my understanding. I now see that sexism is as important as racism in liberation struggle. Black women and men have to address white dominant society as well as male domination from both within and outside the black community. Black feminist thought has broadened my understanding of how various forms of oppression criss-cross and often collide.

I now also see that my experience of trying to live up to a "man-of-the-house" sex role is shared by many of the men in my family. I watch my male relatives mask their depression with jokes that project their sense of worth-lessness onto the women in their lives. I worry for them and more so for the women they claim to love. I see how the men's penchant for domination in the home has wreaked havoc on their partners. There is a cloud of anxiety that covers these women. That cloud is the threat of violence that lingers in the air after the man has publicly ridiculed, demeaned, or yelled at her. I am torn up inside even as I try to figure out how to intervene.

I once feared that any act of intervention would be met with resistance by the men and would result in increased violence in the home. I now better understand the root causes of this pain and anger. Rather than being a model for healthy relationships, patriarchy is actually the very force responsible for their demise.

I try to speak affirmatively to these men in my family, offering them alternative ways of viewing themselves as men, keeping myself accountable to the pain and anguish that I know very well. I know that I must not wait for a tragedy to occur. I must remain in constant communication with the hope that conversation can offer a process for change. I share with my family and with myself the belief that love is justice in its most intimate embrace. As such, we men must make every effort to see the women in our lives as equal partners and we must respect them as individuals with ambitions and desires that transcend our own.

It has been ten years since I embraced feminist thought as a guide for my personal life and political activism. In that time, I have given talks and workshops on resisting negative socialization and internalized oppression. One of the issues I am constantly confronted with is how to talk about the matrix of oppressions in a way that is both direct and accessible. I find that all too often some folk want to hide behind their personal oppression. For example, when I give talks on racism and how race impacts our understanding of sexist oppression in the United States, it's not unusual to meet resistance from white women in the audience. More than one white woman has tried to deflect any consideration of how she may experience white privilege even as she must contend with sexism. At the same time, I often meet white men who claim a profeminist outlook but who approach me with questions that suggest male domination only exists within the black community. There is a continuing challenge to appreciate the ways that race and class impact how sexism is experienced in this country.

There is a different gendered experience for a black woman or a woman of color and a white woman. Women of color scholars and activists have written about this for years. I have witnessed an increased interest in feminist thought in the black community thanks to the works of bell hooks, Angela Davis, Alice Walker, Joy James, Barbara Smith, Audre Lorde, and many others. My black female peers are pioneering a body of scholarship and engaging in feminist activism that speaks directly to this hip-hop-inspired generation. Yet progress is still slow. While the legacy of racism has made it difficult for feminist thought to have the radicalizing effect it could have within the black community, sexist black men have used that racism to trump any real discussion of sexism within the black community.

In the United States, black masculinity is a manhood that, in the main, has braced itself against the onslaught of a biased and bigoted society. Racism constantly threatens our well being and our very existence. This defensive posturing often leaves us detached from our feelings. In a society that views us as predator and prey, we are inclined to be on guard at all times. Yet our self-protective posturing often manifests in a hypermasculinity that is predicated upon domination and that sees violence as a primary option to resolve problems.

This perversion of manhood took its ultimate and most personal form in the murder of my father in January 2000. My father had recently begun dating a woman who had left an abusive relationship. My father's murderer was this woman's former lover who resorted to the most violent expression of male domination. In his sexist mind, the woman was his property. He did not recognize her agency or her right to create a life outside of his desires. When she began dating my father, this man struck out. He ambushed and attacked my father and his woman friend. My father was stabbed so severely that he died before the rescue workers arrived. The woman spent a few days in the hospital recovering from her wounds.

The murderer was a respected man of the community who was considered upstanding by most people who knew him. He was not crazy. He was socialized to view women as mere property and to exercise power even to the point of violence, especially when he believed his so-called manhood was being challenged.

As long as domination and violence are considered central parts of masculinity, I worry about the future for my two boys. At ages eleven and eight, they are still becoming aware of themselves in the world. I am learning how quickly sexist socialization can take place. The system is relentless; it bombards my sons with sexist and racist messages on a daily basis. Their mother and I go to great lengths to provide our sons with alternative ways of understanding themselves as boys so that they can resist sexist indoctrination. Yet, despite all our intervention, it seems that every aspect of their young lives is filled with sexist instruction. The same old sexism has been revamped for the computer age. Female cartoon characters are portrayed as damsels in distress who are in constant need of a male hero to save them. In video games, the same is true but with added violence and grossly sexualized images of the female body. My response is to aid my sons in making better choices about the kinds of cartoons they watch and video games they play. I read books with them about women athletes who excel in sports. Their mother has taken them to see the WNBA play live.

It is my fervent hope that anti-sexist, anti-racist interventions will serve my sons well as they grow from boys into men. I will certainly be there to provide an example of manhood that is not an expression of force, superiority, and violence but rather an expression of love, respect, justice, accountability, integrity, and peace.

STEPPING OUT OF BOUNDS

Nathan Einschlag

One day the shit just hit me. I understood. Everything that I had questions about, everything that I had stressed about for the last year of my life, finally seemed to have an answer. I simply wasn't like them. I'm six feet tall and weigh one-eighty. I can bench press 225 pounds. But on the team, I stuck out like a weed in the concrete. In the locker room, on the basketball court, in the words I spoke, by my actions. Everything about me was different. I saw things differently. I was from a different place.

Growing up in the immigrant neighborhood of Jackson Heights in Queens, New York, I had seen things that the kids at my fancy college only read about in magazines, or saw on TV. I knew what happened to the drug and alcohol addicts: They died. I saw young abused girlfriends pushing strollers on the way to the local elementary school to pick up their sons and daughters. It was routine to pass prostitutes on my way to the subway late at night. I was from a neighborhood where my senses were trained to keep me aware and out of harm's way. I always watched one block ahead, spotting shadows, and keeping my distance from the men on the corners. I never went down a too-quiet block for fear of what might lie ahead. My actions made me strong. I walked with my head up and a swagger that can only be learned in New York City.

I made a decision when I was young that I would be focused, and not be dragged into the streets like so many before me. I put my heart and soul into basketball and the senses that I honed walking those late night blocks all my life did not fail me. It was love. Basketball embraced me. Sophomore year I made the varsity basketball team at Fiorello H. Laguardia's High School of Music, Art and Performing Arts. My junior and senior year I started. Senior year we were division champs with a thirteen-three record. It was a high point in my life and an experience I will never forget. It would be time to move on, however, and I said goodbye to my high school team.

Soon after graduating I walked onto my college men's Division III basketball team. I thought I was ready. I had no idea that college would be so much different from high school. Things changed drastically for me my freshman year.

Girls approached me all the time. Drunk girls. Eyeliner girls with their eyes halfway shut, holding red plastic cups full of beer. Those same girls would be all over the lacrosse players who would call them sluts later that same week. Girls didn't see the guy I was, just a freshman trying to get to know people. They saw the basketball logo and didn't need to know anything more about me. They thought I must be like all the other guys who pushed up the girls' skirts as they walked by or pretended to trip while grabbing girls' breasts. "Dude, get a drink. Stop being so uptight," they'd say. I didn't want a fucking drink. Where were the kids who wanted to listen to music and get on the dance floor?

I once came back to my room where I stepped over two girls lying on the floor in my hallway. They could have been waiting for me, or for anyone who walked by and was interested in quick, easy sex. College was nothing like I had expected.

The kids on my high school team were the most creative and talented teenagers in New York City. We didn't pound 40s on a Monday night. We didn't drive drunk for fun like my college teammates did. All we needed was a ball and a court. Nothing made us happier. Off the court we argued about who had the flyest sneakers or who was a better rapper, Nas or Jay-Z.

We didn't buy sixteen-ounce cans of Miller Lite instead of eight-ounce cans, thinking that the girls would get drunker because they have twice as much alcohol. "The girls don't notice," my college teammates assured me. I didn't enjoy being affiliated with this team I was on now. This didn't seem to matter to my teammates, though. I was only seen as a freshman athlete who needed to be broken in.

When I turned down drinks, girls would ask my teammates what was wrong with me, and why I was such a weirdo. They called me strange because I would not objectify them. The gender roles at my school were like nothing I'd experienced. Girls were doing male athletes' laundry while the players poured beer on the girls.

To make matters worse my coach was not playing me. He didn't seem to take a liking to me either. I was serious in practice and I listened, two qualities I learned from the coaches for my previous teams. The other freshmen were rowdy and rude. Some upperclassmen were hotheaded and didn't look Coach in the eye when he talked to them. I thought it was disrespectful, but Coach seemed to respond well to their bad behavior. He took my silence as a sign that I was lethargic and unmotivated. I had such a strong desire to play, but my coach decided instead to question my masculinity. "I need to HEAR you, NATE! TALK LOUDER!" he'd yell. "GODDAMNIT! SCREAM SOMETHING!"

Talking is a vital part of basketball and I didn't have a problem doing it. But it was more intense with Coach. No play was done hard enough or loud enough. Maybe if I had brought beer to practice and pictures of me taking advantage of a passed out girl (like some of the other guys did) then I would have been seen as a real basketball player and gained my coach's acceptance. But at the time the thought hadn't crossed my mind. And I wouldn't have done it, anyway.

Off the court people treated me differently, too. I'd hear things like, "Dude, if you weren't on the team I'd probably make fun of you, too. Fuck it, though. You're cool. Bitches seem to like you." Thankfully, girls showed me attention. At least I was a cute weirdo on the basketball team and not some freak-fag theater major, they'd tell me. I couldn't tell my teammates that I was minoring in theater. I didn't need to give them any more ammunition.

I loved basketball, but it was ruining my life. I wanted to show Coach that basketball was my priority. I stopped telling him I'd have to miss practice for tutoring sessions or class requirements. I would show up at study groups late and still sweaty from practice. I'd convince the ushers at the theater to let me in late. I feared missing practice.

Coach seemed to love his players' bad attitudes. They were rich kids who didn't think about their parents' money or care too much about education. Their father's business would hire them, so what did a C-minus or a D-plus here or there matter? My priorities were different. I didn't have time to stay and bullshit about "bitches and beer" in the locker room. I didn't care if Susan was wearing a low-cut shirt today in Philosophy, or that she almost fell down the stairs drunk last night at the soccer party. *It wasn't their fault that they gave her the beer. No one told her to drink so much. This is college not kindergarten.*

I had reading to get done. I had papers to write. I had college to attend to. I always felt like the odd man out, but now I started not to care. This isn't what I wanted from a basketball team. I didn't feel like part of a team, even if the school saw and treated me like I was on one. Something was changing; it was me.

I'd talk to my old friends on the phone about school. I'd tell them that things were going well and that I was adjusting fine. The next party I went to, I bought in for a red plastic cup. It was soon full of beer. "Maybe they're right and I do need to loosen up," I thought. I had practice late the next day, and wouldn't have to worry about being hung over. If I teased a few girls that night, cursed and yelled, and tried to be like one of the guys, maybe I'd finally get some playing time. If Coach saw that the guys liked me better, then maybe he'd take notice of my game and play me more.

Not only was I slow in practice the next day, but Coach laid into me extra hard. The guys didn't see me in any new light, and I still felt like the odd man out. Nothing was going to change the situation I was in. My teammates were sexist and ignorant. It would be so easy to be like them. I could just kick back, get wasted, and blame my actions on intoxication. But I wasn't about to let this happen. I made a decision that would separate me from the team and cost me one of the things that I held closest to my heart.

I quit the basketball team after a year and a half. Feeling more comfortable at school now, I shed the basketball reputation. I am no longer the cute, weirdo athlete on campus, but Nate, "the quiet kid who I see in the library and I think is gonna be in that play next week." The girls are a little shyer when they approach me now, especially the ones from the parties I used to go to. I'm not like the other guys and they feel embarrassed and a little ashamed. I still hear them whispering about when I was on the team and what they thought I was like, but I also hear the truth now. "That's Nate. He's such a man."

Had I known what a shock I was going to be in for when I started college, had I known it was going to be so much different from what I was used to at home, in high school, I would not have taken a backseat to my teammates' obnoxious behavior. Had I understood the hypermasculine jock culture that existed in Division III sports before I joined the team, I would have promised myself that I would be more vocal, challenging the things that my teammates thought were fun. Instead I was silent. I let people categorize me, and let them think I had the same beliefs and interests as the guys on my team. I never told my coach how I felt until the day I quit the team. He'd had the wrong impression of me, about how to approach me. I will always look back and wish I had been more honest with the staff and my teammates about how I was feeling.

But I will also look back at my college basketball career as one of the most influential times of my life. I learned more about myself during that year-and-a-half of struggle than I did during my entire life before that. By turning my time on the team into a learning experience, and growing from that experience, I know that I made the right decision to leave college basketball. The athletes at my school haven't changed their behavior, but by sticking to my principles and by not letting people categorize me, I have stayed true to myself. I can fight gender stereotypes with my words and with my actions. I know there's another way for men to be.

GROOMING MASCULINITY: CLEANS YOUR BALLS, YES. BUT WHAT ELSE DOES IT DO?

Michael J. Murphy

Sexist and misogynist images in the media are increasingly unacceptable. Don't get me wrong: These still exist—in advertising, the Internet, and especially in pornography. But you only need to flip though a popular magazine from the 1950s or 1960s to realize that things have changed. Sort of. Susan Douglas uses the term "enlightened sexism" to describe the persistence of sexist media despite feminist efforts. It's not that sexism has gone away or become unfashionable; it's that media consumers are more educated and aware of these issues. Conscious of the irreversible damage one slip-up can do to that valuable commodity known as The Brand, sexist marketers are hyperconscious about avoiding egregious sexism and misogyny—unless, that is, it will sell the "merch." Then, all bets are off. One place this is especially true is when it comes to marketing and advertising grooming products for young guys. Starting in the 1980s, marketers discovered a yet-to-be-exploited niche market: men. You don't need a cultural historian or a media studies professor to tell you that the commercial landscape is now littered with ads for AXE, Old Spice, Dove+Men, Gillette, and other brands hawking sprays, lotions, potions, and promises.

But how should a wannabe-feminist guy understand these? You've watched Jean Kilbourne's videos about advertising and read Michael Kimmel's books about hypermasculinity. But nothing about the objectification of women or the eroticization of violence prepared you to deal with the barrage of images of fit guys with shredded six packs telling you you're not a "real man" unless your hair product gives you that "I-don't-care-how-my-hair-looks" look. Aren't marketers' discovery of men and the depiction of the male body the way that women have long been depicted, a form of equality? How can an ad be sexist if it doesn't even *depict* women? This is where profeminist guys need to pay close attention and sharpen their feminist media analysis skills. Sexism in advertising hasn't gone away, it's just gone into stealth mode and we need to keep pace.

Case in point: those AXE ads plaguing television, Facebook, magazines, and YouTube. You know the ones, where some average-looking dude sprays on a toxic amount of body spray and women—often lots of women—fall all over him. Or the ads for shower gel depicting mud-covered women begging (the presumably male) audience to "get dirty." Or my favorite: the guy uses AXE "Dark Destiny" body spray, turning him into a "chocolate man," making him irresistible to women who want to (literally) eat him alive. The AXE ads are sophisticated pieces of modern advertising that intentionally sidestep old questions about the sexual objectification or commodification of women. Instead of women being turned into objects for sale—food, drink, cars, etc.— here, it's men who are the consumables. Instead of literal or metaphorical gang bangs, where groups of guys victimize or gang rape a woman, AXE ads feature men as the passive recipients of women's . . . uh, "attentions." Such ads ping a feminist guy's sexism detector but resist easy analysis. These ads seem to turn old stereotypes on their heads, righting millennia of wrongs against women, showing bros at the mercy of the ladies for a change. Sure, it's objectification and exploitation but men are the targets this time. Isn't that a form of equality? And isn't equality what feminism's all about?

Answering these questions requires us to develop some new cultural analysis skills. I want to demonstrate this approach using a notorious Internet ad for AXE shower gel, but the approach taken here is applicable to many other forms of pop culture. By applying this approach, we can see that the spate of new ads for men's products don't represent any radical departure from more blatantly sexist ads.

"Cleans Your Balls," was an Internet advertisement for AXE shower gel and the AXE "detailer" (a scrubby sponge) released in early January 2010. By mid-2012, the ad had attracted over 2 million YouTube views, inspired several copycats, and won a Gold Lion medal at the 2010 Cannes International Advertising Festival. Parodying the format used by television's Home Shopping Network, the commercial is set in a brightly lit studio with a large central desk, celebrity spokespersons, and an overly enthusiastic audience. The commercial features spokesperson "Denese Saintclaire" and tennis star "Monica Blake" (played by Emmy award-winning actress Jamie Pressley) who tell guys that "No one wants to play with dirty equipment!," then demonstrate how AXE shower gel and the AXE detailer "cleans your balls"—golf balls, tennis balls, soccer balls, and the like. The humor in this commercial stems from its flawless imitation of an infomercial, itself an obviously staged per-formance, and the sexual implications of the word "balls" (dirty balls, ball sack, fuzzy balls)—a double entendre that neither the audience nor hosts seem to comprehend. What amounts to a three-minute-long adolescent male joke concludes with an overview of the AXE product line and a telephone number that viewers can call to receive a free "detailer."

While the sexual innuendo in this commercial, and images of oblivious women playing with men's "balls," are problematic, they obscure the ad's real message: Anxious young men have nothing to fear from women's accomplishments because ultimately women lack the right anatomical equipment to successfully compete. To fully comprehend the gendered messages in this and other ads for men's personal products, we need to understand three things: (1) the targeted customer and his concerns; (2) the gendered associations of the product being advertised; and, (3) the historical use of bodily metaphors to oppose feminist aims.

Advertising for grooming products like AXE is generally aimed at eighteen- to twenty-four-year-olds. Marketers target this age group because they know if they can get us hooked on a brand when we're young, we're likely to stick with it for the rest of our lives. But young men are also the hardest market segment to reach through traditional media like television and magazines, which is why "Cleans Your Balls" debuted as an Internet ad. You don't have to be a psychologist or sociologist to know that the typical young heterosexual male is anxious about masculinity. This is because, while they're biologically male, they're still working out for themselves what it means to "be a man." The marketers who developed the AXE campaign identified and intentionally targeted a group of young men they term "novices" because of their insecurity, inexperience, and low self-esteem. These guys are eager to get with girls but inept at doing so. But while they obsess about girls, the kind of masculinity they idealize is strongly opposed to any behavior or appearance that might be construed as feminine. This leads to an awful lot of risky and dangerous behavior designed to establish young men's masculine credentials: fast driving, hard drinking, physical violence, or reckless sexual hookups.

"Novice masculinity" also presents a serious challenge to marketers of bath and beauty products—the category that includes products like AXE, which have long had feminine associations. At least since Ancient Greece, over-attention to one's beauty or physical appearance has been considered feminine, whether undertaken by men or by women. This is why there are so many images in Western art of women gazing into mirrors, and why the myth of Narcissus (the Greek god who saw his own reflection in the surface of a pond, fell in love, and fell in and drowned) is seen as a cautionary tale about what happens to men who become overly concerned with their appearance rather than their accomplishments. It's also why women in advertising are often depicted touching themselves while men are usually depicted reaching out to engage the world around them. Long-held gender ideals encourage women to be decorative objects (ornaments) and men to be active agents (instruments). Because bath and beauty products are fundamentally about caring for one's self and appearance, and not primarily about affecting the world beyond one's self, they are typically gendered feminine. But while modern advertising has played a major role in perpetuating these associations, they now are hindering the beauty industry's growth. As any trip to a department or grocery store will show, the market for women's bath and beauty products is saturated and any growth will depend on finding and developing new markets for new and existing products. On the whole, male consumers represent an untapped market for grooming products. But given their longtime associations with the feminine, how do you make such products "safe" for men, especially the young men who comprise AXE's target market, who are overly sensitive to being perceived as feminine?

One way is to anchor masculinity in the male body, a perennial shelter for anxious men. Historians of gender have noticed that when women get powerful, men get biological. In the nineteenth century, when feminists were agitating for the vote, a common objection was that women's biology (especially their reproductive anatomy) made learning and voting for women unwise, even dangerous. The argument went like this: Women were fragile delicate blossoms with only enough energy for education or reproduction, not both. If they went to college or participated in public life, the blood would rush from their "lady parts" to their brains, and they'd be left unable to reproduce, much to the detriment of the human race. Moreover, women's monthly hormonal cycle made them irrational beings unsuited for rational decision making. Only men were biologically able to survive the dual demands of voting *and* insemination. (Yes, really!) Though long discredited, this is the logic behind TV pundits' claim that female political candidates can't be trusted because they might drop the bomb at "that time of the month." Whenever a woman proves she can do anything a man can, she blurs the social differences between the sexes. History shows that the response is often an effort to justify social inequality through appeals to (real or imagined) biological sex differences. This often happens at a time when the balance of power among the sexes is undergoing fundamental shifts—as in right now when more women are earning high school and college diplomas than men, and women are gaining ground in professions previously dominated by men. Therefore, it is no accident that the "Cleans Your Balls" ad is an extended play on the double meaning of the word "balls," a slang term for male testicles. Humans are a weakly dimorphic species, meaning human males and females are more similar than different in outer appearance, unlike say, black widow spiders or pea fowl. Despite our outer similarities, the area in which we are most different is our reproductive anatomy which is why vaginas, testicles, and penises play such a large role in political and cultural discourse aimed at justifying social inequalities between the sexes. Nor is it unimportant that the particular male organs so slyly referenced in the "Cleans Your Balls" ad often serve as a metaphor for those oh-so-masculine qualities of bravery, courage, and moxy.

How does this help us understand the "Cleans Your Balls" ad? Remember that advertising always makes a promise to potential consumers. If you buy this product, then you will become something different: thinner, hotter, sexier, smarter. The "Cleans Your Balls" ad is attempting to market a product with feminine associations to male consumers who are inordinately concerned with masculinity because of their age and wider social changes that are shifting the landscape of gender and power. It does this by assuring young males that, no matter how much men start to care about physical appearances, their male anatomy still makes them men—the implication being that, because women don't have testicles, they'll never have the "balls" to do what a man can do. In other words, men are entitled to everything that is now and has ever been considered masculine by virtue of the fact that they're male (and women aren't because they're not). The "Cleans Your Balls" ad makes bathing safe for insecure males by reminding them that they still have "balls"—code for masculinity and male entitlement. Wash all you want guys, you'll still be men! Moreover, the AXE ad implies that the connection between male anatomy and male entitlement is so "male" that women can't even understand it. The function of pretty spokespersons like "Denese Saintclaire" who seem oblivious to the sexual connotations of words like "balls" and "ball sack" is to assure anxious young men that, really, they have nothing to fear from competent, professional, beautiful women because such women just don't get it. So, the message sent to and about young men and women is doubly damaging. Young men are growing up in a world where women have more political and economic power than ever before. AXE ads like "Cleans Your Balls" make the false promise to young men that, even if a woman can do your job better than you or has more education, your anatomy still guarantees that you're a man with all that men are entitled to. It also tells them that the connection between maleness and masculinity is so strong and secure that those women who work hard to get what men have always taken for granted will still be too dumb (but pretty!) to realize that they're (anatomically) disqualified before the race even begins. And it teaches this extraordinarily conservative and reactionary lesson through a humorous advertisement that was deemed too risqué for television, yet groundbreaking enough to receive an industry award for innovation. Not exactly a lesson for success—for either men or women.

The spate of new ads for men's products does not represent any radical departure from the more obviously sexist ads of the 1950s and 1960s or more recent years. It is just that now the sexism has gone underground. Excavating it requires some historical knowledge, sustained attention, and thoughtful analysis—three possessions in short supply in our fast-paced media landscape which discourages us from focusing on one thing for any length of time. But if we want to understand what sexist media looks like at the dawn of the twenty-first century, we need to stop surfing the surface, hit the pause button, and start looking really carefully. My analysis of the "Cleans Your Balls" ad suggests the kinds of knowledge, analytical skills, and angles of approach now required to unpack the sexist messages in today's advertising and marketing. No longer is it sufficient to ask whether women are treated like objects or subjected to (real or implied) violence—though these are still a regular and troubling occurrence in advertising imagery. Now, if we want to understand the gendered cultural work of advertising, we need to also consider the larger social context in which the ads appear, the gendered associations of the product being advertised, and the nature and concerns of the targeted market. Advertisers and marketers are smarter and more sophisticated than ever before, though their messages are really old and tired. But in order to see this, we need to sharpen our cultural criticism skills, read more widely, and think a bit differently about how sexism rears its ugly head.

SEARCHING FOR THE COLORFUL FACES OF MUSLIM MEN

Amanullah De Sondy

W hat does a Muslim man look like?
As a scholar, teacher of Islam, and as a Muslim, I help my students grapple with this difficult question every day. Just as there are no two Christians or Jews alike, no two Muslims are the same. Yet we are bombarded by media with a fairly monolithic picture of Muslim men, which quite easily extends to singular ideas about Islam. We are repeatedly shown a Muslim man with a big beard, which takes on the meaning that Muslim-man-with-a-beard always equals a Shari'a-loving extremist. Laugh or cry at such generalization, this is the reality of Muslim and Islamic stereotypes. Before my students pick up a book introducing them to Islam, they have already been inundated with stereotyped images of Muslim men and women, and these images are firmly lodged in their minds. The challenge for me is to provide broader images of Muslim masculinity, and to present a variety of different ways that Islam is lived from Sunni to Shi'a to Ahmaddiya to Ismaiili to Alawi.

Consider some of the Orientalist art that comes to mind when we think of how Western painters have portrayed Muslims. These depictions in the past have been of the bearded, turbaned man playing a musical instrument with semi-clad, face-veiled, belly-dancing women. The seduction of the exotic mesmerizes many for different reasons. For some, it shows the alleged superiority of the Western world and, for others, there is curious intrigue. Either way, what still remains is an image that plays a role in creating prejudice and stereotypes, labels that are at odds with the actual diversity and variety of Muslim men globally. These images build bridges and burn them as the often-repeated mantra, Islam-versus-the-West, is sustained and glorified through such visual discourse. Although Edward Said's work on Orientalism reminds us that exoticizing the Eastern man is no longer acceptable, the problem continues.

This matters because we live in troubled times. The atrocities of 9/11 in the United States, 7/7 in the UK, and other world terror events, have fed our imagination about what Islam is and what a Muslim man looks like. The images of Saudi men in their passport photos that were shown on TV screens in every news show following the attacks of 9/11 quite powerfully promoted stereotypes about Muslim masculinity as dangerous. Today, when we think about Saudi Arabian men, we are likely to think of the suicide bombers of 9/11. We should never underestimate the power of the media in promoting extremely negative stereotypes about race, ethnicity, religion, and nation of origin. We must pay careful attention to the links between our prejudice about people and our politics toward nations.

My interest in Islamic masculinity began when I took courses on women and religion in Scotland. During a public lecture by a Muslim feminist scholar, I raised the question whether it was now time to focus on Muslim men and to explore the social constructions of Islamic masculinity. I argue that it is.

So what does it mean to be a Muslim man? What effect do images have on the way in which we understand our own masculinity? When I was growing up in Glasgow, I joined a couple of Muslim youth groups. They were gender-segregated. In our youth group boys' club, for instance, our regular gathering consisted of a general Islam talk during which the boys sat and listened, probably only because the organizers planned a sporting activity to follow. These sports events included boys-only swimming, football, archery or, sometimes, wrestling. The cultural and social norms of gender segregation in most Islamic societies have helped to uphold particular norms and roles for Muslim men and women. Muslims in Diaspora, whose parents arrived predominantly from South Asia and the Middle East, have attempted to uphold the same gender-segregated traditions in social and religious gatherings.

However, there is growing discomfort with gender segregation among a new generation of Muslim men and women growing up in the West: Asra Nomani refused to enter her West Virginia town mosque from the back door and sought a more central role for women in her community; Amina Wadud led mixed-gender prayers, an international act that encouraged gender- and sexuality-inclusive congregations to emerge; in Toronto, El-Farouq Khaki, a leading gay Muslim activist and lawyer, works tirelessly on issues of gender equality, sexual orientation, and progressive Islam. Khaki, along with his partner Troy Jackson and their friend Laury Silvers, established el-Tawhid Juma Circle, the first mosque for all gender identities and sexual orientations. This has led to the founding of a number of inclusive Muslim congregations around Canada and the United States. These congregations play a significant role in welcoming Muslims who don't feel comfortable in "mainstream" mosques. A recent visit to South Africa introduced me to the work of The Inner Circle, an organization set up in Cape Town by Imam Muhsin Hendricks, that focuses on issues concerning sexuality and spirituality. Hendricks was rejected by the Muslim community when he came out as gay. Hendricks, who is divorced and the father of three children, is now married to his Indian partner.

Along with progress in shifting religious institutions, we are also beginning to see a real challenge to hegemonic Muslim masculinity through books and film. The work of author Michael Muhammad Knight, for example, is a powerful expression of dissent. His book, *The Taqwacores*, is a novel about a fictional group of punk Muslims based in Buffalo, New York. The men and women in this story challenge every norm and assumption about Muslims and Islam—from a burqa-clad Muslim woman who crosses out the anti-women passages of the Qur'an, to men who are high on intoxicants seeking the fun and frolics of love, sex, and rock & roll, to a gay Muslim who is supported and affirmed by those who love him. Yet these characters in *The Taqwacores* still show a commitment to their Islamic belief by holding interestingly astute Friday congregational prayers in their home. The movie based on Knight's novel features compelling scenes of Muslim men committed to their faith and also participating in acts of so-called debauchery. These scenes powerfully blur the edges of what is sacred and profane, dichotomies that scholars of religion have tried to keep separate. But when we see these lines blurred in the portrayed lives of these Muslim men, our rigid categories and expectations of Muslim masculinity are challenged.

For too long we have been bombarded by movies that show Muslim men as villains, as barbaric, as wearing strange clothing, as plane hijackers. Renowned Egyptian-born journalist Mona Eltahawy asks in her *Time* magazine article, *Why is it we always see images in media that portray angry Muslim men with long beards and burning the U.S. flag?* Eltahawy has a point.

I'm not saying that these images are always incorrect. There are lunatic Muslim men and women out there who want to do horrible things to people through their interpretation of Islam. But why don't we see the vast majority of Muslim men and women who are peace-loving and want to build bridges? Fortunately, a recent wave of movies has attempted to challenge negative stereotypes and provide more diverse portrayals of Muslim masculinity. These movies rarely make the big screens; one needs to work hard to find these movies outside the mainstream.

Three such films have been produced post-9/11, and challenge us to see and hear a broader variety of Muslim men. The first movie is *Monsieur Ibrahim*. In this movie, a Muslim grocery store owner in Paris, Omar Sharif, befriends a young Jewish boy (Momo, short for Moses). Momo lives with his father, who later leaves him and commits suicide. Ibrahim adopts Momo and there develops an interesting cross-generational, cross-religious relationship that sees the two travel through Europe to Ibrahim's home town. Ibrahim takes Momo to different places of worship to educate him, yet throughout the movie his love and affection for Momo as his adopted son are never extended to trying to convert him to Islam. Ibrahim does continually comment that he is at peace with his life because "he knows what is in his Qur'an." At the end of the movie when Ibrahim dies, Momo inherits the local "Arab" shop and Ibrahim's Qur'an, only to find a blue, dried-up flower. The movie challenges the way in which Ibrahim, as a Muslim man, held strong to the letter of the text but equated all that it contained to the beauty of flowers.

The second movie is *Ae Fond Kiss*. This movie is directed by Ken Loach and set in Glasgow, Scotland. The protagonist of the story is a Glaswegian Muslim, Kasim. Kasim is conflicted between the sense of identity that his parents brought back from Pakistan and the Scottish culture in which he is growing up. Kasim meets a Catholic high school teacher, Roisin, with whom he falls in love. This creates a lot of difficulty not only for him but also for her: Roisin balances her personal life with being a Catholic high school teacher, reprimanded by her priest for living with Kasim out of wedlock and with a non-Catholic man. The movie ends with a showdown between Kasim's family, Kasim, and Roisin. This final, powerful scene finds Roisin playing at the piano as she asks Kasim if he has returned home to pick up his belongings. Kasim asks, "That depends . . . will you grow tired of me?"

In typical Roisin fashion, she teases him with "Absolutely." The couple embrace and kiss, leaving the audience unsure about the outcome of this rocky love affair. The movie portrays complicated images of Muslim masculinity *vis-à-vis* Kasim, who presents a much more intimate, loving, sexual Muslim masculinity compared with his first-generation father.

The third movie, *Sabah*, is based in Toronto, Canada, where a family from Syria are trying to balance their Syrian culture with the environs in which they find themselves. Sabah is a forty-year-old Muslim woman who falls in love with a white, atheist, Canadian carpenter who seems to get a lot of business from local churches to make crosses. Sabah's brother, Majid, who takes charge of the family after their father's death, begins as a strong patriarch but as his sister's love relationship develops, his niece resists an arranged marriage, and his own wife conducts an affair with her Arabic teacher, we begin to see a very different Muslim man. Majid is a Muslim man who confronts his vulnerability as he discloses the immense pressure he has been under in supporting the family. Majid is seen crying at one point as he talks to Sabah about sacrifice. Not all stories have a happy ending but the poignancy of this film highlights how we are usually bombarded with such negative and bloody images of the Muslim man. This movie highlights a Muslim woman. But this movie is also significant because of the varieties of masculinities that are presented: an older, patriarchal brother/son, a deceased father, a non-Muslim/Canadian lover, and a young tattooed Syrian student are just a few of the interesting characters who bring this movie to life.

Like the characters in these on-screen movies, no two Muslim men are alike off-screen. This message bears repeating, not just for those looking *at* Muslim men but also *for* Muslim men who must begin to accept that we don't all look the same, act the same, and wear the same clothes. Some Muslim men have beards, some do not. Some dress in traditional clothing and some do not.

It sounds simplistic but I'm shocked at the number of times that I have been asked about things I wear.

Recently, after giving a lecture on Qur'anic masculinities, I was asked about the significance of a ring I wore on my pinky finger. Quite surprised at the question, it once again reminded me of how powerful different images of Muslim men are in allowing people to make conclusions. Sociologists and anthropologists inform us that masculinity is constructed through interactions with all that surrounds a man, so the way in which boys grow up to identify as men depends on how they are brought up. We also know that Islam has never thrived in a vacuum, it is dependent on the ways in which men and women have constructed and presented it to the world, albeit from a prophet who is said to have received divine revelation. How one reads the history of Islamic civilizations plays an integral role in shaping the image of the Muslim man. One version of Islamic history describes the prophet who mended his own clothes and, in another version of Islamic history the same prophet had multiple wives and was commander-in-chief in battle. The version we turn to can promote and infuse a variety of different Islamic masculinities. But in a world then and now that is still very much based on a butch, virile, heterosexual man, it goes without saying which reading and image of the prophet has played the dominant role in depicting and constructing the Muslim man.

Better understanding the possible varieties of Islamic masculinity will inextricably affect the way in which Muslim men see and understand Muslim women. For far too long men have understood Muslim women through the lens of the dominant, hegemonic strand of Muslim men who seek to strengthen their own hegemony through their role as husbands, fathers, householders, or even warriors. The times are changing where Muslim men and women who do not fit these limiting roles are seeking their own emancipation among Muslim men and women, and also extending the voice of Muslim feminists against hegemonic masculinity. It will take hard work to seek the varieties and diversity of Muslim masculinity but it will certainly help in understanding how complex the times we live in are without generalizing and stereotyping. When young Egyptians led a revolt against a tyrannical regime, as part of the Arab Spring begun in 2010, it allowed Westerners to finally realize that Arabs are actually quite like us. And when we begin to understand each other, regardless of where we live or how we might pray, we begin to build links and strengthen communities, societies, and humanity, notions that are sorely needed in the world today.

HOMBRES Y MACHOS

Alfredo Mirandé

My formative years were spent in México City in the *colonia* of Tacuba, near *el árbol de la noche triste* (the tree of the night of sorrows), a tree where according to Mexican folklore and legend Hernán Cortés was said to have wept after the Aztecs soundly defeated his forces. Over the centuries the tree had been bent by the force of its own weight and was now almost on the ground. I did not understand the historical significance of the old tree at the time, but it was very much a part of my daily life as a child.

We lived in Tacuba near *el árbol de la noche triste* in an extended family with my mother's oldest sister (Márgara) and oldest brother (Juan), and their respective families. *Los* González-Ochoa were from the village of Sayula, a historic community in the state of Jalisco. The first house on the right as you walked in the front gate, which was always open, was occupied by my Tío Juan, his wife Mariana, and their two sons. Tía Márgara, her husband Miguel, and their two daughters occupied the second house. I lived in the last and smallest of the houses, "*el tres*," with my parents, Rosa María and Xavier, and my two older brothers, Alex and Gordo.

The most lasting impression I have of my *tíos* is that they were sort of *matones* (tough guys), burly, pot-bellied men who smoked, swore, drank tequila, and carried weapons. They were much like the Mexican bad guys in films like *El Mariachi, Desperado,* and *Somewhere in Mexico.* Tío Miguel was a military man, a general in the Mexican army, who dressed in his uniform and carried a .45. Juan was a civilian, sold tequila wholesale for a living, and also often carried a gun and shoulder holster. Another *tío,* Manuel, lived in Puebla. He was married to my mother's sister, Ana Luisa. Manuel was also in the military, had entered the Mexican Revolution when he was only fourteen, and had become a professional military hit man. He was said to have executed hundreds of men during (and after) the Revolution, executions that were both formal and informal. My father was never in the military and never carried a weapon. He was athletic and strong, and he didn't smoke, drink, or swear.

Our extended family and neighborhood was like a small community. One of the most vivid memories that I have of Tacuba was an incident that happened when I was around six. It was in the afternoon. There was a lot of noise and yelling, as the entire neighborhood gathered around Tío Juan's house. We could hear arguing, screaming, and swearing. Juan was drunk and beating Tía Mariana. My father jumped over the short picket fence and attempted to stop the beating. Because it was unheard of for one household to intervene in the private affairs of another and because we could sense the danger, it was a very dramatic moment as we watched my drunken uncle coming after my father. My dad was a skilled boxer. He hit and jabbed at Juan and then deftly circled around him, intending more to dissuade him than to seriously hurt him. As my uncle's face bloodied and it became clear that my father was getting the better of the fight, Juan ran into the house and emerged from the kitchen with a butcher knife. My father looked frightened and was certainly alarmed but he didn't run. He continued to dance and jab with Juan pursuing, coming forward, threatening him with the knife. What happened next was even more incredible, as my mother somehow entered the yard and stepped between her husband and her older brother. She proceeded to belittle Juan, asking, and pointing at her brother,

> How can you call yourself a man if you go around beating up defenseless women? What kind of a man needs a knife to fight an unarmed man? Put down the knife and let's see what kind of a man you really are.

Humiliated, Juan put down the knife and went inside the house.

I never thought much about the incident, but in retrospect I believe that it had a profound effect on my development, my identity, and my notions of what was considered good and bad behavior in a man—and in a woman. I learned early, for example, that one of the worst or lowest things that a man could do is to hit a woman. I also learned from this and other examples that it is important and honorable to stick up for and defend people who are wronged, abused, or treated unjustly. But most importantly, I learned that strength of character and valor are not gendered qualities.

My *noche triste* occurred when my father returned from location in Morelia where he had been working as an extra in the film *Captain from Castille*, ironically a film about Cortés and the Conquest. My father had been gone for a long time. I was happy to see him and he brought us a lot of presents. But later that evening, there was a big fight, and after my parents argued all night, they separated. Years later my mother related how after she had been fighting with my dad and was very sad and depressed, she had gone to *el árbol de la noche triste*. As she cried by the tree she said she thought about how both she and Hernán Cortés had been in the same situation: depressed, weeping, and alone.

When my parents separated, my brothers and I moved with my father to live with his mother, Anita, and my great-grandmother, Carmela (Mama Mela) in Tacubaya. Grandmother Anita was a petite, energetic woman, while Mama Mela was tall, dark, and stately. In Tacubaya, we were surrounded by family again, but now it was the Mirandé-Salazar family on my father's side. His family was smaller because he was an only child and because his father's two siblings, Concha and Lupe, never married or had children. My grandfather, Alfredo, died when I was about two years old, but I remember him.

In Tacubaya we lived in an apartment house that my grandmother owned. We lived in the first apartment, and my great-aunts, Concha and Lupe, lived in *el seis* (number six). Concha had been an elementary school teacher and Lupe was an artist. They were retired but very active; both did a lot of embroidering and Lupe was always painting. I was very fond of *las tías*. They always seemed old and very religious, but I was very close to my aunts and loved them deeply. They wore black shawls and went to church early each morning. When I wasn't playing on the patio, I was usually visiting with my aunts. They taught me catechism, and Lupe was my *madrina*, or godmother, for my first communion. I would spend hours with *las tías*, listening to their conversation and stories about my grandfather and about the Mexican Revolution.

I was named Alfredo after my grandfather and I strongly identified with him. My family said he was a great man and that they would be very proud and happy if I grew up to be like him some day. Actually, I had no choice—my family expected that I was destined to be like him, since I was his namesake. They said I had the privilege and the responsibility that came with the name, and, like him, I too would be a great man some day. To my family, my grandfather and I were linked because we were both Mirandé and Alfredo, but also because we were both men. I did not realize it at the time, but my teachers—*las tías*, my grandmother, Mama Mela, and my mother and her sisters—were socializing me into my sex role.

I don't know very much about my Grandfather Alfredo, except that he was of humble origins and he was a self-made man who pursued a career as a civil engineer. He was committed to bringing about social justice and distributing the land held by the *hacendados* (landowners) among the Mexican *peones* (laborers). He served as a civilian under Emiliano Zapata, making cannons and munitions. According to historian John Womack, my grandfather was one of Zapata's key assistants and worked for some time as a spy in Puebla under the code name Delta. While he was in hiding, my grandmother took in other people's clothes to mend and launder to earn money so that the family could survive. My aunts said my grandfather grew disillusioned, however, as the Revolution did not fulfill its promise of bringing about economic and social justice.

Tía Concha and Tía Lupe had several photographs of Alfredo in their tiny, crowded living room. In one picture he is standing proudly in front of a new, experimental cannon that he built. The story I was told was that a foolish and headstrong general, anxious to try out the new cannon, pressured Alfredo to fire it before it was ready. My grandfather reluctantly but stoically complied and when the cannon exploded he suffered severe burns all over his body, almost dying as a result. It took my grandfather months to recover from the accident.

As I think back on these stories I was told as a child, I understand that most were designed to impart certain morals and values. What I learned directly from my *tías* and, indirectly, from my grandfather, was that although it was necessary to stand up for one's principles, war and personal conflicts should be avoided, if at all possible. I understood that I should strive to be on a higher moral plane than my adversaries.

Alfredo was intelligent, strong, and principled. But what impressed me most is that he was said to have been incredibly just and judicious. Everyone who knew him, including my mother, said he treated people of all educational and economic levels fairly, equally, and with dignity and respect. Alfredo lived in a society and a historical period in which women were relegated to an inferior status and were largely controlled by men. Yet I also know that he and my grandmother shared a special intimacy and mutual respect.

I now realize that I was raised by strong and powerful women, and that most of what I understood about being a man was learned from women. My great-grandmother, Mama Mela, possessed an uncommon dignity. My Aunts Concha and Lupe were traditional, strong, and independent. But the woman that stands out most in my mind is my mother's oldest sister, Tía Márgara.

Márgara was a large, imposing figure and probably weighed well over two hundred pounds. In her youth Márgara was a tall, attractive woman, and she had a wonderful sense of humor and an incredible singing voice. But *la tía* also had a foul mouth and seemed always to be complaining about some *desgraciados* (bastards) or *hijos de la chingada* (sons of bitches). Ironically, she embodied many stereotypically macho traits. She swore, was a chain smoker, gambled, drank tequila, and loved to sing *rancheras* (Mexican country ballads) and belt out the *gritos* (yells) with the songs. She was the female counterpart to my stereotypically macho *tíos*, but more memorable because she was a woman.

What I remember most about *la tía* were the numerous confrontations and fistfights she had with both women and men. Márgara liked to knit, but she also liked to fight. She usually carried long, sharp knitting needles, which she would often use as weapons. I recall one incident in particular: Márgara got out of the car during a traffic dispute, pulled a cab driver from his vehicle, and proceeded to beat him with her fists. Everyone said, "*Era muy brava*" ("she was very tough"). Her physical assaults were of legendary proportions and were always, it seems, accompanied by verbal abuses and denunciation of her victims, so that in the end, her adversaries were not only physically bested, but also subdued and humiliated.

The problem was that these stories from my childhood were at odds with the images of men and women that were prevalent in popular conceptions of Latinos and in academic social science literature. Latinos in general, and *mexicanos* in particular, have been characterized as heirs to a cultural heritage that is said to be driven by the simultaneous veneration of the male and denigration of the female, a heritage in which men are powerful and controlling and women weak and submissive. Because of my own biography and my increasing concern with portrayals of Latino masculinity and machismo, I was drawn into a project to separate the macho myths from the realities of manhood.

From my social science training and from watching my own family, I knew that this machismo stereotype couldn't possibly be the whole story of Latino manhood. My father and my grandfather were not stereotypically macho, and my mother and aunts, especially Márgara, were hardly passive and dependent. Even if there is a cultural concern with outward displays of masculinity and *hombría*, this is certainly not unique to Latino cultures. There are many societies that have focused on manhood, that have ritualized masculine rites of passage, and that value outward masculine displays.

I decided to research the historical roots and contemporary manifestations of Latino masculinity because I wanted to explore the diversity and variety of masculinities. I wanted to understand Latino men but in the end, the results revealed as much about me as it did about the men I studied. I launched my research project on masculinity by doing in-depth interviews with Latino men because I was dissatisfied with the images of Latino men and masculinity found not only in the academic social science literature but also in the society at large. These images had been used to perpetuate negative conceptions of *mexicanos/as* and to legitimate our economic and political subordination and maintain our subordination.

My goal, both personal and professional, was to conduct a study of Latino men that did not begin with the premise that Latino culture and Latino masculinity was inherently pathological and negative. I wanted to look at Latino men in a way that reflected the richness and complexity of Latino culture—a study, in other words, that would incorporate those who were as different and diverse as my father, my uncles, and my *tías*. I wanted to capture the images that Latino men themselves have of machismo, masculinity, and fatherhood. I felt it was important to learn more about how Latino men saw their roles as fathers, as husbands, and as men, and the qualities or attributes that they most respected and admired in a man. Finally, I wanted to place my research findings within a meaningful historical context.

I found in a roundabout way that contrary to what many scholars claim, negative machismo, or exaggerated masculinity, was neither a response to the Conquest nor an extension of pre-Columbian warring Aztec society. Instead, like Catholicism and many deadly diseases, negative machismo was imported and imposed on the indigenous population via the Conquest. The small band of *conquistadores* who conquered and subjugated millions of indigenous people under the leadership of Hernán Cortés appears to be the historical prototype of negative machismo. Though it is said that the Conquest was divinely ordained in order to convert the "heathen natives," the *conquistadores* proved to be cruel, violent men who committed numerous atrocities and *chingaderas* in the name of God, crown, and king. The *conquistadores* appear to have embodied what Evelyn Stevens calls "The Seven Deadly Sins of Machismo": extreme pride, wrath, lust, anxiety, callousness toward women, an obsession with the number of conquests, and belief in male hypersexuality.

Aztec society was hierarchical, militaristic, and characterized by a clearly delineated sexual division of labor. But war and violence were not ends in themselves. War and the sacrifice of enemy prisoners were justified as necessary in order to satisfy the gods and continue the cycle of life. Across social classes, the Aztec masculine ideal also included such attributes as being humble, modest, contrite, selfless, and not giving in to impetuousness or self-indulgence.

Two polar and conflicting images of Mexican masculinity emerged from my project, corresponding roughly to Spanish and Aztec conceptions of men. A majority of my respondents did not identify with being macho. They saw machismo as a negative or synthetic form of masculinity, characterized by profound feelings of inferiority or inadequacy in men, male dominance, and the subordination and denigration of women. This finding calls into question the idea that machismo, at least as it has been traditionally conceived, is somehow a positive or desired cultural trait or value.

Although a minority of respondents identified with being macho and had a positive conception of the term, these men were careful to distinguish between being macho (male) and being *machista* (sexist). Rather than linking machismo with pathology, violence, or the denigration of women, for these men, like my dad, it meant adhering to a code of ethics—similar to the Aztec code—that guided behavior and included attributes such as being honest, respectful, modest, sincere, loyal. Perhaps most importantly, this perspective on machismo includes the expectation that men ought to stand up for their rights and beliefs. The worth of a person, according to this view, is measured not by external attributes, such as physical strength, sexual prowess, fighting ability, or drinking behavior, but by internal qualities and especially the strength of one's character. A man who claims to be *muy macho*, who thinks he is *chingón*, who goes around holding his genitals and committing numerous *chingaderas*, who beats up women, or who is otherwise fixated on proving his manhood is, by definition, not macho. A real macho is confident in his sense of self and in his masculinity and doesn't need to prove it to anyone, and most certainly not to himself.

Another important, and paradoxical, conclusion is that the positive sense of being macho is essentially an androgynous quality, as *la hembra* (the female) is the feminine counterpart of *el macho*. *Hembrismo* (femaleness) is similarly demonstrated by internal qualities such as pride, dignity, courage, persever-ance in the face of adversity, and selflessness, not by external attributes like toughness, physical beauty, large breasts, sexuality, or excessive femininity.

Looking back on my youth, I saw that I was provided with a wealth of positive and negative images of masculinity and femininity. As I reflected on the family folklore surrounding my father confronting Tío Juan as he was beating up his wife, I realized it took bravery for my father to get involved in a family squabble and to stand up to his brother-in-law. But I also came to realize that it probably took even more courage for my mother to intervene. She was, after all, the youngest of seven children, and a woman. She grew up in a small village in an era when women ostensibly occupied subordinate roles and did not interfere in the affairs of men. By intervening in the physical confrontation between two grown men (her older brother and her husband), my mother not only challenged her older brother but also, indirectly and symbolically challenged her husband and the (allegedly) traditional sub-ordinate role of women. Perhaps gender roles are not as rigid or as predictable as mainstream thought would have us believe.

Machismo and conventional conceptions of masculinity (and femininity) have typically been associated with backward rural Chicano/Latino culture. The assumption has been that modernizing and adapting to American culture would eventually lead men to reject traditional gender roles. My research, however, revealed something quite different.

Men who had greater ties to Latino culture—those who were born outside the United States or who preferred to be interviewed in Spanish—generally had more negative views of machismo and were less traditional in their con-ceptions of gender. Although most men responding to my survey thought of machismo as something negative, the men with stronger ties to Latino culture were *overwhelmingly* negative in their views of machismo. What's more, the men with stronger ties to Mexican/Latino culture and those with lower socio-economic status were more likely to identify being self-centered, or *egoísta*, as a negative quality in a man.

What this means is that contrary to stereotypes about poor and working-class Latino men being macho, there is actually a distinctive Mexican cultural ethic surrounding manhood and masculinity. A man's success is measured not so much by external qualities, such as wealth, education, or power, but by internal ones such as being honest, responsible, and hardworking, sacrificing for one's children, and, most of all, not being selfish. In the working class, a man who has an honest job, who works hard to provide for his family, and who is responsible is considered a success and a good man and father. One who does not look after his family is not considered successful as a man, regardless of how much money he has or how important his job is. One of the lowest things that a man can do, according to this ethic, is to be selfish and irresponsible (*egoísta*) or to succumb to such personal vices as drinking, drugs, gambling, or womanizing. Worst of all is failing to take care of the family.

These contradictory views of machismo and masculinity can be reconciled if we see masculinity in Chicano/Latino cultures not as conforming to either the positive or negative conception of machismo, but rather as representing the horns of a dilemma or choices faced by men. Since there is not one, but various, masculinities, a man is evaluated according to whether he is being responsible or irresponsible, honest or dishonest, *egoísta* or selfless. The findings also call into question the assumption that poor or working-class men are more likely to be more patriarchal and that as people get more education and better-paying jobs they will become more gender egalitiarian. My research findings did not support the assumption that socioeconomic status is a critical determinant of gender role attitudes and behavior or the related assumption that traditional masculinity is somehow more prevalent in the working class. Unfortunately, since racial oppression and class oppression go hand in hand, it is often difficult, if not impossible, to separate the relative influence of race and of class on beliefs and behavior.

The Bem Sex Role Inventory (BSRI) is a measure of masculinity and femininity that has been widely utilized in social science research. Contrary to what I expected, men who had more education or higher incomes, those engaged in professional occupations, and men who opted to be interviewed in English, scored higher on the masculine component of the BSRI and were less—not more—androgynous.

Surprised by these findings I developed a second tool to measure the data: the Mirandé Sex Role Inventory (MSRI), which looks at masculinity and femininity within a cultural and situational context. The MSRI produced findings that were more consistent with my expectations. Respondents with more education, higher incomes, and those who were professionals, were generally less traditional on this measure.

What this told me was that much of what we assume to be universal when it comes to gender roles and masculinity and femininity is, in fact, culture specific. The dominant sex role paradigm that has prevailed in the social sciences, for example, assumes that aggression and assertiveness are masculine traits, and that being emotional, affectionate, and showing one's feelings are feminine qualities. Ironically, the stereotypical view of a "macho man" as cold, insensitive, and emotionless is actually more consistent with Anglo than with Latino conceptions of masculinity. Superheroes like Rambo, Superman, and Batman epitomize this image of white masculinity. In Chicano/Latino culture it is permissible and desirable for men to be emotional, to show their feelings, and to kiss, hug, be affectionate with male children, and to even cry on occasion. Latino men can at once be warm, loving, and tender, and self-reliant, self-sufficient, and willing to take a stand. And I assure you that if we had a Superhero, he most certainly would cry.

Raewynn Connell, one of the leading voices in the new masculinity scholarship by men, points out the complicated nature of what she calls "masculinities" and calls for us to reject hegemonic masculinities. Ironically, Connell and other new scholars interested in men and masculinity have engaged in their own brand of hegemonic discourse by ignoring masculinity among Latinos and other subordinated communities and by assuming that we can understand all masculinity by focusing on Euro-American theoretical models. In Connell's book *Masculinities* she talks about working-class masculinity and mentions in passing Robert Staples's pioneering work on black men. But Connell largely ignores other people of color. This oversight isn't unique to Connell, but she certainly represents the problem. I fully endorse the call for ending hegemonic masculinities and believe that perhaps the most important conclusion that can be drawn from my research—along with what I know from growing up male in my family and the culture—is that there is not a single Chicano/Latino masculinity, but a variety of masculinities that are not only different, but often contradictory. We should remember that these masculinities are not a subset of the dominant masculinities and that they are as complex and varied as Euro-American masculinities.

Part II

The Politics of Sex and Love

INTRODUCTION

In this section men write about pornography, love, relationships, and lust, and articulate some provocative views on homophobia, biphobia, and racism in the gay community. These writers navigate the minefields of power, domination, and consent, and move our collective efforts one step closer to understanding the contemporary sexual landscape in more accurate and nuanced ways. These crucial conversations bring discussions about sex out of the locker room and out of the classroom.

In "Just a John?: Pornography and Men's Choices" Robert Jensen argues that pornography is not really about sexing up and getting off: Pornography is actually about gender inequality and women's subjugation. Because we live in a culture that buys, sells, and trades women's bodies, Jensen asks men who use porn to take a cold, hard look at why they do so. Pornography, he argues, is just another form of buying women's bodies. Instead, there are creative possibilities for new ways of enjoying sex and pleasure that do not require the old tropes of male violence and sexual control of women.

The issue of pornography, pleasure, and power has been ground zero for ongoing feminist debate.[1] The arguments fall roughly into two camps. Some feminist thinkers claim that pornography—and by extension, sex work—is a legitimate source of women and men's pleasure and employment.[2] Civil libertarians such as Nadine Strossen argue that to quash the supply or distribution of pornography amounts to censorship.[3]

An alternative argument about pornography, notably represented by Andrea Dworkin and feminist legal scholar Catharine MacKinnon, is that pornography is a form of forced sex, and that it institutionalizes gender inequality and eroticizes male supremacy and female subjugation. To MacKinnon, pornography does not simply harm women, it *is* harm.[4] For black women, and other women of color, this issue is exponentially complicated because of America's "brutal history of racialized sexual coercion and violence."[5]

Some who oppose pornography want to get rid of it. Some argue for increased porn literacy as a genre of critical media studies.[6] Others maintain that having more independent or queer porn, or more women in positions of power as sex industry executives and directors, will improve pornography's impact on women. Women who run Internet porn companies or video companies, or who work as porn actors and models, claim these options provide ways to earn money and, for some, to creatively explore their sexuality. Recent feminist scholarship presents a variety of viewpoints on sexuality and consent, and questions of gender, power, and exploitation.[7] Jensen, however, is unconvinced that pornography is anything but exploitation. Fear of censorship, he argues, prevents us from confronting what pornography actually reveals "about the cruelty of our culture, and the white supremacy and misogyny that abounds in America."[8]

Personal accounts by those describing their first-hand experiences consuming or producing pornography force us to rethink the line between empowerment and exploitation, along with rethinking the assumptions of heteronormative sexuality and conventional masculinity. Queer porn actor Ned Mayhem writes, "Before I did porn, even as I conformed to these [conventional] standards of masculinity, I desperately wanted someone to look at my naked body with the same immediate arousal with which I looked at naked women." Sut Jhally, Professor of Communication and Executive Director of the Media Education Foundation, comments that all of us present ourselves to be watched and gazed at. We all "watch attractive strangers with sexual desire. To treat another as an object of our desires is part of what it means to be human."[9] The problem arises when women are presented as nothing more than objectified sexual desire and men are presented as only agents of sexual objectification. This wrings out the complexities of human desire and the politics of gender and power. Picking up on this point in his essay, "Male and Queer in the Porn Industry," Mayhem problematizes assumptions about who does porn, who uses porn, who likes to be watched and who's doing the watching, writing that "the experience of being *consensually* sexually objectified can be fun and empowering."

Marcus C. Tye's intellectually incisive essay, "Bye-Bye Bi?: Bailey, Biphobia, and Girlie-Men" raises the issue of biphobia, the fear of bisexuality. Tye explains how academic research on sexuality is conducted and interpreted in ways that leave bisexual men like him invisible. When academic research refuses to acknowledge male bisexuality, men are led to believe that they have only two sexual options: to be either homosexual or heterosexual.[10] When, in turn, the media assumes that men are either homosexual or heterosexual, our cultural biphobia is revealed and reinforced. Tye raises important questions about how we conduct research on sexuality, how mainstream media interprets this research, and how unexamined bias and presuppositions about sexuality precede this. Mainstream media love bisexual women, but fear bisexuality in men. And when bisexual men remain invisible and unrecognized, fears about masculinity and sexuality are encouraged to flourish.

In "Darker Shades of Queer: Race and Sexuality at the Margins," C. Winter Han addresses the problem of racism in the gay community. "By now," Han writes,

> I've listened with a mild sense of amusement as countless gay leaders, an overwhelmingly white group, attempt to explain that their oppressed status as sexual minorities provides them with an enlightened sense of social justice that enables them to understand the plight of those who are racially oppressed.

Yet queer neighborhoods, magazines, storefronts, and bars within the gay community bring new meaning to the term "whitewash." One need only look as far as the personal ads to find phrases like "No femmes, no fats, no Asians." "Sadly," writes Han, "racism isn't just about how we are treated, it's also about how we treat ourselves."[11]

In their essay "Let Us Be Seen: Gay Visibility in Homophobic Poland," Tomek Kitlinski and Pawel Leszkowicz describe how risky it is to be out and gay in Poland. Poland is dangerously homophobic, they explain. Some high school textbooks still teach that being gay is an illness. Furthermore, homophobia goes hand in hand with misogyny and anti-Semitism in Poland: At feminist and gay demonstrations, counter-demonstrators commonly shout, "To the gas! We'll do to you what Hitler did to Jews." In their essay, Kitlinksi and Leszkowicz describe a bold and public nation-wide photography project that featured same-sex couples on billboards and in art galleries. The campaign was intended to confront the issue of gay and lesbian visibility in Poland and to resist the country's homophobia.[12] The authors believe that activism, art, and academic research are effective forms of dissidence, and hold out great hope for the "day when prejudice, discrimination, and violence will be abandoned—in Poland and globally."

In the next essay, "The Real Slim Shady," Ryan Heryford writes about navigating heterosexual relationships and his sense of self as a feminist-minded man. Heryford's perspectives on gender conflict with those of his girlfriend in perhaps unexpected ways: She likes Eminem; he prefers the Dixie Chicks, contradicting gendered stereotypes about masculinity and "being hard." Heryford tries to understand why some women prefer guys who treat them badly and wonders why these women put themselves in the path of violent, dangerous men. Heryford's best friend Matt is in a relationship with just such a woman. Matt, a gentle sort of guy, tries to get tough with his girlfriend Sarah. When this backfires, they break up, and both Matt and Heryford are left questioning the meaning of masculinity, aggression, love, control, and tenderness.

1. Some of the late-twentieth-century feminist perspectives on sexuality are chronicled in Ann Snitow, Christine Stansell, and Sharon Thompson, eds., *Powers of Desire: The Politics of Sexuality*. New York: Monthly Review Press, 1983. Also see Carole S. Vance, *Pleasure and Danger: Exploring Female Sexuality*. London: Pandora Press, 1989. Publication of this latter anthology followed the contentious 1982 Scholar and Feminist Conference on the politics of sexuality, held at Barnard College, New York.

2. Carly Milne, ed., *Naked Ambition: Women Who Are Changing Pornography*. New York: Caroll and Graf, 2005; Jill Nagle, ed., *Whores and Other Feminists*. New York: Routledge, 1997; and select essays in Merri Lisa Johnson, ed., *Jane Sexes It Up: True Confessions of Feminist Desire*. New York: Four Walls Eight Windows, 2002. The term "pro-sex feminists" has been used to describe so-called third-wave feminists who support the freedom to do sex work and to use pornography. This is a misnomer. I am unaware of analogous feminists who could be called "anti-sex." The central issue is, rather, power and sexual consent, not whether one is for or against sex.

3. Nadine Strossen, *Defending Pornography: Free Speech, Sex, and the Fight for Women's Rights*. New York: New York University Press, 2000.

4. To support her argument that pornography does not represent harm but is in and of itself harm, MacKinnon compares pornography to signs appearing above water fountains in the race-segregated South. Just as pornography is harm, a sign stating, "Colored" does not represent harm, but is itself the harm. Catharine A. MacKinnon, "Not a Moral Issue," *Yale Law & Policy Review*, vol. 2 (Spring 1984): 325. See also, Gail Dines, *Pornland: How Porn Has Hijacked Our Sexuality*. Boston: Beacon Press, 2010.

5. Mireille Miller-Young, "Hardcore Desire," *ColorLines*, Winter 2005–2006: 35.

6. Shira Tarrant, "Pornography 101: Why College Kids Need Porn Literacy Training," *AlterNet*, September 15, 2010. http://www.alternet.org/media/148129/pornography_101%3A_why_college_kids_need_porn_literacy_training?page=entire (accessed June 25, 2012).

7. See, for example, Tristan Taormino, Constance Penley, Celine Parrenas Shimizu, and Mireille Miller-Young, eds., *The Feminist Porn Book: The Politics of Producing Pleasure*. New York: The Feminist Press, 2013; and Ronald Weitzer, ed., *Sex for Sale: Prostitution, Pornography, and the Sex Industry*, second edition. New York: Routledge, 2010.

8. In his 2007 article titled "A Call for an Open Discussion of Mass-Marketed Pornography," Jensen suggests that just as we would not mistake concern about McDonald's nutritional content with being anti-food, "pursuing a healthy sexuality does not mean we have to support toxic pornography." Only four days after this article was originally published, it generated more than 400 comments and copious reader debate. See http://alternet.org/mediaculture/47677/, and http://www.alternet.org/sex/47987/.

9. Sut Jhally, dir., *Dreamworlds 3 (Abridged): Desire, Sex & Power in Music Video*. Northampton, MA: Media Education Foundation, 2007.

10. Mainstream interpretations of the Academy Award-winning 2005 film *Brokeback Mountain* is a prime example of Marcus C. Tye's point about bisexual invisibility. The protagonist characters are routinely described as gay cowboys, but the film actually

shows them as bisexual. The public misframing of this film "results from our culture's ongoing tendency to polarize, dichotomize, and oversimplify issues of sexuality and sexual orientation." See Harry Brod, "They're Bi Shepherds, Not Gay Cowboys: The Misframing of *Brokeback Mountain*," *Journal of Men's Studies*, vol. 14, no. 2 (Spring 2006): 252. Jennifer Baumgardner raises similar points in her book, *Look Both Ways*. See Jennifer Baumgardner, *Look Both Ways: Bisexual Politics*. New York: Farrar, Strauss and Giroux, 2007.

11. For self-reported accounts by young gay Asian males living in Anglo-Australian environments and discussion about the impact of white archetypal masculine ideals on body-image concerns, see Murray J.N. Drummond, "Asian Gay Men's Bodies," *Journal of Men's Studies*, vol. 13, no. 3 (Spring 2005): 291–300.

12. Kitlinksi and Leszkowicz further explore art, xenophobia, homosexuality, democracy, and activism in their co-authored book, *Love and Democracy: Reflections on the Homosexual Question in Poland*. Krakow: Aureus, 2005.

JUST A JOHN?: PORNOGRAPHY AND MEN'S CHOICES

Robert Jensen

There has been much talk about the need for men to love each other and be willing to speak openly about that love. That is important; we need to be able to get beyond the all-too-common male tendency to mute or deform our emotions, a tendency that is destructive not only to ourselves but to those around us. Many have spoken about our need to nurture each other, and that's important, too. But it's also crucial to remember that loving one another means challenging ourselves as well.

I would like to challenge us all—in harsh language—to address men's use of pornography. In an unjust world, those of us with privilege must be willing to do this, especially out of love. The challenge is this: Can we be more than just johns?

Let me start with a story that a female student at the University of Texas told me. She was on a bus traveling from Austin to Dallas for a football game. The bus was chartered by a fraternity and many of the passengers were women. During the trip, someone put into the bus's VCR a sexually explicit video. Uncomfortable with the hardcore sexual images of women being used by men, the female student began a discussion with the people around her about it, and one of the men on the bus agreed that it was inappropriate. He stood up and said to the other men, "You all know me and know I like porn as much as the next guy, but it's not right for us to play this tape when there are women on the bus."

No doubt it took some courage for that young man to confront his fraternity brothers on the issue, and we should honor that. But we should recognize that his statement also communicated to his fraternity brothers that he was one of them—"one of the guys"—who, being guys, naturally like pornography. His objection was not to pornography and men's routine purchase and use of women's bodies for sexual pleasure, but to viewing it with women present. He was making it clear that his ultimate loyalty was to men and their right to use women sexually, though that use should conform to some type of code of chivalry about being polite about it in mixed company. In doing that, he was announcing his own position in regard to sex. He was saying, *I'm just a john.*

PIMPS AND JOHNS

A john is a man who buys another human being for sex, typically through an intermediary: the pimp. Men sell women to other men for sex: pimps and johns.

There is a lot that could be said about the current cultural practice of using the term "pimp" in a wide variety of other contexts—for example, the MTV show "Pimp My Ride." We live in a world in which men who sell women are glorified. It is also a world in which the dominant white culture implicitly defines a pimp as black and then alternately celebrates and denigrates them. The confluence of racism and sexism in these cultural trends deserves discussion. But I want to concentrate here not on the pimps, but on the johns, on the men who buy women for sex.

I assume that many men reading this masturbate, or have masturbated, to pornography. That makes us johns. I don't mean that most men have necessarily bought a woman from a pimp in prostitution, though no doubt some of us have. I'm talking, instead, about the far more common experience of pornography. In my childhood and young adulthood, I was sometimes a john. Virtually every man I know has been a john. In pornography, the pimp is called a publisher or a video producer, and the john is called a fan or a pornography consumer. But that doesn't change the nature of the relationship: It involves one person (usually a man) selling another person (usually a woman) to a third person (usually a man). What this means is that pornography is a mass-mediated conglomeration of pimps and johns. When you masturbate to pornography, you are buying sexual pleasure. You are buying a woman. The fact that there are technologies of film or video between you and the pimp doesn't change the equation. Legally, it's not prostitution and legally, you're not in trouble. But you are still a john.

THE PORNOGRAPHY THAT JOHNS LIKE

At this point, let me define a few terms. Pornography comes in all forms and all kinds of people consume porn. In this discussion, however, I'm specifically referring to heterosexual pornography. I'm using the term to describe the graphic, sexually explicit material that is consumed by heterosexual men.

These DVDs, videos, and Internet sites comprise the bulk of the commercial pornography market. There are three consistent themes in heteronormative pornography:

1. All women want sex from all men at all times.
2. Women naturally desire the kind of sex that men want, including sex that many women find degrading.
3. Any woman who does not at first realize this can be turned with a little force.

The pornography industry produces two major types of films: features and gonzo. Features mimic, however badly, the conventions of a Hollywood movie. There is some minimal plot, a little character development, and a bit of dialogue, all in the service of presenting the sex. Gonzo films have no such pretensions; they are simply recorded sex, usually taking place in a private home or a starkly decorated set. Gonzo porn often starts with an interview with the woman or women about their sexual desires before other men or women enter the scene.

All these films have a standard series of sex acts, including oral, vaginal, and anal penetration, often performed while the men call the women "bitch," "cunt," "whore," and other, similar names. As they are penetrated, the women are expected to say over and over how much they like the sex. As pornography like this has become increasingly normalized—and readily available throughout the country by increasingly sophisticated technology—pornographers have pushed the limits of what is acceptable in the mainstream. As one pornographic film director put it, "People want more . . . [so we] make it more hard, make it more nasty, make it more relentless."

The commercial pornography industry grew steadily during the late twentieth century and seems to have peaked in the mid-2000s. In 2005, 13,588 new hard-core video/DVD titles were released,[1] but in subsequent years the recession, piracy, and DIY (do-it-yourself) pornography ended the wild growth of previous decades. While there are no absolutely reliable statistics on the industry's revenues,[2] annual sales in the United States are commonly estimated at $10 billion or higher,[3] while worldwide revenues have been put at $57 billion.[4] For comparative purposes, the Hollywood box office—the amount of money spent in the United States and Canada to go out to the movies—was $10.2 billion in 2011.[5] Because there is no way to chart the amount of money generated by pornographic web sites, and because there is so much pornography available online for free, it's more difficult than ever to chart the amount of sexually explicit material available.

MEN'S CHOICES AND RESPONSIBILITIES

We know there are women who consume pornography and a few women who make it. In this society, that's called progress. Feminism is advanced, some argue, when women can join the ranks of those who buy and sell other human beings.

This argument is a predictable result of the collaboration of capitalism and patriarchy. Take a system that values profit over everything, and combine it with a system of male supremacy, and you get a situation where pornography is increasingly mainstream and normalized; it is made into everyday experience. Pornography is profitable when men take it as their right to consume women's sexuality. When women join in the patterns of producing and consuming pornography, they join in a practice of exploitation and objectification.

When confronted with this, men often suggest that women choose to participate in pornography, so there's no reason to critique men's use of porn. We should avoid the temptation to take that easy way out. I'm going to say nothing in regard to what women should do, nor am I going to critique their choices. I don't take it as my place to inject myself in the discussions that women have about this.

I do, however, take it as my place to talk to men. I take it as a political and ethical responsibility to engage in critical self-reflection and to be accountable for my behavior, at the individual and the collective level. For men, the question is not about women's choices. The real issue is about men's choices. Do you want to participate in a system in which women are sold for sexual pleasure, whether in prostitution, pornography, strip clubs, or in any other aspect of the sex industry? Do you want to live in a world in which some people are bought and sold for the sexual pleasure of others?

When we ask such questions, one of the first things we will hear is: These are important issues, but we shouldn't make men feel guilty about buying sexual pleasure. Why not? I agree that much of the guilt people feel is rooted in attempts to repress human sexuality. This sort of guilt is unfortunately part of our society's cultural and theological history, and it is destructive. But guilt also can be a healthy emotional and intellectual response to the world and one's actions in it.

Johns should feel guilty when they buy women. Guilt is an appropriate response to an act that is unjust. Guilt can be a sign that we have violated our own ethical norms. It can be part of a process of ending the injustice. Guilt can be healthy if it is understood in political, not merely religious or psychological, terms.

Buying women is wrong not because of a society's repressive moral code or its effects on an individual's psychological process. It is wrong because it hurts people. It creates a world in which people get hurt. And the people who get hurt the most are the people with the least amount of power. When you create a sex-class that can be bought and sold, the people in that group—in this instance, women—will inevitably be treated as lesser, as available to be controlled and abused.

The way out of being a john is political. The way out is feminist analysis. And I'm not referring to a superficial exercise in identifying a few "women's issues" that men can help with. To borrow from Karl Marx, feminist analysis provides ruthless criticism of the existing order. Feminist analysis of pornography will not shrink from its own discoveries. Nor will this analysis shy away from conflict with the powers that be.

We need to engage in this ruthless criticism. Let's start not just with pornography, but with sex more generally. One discovery, I think, is that men are often johns, and that the way in which johns use women sexually is a window into other aspects of our sexual and intimate lives. For many men, sex is a place where we display and reinforce our power over women. By that, I don't mean that all men use sex that way all the time. What I mean is that this pattern of relationships is readily visible in our society. Women deal with it every day, and at some level most men get that.

The issue is not just about pimps and johns and the women who are prostituted. It's about men and women, and sex and power. If you've been thinking, "Well, that's not me. I never pay for it," don't be so sure. It's not just about who pays for it and who doesn't. It's about the fundamental nature of the relationship between men and women, and how that plays out in sex and intimacy.

And if you think this doesn't affect you because you are one of the "good men," then take a closer look. I'm told that I am one of those good men. I work in a feminist movement. I have been part of groups that critique men's violence and the sex industry. And I struggle with these issues all the time. I was trained to be a man in this culture, and that training doesn't evaporate overnight. None of us is off the hook.

WHAT IS SEX FOR?

No matter what our personal history or current practice, we all might want to ask a simple question: What is sex for?

A male friend once told me that sometimes sex is like a warm handshake, nothing more than a greeting between friends. Many people claim that sex can be a purely physical interaction to produce pleasurable sensations in the body. At the same time, sex is said to be the ultimate act of intimacy, the place in which we expose ourselves most fully, where we let another see us stripped down, not just physically but emotionally. Certainly sex can be all those things to different people at different times. But isn't that a lot to ask sex to carry? Can one human practice really carry such a range of meaning and purpose? And in a male-supremacist culture in which men's violence is still tacitly accepted and men's control of women is often unchallenged, should we be surprised that sex becomes a place where that violence and control play out?

This isn't an argument for imposing a particular definition of sex. It's an invitation to confront what I believe is a crucial question for this culture. The conservative framework, often rooted in narrow religious views, for defining appropriate sex in order to control people is a disaster. The libertarian framework that avoids questions of gender and power has also failed.

We live in a time of sexual crisis. That makes life difficult, but it also creates a space for invention and creativity. The possibility of a different way of understanding the world and myself is what drew me to feminism. I was drawn to the possibility of escaping the masculinity trap set for me, and the chance to become something more than a man, more than just a john. I was drawn by the possibilities of becoming a human being.

1. "State of the U.S. Adult Industry," *Adult Video News*, January 2006, p. 154.
2. Jonathan Silverstein, "Is Porn a Growing or Shrinking Business?" *ABC News*, January 19, 2006. http://abcnews.go.com/Technology/story?id=1522119#.T9Z-fbXvWSo.
3. Frederick S. Lane, *Obscene Profits: The Entrepreneurs of Pornography in the Cyber Age*. New York: Routledge, 2000, p. xiv. For a critique of these estimates, see Dan Akman, "How Big is Porn?" Forbes.com, May 25, 2001.
4. An often-quoted source for this figure is the Internet Filter Review. http://internet-filter-review.toptenreviews.com/internet-pornography-statistics.html.
5. Motion Picture Association of America, "Theatrical Market Statistics, 2011." http://www.mpaa.org/Resources/5bec4ac9-a95e-443b-987b-bff6fb5455a9.pdf.

MALE AND QUEER IN THE PORN INDUSTRY

Ned Mayhem

I am a queer porn performer. I have sex with many different people irrespective of their gender—often people I've just met—and I sell images of these sex acts on the Internet to pay my bills. I am also a Harvard-educated, cisgendered white man who owns his own small business while working on a PhD in experimental quantum nanoelectronics. This will not be a sad story; no downward spiral led me to monetize my sex life. Despite some important systemic problems in the adult industry, porn has not scarred me physically or emotionally. I love my work, I consider it to be ethical, important, challenging, and fun, and I am in a healthy long-term relationship that I hope will last for the rest of my life. I want to talk about the lessons porn has taught me about gender—lessons that I never would have internalized without stepping in front of the camera.

Participating in the adult industry is, in many ways, what allowed me to come out as queer, though mainstream porn has not always been supportive of that part of my identity. When I started in porn, I was straight. I do not feel that I was lying to myself or to others about my sexual orientation. I enjoyed having sex with women, and the idea of interacting sexually with a male body seemed vaguely icky and uncomfortable to me. In my most private fantasies I was occasionally aroused thinking about fiddling with penises, but only after doing elaborate mental gymnastics to temporarily put aside my discomfort with the idea. Compartmentalizing the ick-factor did not make it go away and I assumed this meant I would not enjoy making my private fantasy into reality. I knew that talking about these fantasies would only make people assume I was a closeted homosexual. I really did enjoy dating women very much, so I kept my occasional male–male fantasies to myself.

Appearing in porn changed my perspective on heterosexuality, although porn started with a heterosexual relationship. When I began dating my partner, she had already been performing in porn under the name Maggie Mayhem. We had been seeing each other (i.e., sleeping together casually) for a few months when she invited me to a filmed live sex party. I was nervous, but I agreed with very little hesitation. Maggie's enthusiasm for screwing with people's preconceptions about porn performers, and for using sexual expression to stand up for the rights of marginalized people, was fascinating and infectious. All of the sexual and intellectual exploration and personal growth that I intend to describe here come as a direct result of Maggie's loving mentorship and the influence of her nuanced but uncompromising principles. Toward the end of my first filmed sex party, under Maggie's libidinous encouragement, I stepped naked in front of the camera and penetrated her in front of a live Internet audience. I immediately liked it.

For the first time in my life, I proved to myself that I have the confidence to disregard social stigma. It was a very liberating feeling, even more so when the edited footage went up on the Internet with my newly minted stage name. I knew that appearing in porn might close doors for me, but that was part of the appeal. I had always been very cynical about the way people are valued in our society and, as a white guy with a top-tier education, I have always been valued more highly than I deserve. It's easy to talk about how the hierarchy of privilege is bullshit when you're perched at the top of it, and it's easy to talk about destigmatizing marginalized groups while belonging to none of them. I was so privileged I was afraid of losing important opportunities by doing controversial things, but that fear had been holding me back from doing much of anything with my life except following society's expectations for me from college to grad school to research. Performing in porn felt like putting my money where my mouth was for the first time by doing something I believe in, despite the possibility of social stigma or employment discrimination.

Of course, in porn I am also privileged. Being a man in porn means that I am not slut-shamed or threatened with sexual violence on a regular basis, as my partner is. As a man, people do not assume that doing porn means I am stupid, drug-addicted, or a traumatized victim of sexual assault. Being Caucasian in porn means I don't have to look for work exclusively on sites that fetishize my ethnic background. Being cisgendered and having a normative body type means that I am offered more work, and I am not publicly mocked or insulted by the same companies that hire me. It took a hell of a lot less courage for me to get in front of that camera than it does for anyone who doesn't look like me.

Yet, for me, porn was a very important first step toward genuinely not caring what people think about my identity. I had been trying for many years to overcome the internalized shame our culture heaps onto any expression of sexuality outside of a rigidly defined patriarchal structure. I suddenly realized that I hadn't fully overcome this shame because I had been trying to be shameless only in my private life and to keep that relatively secret. With porn, I was finally shifting from private shamelessness to public shamelessness, which opened doors in my psyche.

As I internalized this shift, I found that the mild disgust I had felt when I thought about sex with men slowly vanished. I started thinking about sex with men without fear of what my feelings might imply about my identity. It felt like I had already come out, the hard part was over, and I could play with whatever kind of genitals I wanted and take them or leave them. It didn't take long before I added "queer" to my public identity, and started having guilt-free sex with men for fun and profit. Maggie and I have never been sexually monogamous, and she thoroughly encouraged this new development in my sexuality.

Exploring sex with men for the first time was exciting, but I was eager to do gay porn for another reason. I wanted to be the center of attention. Porn is made to sexually arouse, and any given piece of pornography is designed to sexually arouse a certain type of person. We call this "the gaze"— the assumed perspective of the intended audience. Most mainstream porn is made for a heterosexual male gaze. Female bodies are the currency of arousal, and male performers are usually headless stunt cocks—unobtrusive foil characters at most, who should be mostly silent and need not be particularly charismatic or good-looking. The assumption is that it would make the (male) audience uncomfortable to sexualize a man's body. As a result, male performers avoid a lot of the intense stigma and shaming that female performers are subjected to, but it is also difficult for male performers to make a name for themselves or to build a fan base.

In contrast, gay porn is made for a homosexual male gaze. Here, the male body is meant to be the visual trigger for arousal. I wanted to be that trigger. I wanted people to look at me and get turned on. Heterosexual men are rarely thought of as visually arousing. Manliness means agency, and men are supposed to be desired for their power, skill, or confidence. For a man to pay attention to his appearance is considered feminine, and is looked down upon by straight men. Before I did porn, even as I conformed to these standards of masculinity, I desperately wanted someone to look at my naked body with the same immediate arousal with which I looked at naked women. I did not think that this would ever be possible. I was sometimes desired for what I could do with my hands or penis or words, but that is different from being desired purely for the aesthetic of my physical appearance. I wanted to be the object of a sexual gaze.

This may sound like I am glorifying the experience of being objectified. In a way, I am. The experience of being *consensually* sexually objectified can be fun and empowering. Many men never have a chance to experience this and I believe they should—but consent is key. Women are routinely made the objects of a sexual gaze without their consent, often in nonsexual contexts, and that is used to devalue them. A lot of homophobia among straight guys involves the fear of being objectified nonconsensually by a homosexual male gaze in much the same way that women are by heterosexual male gaze.

I have not yet mentioned a female gaze. Very little porn is made for a female gaze, and none of it is mainstream. I have heard it argued that women are simply not aroused visually the way men are, or that they are for other reasons not capable of enjoying porn the same way. I call bullshit. Women do not make up a large percentage of porn consumers because there is a strong social stigma against women buying porn, and because those who overcome this stigma are disappointed to find that almost all porn is made for a male gaze. I have friends who are shocked that many of the straight female porn consumers enjoy gay male porn. I believe my friends' shock stems from the ingrained idea that male bodies are not visually arousing, or that women are simply not visually aroused. Our culture teaches this idea to people from a young age, and many act as if it were true. Let me say it one more time, from my experience as a male porn performer and producer: This is bullshit. Once my partner and I started making our own porn, which was unafraid to sexualize my body, we found that all of our biggest fans were women.

Gay porn allowed me to be objectified on my own terms, and I enjoyed it. However, I found that doing both gay and straight porn put me under fire from two sides. Some gay performers would see my female partner and turn up their noses at me, calling me "gay for pay." Gay for pay is a term used to describe straight men who perform in gay porn to get more work. The connotation is that these performers take work away from genuine homosexuals, who presumably make better gay porn because they enjoy what they're doing and understand the gaze of their audience. As a queer performer who enjoys sex with men in my personal life as well as on camera, this attitude felt isolating to me.

The response from the straight porn world was even more brutal. Male performers who do both gay and straight films (so-called "crossover" performers) are considered by most of the mainstream straight porn world to be irresponsible HIV risks. This is demonstrably absurd. To perform in straight porn (and most gay porn), performers are required to be tested monthly for Chlamydia, Gonorrhea, and HIV. The HIV tests we use are RNA based, with a "window period" of less than two weeks (rather than six months for a standard antibody-based HIV test). The results of these tests are shared within the industry. If straight porn performers were getting HIV at a high rate, we would know. They are not. Every time a positive HIV result comes up, it is a scandal. This happens once every several years, usually due to off-camera activities, and the performer immediately retires. Given the size of the porn industry, this makes the HIV rate in porn far lower than that of the general U.S. population. Nonetheless, so-called crossover performers have been publicly condemned and privately banned by some major players in mainstream straight porn due to a perceived HIV risk that has far more to do with homophobia than epidemiology.

Despite the divergent gaze and disinclination to share talent between gay and straight porn, I was discouraged to find that both genres perpetuate the same strict standards of prescriptive masculinity for their male performers. I expected this from the hetero crowd, but as a newly minted queer, I was shocked at the extent of stigma against male femininity in gay porn, and in gay culture generally. It is clear that straight culture uses traditional standards of masculinity to perpetuate homophobia by equating male homosexuality with femininity, but I expected to find gay communities more supportive of feminine men. Instead, in porn casting calls and Craigslist personal ads, I found the same stigmatizing words repeated: "straight-acting only," "no femmes," "please be masculine." Any man who even vaguely resembles a feminine homosexual stereotype (lisp, limp wrist, fashionista, for instance) will be mocked and shunned by gay men in the same ways many of them were by the jocks in their high schools.

By most of these standards I qualify as "masculine." My experiences in porn, both gay and straight, made me think hard about what made me masculine and why. I had to step back and rethink some of the experiences I had growing up. Like most adolescent boys, every minute aspect of my awkward social presentation was picked apart, and I was rewarded for presenting masculinity and punished for presenting femininity. Everything from my posture, my sports prowess, personal confidence, the violence I showed in dominance battles, my willingness to hurt others, the interest I showed in sexualizing women, and the extent of my participation in misogyny, were all used to evaluate my social merit. The rewards and punishments did not come only from peers; teachers, authority figures, and media representation participated in masculinizing my peers and me. Sometimes this took the form of codified rules rewarding traditional manly behavior. At other times reward or punishment was the difference between a warm smile from a teacher or a disappointed shake of the head. To a large extent I played along, as most do. They were offering me power and privilege in exchange for my performance of masculinity, with the implication that the masculine ones are the ones who most deserve these perks. Many men's whole lives revolve around this internalized reward system based on their performance of masculinity.

Both mainstream gay and straight porn subject their male performers to this strict standard of prescriptive manliness. I started in the porn business to help me stop caring what people thought of me, so I was unwilling to continue making my appearance live up to a standard I believe is harmful. The more I thought about the depiction of masculinity, especially in sexual performance, the more important it seemed. It is clear that the intense judgment applied to women based on their performance of gender roles is a major symptom of ingrained sexism in our culture. Because men are predominantly the aggressors in sexism and sexual violence, the way we socialize men to perform masculinity is a major cause of these problems. During adolescence, young men are handed privilege on the condition that they participate in abusing it, justifying retroactively the abuses of generations before. Masculinity and male hierarchy are intimately linked to perceived sexual prowess, so the depictions of masculinity in porn are especially important to the way gender dynamics will play out in the next generation. I decided that if I am going to invest a large portion of my time participating in this performance, I want to be much more transgressive about it than I could possibly get away with in mainstream porn.

Luckily, there is other porn being made. Just as I was getting fed up with the standards of the adult industry, I found my local indie queer porn scene. The San Francisco Bay Area is home to a growing network of small artisan porn studios turning out really hot content designed to challenge prevailing ideas of what sexuality and gender performance should look like. The label "queer" is liberally self-applied in this group as a general term to signal rejection of prescriptive gender norms in terms of identity, presentation, and orientation. Performers of widely varying ethnic backgrounds, body types, and genders are depicted having the types of sex they actually enjoy, described with marketing language they are comfortable with. By giving sexually marginalized groups a medium to express their sexuality on their own terms, porn is used as a tool for education and empowerment. The results are both inspiring from a political standpoint and, to me, far more arousing than most porn I had seen elsewhere.

By this point Maggie and I had fallen very sweetly in love, and I had taken her stage name. It wasn't long before we started our own DIY porn website entitled Meet The Mayhems. We were inspired by some progressive role models in queer porn, and we were skeptical of the ethics, technical standards, and business models of all the big players in the industry (and especially of all the tools available to small adult startups).

We wanted a way to monetize our content on our own terms with little to no startup capital. To make this possible, we had to do everything ourselves, from programming and web development to videography, editing, legal issues, and publicity. This work gave us the freedom to present masculinity and femininity in new ways, to show hot sex acts we always wanted to see in porn and rarely did, and to find our own audience and create our own market. Nine months after the launch, our work was recognized by the Feminist Porn Awards in Toronto, and our small membership has continued growing steadily.

The next step for our site is to make the tools we developed, and the information we learned, available to other independent performers who may not have the technical background or the free time to build it all from scratch. By giving performers the tools to take control of their own representation, we hope over time to undermine the mainstream porn industry's exaggeration of cultural gender standards. There are specific expectations for men in porn, but even more harmful are the expectations for people of color, transgendered performers, or performers of different body types. It is generally not for me to decide what is offensive or empowering for marginalized groups to which I do not necessarily belong, especially when it comes to sexual fantasy and media representation. When using independent porn as a tool for sexual expression and social change, it is important to give a diverse range of performers access to that tool.

Working in the porn industry has taught me an immense amount about my own sexuality and gender presentation, and has forced me to face some uncomfortable truths about my culture. Portraying masculinity and queerness in porn in new ways can help change the cultural weight of these identities. I hope the work that we've done building Meet The Mayhems will prove relevant to undoing the layers of stigma I experienced both as a model starting out in porn and as an adolescent starting out in manhood. I do porn because I want to show people that it is okay for them to experience sexual pleasure any way they please with any partners they want, within the bounds of mutual consent. A growing number of pornographers share similar mission statements, and I hope that as a result fewer people will feel personally judged when they look for sexy images on the Internet.

BYE-BYE BI?: BAILEY, BIPHOBIA, AND GIRLIE-MEN

Marcus C. Tye

I am standing in front of an electric sliding door to the library. It doesn't open. I flap my hand over my head toward the sensor. Still the door doesn't open. Long seconds pass, with three thoughts running through my mind.

1. Did I look vaguely effeminate with all the hand flapping?
2. Decades into a supposed feminist revolution, what is a trained psychologist doing with 1950s' notions of what type of hand motions are manly and womanly?
3. Perhaps, as the *New York Times* had recently suggested, I didn't exist. Maybe that was why the door wasn't opening.

The *Times* didn't say that I, Marcus C. Tye, didn't exist, but that week published an article stating that male bisexuality, and male bisexuals, aren't real. We're all gay, straight, or lying: gotta pick sides, which I'd rather not. So does that mean I don't exist? And why do men have to pick teams?

Every now and then the *New York Times* has an article on male sexuality. It usually becomes the most frequently emailed article, especially if it concerns sexual orientation. "Straight, Gay, or Lying?" almost topped the most emailed charts for a whole week, mostly holding steady at number two, at times trumping reports on the London Underground bombing that happened the same week. But ever since this *New York Times* article grabbed popular attention in 2005, not much has changed when it comes to how mainstream media interprets and presents information about male sexuality in limited and biased ways.

While this suggests that the supposedly liberal, East Coast educated elite are actually closet *E!* cases, it also suggests a certain public fascination with male sexuality. A consistent theme emerges over the years: Articles on the down-low, brokeback marriages, and the like all reach the conclusion that males are straight or gay, and anyone who doesn't pick sides is being dishonest. I think this says more about mainstream notions of masculinity and how scientific research is interpreted in popular media than it says about male sexuality (bi or otherwise). But first I should explain the "Straight, Gay, or Lying" article.

As one might expect, the original scientific paper that underscored the *Times* report is filled with quadratic regressions and absolute residuals. The statistics tell a very different story than the one reported in the media, even the supposedly veridically exhaustive *Times*.

The original paper was written by Gerulf Rieger, Meredith L. Chivers, and J. Michael Bailey of Northwestern University. Of the three, Bailey is by far the most well known, a tenured professor and former chair of the psychology department at Northwestern. He's a heavy-hitter in the research field of sexual orientation and gender, who got somewhat bloodied by transgender activists for his book *The Man Who Would Be Queen* and his theories on transsexuality.

This particular paper on sexual arousal in males involved taking self-identified heterosexual, bisexual, and homosexual male volunteers, recruited from gay-oriented magazines and an unidentified "alternative" newspaper. As is typical in these experiments, participants are instructed on how to put a small rubber-band-like device on their penis, and then are shown straight or gay porn as well as visual stimuli that, for most people, are completely non-sexual. (Think carrots. Although there have been reports of men with erotic attraction to carrots, it's so rare it doesn't even warrant a special name.) The plethysmograph records how stretched the band is, i.e. how engorged the penis is.

A great many people won't participate in this type of research, so samples suffer considerably from selection bias. Of the ones who are willing, some men are intimidated by the situation and have no arousal at all: what we in the psychological science business call a floor effect. Their floppy data are thrown out. Some men are generally very horny and highly aroused throughout the experiment. Their rock-solid arousal becomes statistical noise that cancels out, too: a ceiling effect. A running joke in the field—partly true—is that this ceiling effect happens especially often when the volunteers are young male college students.

So what we're left with are guys in the middle range of arousal, a subset of a subset of half the population. Arousal studies are possible with women, and show less of a relationship between genital arousal and subjectively reported arousal than with men, but that's a topic for another essay, as the Rieger paper only looked at males. Sorting through all the statistics, the results were simple: Rieger, Chivers, and Bailey found that gay men got hardest looking at gay porn, and straight men got hardest looking at straight porn. A no-brainer. More interesting was that most self-identified bisexual men got much harder looking at gay porn. And, these bisexual men responded no more to straight porn than the straight guys did to gay porn. So, from their penises' perspective, they responded like the gay guys. A few were opposite: They got much harder from straight porn, and gay porn didn't do anything more than it did for the straight-identified men. Sounds like the *New York Times* got it right, right?

But what's most interesting about the study, and what wasn't reported at all in any mainstream press, is that all three groups in the study—gay, straight, or bi—showed more arousal to any of the porn than they did to neutral stimuli.

The media misreported that bisexual men expressed "exclusively" gay or straight arousal, meaning they got aroused by depictions of men or women, but not both. But what Rieger, Chivers, and Bailey actually found and reported in their study was that the bi men responded *like* straight or gay men: Straight guys actually got somewhat hard at the gay porn, gay guys got somewhat hard at the straight porn. Sure, they got much harder to their preferred stimuli, but they all showed moderate arousal to their non-preferred stimuli, higher (and statistically significant) than to neutral non-sexual stimuli, so we're not talking about a ceiling effect.

The authors could have concluded from their data that the bi-identified men were just being honest about experiencing some bisexual arousal, which, based on their research, is evidently almost universal in men. Instead they concluded that male bisexual identity isn't consistent with the data, that there are really just two teams, like most people continue to believe. There were other problems with the study that fueled the misreporting, such as the use of Alfred Kinsey's earliest pioneering-but-outdated one-dimensional scale of sexual orientation, rather than a more modern grid like Fritz Klein's that separately identifies arousal to males and females, and more importantly breaks out attraction, behavior, fantasy, preference, and emotional bonding. Instead, they collapsed Kinsey's seven-point scale (0, exclusively heterosexual, to 6, exclusively homosexual) into a trichotomous "what team are you on?" identity question.

The media headlines could have—and *should* have—read that the 96 to 98 percent of guys who identify as heterosexual are in fact bisexual in arousal to a small but measurable degree, because if you get down to it and show them gay porn and check out their penises, you're going to find they aren't quite so 100 percent straight as they say. Even if some of the straight-identified men were closeted homosexuals, it wouldn't account for the fact that some arousal to gay porn was typical of the average straight male. Most gay men openly acknowledge an occasional heterosexual experience, so I think it's more interesting to consider the unacknowledged same-sex sexual potential of the 96 to 98 percent of guys who identify as heterosexual.

So, why didn't the *Times* hit on this? Why not title the article "*Bi* or Lying?" Why the ongoing focus on the closeted gay male living on the down-low or in a brokeback marriage, the barely disguised biphobia? Isn't it even more newsworthy that the overwhelming majority of straight-identified men apparently are experiencing and suppressing moderate same-sex arousal? After all, straight men are not generally socialized for sexual restraint.

I think the answer is because the myth of the straight male is integral to our culture's conceptualization of masculinity. Acknowledging the truth is too threatening—both for men and women. Furthermore, keeping the myth alive is essential to social conservatives' goal of keeping gender and sexuality in check. This is nothing if not a power issue.[1]

EVERY MAN'S FANTASY?

In a shopping mall in Sydney, Australia, I once saw a poster of two women, looking like very attractive identical twins, about to embrace. Their unbuttoned shiny jackets revealed large bosoms about to make contact. Underneath was the caption, "Every Man's Fantasy." Bisexual behavior among women is a frequent element of heterosexual male porn, suggesting that quite a few women are at least a little bit bi (or at least, their heterosexuality will not be diminished by a little experimentation).

Notwithstanding all the suggestiveness of semi-naked, buff young men cavorting with one another in Abercrombie & Fitch advertising, the suggestion of male bisexual behavior remains just that, a suggestion. The guys are just horsing around. Unlike the women in the ad in Sydney, they're not really about to start making out. Men and women both take great pains to ensure that male–male sex is a line that just isn't crossed by "real" men, no matter how homoerotic the horseplay gets. I have yet to see a caption stating "Every Woman's Fantasy" underneath an image of two guys about to get it on.

Despite the alleged popularity of gay male friends, gay television characters, and even the appeal of gay male pornography among straight women, a lot fewer women actually report the fantasy of a guy-guy-me three-way, than straight men report the fantasy of a woman-woman-me three-way, so it's a taboo that is reinforced by women just as much as by men. Gay men can go there, but not straight men. And remember, you've got to pick sides.

It's clear there is a cultural double-standard about same-sex behavior in heterosexually identified men and women. A careful read of the literature produced by Rieger and others shows that the 100 percent "red-blooded heterosexual male" turns out to be a myth (or almost as rare as the exclusively gay male; that is, 2 to 4 percent of the population). Research suggests that the typical heterosexually identified male experiences some arousal to same-sex erotic stimuli. The amount of arousal is modest, but is far more than nothing. I'm not suggesting we're bonobo chimpanzees at heart, and that absent the prohibitions of culture we'd all be rolling around under the rainforest canopy. That would be a misread of our evolutionary heritage, which suggests that it is impossible to separate out the interaction of culture with biological tendencies in *homo sapiens*. It's an intellectual fallacy to suggest there is a single natural state of human behavior. Instead we observe behavioral tendencies that vary between individuals and even within individuals across time, with culture shaping the likelihood that such behavioral tendencies will occur, the manner of their display when they occur, and whether we feel guilty or proud about the behaviors.

It *is* natural for culture to influence our behavior, but its greatest influence is on our beliefs about our behaviors and our identities. When it comes to having sex, culture has a far greater influence on our sexual identities and how we feel about our sexual practices than on the sex itself. Into carrots? Whether you're ridden with guilt and believe this desire is a hellfire-damning abomination, or whether you think it's no big deal, is culturally determined. Men are a little bit bisexual, but whether most men recognize or accept this is the result of social learning.

So, why aren't we now reading articles about expanding horizons of male bisexuality? Why don't we see the fantasy played out on TV commercials for the enjoyment of straight women, whereas we see female bisexuality played out for men? Why do research articles gloss over their own findings that show that exclusive male heterosexuality isn't really that exclusive? And why do we see most heterosexually identified men continue to vehemently say they are 100 percent exclusively heterosexual? I think the self-brainwashing is strongly related to what I'll call "the girlie-man effect."

At its heart, the joke of the girlie-man involves a male who violates gender role expectations: a physically weak male, one who has an unmanly wave of the wrist, an unmanly mode of speech, an unmanly build. It's a joke that doesn't apply to women. Certainly, women who violate gender role expectations of femininity may face disdain, discrimination and often violence, and certainly, women face enormous pressure to conform to ideals of thinness and beauty, but there is no exact female-on-female equivalent to the nervous locker-room laughter from males that mocks another male who fails to live up to expectations of strength and masculinity. Strong women may have their sexuality mocked, and male androgyny or metrosexuality is from time to time mocked in popular media, but there is no feminine analog of the girlie-man, no boyly-woman touchstone of mirth. We certainly don't have contemporary female politicians publicly suggesting that their female opponents are boyly-women or ball-busters. It doesn't fit in quite the same way.

Consider iconic "manly men" film stars: Arnold Schwarzenegger, Sylvester Stallone, the later Tom Cruise. This role is often one of exaggerated secondary sexual characteristics, hypermasculinity, and traditional male gender roles: pumped biceps, which require a dedicated personal trainer or the abuse of steroids, a booming voice, physical strength and conquest, provider and protector—the opposite of the girlie-man. The man's man doth protest too much: As many scholars have noted, women today have more flexibility in normative roles—even in clothing—than men. Social conservatives are upset about feminism not just because of expanded opportunities for women, but because equality means a sharing of privilege previously reserved for men, and a diminishment of male power and control. The battle against feminism has been lost in the courts, and so threatened and diminished males cling to anti-quated archetypes of masculinity for their sons. These sons in turn perpetuate the myth that maleness is defined by vast innate differences, and exaggerate those differences that do exist. No "real" boy wants the shame of growing into a girlie-man.

No longer assured of being head of state, head of corporation, or even head of family, the average boy still receives the vestigial imperative of former male privilege: a message that he must still be a real man, and that all real men are strong, and are powerful. No wrist flapping, no girlie pretentions, and certainly no acknowledging of non-heterosexual impulses. That's grudgingly OK for the gays, but not for the rest of mankind.

Of course, daughters are indoctrinated into this cultural ideal, too, and they perpetuate it just as strongly. Most heterosexual adolescent females desire a pumped-up "real man" over a metrosexual, and many adult women would be horrified if "their" man turned out to have any sexual interest in other men. The main reason bisexuality among males isn't acknowledged yet is that if it were, it would accelerate the perceived erosion of male power.

That most women still prefer the heterosexual male myth shows just how far we still have to go. That so many sexuality researchers and journalists cooperate in the myth of exclusive male heterosexuality shows how ingrained the myth is, how difficult it is to see beyond our own childhood indoctrination. So, we collectively sideline the real findings of the plethysmograph, and instead falsely conclude that science shows an absolute dichotomy between male and female, gay and straight, rather than the dazzlingly complex diversity that science truly reveals, and that feminism frees us to celebrate.

Of course, there is a cost to males for holding on to these vestiges of male power. The consequence for the typical, mostly heterosexual man, goes far beyond a diminished range of sexual partners. It is a confining prison of gender role conformity, of having to be manly in gesture and speech and body. It results in men amping up innate biological differences, heightening secondary sexual characteristics such as muscle mass and lately even height, with parents administering growth hormone to boys. The prison of traditional masculinity fuels steroid abuse, limits career choices, and involves a continuous barely conscious self-monitoring, a self-censorship, a mismatch between potential and what is realized in many aspects of life. Women are not spared either. A corollary is the popularity of breast augmentation among women, again amplifying innate but modest differences in physique.

Our ideas about masculinity are still easily threatened. We see this in the ways that bisexuality in so-called straight men is covered up and ignored—even feared. More radical, accepting change has been kept at bay, for now. But on the insightful edges of our culture, a willingness among both men and women for ostensibly heterosexual males to explore and acknowledge bisexual behavior (if not identity) suggests that liberating forces will eventually come for men, too.

1. In 2012, A.M. Rosenthal, David Sylva, Adam Safron, and J. Michael Bailey conducted a study of male bisexuality with more careful selection of participants, and did find a distinctive bisexual arousal pattern in bi-identified males. This "bi guys are telling the truth" study received little media attention. See "The Male Bisexuality Debate Revisited," *Archives of Sexual Behavior*, vol. 4, no. 1 (2012): 135–147.

DARKER SHADES OF QUEER: RACE AND SEXUALITY AT THE MARGINS

C. Winter Han

By now, I've listened with a mild sense of amusement as countless gay leaders, an overwhelmingly white group, attempt to explain that their oppressed status as sexual minorities provides them with an enlightened sense of social justice that enables them to understand the plight of those who are racially oppressed. As sexual minorities, they say they share a history of oppression. This "shared history of oppression," they explain, provides them with exceptional insight and somehow absolves them of blame when it comes to the racial social hierarchy. Certainly, this view is not unique. People of color also believe that they possess special insights when it comes to social justice. Yet, two things are bitterly clear about our "shared" American experiences. One, a shared history of oppression rarely leads to coalition building among those who have been systematically denied their rights. More devastatingly, such shared experiences of oppression rarely lead to sympathy for others who are also marginalized, traumatized, and minimized by the dominant society. Rather, all too miserably, those who should naturally join in fighting discrimination find it more comforting to join their oppressors in oppressing others. In fact, they trade in one oppressed status for the other. Doing so, many gay white folks become more racist than non-gay folks while many people of color become more homophobic. As a gay man of color, I see this on a routine basis, whether it be racism in the gay community or homophobia in communities of color. And it pisses me off.

Psychologists have theories, I'm sure, about why such things happen. Perhaps some of us feel some comfort in the ability to claim at least a small share of the privileges and benefits of belonging to the so-called majority group. Maybe gay white folks use their race to buy into the mainstream while straight people of color use their sexuality for the same purpose. If they have something in common with those with power, perhaps some of that power will trickle down or rub off on them. I doubt it, but it's easy to believe. It's even comforting. What easier way to make oneself feel better than to marginalize others. But for now, it doesn't really matter why they do what they do. I'm not interested in why it happens. Rather, I'm interested in exposing it, condemning it, shaming it, and stopping it. Many gay activists want to believe that there aren't issues of racism within the gay community. As members of an oppressed group, they like to think that they are above oppressing others. Yet, looking around any gayborhood, something becomes blatantly clear to those of us on the outside looking in. Within the queer spaces that have sprung up in once neglected and forgotten neighborhoods, inside the slick new storefronts, in trendy restaurants, and on magazine covers, gay America has given a whole new meaning to the term "whitewash."

Whiteness in the gay community is everywhere, from what we see, what we experience, and more importantly, what we desire. Iconic media images in television and film, such as *Queer as Folk, Queer Eye for the Straight Guy, The L-Word*, or the domestic partners Mitchell and Cameron in *Modern Family*, promote a monolithic image of the gay community as being overwhelmingly upper-middle class—if not simply rich—and white. These images aren't new. Flipping through late night television, I'm often struck by how white and rich gay characters are whether they are on reruns of the *Golden Girls* or rebroadcasts of *Making Love*. The only difference now is that there are more of them, and they aren't so angst ridden about their sexuality. We now live in a country where gay TV characters are out and proud instead of languishing in perpetual shame, hiding in the shadows. They revel in their sexuality, at least on the screen. I can't help but think, though, that their revelation comes largely from their privilege of whiteness, the privilege to "be like everyone else," with only one minor difference.

Even the most perfunctory glance through gay publications exposes the paucity of non-white gay images. It's almost as if no gay men or women of color exist outside of fantasy cruises to Jamaica, Puerto Rico, or the "Orient." To the larger gay community, our existence, as gay men and women of color, is merely a footnote, an inconvenient fact that is addressed in the most insignificant and patronizing way. Sometime between Stonewall and *Will and Grace*, gay leaders decided that the best way to be accepted was to mimic upper middle-class white America. As a sexually marginalized group, the idea is to take what they can from the dominant group and claim it as their own. Rarely a day goes by when I don't read something, by some gay "leader," about the purchasing power of the gay "community."

Sometimes, racism in the gay community takes on a more explicit form aimed at excluding men and women of color from gay institutions. All over the country, gay people of color are routinely asked for multiple forms of identification to enter the most basic of gay premises, the gay bar. Some might argue that this is a minor irritant. But in a country where gays and lesbians are expected to hide their sexuality while in public spaces, gay bars and other gay businesses provide us with the few opportunities to freely be ourselves. Denied access to the bars, gay men and women of color often lose the ability to see and socialize with others like us who also turn to these allegedly safe places for not only their social aspects but for their affirming aspects, as well. Isolated incidents might be easily forgotten, but news reports and buzz on various online forums expose such practices as endemic in gay communities. From New York to Los Angeles, from Seattle to Miami, the borders of gayness are patrolled by those who deny the existence of gay men and women of color. And much like a neighborhood with more than six black families is quickly labeled "black" and, hence, avoided by many white buyers, a bar with more than six non-white folks is quickly labeled "ethnic" and avoided by the white clientele. Except, of course, those on the prowl for something "different" to whet their sexual appetite. In so many ways, their actions are nothing more than a cheap version of sexual tourism.

More importantly, gay men and women of color are routinely denied leadership roles in gay organizations that purport to speak for all of us. In effect, it is the needs and concerns of a largely middle-class gay white community that come to the forefront of what is thought to be a gay cause. Interjecting race in these community organizations is no easy task. On too many occasions, gay men and women of color have been told not to muddy the waters of the primary goal by bringing in concerns that might be addressed elsewhere. When mainstream gay organizations actually address issues of race, gay white men and women continue to set the agenda for what is and is not considered appropriate for discussion. During one community forum on race, the organizers, again an overwhelmingly white bunch, informed the audience that we would not actually talk about racism, as "everyone is capable of racism." With one sweeping generalization, this group of white men trivialized the everyday experiences of the men, and a few women, of color in the audience by denying our personal experiences and by turning the accusation back on us. It's a funny feeling to sit in an audience as an Asian gay man and watch as middle-class, white men claim victimhood in racist America. Ultimately, isn't that what their claim that "everyone is capable of racism" boils down to? Isn't what they're really saying is that they are also victims of racism?

Sadly, racism isn't just about how we are treated. It's also about how we treat ourselves. The primacy of whiteness in the gay community often manifests as internalized racism. In his online essay, "No Blacks Allowed,"[1] Keith Boykin argues that "in a culture that devalues black males and elevates white males," black men deal with issues of self-hatred that white men do not. Boykin argues that this racial self-hatred makes gay black men see other gay black men as unsuitable sexual partners and white males as the ultimate sexual partners.

This desire for white male companionship is not limited just to black men, and neither is racial self-hatred. Rather, it seems to be pandemic among many gay men of color. Even the briefest visit to a gay bar betrays the dirty secret that gay men of color don't see each other as potential life partners. Rather, we see each other as competitors for the few white men who might be willing to date someone considered lower on the racial hierarchy. We spend our energy and time contributing to the dominance of whiteness by putting white men on the pedestal while ignoring those who would otherwise be our natural allies.

The primacy of white masculinity in the gay community is no accident. It is a carefully choreographed racialization of men of color that mimics the masculine hierarchy in straight communities. Related to the "middle-classing" and "whitening" of gay America, images of gay men have mirrored the mainstream. No longer the Nellie queens of the 1960s, stereotypical images of gay men have changed from swivel-hipped sissies to muscle-bound he-men. So ingrained is the image of the "ideal" man within the gay community, "straight-acting" is a selling point in gay personal ads.

But masculinity doesn't exist in a vacuum. Masculinity is built upon the femininity of Others. Lacking female femininity, the gay community thrusts this role upon Asian men. Given the way that Asian men are gendered in the mainstream, this isn't a difficult task. If gay white men are masculine, they are masculine compared to gay Asian men. If masculinity is desirable and femininity is not, then clearly white men are desirable but Asian men are not.

While black men have escaped the feminization inflicted on Asian men, their masculinity is also heavily gendered. Rather than lacking masculinity, they are hyper-masculine, outside of the norm and thus to be feared. Gay Latino men and gay Native American men fare no better in the gay imagination. In the gay white mind, they are exotic beings who exist for the pleasure of white male consumption. Much like heterosexual male claims to the right of sexual consumption of women, many gay white men have claimed the right to pick and choose what they want from their sexual partners by positioning whiteness as a bargaining tool in sexual encounters.

Ironically, we strive for the attention of the very same white men who view us as nothing more than an inconvenience. "No femmes, no fats, and no Asians," is a common quote found in many gay personal ads, both in print and in cyberspace. Gay white men routinely tell us that we are lumped with the very least of desirable men within the larger gay community. In this way, we are reduced to no more than one of many characteristics that are considered undesirable. Rather than confronting this racism, many of my gay Asian brothers have become apologists for this outlandish racist behavior. We damage ourselves by not only allowing it, but actively participating in it. We excuse their racist behavior because we engage in the same types of behavior. When seeking sexual partners for ourselves, we also exclude "femmes, fats, and Asians."

The rationale we use, largely to fool ourselves, to justify the inability of seeing each other as potential partners and allies is laughable at best. Many Asian guys have told me that dating other Asians would be like "dating [their] brother, father, uncle, etc." Yet, we never hear white men argue that dating other white men would be like dating their brothers or fathers. This type of logic grants individuality to white men while feeding into the racist stereotype that all of "us" are indistinguishable from one another and therefore easily interchangeable.

Some of us rely on tired stereotypes. Boykin writes about the professional gay black man who degrades other black men as being of a lower social class while thinking nothing of dating blue-collar white men. The Asian version is that they are "Americanized" and looking for "American" men. In effect, we help white men oppress other men of color by buying into the racial social structure that the former group has created.

This self-hatred and willingness to join our oppressors in oppressing others is clearly evident in a column posted on Advocate.com. Jasmyne Cannick, a self-described black lesbian, argues that we should not extend any rights to "illegal" immigrants until gays are granted full rights. When did equality become a zero-sum game? Does extending human rights to immigrants somehow limit the amount of equal rights left for us? This is as absurd as claiming that extending marriage rights to gays and lesbians would somehow weaken heterosexual marriages. Extending rights to immigrants does not limit our rights in any way. To the contrary, it reinforces the commitment to equality and fairness for everyone, including gays and lesbians. As for Cannick's argument that these immigrants are "illegal," I might remind her that until the Supreme Court ruled on *Lawrence v. Texas* in 2003, millions of us were engaging in the horribly illegal activity of loving someone of the same sex. Thousands of us also got married "illegally." Why does Cannick believe that we have the right to challenge laws that brand us or our actions illegal, while others do not share this right? Clearly, those with the real power at the *Advocate* wanted to make a statement and found a pawn in Cannick. Her willingness to stand so firmly against granting rights to "illegal" immigrants simply reinforces the erroneous belief that it is acceptable for some members of society not to have the exact same rights enjoyed by others. Shamefully and unapologetically, Cannick quotes Audre Lorde at the very same time she uses the master's tools to build a fence around another oppressed group.

If we are invisible in the dominant gay community, perhaps we are doubly so in our own communities of color. If we are a footnote in the gay community, we are an endnote in communities of color—an inconvenient fact that is buried in the back out of view. We are told by family and friends that being gay is a white problem. We are told, early in life, that we must avoid such stigma at all costs. When we try to interject issues of sexuality, we are told that there is precious little time to waste on trivial needs while we pursue racial justice. Cannick writes that "lesbians and gays should not be second-class citizens. Our issues should not get bumped to the back of the line in favor of extending rights to people who have entered this country illegally." I've heard that exact sentence elsewhere. In fact, nearly verbatim, except "entered this country illegally" was replaced with "chosen an immoral lifestyle." See how that works? Master's tools.

I've seen those who are marginalized use the master's tools in numerous instances, now too legion to list. Citing Leviticus, some people of color who are also members of the clergy have vehemently attacked homosexuality as an abomination. This is the same Leviticus that tells us that wearing cloth woven of two fabrics and eating pork or shrimp are an abomination punishable by death. Yet not surprisingly, rarely do Christian fundamentalists picket outside of a Gap or a Red Lobster. If hypocrisy has a border, those yielding Leviticus as their weapon of choice must have crossed it by now. It must be convenient to practice a religion with such disdain that the word of God need only be obeyed when it reinforces one's own hatred and bigotry. How else do we explain those who condemn the film *Brokeback Mountain* based on their religious views while, in the same breath, praise *Walk the Line*, a movie about two adulterous (Christian) country singers?

More problematic is that we choose to practice historic amnesia by ignoring the fact that Leviticus was used by slave owners to justify slavery by arguing that God allowed the owning of slaves and selling of daughters. Anti-miscegenation laws, too, were justified using the Bible. In 1965, Virginia trial court judge Leon Bazile sentenced an interethnic couple who were married in Washington, D.C. to a jail term using the Bible as his justification. In his ruling, he wrote, "Almighty God created the races white, black, yellow, malay and red, and he placed them on separate continents. The fact that he separated the races shows that he did not intend for the races to mix." Scores of others also used the story of Phinehas, who distinguished himself in the eyes of God by murdering an interracial couple, thereby preventing a plague, to justify their own bigotry. Have we forgotten that the genocide and removal of Native Americans was also largely justified on biblical grounds?

Have we simply decided to pick and choose the parts of the Bible that reinforce our own prejudices and use it against others in the exact same way that it has been used against us? Have we really gotten so adept at using the master's tools that he no longer needs to use them himself to keep us all in our place?

Given the prevalence of negative racial attitudes in the larger gay community and the homophobia in communities of color, gay people of color have to begin building our own identities. For gay people of color to be truly accepted by both the gay community and communities of color, we must form connections with each other first and build strong and lasting coalitions with each other rather than see each other as competitors for the attention of potential white partners. We must begin confronting whiteness where it stands while simultaneously confronting homophobia. More importantly, we must begin doing this within our own small circle of gay people of color. We must confront our own internalized racism that continues to put gay white people on a pedestal while devaluing other gays and lesbians of color. Certainly, this is easier said than done. The task at hand seems insurmountable. In Seattle, a group of gay, lesbian, and transgendered social activists from various communities of color have launched the Queer People of Color Liberation Project. Through a series of live performances, they plan on telling their own stories to counter the master narratives found within the larger gay community and within communities of color.

Certainly, gay people of color have allies both in the mainstream gay community and in our communities of color. Recently, Khalil Hassam, a high school student in Seattle won a national ACLU scholarship for opposing prejudice. Hassam, the only Muslim student at University Prep High School, decided to fight for justice after a Muslim speaker made derogatory comments about homosexuals. Despite his own marginalized status as a Muslim American, Hassam confronted the homophobia found within his own community. Examples such as these are scattered throughout the country. Nonetheless, there is much more that allies, both straight and gay, can do to promote social justice. We must see gay rights and civil rights not as exclusive, but as complementary. All too often, even those on the left support "other" causes out of a Niemoellerian fear of having no one left to speak up for us if the time should come. I propose that the motivation to join in political efforts should come not from such fears, but from the belief that there are no such "other" causes. Rather, as Martin Luther King, Jr. reminded us, "an injustice anywhere is a threat to justice everywhere." We must remind ourselves, contrary to what Cannick may want us to believe, that social justice is not a zero-sum game. Granting rights to others does not diminish our rights. It is the exact opposite. Ensuring that rights are guaranteed to others ensures that they are guaranteed to us.

Ultimately, the crisis for gay men of color is one of masculinity. The centrality of masculinity within the gay community leads to rejecting all those outside of the masculine norm. Likewise, the centrality of masculinity in communities of color leads to stripping away masculinity based on stereotypical perception of homosexuality. Gay men of color are told, by both communities, that we are somehow not masculine enough to be full members in either community. Some of us have tried to attain this mythical masculine norm. We spend hours at the gym toning our bodies and building our muscles to fit with the gay masculine norm. Some of us disguise our speech, alter our style, and we watch our steps in an effort to appear more straight to the untrained eye. And while a few of us may escape the cage of the masculine abnormality, we leave our brothers behind. "You're pretty masculine for an Asian guy," we are told. "You don't act like a black guy," they say. Ironically, both of these betray the cage of acceptable masculinity that binds us to the mythical norm. Asian men are not masculine enough, black men are too masculine. The narrow range of acceptable masculinity is reserved for white men—gay or straight—because, ultimately, it benefits them. Rather than see the explicit racist statement embedded in this compliment, we secretly blush and giggle at the attention. I can't speak eloquently or competently about lesbian experiences with the expectations of femininity they experience. Yet, whenever I listen to my gay Asian sisters speak of needing to be more lipstick to attract the butch white woman, I wonder what's happening over there in the lesbian community. It sounds vaguely familiar.

The real solution lies not in mimicking the masculinity found in the larger society, but in abolishing it. We need to think about re-envisioning what it means to be masculine and, for that matter, what it means to be feminine and the social value we place on each of these categories. Sadly, I don't have the answers, at least not yet. But I can't help but feel that feminist scholars who attack the gendered hierarchy have a point. Perhaps one of them will find the answer some day. Until then, I can continue to make sure that concerns regarding race are brought up in the gay community and homophobia is confronted in communities of color. Perhaps one day, I won't need to do either.

1. http://www.keithboykin.com/sexuality/interracial.html.

LET US BE SEEN: GAY VISIBILITY IN HOMOPHOBIC POLAND

Tomek Kitlinski and Pawel Leszkowicz

It was a freezing Sunday afternoon in winter. We stood holding hands in the heart of Poland's capital, Warsaw, in a park next to the Monument of the Unknown Soldier. The statue of this soldier represents the model Pole. But we had made a decision to participate in an unsoldierly, non-military, civil campaign to resist Poland's homophobia in an action of gay and lesbian visibility. In front of us a young photographer, Karolina Bregula, held her camera, asking us not to pose, but to be natural and smile. The smile was a problem. We remained stiff and cold because two men holding hands as a loving couple was a very unusual thing to do in Polish public space.

The park was crowded with strolling people who pretended not to look at us. After thirty minutes of discomfort we welcomed the end of the session with relief. Now we could go back to passing for straight. By giving our real faces for a public campaign we joined twenty-nine other gay and lesbian couples in contributing to the first, large-scale coming out event in Poland's history.

The "Let Us Be Seen" campaign for gay and lesbian visibility was inspired by feminist art; the idea that art can be a participatory tool used to demand our rights. This project was intended to counter Poland's prejudice and gay invisibility through positive and viewer-friendly images. It ignited a storm of hatred. The far-right militia group, the All-Polish Youth, threatened the exhibit, and some community leaders refused to host the show. In the end, though, the photo exhibit provided visibility and strength for Poland's gay community. At equality parades where gay demonstrators are frequently attacked with stones, eggs, bottles, and slurs, activists now shout back, *Let us be seen!*

POLITICS

A bit of background is in order to better understand the importance of the "Let Us Be Seen" photo exhibit.

In our opinion, Poland's political transition has gone terribly wrong. In the 1990s, totalitarian communism gave way to fundamentalism instead of liberation. This has meant free elections and travel without granting sexual freedom to women and minorities. Social and economic constraints have not only remained, but increased. Poland is currently misogynist and homophobic. Some high school textbooks still teach that homosexuality is an illness. On May 7, 2004, one week after Poland joined the European Union, members of the nation's leadership, the ultra-conservative League of Polish Families, attacked the Krakow Feminist and Gay Parade of Equality with caustic acid.

The All-Polish Youth is a subset of this far-right political party. With its roots in Poland's interwar anti-Semitism, the League of Polish Families and the All-Polish Youth are staunchly homophobic and actively anti-gay. They also aim to deprive women of rights. Abortion has been criminalized in this country since 1993, but the League wants a total constitutional ban. In the early twenty-first century, far-right ideology isn't at the margins, but at the very center of Poland's politics.

Anti-gay arguments are made in the media about religious prohibition, sin, medical pathology, unnatural behavior, gay men's promiscuity, and gay men as pedophiles. In order to scare Poles into voting against EU membership, the League of Polish Families argued that Western liberalization promotes homosexuality. Posters appearing in the far-right and nationalistic press featured images of a same-sex couple with a child to symbolize Western Europe's moral depravity.

In a country where Roman Catholicism currently underscores a virulently conservative political ideology, gay men and lesbians in Poland bravely appeared in the public photos for "Let Us Be Seen." The project started in March 2003 and was initially planned as a public art campaign displaying same-sex portraits on city billboards. In this way, same-sex couples holding hands would inhabit the streets with straight couples and other passers-by as equal parts of society.

But the billboards were only seen for two weeks. The mayors of Warsaw and Krakow would not support the use of public space for the exhibit. The commercial company that owns the billboard sites withdrew from the project. Although the photos were deliberately hung high enough to deter vandals, paint was splashed on them in hostile attempts to destroy our efforts.

Since the streets proved inhospitable, art galleries instead functioned as alternative platforms for exposure. The All-Polish Youth threatened gallery openings with violence and members of the group were responsible for a fear campaign directed toward the exhibit. Yet although some cities banned the shows and skinheads destroyed many of the photos, "Let Us Be Seen" was still very successful in Warsaw and Gdansk. To promote continuing success, as small as these steps may seem, a feminist–gay alliance is badly needed.

Feminism helps us survive in Poland. Women's struggle for equality inspires the gay rights movement. Feminists teach us to resist oppression in a country where gays are despised, disrespected, and discriminated against. Moreover, misogyny and homophobia go hand in hand with anti-Semitism. At feminist and gay demonstrations, counter-demonstrators commonly shout, "To the gas! We'll do to you what Hitler did to Jews."

Feminists spearhead opposition to this sort of prejudice and hatred. The civil rights activities that started in the 1980s in conjunction with international feminism have become stronger every year. The Gay Pride Parade, organized in Warsaw since 1995, is increasingly visible in spite of bans and attacks. Similarly, the liberal Jewish community also supports the gay rights movement under the motto "minority for minority." In a statement by Poland's reform synagogue, Beit, for example, the congregation openly spoke out on behalf of Warsaw's Gay Parade of Equality on June 10, 2006.

Recently, the director of a large public art gallery in Poland organized a town-hall meeting about gay and lesbian rights to welcome the exhibit of "Let Us Be Seen." There was an unexpectedly high turnout of activists and academics. The All-Polish Youth also came. Pawel was asked to moderate the meeting. We asked for police protection.

There was a crowd of friendly allies, and a small hostile group that was outspoken and visible. Pawel had to control a militant group of skinheads and religious fundamentalists from the All-Polish Youth and the League of Polish Families. These men wanted to speak the most, voicing their prejudices against gay men. The rest of the participants—around one hundred people, mostly students and some local journalists—occasionally stood up to the attackers.

Pawel managed to calm the members of the All-Polish Youth by allowing each person to speak, if only once. Miraculously, this worked and many opinions were presented. Our face-to-face meeting with far-right fundamentalists confirmed for us that post-Communist nationalism in Eastern and Central Europe is carved from racialized, sexualized, masculinist hatreds and that, in a context of limited visibility and political power for marginalized groups, coming together to talk is an even more pressing need. Instead of excluding women and sexual minorities from discussion, there is an urgent need for openness and political hospitality.

HOPE

There is also another, more optimistic, part of the story. "Let Us Be Seen" provoked not only hostile reaction, but also positive media support. There was a debate on TV, on the radio, and in the press. The Polish edition of MTV had a regular ad featuring portraits of same-sex couples from the photo campaign.

Polish video clips with fragmentary images of same-sex love started to appear. The photographed couples were suddenly sought by the media to participate in talk shows and journalistic photo-stories. For a while "Let Us Be Seen" was a hot subject.

The challenge, though, remains serious. Men enjoy a monopoly of Poland's power. Mainstream media (particularly the state-run media) foregrounds misogynist and homophobic sitcoms, commercials, and news broadcasts. The ideology of the heterosexual reproductive family is relentlessly circulated. Homosexuality is still largely invisible and taboo. But alternatives are possible.

Poland's feminist band Duldung sings that ours is a "dictatorship of white beetroots," slang for macho, militarist, homophobic Poles. It is our conviction that activism, art, and academic research are forms of dissidence. We believe that writing, discovering, and interpreting the history of women and gays is a crucial political task. We promote democracy, pluralistic society, human rights, equality, and toleration. We believe that contemporary knowledge about the variety of human sexuality, and freedom from religious pressure are important. Together, we dream of a day when prejudice, discrimination, and violence will be abandoned—in Poland and globally. We shall overcome.

THE REAL SLIM SHADY

Ryan Heryford

I usually miss. Something always goes wrong. My knees buckle, or the dryer bell rings in the other room. I turn my head and my hips follow. My dick sways too far to the left or sometimes to the right, and a splash lands on the rim or the back of the seat, sometimes onto the puke orange rug we keep at the base of the toilet. I'm always stealthy. I snatch a tissue square and wipe off the stray drops, throwing them back into the bowl. I've never been caught. OK, I've only been caught a few times.

My girlfriend believes it is romantic to have that freedom of walking in on me while I pee. Perhaps, it is through this little ritual of ours that all of my elaborate masks which I have polished for her, all of my adorned statements about nothing at all, are reduced only to this: a body, pale, untrimmed, with a dick that usually sways too far to one side, dripping piss onto the white tiles below. So that she might say—"You peed on the floor."

"I'm sorry. I'll clean it up."

"No you won't. You'll clean some of it up. And some it will seep into the cracks, or make a puddle behind the toilet bowl. And it will dry and get warm when I turn the heat up. And it will stink like all hell. But you won't notice. You never notice. Only I do."

"I'll clean it up. I'm sorry. This is ridiculous anyways. Why don't they ever put urinals in people's homes? Only seats. It's unnatural. It isn't natural to pee into a seat. Even with the rim up. The diameter isn't wide enough. It's like a carnival game without prizes. Only punishments."

"Don't be a prick about it. If it means this much to you, don't clean it up at all. I'll just suffocate from the stench. And when my body is cold and dead on the bathroom floor, you can pee all over it." She usually sighs now, and then she says: "Christ, you're just like every other guy I've ever dated."

This is when the fight begins.

We fight precisely because I am not at all like any other guy she has ever dated. I am lanky, uncoordinated, and my cologne smells like a teenage girl's body wash. I go to bed by eleven and I am up at seven. I usually skip breakfast. I eat soy processed imitation meat patties for lunch. And sometimes, if I'm feeling adventurous, I'll go and see a movie in the evening. But only after reading numerous reviews and repeatedly verifying the show time. If my car broke down on the way to the theater, I wouldn't even know how to open the hood. I would probably call my mother. Most likely, I would cry.

These traits are incomparable to the other men who have come and gone throughout her life: a Jewish cocaine dealer with a pit bull and Samurai swords; a high school rugby all-star who punched out the coke dealer during a gang fight at the homecoming dance; a car mechanic with a pot farm in his basement and a gold chain that read, *Ain't No Secret I'm a Full Grown Man*. At this point in the argument, I will bring up each one of these characters by order of their deficiencies, and then tear them down by order of my insecurities. The truth is, I am severely jealous. While they dueled out their shortcomings with the sharp edges of their inflated masculinities, mine shrivels away, deflated in its holster. And the only link that I have to any of them as men is that we have all dripped pee along the rim of our girlfriend's toilet seat.

She would tell me not to panic. She never really cared for any of them. When they made love, she would always close her eyes. She would fantasize about someone else, someone who ultimately understood her. Often, she would conjure up the image of her favorite musical artist—Eminem.

I imagine that the image isn't too hard to conjure. His figure is plastered all across the bedroom. A *Rolling Stone* clipping of Marshall Mathers in a suit and tie with roses in his arms, lying in his unsealed grave, is tacked up next to her nightstand. Slim's very own plastic action figure hangs above our door, a three-centimeter chainsaw glued to his left hand. My personal favorite is the poster, duct-taped to the ceiling above the bed, where he's standing tall, stark naked, holding a two-foot bong over the patch of poster where his dick ought to be.

When we make love, when she is on the top, I don't have to conjure up anything at all. There he is, his dark brown eyes staring hard into my baby blues, that lifeless expression on his face which seems to say—"Yeah, I trickled a little bit of piss onto the toilet seat. So what, pussy?"

I asked her to take them down. It wasn't happening. She's been playing his albums since she was thirteen. "What the hell is so fascinating about him, anyways?" I asked. "He's a misogynist pig, a racist, anti-Semitic. He hates homosexuals. He hates everything and everyone just for the sake of hating."

"Because he never backs down," she told me. "He'll always be the last one standing."

"Standing for what?" I asked.

"Standing for his pride, his manhood."

My best friend Matt is a skinny feminist with knee problems, lactose intolerance, and an extensive collection of Ani DiFranco records, who thinks that he stands stronger than any of the Slim Shadys out there. But Matt doesn't have to stand up, he tells me in our ongoing e-mail conversations. Matt "relinquishes power!" saying, "Yeah, I have power; but here, you fucking take it. That is hard! And all the fucking cock-wielding assholes (whose heads I've fought myself from wanting to tear off, whose throats I've fought myself from wanting gleefully to defecate down). They're the real unformed ones."

But he doesn't really mean any of this.

"Actually," he writes, "that line about wanting to tear off their throats is a slightly altered rendition of wanting to wash their feet. I turned it around toward anger, frustration, and fury, because I wanted to seem a little hard, which I am not really. But I keep it alive for the sake of other's passions."

Dirty feet can be sexy sometimes. They are a sign of one's rugged, untamed manhood; that brown-eyed expression that says, "So what, pussy?" But dirty feet grow calloused, gather diseases; they become unfit to walk upon. Matt's need to clean these feet doesn't comes from hatred. It comes from a desire to love.

Matt has always told me that to love the one you are with is to love everyone they've ever loved. "What you must love is the entity," he writes, "that part of your girlfriend which was and is that previous relationship. You must love her love (all bad and good included). I think one of the biggest flaws is what I call 'historical re-visioning' of relationships. That's when we look back on an old relationship, based on where it ended, and revision everything that happened. This is often an important phase of recovery or learning to live with the relationship's end. But it can't stop there. At some point, we must go back and learn to love the relationship on its own terms, particularly for those involved, and also for their new partners."

I've taken Matt's advice into my own heart. I have gone back through the catalogue of all my girlfriend's ex-boyfriends and attempted to envision the love that was once there. I have spent hours alone on our bed, listening to each of Slim's tracks, my eyes tracing the muscles of his plastic action figurine, juxtaposed with my own scrawny flesh and bones reflecting off the bedroom mirror.

But I listen to folk music. I listen to soft and deftly placed guitar rhythms, honky-tonk pianos and bluesy vocalists who dwell upon each word they echo. I detest thumping bass beats, cars with rims and sound systems, weight rooms that smell like testicles and chlorine. If she and I had never met, had never loved one another so deeply, I wouldn't even have befriended these men, we wouldn't have even struck up a conversation. I would have tossed Slim Shady's CD out the window of my Jeep Wrangler, the one with the Dixie Chicks slogan taped to the bumper.

To love those men whose piss has already stained your partner's toilet seat is a dangerous task. It requires endless self-comparison, reflecting on all that it means to be both human and the socially conditioned monster that we call "man."

Even Matt was ultimately destroyed by his own manifesto. In order to love his girlfriend, Sarah, he not only needed to love Garret, her manic depressive ex-boyfriend, but he also needed to love the man with whom she was having an affair.

Sarah met Garrett when she was fourteen years old. They started fucking right away. It wasn't particularly romantic. He held a switchblade to her throat. In the parking lot behind the middle school cafeteria, in the back of her aunt's station wagon. He held a switchblade to her throat and he fucked her until he had finished. Then they would walk back to her mother's house. If she didn't hold his hand tight enough, or if she looked over toward the tanned German boy who spread mulch across her neighbor's front lawn, Garrett would slap her hard across the mouth and remind her of what a goddamn slut she could be. They did this for five years, and then he disappeared. He was found, a few months later, dead from a heroin overdose, outside of a Los Angeles erotic massage parlor.

Sarah graduated from her small-town, blue-collar Connecticut high school, and moved to big-town, blue-collar Baltimore where she met Matt. I can't imagine that their love for each other was ever perfect. I can't imagine perfect love. But the role that Matt played in Sarah's new life was drastically different from her ex-boyfriend. Matt was sensitive, communicative, thoughtful and always kind to her. They carried this love for three years, and then, in the fourth, things began to wither.

"She wasn't connecting physically to me anymore," Matt tells me by e-mail. "She wasn't interested at all in sex. She didn't find me physically attractive."

Despite the anguish and trauma that Garrett had brought into her life, Sarah still yearned for a man who would stand up and be a Real Slim Shady, someone who would subjugate her, dominate her, set her in her place so that she might know where she sat. With Matt, things were more complicated. All of the power structures that Garrett had laid out to define her as a woman were gone and now she had to learn what it meant to live as a human. In a moment of retreat, she found Ben, a computer graphics designer who lived in the apartment below, who had fighter jets tattooed across his biceps, and sixty-pound weights lying beside his leopard-print comforter.

"One thing was for sure about Ben," Matt writes. "He was condescending to her. This much she said. He looked down on her, and treated her like a sex toy. And the idea that she would allow herself to be treated like that was so disturbing because of how much I valued her."

Matt's efforts were based in love, at first. Despite his own hurt that he felt inside, Matt asked Sarah more and more questions about Ben. He tried to know and love Ben as something separate from the violent, masculine images that he had conjured up for himself. But the more that Matt learned about Ben, the more hatred he felt toward him. And through his hatred, he slowly started to become the thing that he most feared and detested.

"I literally tried everything to revive our relationship. The most prevalent and prominent of which was to go hard, to become a cock-wielder, to try and demand that she stay, to put up a fight."

It was when the boundaries were broken that Matt's own persona became the most dangerous and violent part of their relationship.

"Just before the Ben incidents, we had been trying simulated rape (wrestling sex, anyways). And so I thought I would try to spring that on her spontaneously."

He tossed her spine against the wooden backboard of their bed. He pulled her hair back into the space between the metal frame and the wall. He held her hands over her head, and wrapped the space between his thumb and his index finger, tight around her neck. He unzipped his jeans. She started to cry. And then she started to scream.

"The desperation of my attempted role play made it too real. That type of thing has to happen when trust is at its strongest, not weakest. It really broke down. She was very upset, crunched up in a ball on the bed. I was apologizing. Saying that I didn't know how to let her go. And then I saw myself in her full-length body mirror, which was at the foot of her bed, leaning from the ground to the wall, behind a milk crate, on top of which was an open laptop. When I saw myself in the mirror, several things happened:

1. I wanted to lose control of myself.
2. I hated myself for wanting to lose control.
3. I wanted to do whatever it would take to win her back. Anything to make her stay. In a way, it all culminated in a particular loss of control. Although somewhat dramatically contrived, in the end it was not."

Matt punched the mirror from a kneeling position by their bed. He hit where the mirror's hypotenuse was furthest from the wall. It burst, into his knuckles, all over the floor, into Sarah's laptop keys. Blood was everywhere. He went to her and apologized again. He kissed her on the forehead.

"Perhaps more gently than I ever have in my life with anyone."

He told her he was going and then he left. It was the end of their relationship.

Matt's single now. Sarah has taken up with an army reserve trooper named Bill. They live in an apartment above Bill's father's hardware store in a suburb of Chicago. Matt has moved back in with his mother. He's still learning how to love and how to be human. He sent me another e-mail yesterday:

I read an incredible, incredible line last night in a book, while I was in bed. Two people in love were about to have a sexual encounter. It was building up. And one of them, he felt such a forceful and urgent surge to love—not just to touch, but to love. I think it was described as a river pushing through a small culvert in a mountain ridge. A force—*"It was the violence that made him gentle, for it frightened him."* And that's exactly it, sometimes for me. It is the sheer, untamed force of feelings, the violence of emotion that causes me to be so gentle. Because I am frightened of what it could do to her and to me.

Sometimes, in my own dreams, I tear down my girlfriend's posters along the bedroom walls. I lay them out across the cold white tiles beneath the toilet bowl. I unzip my pants and begin to dribble thin streams of urine across the curves that move over the chest and the shoulders and the arms of the Real Slim Shady. Some nights, I catch my reflection in the bathroom mirror. I see my own baby blues wither and shrink, the dark black of my pupils consuming everything as I let out a few last drops onto the poster's hard brown eyes, thinking—"So what, pussy?"

Part III

Dealing With Violence and Abuse

INTRODUCTION

Violence and abuse impact men as perpetrators, as partners to those who have lived through it, and as victims and survivors themselves. Many men are personally and professionally engaged as violence-prevention educators and as direct-service providers, working to end the cycle of emotional, physical, and sexual abuse that impacts so many in our communities. In her book *Rose: Love in Violent Times*, author Inga Muscio describes a continuum of destruction spanning "passive" violence and everyday micro-aggression, bullying, racism, ecocide, rape, and international war. "Most forces of violence *are* bigger than any individual," Muscio writes. Yet forms of violence "live in our most intimate lives, inform our own choices and relationships. If we want to have a better world, we cannot shy away from these complexities."[1]

The men writing in this section do not shy away from these complexities of dealing with accountability and silence. Each author addresses these complexities by disclosing their own abuse, addressing their accountability as abusers, or by describing action as allies in preventing and ending gender-based violence.

There are some signs of long-overdue improvement in this regard. The FBI, for example, announced in January 2012 that after 80 years, it was finally revising its archaic definition of rape. Until then, the FBI only counted rape that included penetration of a penis into a vagina by force. That meant that coerced rape, men's rape, drugged rape, anal or oral rape, and rape by objects or fingers didn't even count as rape to the FBI. This revised FBI definition of rape includes any penetration, no matter how slight, of the vagina or anus with any body part or object, or penetration of the mouth by a sex organ of another person, without the consent of the victim.[2] This more accurate definition of rape improves reporting and response measures for women. Significantly, it also means that men who are raped can now be counted. This helps create advocacy measures, support teams, and legal procedure to better serve all victims and survivors, including members of the male, transgender, and intersex communities.

All too often, though, mainstream media reports and everyday conversations about violence, abuse, and sexual assault are shrouded in myth and inaccurate data. As author Jessie Klein makes clear in her work on bully culture, we must be collectively willing to examine the specifically gendered patterns of violence. In the past three decades, there have been at least 191 school shootings across the country. According to Klein, "multiple studies show that since the eighties, social isolation has tripled among youth and adults; depression and anxiety rates have soared and afflict youth at increasingly younger ages. Empathy has decreased."

Gender is a crucial yet often avoided component of this social problem. When the media reports on "school violence" as if it were a gender-neutral phenomenon, this distracts us from effective solutions. In 10 percent of school shootings since 1979, boys targeted other boys who were involved with their ex-girlfriends; or they attacked people in their schools after their girlfriend broke up with them. Over 20 percent of the shootings were related to violence directed at girls or women—often after the male perpetrator felt rejected by them, creating a perceived threat to his masculinity.

In about 50 percent of the shootings, boys responded to different forms of masculinity challenges. Boys are currently expected to be athletic, powerful, unemotional, and able to attract and dominate girls. Those who fail to meet these expectations are often abused, psychologically and physically. Some tragically "prove their manhood" by using guns and violence. Almost 10 percent of the shootings related to gay-bashing. Heterosexually identified boys said that they were enraged when called names associated with homosexuality.

"Keeping discussions about gender and sexuality out of schools," Klein explains, "cements our schools' bully society. Even schools that take bullying seriously often miss the connection to gender."[3] Misdirected attention or misinformation distracts society from effectively supporting victims and addressing perpetrator behavior.

Among other misinformation about gender-based violence is the idea that women attack men, physically or sexually, just as frequently as men attack women, or that huge numbers of women lie in reports that men have raped them. These myths have been debunked by the Centers for Disease Control's National Center for Injury Prevention and Control and by the U.S. Department of Justice.[4]

The California Coalition Against Sexual Assault's[5] Prevention Services Coordinator, Chad Sniffen, explains that myths and misinformation about sexual assault are counterproductive in many ways. A common example is the idea that "many" (in some objective sense) reports of sexual assault from female victims are lies—false reports motivated by greed, regret, or a desire for revenge for a romantic slight. The rate of false or "unfounded" sexual assault reports provided by the FBI or other law enforcement agencies is often used to support this myth. However, most research suggesting high rates of false rape accusations make a key mistake of confusing "unfounded" reports to police with *false* reports to police.[6] Furthermore, explains Sniffen, the following caveats are rarely discussed (or even known) by people making such claims about false reports: First, there is no standard definition or meaning of an "unfounded' case; second, police agencies often identify cases where victims refuse to cooperate at some point in the investigation (regardless of why) as unfounded; and third, victims of traumatic crimes like rape will sometimes recant their reports simply to end the questioning of detectives and defense attorneys about the gory details of the way they were sexually violated. The truth of the matter, Sniffen says, is that when taking these factors into account, there is no evidence that the false reporting rate for sexual assault is any different than the false reporting rate for any other crime—that is, about 2 percent.[7]

As for the myth that women are just as violent as men in instances of domestic or interpersonal violence, the data show that men are disproportionately the perpetrators of violence. According to the U.S. Department of Justice:

> Most violence against both women and men is male violence. Nine in 10 women (91.9%) who were physically assaulted since the age of 18 were attacked by a male, while about one in seven male assault victims (14.2%) were victimized by females. Similarly, all female rape victims in the study were attacked by a male, while about a third of male victims (35.8%) were raped by a female.

Data provided by Darkness to Light, an organization dedicated to confronting child sexual abuse, indicate that one out of six boys survives sexual abuse by the time he is eighteen years old; only 5 percent of perpetrators are strangers.[8] According to the National Crime Victimization Survey, a large-scale study of crime incidents in the United States, 9 percent of victims of rape and sexual assault are male. "While these numbers certainly make clear that the majority of rape and sexual assault cases are crimes perpetrated against women, the data also point to a sizable"[9] number of male victims who deserve consideration by researchers, theorists, advocacy networks, and the media.

Issues regarding masculinity and violence are receiving concerted national attention: In 2012, the Cal Ripken, Sr. Foundation, Men Can Stop Rape, Women of Color Network, the National Resource Center on Domestic Violence, Men Stopping Violence, Coach for America, *Voice Male Magazine*, A Call to Men, and several other prominent organizations joined forces with the Healthy Masculinity Action Project (HMAP). These groups, which are each at the forefront of violence prevention and education, collectively launched an unprecedented, ambitious undertaking to promote messages of healthy, non-violent masculinity across the United States. This action project "will develop new male leadership that role models strength without violence." The Healthy Masculinity Action Project promotes national dialogue and encourages men to be strong and assertive, "as well as caring and connected [to] loved ones, schools, workplaces, nation, and the world."[10] *Boys and Men Healing* is a documentary film built around the stories of three adult survivors coming to grips with what happened to them as children.[11] Jeff Perera is a Program Manager with the White Ribbon Campaign—the world's largest effort to engage men in ending violence against women. One of many younger men speaking up against gender-based violence, Perera explains in his YouTubed TEDx Talk, "Words Speak Louder Than Actions," that the words we use have an impact on the world. There is so much meaning in shared phrases such as "Be a Man, Please, Sorry, Stay, Go, Relax, Stop, Don't, No." Becoming aware of the impact of our words on others, says Perera, means becoming aware of how each of us can impact one another every single day.[12]

Male Survivor, a sexual abuse advocacy and support resource, also works to support men and boys. One component of their effort is dispelling myths about perpetrators and survivors of incest and sexual abuse or assault:[13] The fact is that men and boys can be victims; most perpetrators are not homosexual, if a boy experiences sexual arousal or orgasm from abuse, this does not mean he was a willing participant or enjoyed it; boys are equally traumatized by abuse as girls; boys who are sexually abused by men do not necessarily grow up to be gay; boys who are abused do not necessarily grow up to become offenders; if the perpetrator is female, the impact of assault or abuse is serious.[14] As authors B. Loewe and Anonymous attest in their deeply personal essays, and as the Male Survivor advocacy and support website explains, for any male who has been sexually abused, becoming free of these confusing or misleading myths is an essential part of the recovery process.[15]

In "How We Enter: Men, Gender, and Sexual Assault," B. Loewe reflects on how stories about invincible male power and chronic male sexual desire impact our ability to accurately understand male sexual assault. The idea that men are always stronger than women and that rapists are predatory strangers, for example, are myths that perpetuate rape culture and prevent acknowledging that men can also be victims of sexual assault.[16] "The existence of male survivors actually interrupts these myths," Loewe explains. "Our existence creates a space for redefining or abandoning constructed male identity." Loewe's exploration of sexual violence and masculine identity draws from his experience as a political activist and as a survivor of an assault by two adult women when he was sixteen years old. Loewe's analysis brings insight to the subject of sexual assault, and in doing so, helps end the silence that surrounds it.

Writing under anonymity, the next author presents a courageously frank essay about incest. By intimately describing his personal experience of abuse by his father, Anonymous dispels many of the myths about male sexual assault that pervade mainstream misunderstanding. Grappling with the lifelong aftermath of this childhood sexual abuse, Anonymous says he is unwilling to claim the title "survivor," because that would suggest that he is thriving in some sort of linear progress toward healing. Living with the impact of abuse is way more complicated than that, Anonymous explains in "An Abused State of Mind."

"Prison Breakthrough" takes us inside the Marin County Jail as writer and ex-convict A. Razor waits for transfer to San Quentin Prison. Facing a possible life sentence for a third-strike felony, the judge gives Razor a final reprieve and the chance to confront his unaddressed substance addiction. When he starts working a recovery program inside the jail, Razor "accidentally" finds himself in a therapy group focused on ending violence by men against the women who were their domestic partners. In his first meeting, Razor sits in silent horror as he realizes he is no different from the other men in the room who are there on domestic violence charges. With information and support from the group facilitators, Razor struggles to face his personal accountability as an abuser while he figures out how to make a radical change to stop his part in the cycle of abuse.

Ben Atherton-Zeman, a spokesperson for NOMAS (The National Organization for Men Against Sexism), looks at recent instances of highly publicized youth violence, demanding that we must call it what it really is: *male* violence. "Men's Manifesto 2012" argues that we must redefine masculinity and manhood to include both toughness and vulnerability. Doing so, Atherton-Zeman states, is what will provide better role models for men and boys and will encourage respect, equality, and shared power in relationships with others.

While A. Razor and Ben Atherton-Zeman focus on men's individual accountability within broader structural issues of violence, Eli Hastings describes an *ad hoc* vigilante response to sexual assault. The essays that follow by Grantlin Schafer and Jonathan Ravarino highlight the work of organizations and the strength of collective action. Given the scope of the problems, both individual and institutional strategies are important in preventing and responding to violence and abuse.

In "Violation," Eli Hastings tells the story about group of guys avenging a sexual assault on their female friend during high school in Seattle, Washington. While this example of teenage revenge may be an incomplete, or ineffective attempt to deal with violence, Hastings raises important issues about what it means to respond to male violence with more violence. He also honestly reveals the distress so many men face in dealing with a woman's sexual assault, and not quite knowing what to do about it. This essay invites us to think carefully about how our perceived options impact the form of action we choose to take. Hastings points to the fact that we need the right tools of social awareness in order to avoid recreating that which we seek to end; in this instance, violence.

In "Breaking the Silence One Mile at a Time" Grantlin Schafer describes his experience following college graduation when he took part in a national tour to educate men about ending male sexual violence against women and helping assault survivors recover. The program Schafer joined was conducted by the group One in Four, an all-male group of peer educators.[17] Ending violence against women is a specific topic area around which men are organizing actively and visibly. Men have a role in caring about and taking action against sexual violence for five reasons: Because men rape, men *are* raped, rape confines men, men know survivors, and because men can stop rape.[18]

In "Being a Social Justice Ally: A Feminist's Perspective on Preventing Male Violence," Jonathan Ravarino provides a ten-point plan for men who are social justice allies, particularly those working to end male violence against women. Ravarino provides tools for identifying and dispelling myths about masculinity and sexual violence. He points out why it is politically important that men develop "the capacity to shut up and listen to the actual experiences of women" and why men's role in stopping violence against women is so crucial. Ravarino ends by highlighting mindfulness meditation as an important aspect of doing meaningful and consciously political work.

1. Inga Muscio, "Introduction," in *Rose: Love in Violent Times*. New York: Seven Stories Press, 2010.

2. Shira Tarrant, "It's a Dress, Not a Yes," in Norah Piehl, ed., *Issues That Concern You: Date Rape*. Almondsbury, Bristol, UK: Gale/Cengage, 2012.

3. Jessie Klein, "Gender Is the Key to the Bullying Culture," *Women's Media Center*, March 27, 2012. Available at: http://www.womensmediacenter.com/feature/entry/gender-is-key-to-the-bullying-culture (accessed June 27, 2012).

4. Mark Potok and Evelyn Schlatter report: "There is limited data that women sometimes initiate partner violence, although women involved in mutually aggressive partner relationships were more likely to suffer severe injuries than the men." However, the research study most often cited to support such claims is based on at-risk youth, rather than women, in general. Because the sample is "a very particular subset of the population," these research claims cannot be applied generally. Potok and Schlatter note that:

> The best studies, where the rape allegations have been studied in detail, suggest a rate of false reports of somewhere between 2% and 10%. The most comprehensive study, conducted by the British Home Office in 2005, found a rate of 2.5% for false accusations of rape. The best U.S. investigation, the 2008 "Making a Difference" study, found a 6.8% rate.

Mark Potok and Evelyn Schlatter, "Men's Rights Movement Spreads False Claims about Women," *Southern Poverty Law Center, Intelligence Report*, Issue 145

(Spring 2012). Available at: http://www.splcenter.org/get-informed/intelligence-report/browse-all-issues/2012/spring/myths-of-the-manosphere-lying-about-women. Claims regarding gender symmetry in domestic violence are not supported by the data. For further information on this issue, see http://www.xyonline.net/content/domestic-violence-and-gender-xy-collection.

5. The California Coalition Against Sexual Assault (CALCASA) provides leadership and resources to rape crisis centers, individuals, and other groups committed to ending sexual violence. For more information, see http://calcasa.org/.

6. Mark Potok and Evelyn Schlatter, "Men's Rights Movement Spreads False Claims about Women." Southern Poverty Law Center, *Intelligence Report*, Issue 145 (Spring 2012).

7. Chad Sniffen, personal correspondence, June 28, 2012. For more information on the issue of false reporting in rape cases, see Kimberly A. Lonsway, Joanne Arcambault, and David Lisak, "False Reports: Moving Beyond the Issue to Successfully Investigate and Prosecute Non-Stranger Sexual Assault," *The Voice*, vol. 3, no. 1 (2009): 1–11. Available at: http://ndaa.org/pdf/the_voice_vol_3_no_1_2009.pdf; Joanne Belknap, "Rape: Too Hard to Report and Too Easy to Discredit Victims," *Violence Against Women*, vol. 15, no. 1 (2010): 1335–1344. Available at: http://vaw.sagepub.com/content/16/12/1335.full.pdf; and Stephanie Hallett, "Do Women Lie About Rape?" *Ms. Magazine Blog*, April 7, 2011. Available at: http://msmagazine.com/blog/blog/2011/04/07/do-women-lie-about-rape/.

8. Shira Tarrant, *Men and Feminism*. Berkeley: Seal Press, 2009, p. 108. For further resources and support regarding male survivors of sexual abuse or assault, see Darkness to Light, available at: http://www.d2l.org/site/c.4dICIJOkGcISE/b.6069317/apps/s/content.asp?ct=8670133; Male Survivor, available at: http://MaleSurvivor.org; and 1 in 6, available at: http://1in6.org.

9. Karen G. Weiss, "Male Sexual Victimization: Examining Men's Experiences of Rape and Sexual Assault," *Men and Masculinities*, vol. 12, no. 3 (April 2010): 276.

10. http://www.mencanstoprape.org/images/stories/PDF/Handout_pdfs/hmap-booklet-final.pdf (accessed November 11, 2012).

11. Kathy Barbini, dir., *Boys and Men Healing*, Big Voice Pictures, 2011. Available at: http://www.bigvoicepictures.com/boys-and-men-healing/. See also, Jim Phillips, "Abuse Survivors Tell of Long Road Back from Shame," *The Athens News*, Thursday, April 26, 2012, p. 10.

12. Jeff Perera, "Words Speak Louder Than Action," TEDx, November 27, 2010. Available at: https://www.youtube.com/watch?v=-VBlQJFe_Ik. Also see Jeff Perera's blog, "Higher Unlearning: A Discussion About Men and Masculinity." Available at: http://higherunlearning.com/.

13. http://malesurvivor.org/myths.html (accessed June 27, 2012).

14. "Male Sexual Victimization Myths & Facts." Available at: http://malesurvivor.org/myths.html (accessed June 27, 2012).

15. http://malesurvivor.org/myths.html (accessed June 27, 2012).

16. For resources and information about male survivors, see Male Survivor, available at: http://malesurvivor.org; California Coalition Against Sexual Assault, available at:

http://www.preventconnect.org/19.0.html; and RAINN, the Rape, Abuse and Incest National Network, available at: http://www.rainn.org/.

17. For further information, see http://www.oneinfourusa.org/index.php.

18. http://www.feminist.com/resources/artspeech/mensvoices1.html; http://www.men canstoprape.org (accessed November 11, 2012).

HOW WE ENTER: MEN, GENDER, AND SEXUAL ASSAULT

B. Loewe

My mother took me aside from my eighth birthday pool party to scold me. It was the summer after third grade, and we'd set up a big tent in our backyard. My sister wasn't allowed to sleep in it at night. My mom gave her the same reason she gave for Kate not being able to play in the woods, only this time the evening news agreed. All the mothers were talking about the "Silver Spring rapist." Pat McCall didn't know what rape was. So he and I snuck around to the soda machines and I explained in a whisper in his ear, "Rape is when a man forces a woman to have sex with him," and we ran out screaming toward the shallow end of the pool until I heard my mom call my name in mid-stride. She said that my friends and I were very young, and that I shouldn't share such things because their parents might not want them to know about it yet.

That summer my friends and I inherited our first lesson in sex education: rape mythology. We crafted a common imagery in hushed tones in each other's basements out of earshot of our parents who would be sure to censor us. There were dark men stalking alleys or, in our suburbanized version, the surrounding woods. And there were unsuspecting helpless women who fell victim to their attack, as these men carried out their plot, pushing themselves on top of women and forcing them to have sex. For our young, uneducated, but highly imaginative minds, the story always stopped there. We had no concept of what sex actually was, other than that it was something dirty, wrong, and to be desired like grass stains on church clothes. It was something that women could give us and that some men took from them. We saw the potential power we, as man-boys, were to inherit; the manhood we were to adopt and avoid. We affirmed our own moral purity in knowing that we would never misuse that power. We learned that men are stronger than women, but that rapists are predator-types who abuse the power all men rightfully hold. As far as we knew, potential abusers remained relegated to alleys and bushes, living as a lurking threat. They were not people who played a role in any other part of our lives; not as mothers or fathers, not as neighbors, relatives, partners, or religious leaders. Surely we didn't know any rapists. And, surely, we could not be abused.

As we've grown up, so have many of our understandings about sexual assault. However, the way men respond to sexual assault is still often based on these lessons we first learned as children. And so these attempts at addressing sexual assault perpetuate patriarchy rather than breaking it down. Working with a framework of men-as-attackers and women-as-survivors, our conception of power can only rest in the hands of men. In dealing with sexual assault, this makes "good men" the protectors and avengers and in general makes women preyed upon and in need of prayers. If this is our story, then gender is determined not by our biology, but rather by which end of the knife we're on. If some of our earliest ideas of manhood depend upon having control over women, what does it mean to let go of that handle? Or even further, what does it mean when men feel the steel against their own throats?

Men's groups dedicated to anti-sexist work have done their darnedest to raise consciousness about these issues. Feminist men's groups I've been involved with focus on defying stereotypes by examining how we fit them. In these groups, we get emotional about not being in touch with our emotions. We patiently listen to each other talk about our impatience with our partners. With good reason, we focus on patriarchy as something we, as male-socialized people, do to others. We look at the outward effect of behavior we've internalized in order to be better organizers, better partners, better friends to the people in our lives. Whether we're describing scenarios that involve dominating conversations or dominating other people's bodies, from our position of masculinity, we analyze ourselves as potential perpetrators, always identifying with the person in power. We're willing to examine in depth our effect on a fairy-tale She-ra but we're unable to see ourselves as anything other than a He-Man, Master of the Universe. Examining our own moments of weakness is rarely a topic we talk about. Weakness would be too sharp a point to bring near our identities so inflated with masculinity. We are always strong, always the actor, never the acted upon. Thus, it is difficult to see ourselves as potential survivors, potentially vulnerable.

With patriarchy so pervasive, it's no wonder that men have to struggle so hard to unravel their myths of supremacy. In order to do so, men must confront the very basis of their identity, to acknowledge our own vulnerability, and to begin rethinking and rebuilding meanings of power. This self-examination requires the very tools that the process of becoming men convinces us to abandon. From the time we are young, boys are taught we should not cry or express hurt. As bell hooks explains in *All About Love*, boys "must be tough, they are learning how to mask true feelings. In worst-case scenarios they are learning how not to feel anything ever." At every point that we might imagine living without absolute control, without being masters of our destiny, there is another road sign rerouting us toward expressway erections.

But what happens when our lives and our lessons contradict? More specifically, what happens when men are the victims, rather than the perpetrators, of assault? For me, it took years before this possibility could be considered anything other than a joke.

I never classified my experience as sexual assault because it never fit my definition of abuse. It wasn't forced. It wasn't violent. It was inappropriately discreet; the epitome of "bad touch." Importantly, I was a man-boy and they were women. I knew that as a "red-blooded American teenage boy" I was supposed to want sex all the time and welcome any chance at it.

I believed that I held the social power in that room and I wasn't going to let these two women affect that. I wasn't going to let them affect me. I walked out of that room confused. In all my previous ideas about abusive sexuality, the powerful man overtook or ignored the will and desires of the less-powerful woman. If a woman could do this to me, what did that say about my power and my masculinity? Besides, wasn't this supposed to be kinky? Men are always supposed to want sex so this must be a joke. *Women could never have power over me.*

And thus, as long as I stayed in my manhead, this encounter when I was sixteen years old wasn't an assault. It was a funny story to tell friends because the idea that I could have been acted on instead of being the crafter of my own universe, Charles in Charge, unaffected by the world around me, was absurd.

As long as I relied upon these early lessons of masculinity, sexuality, and power for my self-definition of manhood, I could neither deal with the reality of my own world nor effectively act in solidarity with the women and gender variant people in my life. My desire to maintain my own sense of power debilitated my ability to participate in efforts to actually end sexual violence. Without a broader systemic analysis, activist men's groups deal with every assault case as another individual man gone wrong. For these groups, it's up to men to use our strength and rationale to either bring the perpetrator back into the fold of appropriate manhood or expel him from the circle. The approach perpetuates patriarchy rather than finding strategies to redraw the systems that shape our world.

It wasn't until I was in a men's discussion about sexual assault where, in go-around fashion, people could make comments like "I passed out drunk and when I woke up, someone was on top of me having sex," and then move on to the next person without any emotional content, that my male bonds began to break down. When we wrapped up the group, all I could say was how inadequate it was. The clock struck two hours and we were done. I walked to the nearby rocks and cried.

Later my partner at the time confronted me about the group's collective lack of emotion in the discussion. She asked, "How can you all expect to struggle against sexual violence when you don't let it affect you? When you don't feel it?" I defended the group and said that men deal with things intellectually and that it's a different, not a lesser, way of processing than emotional ways. I pointed to how I treated my own experience of being abused as an example. Then things shifted. This conversation with my partner forced me to realize that I did not have a different experience or a different relationship to my body. I had a detached one, an absence of a relationship with my body. She said, "It's not a different experience, it's half an experience." I agreed. I wanted to be whole.

Most literature on male survivors of sexual assault describes a "feminization process" where men feel "less like a man" after being abused. Often, this state of being is described as standard but temporary, with multiple appeals to survivors to reclaim their traits of traditional masculinity: to be strong, to be courageous. Many resources available to male survivors assure men that they are still "real men" and explain that abuse causes most to question their sexuality and gender identity.

No one should have to survive abuse. But, at the same time, I don't think it's a bad thing for men to have to critically think through gender socialization. One of the effects of having social power, of having privilege, is the ability to live *without* questioning one's identity; to assume, in this case, that hegemonic manhood is natural, normal, and preferred.

The existence of male survivors actually interrupts these myths. Our existence creates a space for redefining or abandoning constructed male identity. Patriarchy may not be the knife whose handle men firmly grasp and wield, but, rather, a double-edged blade that targets some and cuts us all.

It is not in redirecting, but in redesigning, our relations that all of our wounds can heal. With this new framework, I could neither be the Superman hero with the shadowy stranger in the alley as my foil, nor could women remain hapless objects in a world that I, and other men, create.

While men must grapple with the privilege and responsibility that socialization allots us, we can also un-puff our chests and end the posturing. We can strive to be something other than the action figures of our collective imagination.

Having lived through a harsh denial of our invincibility, having our scripts interrupted, we have the chance to either deny our experience—as I did for half a decade—or we can reject the role we're expected to play and improvise a new place for ourselves. We can reinvent a world of sharp contrasts and create a space amongst the subtler tones, to dance in the hues between poles. We can stop viewing life in polar opposites and start becoming human as a way to own up to and fight against male privilege, and to end masculinist patterns of domination over others.

More often than not, discussions about male sexual assault are used by men to avoid responsibility for the power and privilege they maintain. The topic of men as victims, especially victims of the actions of women, is used to obscure the prevalence of male sexual violence. Worse yet, these are used as cloaked conversations coated with allegations of reverse sexism meant to maintain, not reexamine, men's power. Recognizing this dynamic creates an even bigger challenge to understanding that, according to the National Alliance to End Sexual Violence, one out of six boys will experience sexual assault by the time they reach eighteen. By comparison, though, one in three women will be sexually assaulted in her lifetime. What this means is that we need to include men as victims in conversations about sexual assault without decentralizing women's experience and without taking away from the leadership of women and gender variant survivors. We must recognize that while sexual assault affects everyone, it is also a tool of patriarchy that specifically and disproportionately targets those assigned less social power.

Male socialization kept me from understanding that I had been molested, and women's support finally enabled me to identify as someone who was—five years after the fact.

I bring this up crying on a bus ride with a guy friend. I tell him that he doesn't know a thing about my past and I accuse him of assuming that I haven't been abused. In doing so, I assumed the same of him. I was wrong. But he says he never thinks about it. It never registers. But then what do men let register with them? Are we so out of touch with ourselves and so in touch with trying to maintain power that we must deny our vulnerability to everyone? With no space to talk about ourselves as victims, we maintain the tough-guy persona that patriarchy demands of us. As bell hooks writes (again in *All About Love*), "patriarchal masculinity requires of boys and men not only that they see themselves as more powerful and superior to women but that they do whatever it takes to maintain their controlling position." If this is true, what must men do if we are ever to play an effective role in challenging sexual assault in our communities? What is at the core of our identities if we remove superiority over women and moral purity compared to more abusive men? What will give us permission to express our own vulnerabilities? What does real, positive masculinity look like?

To be honest, I rarely feel emotionally equipped to deal with these questions or mentally prepared to write about them. I get a knot in my stomach every time I think about sexual abuse and I have spent days in an inexplicable fog after reading or hearing yet another survivor's account of assault. But I know that we can do better, that our conversations can become more inclusive, that our approach needs to change in order for all our attempts, from pummeling to processing, from ostracizing to education, to ever be effective. I write this because I want to get past the shock, the shock at my presence in survivor's spaces and at my tears in men's groups, to get past the bravado and the bitter days, the binaries and the ghosts I bring to bed. In this society, everyone comes out damaged goods. In setting out to transform the world we must also be ready to transform ourselves. Toward a world of healing, tomorrow is ours.

AN ABUSED STATE OF MIND

Anonymous

I'll cut the chase. Yes, there was penetration.

One South African therapist asked that question in an initial orientation session to determine the severity of my sexual abuse. She asked in that distinct South African accent; and me, having been introduced to talk therapy by a touchy-feely, New York Jewish therapist, was taken aback by that blunt style and I never returned to her. I still had to pay for the session, that was her rule.

This therapist's rates were high and she said with authority that I needed two years on the couch. When I did the math and told her that was a crazy lot of money, she gave me a look and stated that it really wasn't that much to pay since we were talking about the rest of my life.

So within two years I'd be able to live my life healed from the abuse? As if I was never penetrated? I'll never know because I went elsewhere. First, to a therapist who was even worse, saying things like, "Well, I'm not sure if it is a problem, not if you and your father had such a relationship and it was okay." Or, "I have a cop couple that sees me. They play Russian roulette with loaded weapons. Now, that's a bad relationship."

I soon switched to my next, and final, therapist, and stayed for about three or four years, where I guess I turned a corner and began to heal. I also learned that it'll never go away. I'm just able to handle it better, notice when the spiral down begins, and stop myself from hitting bottom. And so it's been that I've avoided hitting bottom for a while now.

For the last month I've been trying to write this essay on being a sexually abused man. I've started writing again and again. It ain't easy. Not the part where I describe what happened. After many years, that's gotten easier; it's making sense of it all that's hard. The most obvious structure would be to start with the abuse, describe the inciting event, then explain all the fall out, the increasing complications, and in the end wrap it up with the "getting of help," and wise words of reflection. And, while some of that is how it went down, it's way more complicated than that. Mainly, there is no ending that I know of yet. The issues, the pain, all the crap just keep coming back. Sure, I can deal with it better, most of the time. I know through experience that if I cope by acting out, extreme self-medicating, or with total disregard for myself, the only person hurt will be me. Correction: The people who will be hurt will be me, and any friends who have to experience me acting out in this way.

Some of the positive things are that I have learned to stop downward spirals when they start, and that I'm still alive. One of my therapists said that is because I have a strong core. Good thing for that.

The list of negative side effects is long and growing. Obviously, my relationship to sexuality has been disturbed, but luckily a lot of people's relationship to sexuality is, so that's not completely out of the ordinary. In some cases, due to my early over-exposure to sexuality, I can appear to be more open and to have fewer issues than the "average Joe." I can conversely also be more repressed and afraid of sexuality than most. It goes both ways. It's complicated. And, while I may have had all this "early experience," since it was done to me, I don't really own it.

Not really owning parts of my life is another real issue, which keeps coming back. Not owning means also that I learned to disconnect from myself when things are not pleasant, like I did when I was being abused. It's helpful now in real life, when life's misfortunes happen and I'm able to ride it out. It's dangerous when my tolerance level for putting up with negative things so easily means that, if I'm not careful, I damage myself. This is what I mean when I say it's complicated. I know these effects are not necessarily reserved for people who went through sexual abuse; many others I've witnessed share those traits, for whatever reason. We humans got many fuck-ups going on.

Like low self-esteem. Lotsa people have it. My therapists tell me that mine is likely from my upbringing and my abuse. But who knows. I don't display the very obvious low self-esteem. I appear rather confident a lot of times. But I know it's there, and at key moments it makes me self-sabotage my life. But again, many folks have those issues.

Also, I carry a lot of fear. I got no balls at all. *No cojones. Nada.* I've never asked a girl out nor have I ever lied on a resume. I exaggerate in the opposite direction. I warn potential girlfriends and employers about all my pitfalls, issues, and problems. I'm still learning to dial down that bad habit a bit and now I try to just say nothing and let folks fill in their opinions.

Again, these are life issues many people struggle with. Fear and trust issues aren't necessarily caused by sexual abuse. But that's where they originate for me, and when I reflect on my life, on all the times I lacked courage, didn't have the "balls," or I didn't stand my ground, the dots line up and paint the final portrait of a wimp, a failure, someone who got knocked down and did not get up and brush off the dust and fight back. Sure I was a kid then, and I've forgiven my inner kid, and all that mumbo jumbo. But I'm still pissed and hurt. And, sure, there are many times when I've been knocked down and it had absolutely nothing to do with the abuse, but the feelings that I have about myself in such moments are the same.

Eventually I stopped him. I was no longer a subject to his will. But I still haven't been able to become totally independent from the influence of his actions all those years ago.

The imagery of someone who's knocked down and overcomes the obstacles to ultimately achieve success seems to be a theme repeated almost daily by politicians, sport heroes, artists, or entrepreneurs. Almost everyone famous, it seems, has an I-got-knocked-down-and-then-I got-up-again story, and the media pushes that trope like it was their bread and butter. Well, it's great they all got back up, and I know they are trying to help me, to inspire me, with their words. But I stayed lying down after a few knockdowns. Sometimes just a single round leaves me lying down and, either way, I gotta accept me, lying down. Sometimes I don't get up, and that's my reality, and it feels just as defeatist as it sounds.

There's that saying that you build on your success. I don't build soaring skyscrapers of accomplishment but sinking hellscratchers of failure! Therapy taught me to focus less on the negative and more on strengthening the positive, no matter how small. While that sounds like simple common sense in my therapist's office, in real life it's hella hard, and at times impossible. And, sometimes, those well-meaning sentences make me just plain pissed off and angry. How can I build on my successes when the main thing I can see of my own life are the failures? It's the prevalent emotion my life has left me with. It's not always that bad, but it sure feels like it sometimes. Yes, I can always find something positive in the day to stop me from cutting my jugular, and that is great, wonderful and all that, but will this one-day-at-a-time, finding-something-positive-even-in-the-small-things way of life ever be over? Can it ever just be normal and can I ever be a normal guy? The answer so far is clearly no.

One issue that definitely has to do with my experience of sexual abuse is my identification with manhood and what it means for me to be a man. Being sexually used by one's father is a surefire way a father establishes his dominance over his son and knocks him down more than a few notches. And naturally it made me feel real small and powerless, and no longer in control of myself. And alone. Though while my father at first tried to convince me that this was a normal coming-of-age thing that other boys were doing, too, I didn't really buy it. And I was definitely not going to ask my buddies, "Hey, how are your coming-of-age sex rituals with your dad going?" I had insecurity and naiveté that my father took advantage of, but I still understood the world well enough to know that wasn't stuff you talked about. And then to make sure I wouldn't, he told me not to tell anyone, and I knew for sure I was screwed; I had been misled and taken advantage of. At the same time that my main male role model turned into my worst nemesis, my own emerging manhood turned into my own worst enemy.

To get away from my dad I did not confront him directly, but I crabbed sideways: I gained weight and lowered personal hygiene, embraced clubs and drug use, and had not a care for what society thought and I kept going as far as I could as a punk with no future.

"No Future" was the punk slogan of the times, and I was embracing it. But a lot of the time I also stayed busy trying to become "regular," the quality my left-leaning, progressive parents hated most. I joined a Christian youth group (I didn't become Christian although I'm thankful to the group for letting me be a part), I had girlfriends, was in a band, and I was into very ordinary things. Being a punk and trying to become regular are two approaches that don't seem to go together, and they didn't. I was a weird teen, for sure, and the times were difficult. But somehow I made it work. I acted out, self-medicated, and I was also able to experience "normal" growing up with my peers. It saved me.

I was also lucky that the arrogant, confident male (like my dad) was not so popular in my circles, so I was able to latch on to the soft metrosexual male image for a while. I could avoid being confident, strong, decisive, and proud of my maleness, and avoid the danger of becoming a man like my father. I could be a questioning, non-threatening, insecure male, ashamed of all the negativity associated with manhood, and still be a part of the scene and—more importantly—dateable!

But serious issues remain. Because I witnessed a violent, selfish form of male sexuality acted out on my body against my will, I fear male sexuality. One result is that I've never been the one who kissed first in any of my relationships. These days, it seems like women want to be with men who are confident, even a bit bone-headed. That means the guy has to make the first move, something I just can't seem to be able to do because in my mind if I move first, I'm making the first move toward abuse. I know intellectually that isn't true, but try explaining that to my emotions. I don't trust my feelings of lust. And sometimes I have such a hatred of being male, since that is what my dad represented to me. Because he was the number-one male in my life for so many years and then he became the number-one evil, I can't stand anything about men sometimes. When I'm feeling like that, I don't fully respect women who like men, either. This has created a number of unhealthy relationships and serious problems in healthier ones.

I've been to sexual-abuse survivor events and there always seems to be a group of women who were abused by men who are anti-male lesbians. I've wished at times that I could join them and say, "Yeah, I'm anti-male, too. I only want to be with women." But the fact is, I remain a man. I haven't had too much luck with finding like-minded men to bond with and, more often than not, they've creeped me out. I really don't trust men.

Sometimes I've wondered if my dad ruined me for other men. Maybe I was meant to be gay but because of the abuse I got turned off to men. Now

I can't be gay nor can I be a typical straight guy, especially since I've had gay sex. In our homophobic culture people think that means you're gay. I like to hang out with the ladies, gossip with my girlfriends, which I know, is *sooo* gay! My mom at times seemed to be hoping I'd come out as a mother-loving gay son who could also be a girlfriend to her, and together with her, face the evil patriarch, since we both suffered from his actions. My mom kept a photo collection of the most flamboyant pictures of me on the living room wall. When I got older and turned more beer-belly ordinary, she continued the timeline, but replaced pictures of me with those of flamboyant Broadway actors. No joke.

The whole sexual orientation thing comes up a lot. "So is your father gay?" I'm asked. It's odd because no one ever wonders about the sexual orientation of a man who abused a girl. They are seen as sick monsters that society needs to be protected from. But with male-on-male sexual abuse, it seems like people would rather not deal with it. That attitude of denial has enabled teachers and priests to abuse boys for ages; it's that attitude that lets a coach see a boy being raped by an adult male in a college shower room and walk away. This attitude was how police brought an underage boy found running naked in the streets back to the abuser he had escaped. The abuser was Jeffrey Dahmer who later killed the boy after the police left him in Dahmer's care. Society's fear of homosexuality gives male abusers of boys a space to hide in because until recently people turned the other way. If they confronted the abuse, they would also have to confront sexuality—and acknowledge there is a difference between sexual abuse and sexual orientation.

When I was younger, and naively still trying to defend my father, I also confused these two. I thought that the abuse must have happened because my dad was gay, but that he couldn't openly be himself because of the conservative times. I told myself he had to marry a woman, but was always repressed and frustrated, and he couldn't help himself from acting out with me.

For many years I regularly went to gay pride marches and supported gay rights with the logic that this would prevent other boys in the future from being raped by their dads because they were forced to lead repressed lives due to a restrictive society. I now know that sexual orientation has nothing to do with sexual abuse, but I still go to the marches when I can, because I believe in gay rights, and the pride celebrations are a lot of fun! Plus, I figure that the better the world sees what love looks like, the more clearly we can understand what abuse looks like. That way people can take action and stop the abusers.

People call me a survivor. It's a silly word and it's really not completely true. Being a survivor also allows me to be very, very lazy in life. After all, what I heard from therapists and read in books is that I survived something that statistically I could be dead from. I understand these statistical odds vary from person to person. While some may survive sexual abuse, a plane crash, or a natural disaster, and they may come out of it with a new lease on life and with fresh vigor go on to great success, I belong to another group that just wants to chill and stay in recovery. Apparently it's a form of post-traumatic stress disorder

The worst is behind me: I'm not getting sexually abused any more; I don't have to see the abuser very often; it happened a long time ago; I've had therapy. And now I really don't want to do anything but sit in the shade, have a drink, and relax. I sometimes wish I could go on to do more than just be a survivor, but then I figure *Why get involved with new things that just may bring new risks and new pain?* I'm extremely afraid of taking risks and so I don't. Just thinking about it stresses me out, but I survive by inaction, by rolling myself up in a ball, freezing in immobility, shutting down like the boy had to, back then. In that sense the word survivor is not at all true because I'm still afraid of living life to the fullest and still afraid of life's painful consequences. Maybe my body is intact and I've learned some coping mechanisms, but my spirit is still damaged. I don't feel like I've fully survived.

Still, I know the daily work of surviving is about keeping it going, day in, day out. The one-day-at-a-time crap. The seeing-good-in-small-things bull-shit. The building-on-success propaganda. The friggin' overused getting-back-up story. In the end there is no way around it. None of it's a tasty pill to swallow and I still gotta swallow.

Recently, my dad had a stroke and was hospitalized, and since then he's been in a long-term care facility. As a result, I've had a lot of opportunity to go home and reassess. Being home, I've also had the chance to catch up with folks I haven't seen in years. These friends have a natural tendency to say supportive, sympathetic words in regard to my father. I appreciate it, yet I feel I need to defuse some of that well-meant support. Since my relationship with my father is not typical—and it's definitely very difficult—I've now started telling these childhood friends about my history of sexual abuse at the hands of my father. After years of therapy and having told the story to my closer friends, I can do it in an almost detached way now. Once people hear the story, it seems like they knew, or they suspected something. They ask how come I'm not angrier. The fact is, I've been very angry. I've spent months kicking and punching my dad in my mind as I practiced martial arts. I'm still angry with that man, but it's starting to feel like a waste of emotions. Staying angry ultimately damages my own well-being and has no effect on him.

Now that the evil man is old, frail, and in a hospital bed, I feel more pity for him than anything else. Still, I know that I can't let my guard down. Even in his weak state, he remains arrogant. He will never believe he did anything wrong, and he will part from this world, thinking he was justified in living his life the way he did. I told my dad yesterday that I will be published for an essay I wrote about abuse. He didn't react and then he got tired and wanted to sleep. As I left the hospital the sun was shining while an intense, dramatic hailstorm broke through. Dang metaphors of my life.

People ask me why I don't confront him. And what? To hear him deny it? Even if he cried, apologized, said he regretted it, it wouldn't change what he did. I'm pretty sure he's done it to other boys, I know that is what he likes, I know he made these choices, and I won't accept an apology. And even if he did apologize, it wouldn't change how I feel: pity for a sick, old, dying man. But I won't give him the pleasure of having a chance to say he's sorry. Fuck that!

Over time I've also noticed that talking about it is sometimes liberating for me but doing so also means heaping a ton of bad stories on well-meaning friends. It feels like I'm forcing them to face the abuse and to try and make sense of such a horrific thing, and that doesn't seem right either. It's just another way my dad's selfish abuse continues to do damage to myself and also to others, since every time I tell a part of the story, my friends have to see the images in their heads and face the abuse themselves. So now there are times when I'm very careful about who to tell, what to tell, or if to tell at all. In the end there are no solutions because I can't make it go away.

Therapy helped but it also made life a lot worse for a long time. Therapy is no magic cure that I used to believe it could be. Though I see the benefits of being able to talk about it all so freely, I miss some of the innocence that self-deception, or suppression, allowed. It seems like I had more freedom and a lot of hope and purpose for my life ahead. Part of me would still like to cling to a world where my imagined version of therapy could make it all good. If this doesn't make sense, that's okay. A lot of this I'm still figuring out. It's complicated. Luckily, I have my friends who give me support and, in turn, I hear their stories and I see how it's complicated for everyone. And now you heard my story, too, and I'm all anonymous and shit, so you won't be able to tell me yours! Sorry, that's the way it's gotta be. But really, thank you for reading and for hearing my story. It's tough for everyone, in many ways, for many reasons, but by reading this, you made me feel less alone.

So thanks for that. It'll never be over, but I know I am not alone. Neither are you. Good luck to both of us.

PRISON BREAKTHROUGH

A. Razor

It was fall and I was on my way back to prison. I'd been through nine months of trial and transformation, and I had seen a potential three-strikes life sentence whittled down to a ten-year, eight-month prison term. Future enhancements assured a severe sentencing guideline for even a minor felony anywhere in the State of California from here on out. I was tired and humiliated that my life had come to this, but eager for a chance to use one of the options my lawyer diligently argued for during my plea negotiations. They offered to put me in treatment for a diagnosed drug and alcohol dependency instead of giving me twenty-five to life. The court received evidence from a psychiatrist that I had been involved in a drug-slinging, violence-infused world and, as the psychiatrist explained, I had developed PTSD. In past sentencing (and there had been many), the court never once suggested that I needed counseling or drug treatment. According to the judge deciding my case now, this was the only opportunity that I would be given. I would have to earn it by first going into incarceration and then proving that I was worthy of a second chance by exhibiting a true change in my behavior while in lock-up. That was all the incentive I needed to engage in whatever recovery programs that were available once I was inside the gates.

I caught my case in Marin County, California. I'd moved to Marin from Los Angeles to get lost in a rural landscape where I could grow marijuana, package narcotics, breed pit bulls, and avoid the law. My trial went down in a Frank Lloyd Wright-designed monolith-of-a-building that looks like some Jules Verne adventure vehicle. At one end of the Marin County Civic Center is a library and offices. Past those are the courtrooms and the legal arm of the county. The building ends in a sheriff's office and an underground jail, buried beneath a conspicuous mound where the building seems to go subterranean.

I surrendered my freedom in the same courtroom where, in 1970, Black Panther member Jonathan Jackson freed three other inmates and took Judge Harold Haley hostage in a failed escape that ended with both of them dead. I thought about that as I rode the elevator down in chains and was taken into booking, and then even deeper into the area of the jail known as the "Pods."

I waited for two weeks in A-Pod for a chance to enter a drug abuse program that was available only in the C-Pod section of the jail. I told the guards that I was hoping to participate in the C-Pod recovery groups, even though my paperwork indicated that my final destination was San Quentin. When I finally entered C-Pod, I was immediately struck by the lack of anarchy and chaos that A-Pod seemed to revel in. There were strict rules around violence and threatening behavior in C-Pod. If you were kicked out of C-Pod for breaking those rules the wait to get back in could be more than a month. If that happened, I would get transported out of Marin County Jail before I got the paperwork I needed to show I'd completed a recovery program. I knew it was time to buckle down and I quickly learned there were many different programs offered that you could get credit or certificates for completing. These certificates were the key to sidestepping a life sentence. The programs ran the gamut from parenting classes to creative writing classes to meditation workshops to alcohol and drug treatment. (Most of the inmates were hoping for a coveted bed in a treatment program, same as myself.)

I decided right away that I was going to throw myself into this, staying out of the usual politics and maneuvering that came with incarceration. I took on every program and class as if it was a challenge to conquer. I wanted the reward of paperwork that would hopefully sway the authorities to write positive reports and that would ensconce me in a drug treatment facility rather than the rack at San Quentin. The difference seemed as distinct as heaven and hell, even though I had never been in a treatment center before. It had to be better than prison and I felt like I would be a real mark if I didn't take advantage of this last opportunity to change my life and break the cycle I had been caught up in for so long.

After a few days in C-Pod, a group of men came in from the Marin Abused Women's Services, or MAWS, as everyone called them. They did a presentation that struck a chord with me. I was nervous about how precisely they described feelings I harbored, and how quickly they cut through my need to protect any true feelings from the world. I kept my real self even from my most intimate partners, the women I had my closest relationships with; the relationships that never seemed to work out the way I hoped.

Mind you, I detested the weakness I perceived in domestic abusers. Nearly half the men I was locked up with in C-Pod were there on domestic violence charges. I thought it was a sign of shoddy criminal commitment that these men allowed themselves to be vulnerable to arrest because of domestic circumstances. I thought a "wife beater" was a petty and disingenuous type of a criminal. Domestic violence was punk shit and most of these guys were just punks with no hustle. I was pretty self-righteous about it.

I figured doing this domestic abuse program would be an easy way to get another certificate. But, in the back of my mind, I was a little concerned about how much I related to the points about violence that the MAWS men made in their initial presentation.

A week later came time for the first group meeting. It was part of an effort called ManKind. The goals of the program seemed simple enough: to end immediate violence by men against the women who were their domestic partners, and to stop the cycle of abuse that had developed in these men's and women's lives. Even if I didn't admit it out loud, I recognized right away that I needed help with my violent reactions toward people. While I was never criminally charged, I had mistreated some of the women I had been in relationships with over the years. I stopped short of identifying with the abusers I was sitting with, still feeling superior to them since my relationship behavior was not legally in question like theirs was. However, as the group got underway, my mind started reeling from the reality I was faced with. I was just like all of these other men.

As the group discussion continued, I became emotionally uneven inside. I struggled in silent horror, realizing that I needed the help that the MAWS men had come to bring us. I barely made it through that first meeting without losing it completely and breaking down into uncontrollable sobbing. I remember asking in my head, *What have I gotten myself into?* and not being sure if I meant the domestic violence prevention group, the sentence I was serving, or my whole damn life up to that point.

There was domestic violence on a fairly regular basis when I was growing up, not just in my household, but also in many families around my neighborhood. The men I grew up with were bikers, gangsters, military, and blue-collar workers. They were besieged on all sides by a changing world. It seemed it was no longer as celebrated to be violent and to be proficient in violence, but many of them still were.

When I was a boy watching this violence happen around me, I knew I didn't want to grow up to be a man who abused women and children. I did not want to use force to be right or to exact revenge. But when I struggled to cope with peer rejection or ridicule, I resorted to violence. Men in my life actually encouraged me when I did this. I started to believe that my feelings of social and financial inadequacy could only be countered properly by an angry and absolute response. The ideal that I swore to as a boy—that I would never be an abuser like the males I witnessed around me—gave way to the idea that some people had it coming if they crossed me bad enough. I learned from the MAWS group that these justifications for violence were part of the Male Role Belief System. If I felt like that belief system was threatened, I reacted with violence. It was time for a change.

As the MAWS volunteers showed up weekly, they continued laying the groundwork for the group-therapy process. In teaching us about male violence, they explained the three basic principles of the ManKind program:

1. Men's violence against women is learned behavior that can be unlearned. By doing so, men will be freed of destructive belief systems that have also harmed them.
2. Men must be accountable for their violence.
3. Community beliefs that support and encourage men's violent behavior must be changed to end abuse, and men have a key role to play in changing those beliefs.

I began to see a pattern that many men have incorporated, to various degrees, in order to feel more in control and have more confidence when they feel threatened. The ManKind program refers to this personality as the "Hitman." It is supported by so many cultural and media depictions of potent male anti-heroes who rage against unjust circumstances or extol punishment upon those who have crossed the line and disrespected them.

The reality is that dramatic depictions of force in movies or TV shows are exaggerated action/adventure/suspense storytelling tools designed to stimulate areas of trauma in order to provoke an excited state of titillation and entertainment. Innocent enough for the masses, but the underlying message, mixed with role models at home and in the community growing up, can be to react with violence when needs are not met or behavior doesn't comply with the "Hitman's" demands. Understanding these connections between cultural messages and learned behavior was a crucial key for me to understand that violence can be unlearned, and that new ways of resolving conflicts in relationships can be utilized.

The second principle MAWS taught us about was accountability. This requires a level of honesty that is difficult, but accountability is eventually the most liberating experience a person can have, in my opinion. In a world where pressures build and fears mount, relationships can get clouded with dysfunctional self-justification and dishonesty. Part of adopting the Male Role Belief System is accepting negative ideas that women are servile opposites, irrational hysterics, or both. Under the Male Role Belief System, women are valued as long as they are fulfilling a pleasing or accommodating role for a man. When a man thinks he's entitled to always be the "Top Dog" or the "Master of the House," then dishonesty about abuse and accountability sets in.

The weekly MAWS' discussions always led to a revelation about how abuse really works. Violence doesn't start with a first punch or slap. Violence starts when abusive men fear their "Top Dog" roles can't be fulfilled. Abuse doesn't start where I assumed it did, and it includes behavior I didn't consider violent before undergoing the MAWS group process.

These actions include spying or surveillance that lead to verbal attacks on the partner's behavior. In some domestic situations, abuse includes hyper-vigilance about where the woman is going, what she is doing, who she talks to, how she conducts herself, and even what she wears. Critical commentary becomes derogatory and abusive in ways that can transform into physical violence. I learned that physical abuse includes throwing things or punching walls. Violence is not only about punching a person. Abuse can also take the form of neglect and withheld emotions and resources that are meant to be shared in relationships.

I realized that if I couldn't own up to my accountability for abuse, then I would be doomed to repeat it. The ManKind program taught me that I could let go of these learned behaviors and reactions so that I might play a part in creating a better world that was less harmful for others and myself. This behavior could be the key to a new world with new possibilities for new relationships that I had never known before.

The process that unfurled every week in the MAWS group was astounding, not only for the effect it was having on myself, but for the effect on all the men present. Even the most boastful violent predator in the group was humbled into silence from that first day and stayed attentive throughout the meetings. There wasn't a complete or immediate conversion for most, which left men in strange conflicted states as they lined up for their cells to be opened and had the opportunity to think for an hour before the doors were popped again for supper. Men would sometimes argue after dinner about the information that was presented by MAWS. But much of that information was undeniable, if not so painful it often made some inmates tear up. The facts were presented in such a way that it was difficult, if not impossible, to deny. The Male Role Belief System was apparent in all of our lives. It was the way we'd engaged with our loved ones and it was the way we intended to behave in the lock-up as well, so it was very de-stabilizing to be exposed to its weaknesses.

Participating in the MAWS group gave me hope that I'd never had before. The only thing missing was a firm commitment to this new life. I knew at that point I would need to volunteer for the hot seat and expose myself in front of the other inmates and the MAWS facilitators, as I had seen other men do. Even though I was not one of the domestic abuse offenders, and even though I had completed enough of the program to get the certificate, I made a commitment to myself in my cell one night: I would volunteer to speak during the next group and lay my soul bare. I would be accountable for my actions and be open to the suggestions and guidance of the facilitator.

This went against every fiber of my upbringing. I was taking a huge step into an unknown world, but one that had begun to appeal. I heard the message and I saw how it was possible for me to change. The groups had humbled me and slowly given me hope at the same time. I wanted to try and honor that gift by participating in the most open and honest way possible. I also realized that changing my life could possibly save my life.

The night before I was to speak up in group, I confided in another inmate who was also participating in the MAWS program. I told him what I was about to do next day and thanked him for the courage he displayed a few weeks before when he volunteered to be the focal point of the group.

At first, he expressed some disbelief. "Man, you participate well and you're due for the certificate. You are not here for domestic violence or anything like that. Why would you want to front yourself off like that?"

I wasn't surprised by his response. I knew I didn't have to do this to satisfy the court, but I felt compelled for personal reasons. I explained it to him that I was haunted by my own violent past. He understood completely and wished me luck.

I didn't sleep well that night and I was anxious the next day when I woke up. The incident I was about to relive in the group was not a positive one, by any means. It wasn't something I wanted to own my part in before starting this program. It was definitely something I had come to deeply regret, but I had learned that regrets don't equal accountability and that I needed to own up if I was going to unlearn the broken Male Role Belief System.

Before the group started, I approached the facilitator to confirm that I was allowed to be the volunteer that day. I could tell from his body language that he was a little anxious. I figured I'd better level with him, so he didn't think I was playing some strange jailhouse manipulation.

"You know this group means a lot to me, and it's not just because I get a piece of paper showing that I completed a program, or because it allows me to look good for the man so I might get a break like everybody is hoping for in here." I saw the look in the facilitator's eye, knowing he was waiting for the bullshit line that would finish it off.

"I mean, that's definitely why I first started coming to the group, no doubt. But something has changed for me because of this group. I want to do my turn in the chair to honor that, but most importantly, because I need to see myself the way you help others see themselves."

The facilitator cocked his head a little sideways at me and said, "The truth is going to be seen. But, the change is only going to happen if you keep pushing yourself to live with that truth as your guide. If you go back to the old Belief System, even in a subtle way, you will either feel an intense discomfort that will put you back on track, or you will start allowing the belief system back into your actions. And from what I know about you so far, those actions will just keep you here forever, or worse."

I nodded to show that I understood. I knew he was right about what would happen if I went backward. I could see how part of me had always been moving backward in strange contrast to how progressive I thought I was. Those old, learned behaviors about what a man was supposed to do in a relationship, in a family, in a community, even in a community of criminals, was ripping me apart inside and I never wanted to be like that again. I wanted to be a safe place for the people I loved to seek refuge in. I wanted to be a source of comfort and compassion. I wanted to be able to receive those same things when I needed them in equal ways without demands or expectations that were based on my gender or someone else's gender.

As the group began and my name was called I could hear my heart begin to beat in my eardrums like an echo of a drum. My throat choked up and my palms were sweaty. I was nervous in a way I had never been. There were two facilitators and one trainee. I would learn a little later that all of these men had gone through the ManKind program and then kept volunteering until they became facilitators themselves. There was a serious bond between these men and they exuded a lot of integrity to everyone in the pod. They spoke clearly and without any condescending tone or attitude. They slowly began to ask a series of questions.

These questions were designed to get at the heart of the dysfunctional Male Role Belief System. There was a lot of interest in this part of the group because we could all identify with values we were raised with, that extolled ideas about what a "real man" is. This part of the process was also a positive moment that almost always brought relief.

The words Honesty, Courage, Integrity, Honor, Power, Strength—even Compassion—were all written on the chalkboard. Each got a moment of pause while the group had a chance to discuss the traits as they were listed, one by one.

Then I got to talk about my partner, the woman who was my wife at the time. I was instructed to come up with the positive attributes about her, the reasons I was attracted to her, the reasons I loved her. I was told to describe what love means to me.

These words were each listed on the opposite side of the chalkboard and discussed in the same way as the first list. The vibe was pretty strong, with lots of feedback from the other inmates. There were some pretty solid identifiers that painted a positive picture of the reasons people want to be in relationships and families. These are the real values that people talk about when they are honest about what would bring them happiness: Loving, caring, and sharing. Appreciating each other for what you can bring to a partnership or household together. Not wanting harm to come to each other, having each other's back. Everyone agreed that these were sensible goals for successful living and relationships. Most of the guys that had been in the group for a while knew what was coming next. It was time to get to the moment of truth, to confront the past and see what my accountability looked like up close.

I knew the incident well in my head, but now I was about to share it in such a naked way in a room full of men I was locked up with. The facilitators were in place, one at the chalkboard, the other standing next to me, guiding me with his voice. I was asked for my most prominent memories of the moments before the incident, starting with the sensations that came to mind— a taste, a smell, a sound, the texture of what was close at hand. I was asked to describe my position, her position, which one of us was standing or sitting, how close we were to each other.

Once the physical setting was established, the facilitators dove into the feelings.

How you do remember feeling in that moment before you became upset, just before you became violent? What were you talking about? What were you doing? What were you thinking about doing? What did you want and how honest were you in talking about it?

We were both intoxicated. I was driving. I wanted her to just go home and not behave the way she was behaving. I said this to her loudly as I drove. She replied with an insult that I reacted to, without thinking, by slapping her with a backhand. She opened the door of the moving vehicle and jumped out as I tried to quickly brake. I pulled over to stop her and make her get back in the car. I was already bargaining in my head. *She made me do that. She should not have said that. Bitch got what she deserved, but now I might get in trouble. Now she has left my control and won't get back in the car.*

I am sorry already. I beg her to be "reasonable." She jumps into a cab. I meet her at home later. Our relationship never recovers. A few weeks later, despite my appeals that I would get anger management support and drink less, she left me and we never reconciled. I was torn up inside. *Why couldn't she understand? What a bitch*, I thought to myself.

Here's what I learned from the group that day: Plainly put, no one can make me be violent. The ultimate abdication of responsibility is to say, "You made me do this, you gave me no choice." It is the biggest lie that domestic abusers believe. It is the biggest lie I told myself. That lie alters the landscape of accountability so that the violent transgression can live. In an equal relationship based on mutual respect, there is no reason for lies. In a healthy situation, with healthy needs, everyone recognizes that each person is a separate entity with equal and valid wants and needs. Good relationships are based on this mutual respect and a positive alliance.

The core of the ManKind program is that violence is a learned behavior and that it can be unlearned, but only if it is aggressively unearthed and exposed. Abusive men use violence to control their victims. Violence is not caused by some "uncontrollable" emotion. It is a decision based on deeply held beliefs about male dominance. Unlearning male violence requires deep honesty.

Most men learn that our value in this world is based on what we can appear to control, on how much we can stay "king of the castle." An abuser becomes more guarded and his defenses go on high alert when a woman claims her ground or when she simply does or says something that conflicts with his opinions. He thinks his supremacy is being challenged. He becomes fearful that he will not get his needs met. This taps in to a learned childhood belief that he will be cheated out of what should be his. He thinks he will lose value as a man, and he will be vulnerable to being victimized and ridiculed while dropping down some invisible pecking order. The fear can quickly boil into a panic. An abuser who feels backed into a corner explodes with anger. This anger is usually in the form of ritual violence that is designed not only to defend, but also to conquer and punish the offending woman whom he now transforms into a dehumanized and contemptible figure. Most men engaged in this behavior will tell you that the woman made them act out in violence. The strategies for this defensive thought process in the aftermath of violence include downplaying the event and asking for forgiveness as a form of bargaining-away any actual accountability.

Hamish Sinclair, the man behind the ManKind program and his own group, Manalive, is very clear that no outside force causes violence. Violence starts with the perpetrator at the moment called "Fatal Peril," when a man feels disrespected, as though his sense of manhood is being challenged. It literally feels fatal, and the abuser thinks it is acceptable to act out his dominance physically and then downplay his part in it later on. This can lead to empty pleas for forgiveness, like I had done.

I lay in my bunk in my cell that night after I shared with the group, quietly tossing and turning over the truth confronting me. I needed to change and I needed to listen to what these guys from MAWS were talking about because it described something that I felt was wrong with me, that I hadn't liked about myself since I was a little kid. The truth I had to accept about myself that night was that I was violently insecure and that I was most likely to turn on the person closest to me. The main evidence was that I had done it already. I had abused women, including my wife. I was no different than those inmates who were in for domestic violence charges. We were all "wife beaters" and we needed help to change or we would do it again. And most importantly to me in that moment, *I* needed help to change. I had needed it for a long time.

MEN'S MANIFESTO 2012

Ben Atherton-Zeman

Reports of men's violence against women dominate our headlines. In homes across the United States and around the world, my gender is perpetrating violence against women in record number.

In 2001, eleven-year-old Nestor "Tito" Nieves was stabbed to death outside a Springfield, Massachusetts, movie theatre by another boy his age. Subsequent news reports indicated that Nieves was going to the movie with a girl that the other boy wanted to date. "That other boy was jealous and got mad," said Nestor's stepfather, Angel Herrera.

Another eleven-year-old boy from Springfield died in 2009. Carl Joseph Walker-Hoover endured daily anti-gay bullying. Since her son's suicide, Carl's mother, Sirdeaner Lynn Walker, has dedicated her life to stopping bullying.

Like Tito and Carl, I went to middle school in Springfield. I learned many things there and elsewhere about what it means to be a man. There were some good lessons: Be strong about your opinions, stand up against injustice, take initiative rather than standing back, and so forth. But there were some lessons I could have done without: Always have a girlfriend, always have the biggest car or make the most money, don't show vulnerable feelings. If a girl doesn't want to kiss you, kiss her really well and she'll "melt." If your girlfriend doesn't do what she "should," it's all right to bring her into line. And if she's going out with someone else, you have the right to a jealous, even homicidal rage against that other person—or against her.

All the popular guys in school seemed to embody these qualities. They were the guys I wanted to be like, and I tried my hardest to be like them. These same role models were on TV, in the movies, and in our popular culture. Any guy who deviated from this got labeled a sissy, gay, or (Heaven forbid) a girl.

The rigid enforcement of gender stereotypes has a body count. The victims are male and female. One in three women worldwide will be raped or abused by a man they know. In the United States, tens of thousands of women have been killed by men who promised to love them. And the very same gender stereotype that helps to create the problem keeps it going: If men speak out against male violence, we are often called misogynist and homophobic slurs.

I was sick of it in 2001 and I'm sick of it now. After Tito Nieves was murdered, I wrote a Men's Manifesto as a call to end male violence. Since then, much has changed but much remains the same. One of the reasons our sons are killing is because we have encouraged it. One of the reasons our brothers and fathers have abused their wives, girlfriends, and partners is because we haven't said, with a unified voice, that this is not a "manly" thing to do. We still need to do more work to change what it means to be a man, what it means to be one of the "cool" and popular guys. Toward this end, I again propose a Men's Manifesto 2012.

I'm proud to be a part of a growing movement—a multiracial, multicultural, global movement of men who are challenging male violence and outdated notions of masculinity. I have been inspired by, taught by, and befriended by men across the world who have dedicated their lives to reducing male violence. Men and boys around the world work for domestic violence programs and rape crisis centers. They donate and raise money for women's groups. They organize and participate in community walks and wear White Ribbons. Men Can (and do) Stop Rape and Men (are) Stopping Violence. There is a growing Call to Men to become part of the solution.

This movement, at its best, strives to be accountable to those who have taught us everything we know about these issues: women. We men have listened to and learned from women. We often forget to give women the credit they are due, and sometimes claim their ideas as our own. But the heart of this growing men's movement rests in the intelligence, kindness, confrontation, and love from the strong women in our lives.

I don't presume to speak for all men in this movement. These are simply things I strongly believe, things I have heard other men say. Things that I think would make the world a bit better.

We are men and boys who are proud to be working to stop male violence. We are proud to be men who welcome non-traditional expressions of what it means to be a man. We will be our own role models, applauding each non-traditional male role model who appears in film and television. As representations of manhood diversify, we will welcome the by-product of such diversity—acceptance and celebration of all varieties of manhood.

We are proud to be gay men and bisexual men. We are proud to be heterosexual men working to end homophobia.

We are proud to be transgender men. As transmen, we may choose to take on some aspects of so-called traditional masculinity while working to undo the very notion that there *is* such a thing as "male" and "female." As men who were once labeled "female," we bring a knowledge of sexism and male privilege to our work as male allies against sexism.

We are proud to be African-American, Latino, Asian/Pacific Islander, Native American men. We are proud to be white male allies against racism and sexism.

We are proud to have survived violence ourselves. We are rape and incest survivors, survivors of intimate partner violence at the hands of women and men.

/ We will work to end all violence against all people, even as we work to end the epidemic of male violence against girls and women.

We love other men. We will boldly express our love of other men with hugs, tears, high-fives, handshakes, holding hands, and kisses—sometimes with sex. We will sometimes choose a man as a beloved life partner.

We love women. Knowing that our gender perpetrates violence and sexism, we pledge to change ourselves and the world. Rather than riding in on a white horse, we will partner with women and support women's leadership in stopping violence and sexism.

We love our families. Those of us who are fathers love our children. We reject the aloof father image. We realize that our children's happiness depends on treating their mother with dignity, respect, and love.

When a boy scores a touchdown, we will continue to praise him with back-slapping celebration. But we won't stop there.

When a boy dresses like a princess, we will embrace him as we embrace the boy who hits a home run. We will embrace boys wearing skirts, boys wearing makeup, boys wearing black, and boys with piercings.

When a boy cries, we will comfort him. We will cry with him.

We will celebrate boys with long hair and short hair—running boys and boys in wheelchairs—ballet dancing boys and cheerleader boys. We will celebrate shy boys, singing boys, kind boys, and poet boys.

We will stand up against injustice. We will speak out against it, and will listen without defensiveness when it is pointed out in us. Rather than hiding behind "I didn't mean to," we will listen to the effects of our actions, not just point out our intentions. Strength as men will be measured not just by how many weights we can lift, but by how well we can listen.

We claim the right to define what's cool. We refuse to be defined rigidly, and will protect anyone who is bullied because he doesn't seem "cool" to the dominant culture. Coolness doesn't have to be aloofness, toughness, unreasonable jealousy, and possessiveness. We declare that it's cool to be tough sometimes, and vulnerable some others. We declare it's cool to support the people we date in their independence: Love isn't about control and sex isn't about coercion. /

We will not use homophobic, sexist, racist, or other oppressive slurs to gain the upper hand with someone else. And when we're called sissy, gay, or girly, etc., we will take it as a compliment. Strength as men will not be measured in opposition to women and things female, but in unity with those things.

We will be men in this way with determination—sometimes quietly, sometimes proudly, and always unapologetically. We will write country western, hip-hop, and rock songs with these voices. We will raise our sons this way, and raise our daughters to be strong and articulate. We will refuse to accept it if others say this isn't the way to be a man. This is our way to be men, and we will not be denied our self-defined manhood.

We realize that we've been raised in a sexist culture, and that we will continue to act in a sexist fashion despite our best intentions. When confronted on our own sexism or male privilege, we pledge to listen instead of being defensive. We realize that it's a gift for women to confront us on our sexism.

We realize that the continuum of men's violence against women goes from murder and physical violence all the way to sexist jokes and objectification. We admit that we have done things along that continuum, and we pledge to stop doing them.

We realize that in pledging to be part of the solution, we also must acknowledge that we have been (and still are) part of the problem.

We pledge to listen to women and learn from women.

We pledge to be accountable to women's leadership in stopping men's violence, and to be accountable to our own male privilege.

We are sick of violence from intimate partners. Gay men, bisexuals, heterosexuals, lesbians, and transgender folks all have the rights to joyful relationships free of violence and control. As the White Ribbon Campaign asks, we pledge to never commit, condone, or remain silent about men's violence against women. We choose to respect, seek equality with, and share power with the girls and women in our lives. We encourage, demand, and expect other men and boys to do the same.

Tito Nieves didn't have to die. He could be a college graduate by now. Carl Walker-Hoover didn't have to die. He could be a part of the growing anti-bullying movement in high schools across the nation. How many murdered wives and girlfriends were going to be the next Maya Angelous, the next Marie Curies? We must stand with each other as we boldly define a new form of manhood, and work for a world free from violence.

VIOLATION

Eli Hastings

For a while I watched the boughs creak and moan and how the raindrops slid and magnified the dance. I dusted off my desk. I looked at the clock six times in five minutes. I tried turning on KUBE 93 FM—ads. I tried C-89—Richard Marx. I tried silence. It wasn't coming out. I wasn't used to having to actually produce anything and I was rusty. The history paper had blindsided me; it was the old bat's way of getting back at us for skipping her class or coming in stoned and tipsy every other day. Apparently she no longer shared our high school's *de facto* policy of turning a blind eye.

The old oak stairs creaked and trundled. A light tap on my door followed and I turned, glad to be distracted. Kristy entered the room. She looked beautiful: her big amber eyes were in full effect and swollen raindrops winked on her lashes. She had her arms wrapped around her from the chill. We'd broken up a year ago. A snap and crackle of lust was born and died in me as I reminded myself she was my surrogate sister now.

She settled in and in the way her gaze darted around the room we'd haunted so many times with our amateur fumbling, I could tell she had something on her mind. She'd been shy about leaning on me since we'd parted; I desperately didn't want her to feel that way. I coaxed her into speaking, but even when she did she wouldn't meet my eyes. She watched the boughs dance through the rain, too.

"Something happened with Craig . . . I . . . I don't know if you know but I was kind of seeing him for a little while."

I didn't know. I winced inwardly, nodded.

"It was in March. He and Eric came over when my mom went to Vegas." She stopped and walked over to the window, giving me her alarmingly thin back. She crossed her arms again and her shoulder blades rose like wings. "We were fooling around and we . . . got to a point where . . ." she hesitated, looking for language. "You know, I wasn't really serious about him." She blew out a breath that was deep but staggered by anxiety anyway. "He tried to rape me."

What crept from my center outward would best be described as nothing—but a very cold nothing. This was more troubling than rage, because with the stillness and the void of emotion, came the promise of its end.

The next morning at eight o'clock I met Fog, Hugh, and Jamie behind the church. We smoked a lot of grass; someone produced a forty-ounce of Mickey's to share. We'd meant to confer—that had been my intention in calling them all the night before. It wasn't supposed to be so quiet between us. The autumn winds beat the church's brick savagely and ripped leaves down over us. Every few minutes one of us would say something like *Man, I can't believe that little fucker* or *I tried so hard to believe he was a homie.*

Thing was, Craig was allegedly a friend. He'd come late to our high school and our crew and determinedly made his way in. He was a scrawny, tenacious kid with beady eyes and shaggy, dirty-blond hair. His doggedness on the soccer field and ability to intimidate in the process of drug deals were unlikely given his build. And the velocity with which he set aside the healthy, childhood pastimes like soccer, and the zeal with which he dove into the dark lake of drugs was disconcerting even for us. We were all experimenting, of course, and most of us were overdoing it. But Craig was the type of kid that liked to take LSD and sit in a darkened room.

It would be easy to call him a spoiled kid with a Napoleon complex from a dysfunctional (possibly abusive) home—and all that was certainly true. Whenever he tired of a night out, even at age seventeen, he'd call his mother who would drive the half-hour or more from their North End home to whisk him away, no matter what state he was in. And, the way that his mother averted her gaze and spoke deferentially, the bags under her eyes, suggested that things weren't ninety degrees straight behind that family's closed doors. But there was something additional, some malevolent thread woven through Craig's spirit that went beyond all this. Something wicked and mocking in his humor, his laugh, his gaze, and something disturbing in his fanatic adoration of flashback rock like Jim Morrison, the sicker songs of Tool, and, of course, Kurt Cobain.

Then again, one on one, there was an intimacy that was almost irresistible. He was generous with food, drugs, what have you, solicitous of advice, humble, and sometimes hilarious. If he could tap into your anger at a mutual friend (or avowed enemy), he'd unload biting mockery on your behalf, emphatically agree with your assertions. We were all adrift in those days, wandering between the school, city parks, parent-free homes, downtown, ducking into whatever crevices we could find to take a swig or a toke. In the pitch and roll of those waters he was expert at lashing his raft to others—but his motives always felt somehow sinister though none of us could point to much in particular. The shared laughs and parties and kindnesses were simply underwritten by an invisible toll.

My skepticism of his true nature remained, even after splitting to California with him for a two-week road trip. Everyone had tried to shed their doubts, but, as it later came out, doubts had continued to roil in everyone's guts. As the forty-ounce emptied and the silence swelled that October morning, I realized I'd conjured a posse. And I realized that's exactly what I'd meant to do; it was no conference.

When he walked out of the decrepit, old building at second period break, Craig had his earphones on. When he saw the way we were standing around, he took them off. Gusts of wind lifted plastic bags and leaves, sent them spiraling past. The word had leaked and nearly seventy kids hung around to see what the Frink Park Kings would do with one of their own—to see, without a doubt, whether FPK had the heart it claimed. On this typically wet and cold Seattle morning came our opportunity to show we were something more than typical, more than a frivolous, little, white, party crew. He approached Hugh. I knew that Hugh still didn't know what he would do. But when Craig spoke, there was simply nothing to say.

"What's up?" The literal question lurked behind the casual greeting. His small brow wrinkled up. He still didn't know; it'd been nearly six months. How could he know?

It's funny, but what I saw in Hugh's face when he swung was not rage, but restraint, pain, doubt. His boxer's fist collided with Craig's insubstantial chest, but not all that hard. Hugh's left hand took him by the neck. I looked in Craig's eyes when my left hand hit his stomach, and I felt the same things I'd witnessed in Hugh. I looked over his shoulder at the frozen football field and distant barbecue joint and housing projects when my right hand connected with his face. I backed off then, feeling equal parts sick and excited. Jamie put all of his 250 pounds behind every kick that he landed. Craig's earphones were tangling his neck and arms. His backpack was heavy and threw him off even more each time he tried to stand. It wouldn't have mattered; Jamie was aiming for his legs now, keeping him flat on the pavement. When the chain-smoking French teacher Mr. B put himself between the two and politely asked Jamie to back off, he did. Mr. B lit a cigarette and strolled away. He was no fan of Craig either. There was no expression on Craig's face as he hauled himself into a crumpled but vertical shape. He was not breathing hard. He met none of the dozens of gazes that burned on him. He trudged away down Alder Street in silence. My friend Ryan half hugged and half restrained me, but it wasn't necessary.

"Don't ever come back, punk," I screamed after him.

And he never did.

The first vague haunting of regret stirred in me as soon as I hit that kid. Of course, the overwhelming emotion was anger, followed closely by sadness, and then guilt (at not having listened to my gut and distanced myself from him sooner). Regret was a distant fourth or fifth and didn't roll close to the surface for many years, really. But, as early as that afternoon, I was told by a female friend that what we'd done was wrong. She was always evolved, sensible—a strange creature to be roaming the scrappy, boozy hallways of high school.

"Rape is an act of violence, you know. Choosing violence to punish it won't work. It will only make things worse in the long run," she said, or something to this effect. I'm sure that I averted my eyes and nodded vaguely at the linoleum floor as I did whenever savvy and mature girls lectured me in those years. The truth of what she was saying didn't press itself upon me for a long time to come.

As months and then years flashed past, it seemed that more people who'd at least tacitly condoned our actions that day changed their minds. It wasn't that the incident was even discussed very often. In fact, Craig's name became a kind of taboo, as if some Godfather of Garfield High School had commanded that he *never be mentioned again in this house*. But the few times the subject did arise—mainly after high school had concluded and we'd gather for reminiscing—and I tested gazes around the room, I could sense condemnation as a few of them turned away. Had anyone overtly questioned or judged our action (aside from well-meaning girls), I would have unloaded invective on them. My attitude, though never stated as such, was: We did *something*, we took action. It fell to us and we had the balls.

Of course I realized as time went on that my female friend had been right—the futility of answering violence with violence, of punishing a would-be rapist with humiliation, was undeniable. And, indeed, when word of Craig filtered back to us, it sounded like he was a mess: squatting somewhere selling drugs, out of school, wandering around with his headphones looking dangerous, and, eventually, living in California where word was he'd been fired from a restaurant for assaulting a female coworker. It's likely that the beating—or more precisely, the humiliation and banishment, because he wasn't truly injured—only compounded the vile need in him to exert power. To say it plainly: We probably made it worse.

But what was the alternative anyway? Try and coax Kristy into the agonizing, shameful, laborious, and probably unsuccessful process of prosecution? Drag her through more noxious emotional fallout than she'd already endured? Allow that little bastard to keep firing his evil eyes at her every day in the hallways, half-tauting, half-warning (as he'd been doing for months)? Allow him the time to frantically assemble allies, to convince (and he was a conniving creature) a small, key group that Kristy was a liar? No, these options conjured nothing but unbridled disgust in me—and, I assume, in Hugh, in Jamie, in others who stood by in solidarity. In that context, at that age, in that school, there was nothing to do but stand up and be men—in the flawed and undercooked way that we knew. And I forgive my friends and myself for our age and our culture and our warped sense of justice. And I'm still proud that we stood awkwardly up.

Recently, a friend of mind told me she had been sexually assaulted—not rape, but not negligible either—by a mutual friend. As I listened to her cautiously unfold the incident, I realized I was scarcely angry. My placidity was partly due to the odd compassion she felt for her assailant, how she mixed that into her account. This came in stark contrast to Kristy's story; Kristy's revelation was partly a plea for retribution.

But it wasn't only that. It was also how my attention flew to our common friend, how I revised him in my mind—not so much as a sexual predator but as someone who is fucked up, suffering, disturbed. I thought about how easy it'd been before for me to ignore the fact of his pain and his struggles and I knew, without a doubt, that his suffering was at the root of his action. That's not to excuse it, of course—if my female friend had pursued prosecution, I would have supported her.

I'm left to wonder if this truly represents evolution in me. I can't help but feel the lack of rage attends a lack of emotional health: After all, such acts *are* reprehensible any way you slice it and *should* cause outrage. Have I come *too* far from the ignorant, delinquent kid that I was then? Have I studied too many Buddhist texts, do I ascribe too much to the power of suffering? Is my loving-kindness overdeveloped? Or have I simply become too cynical by the battering of years, by watching people I love wrong themselves and others with carelessness, selfishness, and even with the best of intentions? I'm not sure.

But I do know a couple of things.

One: While compassion may have twined with anger in my first, surging reaction, a profound sadness at the caprice of betrayal, at the violation of trust and intimacy—things so golden and fragile in this life—remains a very close second.

Two: Neither compassion nor overwrought cynicism are adequate excuses for not breaking out of our fear when it comes time to really *be* men, to stand up against the timeless and shameful tradition of abusing women.

BREAKING THE SILENCE ONE MILE AT A TIME

Grantlin Schafer

Plenty of stares, some thumbs up, a middle finger, countless inappropriate jokes, and the miracle question: Why are you doing this?

Our 37-foot RV complete with our non-profit name, the National Organization of Men's Outreach for Rape Education (NO MORE), was the vessel soliciting those reactions during our national tour of fifty-nine colleges, one U.S. Navy base, a national conference, forty-two states and 35,000 miles. I spent an entire year with three other recent college graduates as part of the One in Four RV tour to educate men about ending rape and helping survivors of sexual assault. The name "One in Four" comes from the national statistic that one in four college women have survived rape or an attempted rape.

We were taking action. We were speaking out. We were breaking the silence: Men were finally talking about men's violence against women. We spoke in a way that gave us credibility. We were not academics lecturing. We did not stand on soapboxes looking down at our audience. The four of us had experienced that approach and knew it did not work.

As we looked out at our audience, we saw reflections of ourselves from a few years earlier. We crafted our message to speak to our peers as guys who did not want to hurt women. Instead, we wanted to empower them to learn how to help survivors and take action to end sexual violence against women.

Change starts with language. We know that most men do not think they are rapists or that they hurt women in any way, so it is not effective to approach men with the assumption that they do. Most men want to be a better friend, boyfriend, family member; presenting ways to be good allies keeps ears open and defense mechanisms down. When we talk about preventing rape and sexual assault, we provide small, simple things that guys can do and say immediately after they see our presentation. We talk about not joking or kidding around about rape and sexual assault. Jokes like "that team just got raped" take away from what rape really means, so the solution is simple: Don't use the word rape out of context.

We can help prevent violence towards women by paying attention to how we talk to our friends, teammates, and peers in locker rooms, on sports fields, and athletic courts. When we hear teammates or friends yell, "Get up, don't be such a pussy" or "You threw that pass like a girl," they are probably not intending to hurt women. However, this language equates women with being less valuable than men. Some men will use this language to justify treating women as though they are weak and inferior. Another simple solution: Don't bring gender into joking.

Finally we urge guys to step up and say something when they hear bragging about getting a girl wasted at a party the night before, taking advantage of her, or other tales of conquest. It is likely that other guys hearing this kind of talk at the breakfast table or around the lockers are feeling uncomfortable, so by standing up and saying something, the others will respect you. Even if some guys act like they don't respect you, remember that you were the one who had the courage to do the right thing.

Our presentation is part of *The Men's Program* titled "How to Help a Sexual Assault Survivor: What Men Can Do." It works. Men who see this presentation have reported a dual benefit from the program: Learning how to help women recover from rape while decreasing men's acceptance of rape myths. Studies show that men who have attended this program report a lower likelihood of raping. When it comes down to lighting a spark of change, our presentation effectively asks guys to make a simple change of language. We do not order them to join activist marches or become different people. We believe that language influences and guides action, so if we can change our language a change in action will follow.

Even though I knew about the research on the success of programs like ours, I was not personally convinced that One in Four's peer education program would work until I went to a national sexual assault prevention conference. I listened to academics give presentations on how to get through to young men. Sitting there in the audience, I felt talked down to. It sounded too much like a classroom lecture. Lectures struggle to be effective because the message is not real, tangible, or applicable to young men. This is precisely why the RV tour does things differently. Giving suggestions to men about how they can help prevent violence is the first step in creating change, but it is not the last.

This movement is working its way toward creating what writer Malcolm Gladwell calls the tipping point. The One in Four program is a realistic and effective catalyst for change. We give the men who are thinking about gender equality and ending male violence against women a chance to put these ideas into action. To date, twenty-five colleges and one U.S. Naval base house chapters of One in Four. This is just a start. As the number of chapters and members of One in Four continues to grow, our communities will become infused with the message that it is not okay for men to rape.

A goal of the One in Four movement is to bring this message to younger men in the military, in college, high schools, middle schools, and throughout our communities. Young adults are experiencing times of growth and learning; these are formative periods. We want prevention and mentoring to thrive. Establishing One in Four chapters in high schools means that members can serve as mentors for middle-school boys. This will work to change social norms from a scene where younger teens often learn sexist attitudes from older boys to environments that model true respect.

The broad goal of the men's movement is to change the definition of what it means to be a man. We are committed to including men as part of the solution to end discrimination, classism, sexism, and violence against women. This new definition and this new generation of men will produce fathers who are outspoken against sexism and who set an example of positive behavior.

One day while we were on the road, a woman approached our RV. She told us about her father's violence. His abuse included repeatedly raping her well into adult life and led her brother to commit suicide. That moment in a grocery store parking lot outside San Francisco refocused me on the big picture. If our message can empower one guy to become an informed active agent of change, we have fulfilled the movement's goal for that day. We have to take it one man and one mile at a time.

BEING A SOCIAL JUSTICE ALLY: A FEMINIST'S PERSPECTIVE ON PREVENTING MALE VIOLENCE

Jonathan Ravarino

Becoming a feminist has been one of the most important steps I have taken in my adult life. It requires continual critical thinking, unending self-reflection, and risk-taking in multiple spheres of my life. The benefits are well worth the effort. I've gained a better understanding of my position as a man in interpersonal relationships and how to make choices that consider my community. Feminism has offered me a sense of freedom from the shackles of male socialization and the bondage of male privilege. Feminism teaches men something that patriarchy ultimately ignores; that when others are oppressed, no one is free.

My decision to become a feminist—or social justice ally—is a form of activism because it involves risk. I have learned that I must go beyond simply adopting feminist principles or engaging in critical dialogue in the safety of my friends. I and other men must serve as social justice allies by actively supporting women. This role involves making a commitment to work directly with men in the interests of women. This can be difficult, to say the least.

Helping to prevent violence against women is an important way of serving as a social justice ally to women. I hope the ten suggestions I offer here demystify the process of feminist activism and provide men with specific strategies to incorporate into their social justice advocacy.

1. CHALLENGE THE MYTHS ABOUT MASCULINITY, PATRIARCHY, AND SEXUAL VIOLENCE

One starting point in becoming a social justice ally is to begin deconstructing masculinity. A useful strategy is to critically examine one's own socialization.

For example, you might start by asking yourself, "What qualities have I been taught makes a man, a man?" Traits like *tough, strong, intelligent, unemotional, provider, protector, and pimp* will probably come to mind. When I've asked men this question, the response has alarmingly and frequently been something to the effect of "not a sissy . . . not a wimp . . . not a fag." Recognizing the misogynistic and homophobic underpinnings of such comments is important because men's collective commitment to rejecting anything female or gay contributes to violence against women and sexual minorities.

Being a social justice ally involves deconstructing patriarchal ideas. If patriarchy is a political system designed to privilege and ascribe power to men, while oppressing and marginalizing women, then we must look at this impact. Patriarchy operates according to myths about gender and this interferes with genuine human development. When I was young, I was encouraged—*required*, actually—to engage in rough and aggressive competition with other boys. And while I often heard the saying "boys will be boys," it took decades before I fully understood the impact that boys' and, later, men's violent behavior has on others. I have come to see the connection between condoning school-aged aggressive behavior and rationalizing the actions of politicians who start wars against less powerful nations.

Men are also taught myths regarding sexual violence against women. One example of how this works is through the rape and sexual assault trials that are highly publicized in American media. Newscasters minimize the behavior of the men by offering statements such as, "So these men got a little crazy . . . What do you expect when men get drunk and there is an exotic dancer in the room . . . Do you really think men like that could rape a woman? . . . Those men don't have to rape women. They could have anyone they want." Equally frightening are the sheer numbers of people who question the behavior and allegations of a sexual assault survivor. Sometimes people doubt a survivor's integrity by saying things like, "She asked for it by turning him on . . . She didn't have to stay, she could have left . . . She is falsely reporting to get the money."

My point here is simple: Myths about sexual violence silence sexual assault survivors and, at the same time, condone men's violent behavior. Men who challenge myths about male socialization, patriarchy, and sexual violence are well on their way to becoming social justice allies to women.

2. SHIFT YOUR LENS OF UNDERSTANDING

Becoming a social justice ally requires developing the capacity to shut up and listen to what women have to say. Doing this means men must shift their lens of understanding. This is not easy since a facet of patriarchy and male privilege is to ensure that men have minimal awareness of the issues affecting women and other targeted groups. One component of male privilege is that men do not have to think about how their presence and behavior impact women.

Listening to women means understanding their experience and the political issues affecting women's communities. Reproductive rights, independent financial security, equal division of labor at home and at work, and a criminal justice system that is accountable to the people, are central issues for women in today's world. I am reminded of a comment made by a feminist friend who recommended, "Listen before speaking and understand before acting."

One area in which I choose to listen more deeply to women involves the issue of violence. I have learned that women engage in multiple strategies to ensure their safety from men's violence. Examples include locking the car door upon entry, walking to one's vehicle while holding keys in the form of a weapon, exercising with mace readily accessible, going to the washroom in groups, and not walking alone at night. I am embarrassed to admit, but I once believed that locking the car door was irrational and that women went to the washroom in pairs only because they wanted to gossip. By doing so, I minimized the legitimate safety concerns of women in my life and likely missed an opportunity to be supportive.

3. ACCEPT THAT MEN HAVE A PRIMARY ROLE IN STOPPING VIOLENCE AGAINST WOMEN

Violence against women is as much a men's issue as it is a women's issue. Helping men accept that they have a primary role in stopping violence against women is not easy. This often requires patience and understanding.

Because men's violence against women does not happen inside a vacuum, dismantling myths about male violence is crucial. One example would be to critically examine the multibillion-dollar pornography industry that equates violence against women with eroticism. Second, is exposing the dangerous idea that if women can't prevent violence then they didn't try hard enough, or they must have done something to provoke it. Some men operate according to this lie. This myth is dangerous because it blames the victim. Whatever a woman does before, during, or after an episode of violence is done in order to survive.

Men are responsible for men's behavior and thus only men can stop men's violence against women. Nothing women do—and I mean absolutely nothing—warrants sexual violence or domestic assault.

4. AVOID WORKING ALONE

Political activism requires the emotional and physical support of others, and becoming a social justice ally to women is no exception. It is crucial that men join established organizations that work for gender justice and that hold men accountable. This encourages long-term engagement in the struggle. As a mentor once stated, "Women don't need fly-by-the-seat allies; women need men who are committed."

There are many organizations focusing on social justice and the issue of violence against women, including The White Ribbon Campaign, A Call to Men, and Men Can Stop Rape. Becoming a member of established organizations enables allies to become informed about issues affecting women and to learn ways of becoming politically active. The White Ribbon Campaign, for example, is an international organization committed to supporting the lives and safety of women and has become an invaluable resource for networking and receiving important mentoring services. Barring all else, one way to get involved is to give money. Financial contributions are central to helping social justice groups stay afloat and enable them to conduct outreach and educational programming. Financial support also helps rebuild organizations when they are attacked by vandalism or organized efforts to distort their message.

5. DON'T REMAIN ON THE SIDELINES

Becoming a social justice ally requires more than simply joining an organization and putting a logo sticker on one's car. Allies get involved on a political and personal level. Being an ally requires taking serious risk in the face of possible ridicule and alienation—or even hate and discrimination—from others.

The good news is that there are an infinite number of ways to become involved and they do not all call for intense large-scale personal risk or political action. The first step in determining how best to become involved is to make an inventory of your specific strengths and skill sets. You may be good at organizing events, writing newsletters, or speaking to children. You may be better at teaching, research, or facilitating small-group dialogue.

The subject of violence against women is a sensitive one and people tend to feel awkward about discussing sensitive issues. Often we don't want to offend someone or become too emotionally connected to the issue. Failing to engage in a difficult conversation with other men out of fear of making a mistake is a hurdle for both the growth of individual allies and the feminist movement. I encourage men who wish to become social justice allies to keep speaking up and moving forward. Silence feeds violence and we must refuse to be silent. We will all make mistakes along the journey. We must keep working to improve on this.

6. RECOGNIZE MALE PRIVILEGE

Men who are social justice allies are in a unique situation. While we choose to challenge systems of patriarchy, many of us cannot—or do not want to—give up male privilege. Coming to grips with how we continue to experience privilege that we have not earned is a challenge for men to work through.

One thing I do is to take responsibility for my privilege by using it to work for good purposes. Emerging research indicates, for example, that college men are more receptive to learning about rape myths and sexual violence if men provide the workshops or education sessions. In other words, as men, we have unique access to other men. This same-sex dynamic means that men can be effective social justice allies in addressing sensitive topics. I try to stay focused on recognizing the responsibility I have to educate men who, because of persistent sexism, may not otherwise entertain statistics or comments about male violence if presented by a woman.

In my experience facilitating programs on sexual violence, I have noticed that men seem caught off guard when a man gets in front of them and discusses violence against women from a feminist perspective. It could be that men feel less shame and guilt when a man tells them about the impact of violence. I make use of personal disclosures about my own process of learning about violence against women. This seems to help men see me as human, and more like them.

Social justice allies should not run away from their privilege as men but, rather, find ways to use it in the interests of women and social justice. At the same time, it's important to remember that for centuries, female feminists have been confronting men's violence against women. It's not as if male allies invented this concern. We must publicly recognize the contributions and mentoring we have received from women who make up the feminist movement. Men must remain accountable to women's leadership and be open to feedback at every level of the process.

7. CONTINUALLY EVALUATE YOUR GOALS AND INTENTIONS

My professional role as a therapist has given me an understanding that men are socialized to derive self-esteem and self-worth from action-oriented tasks. Men are taught to engage in activities with a specific goal in mind and to do whatever is needed to accomplish their objective. While this may be viewed as determination and discipline, it can also be understood as self-centered behavior that is overly concerned with outcome rather than with process. Social justice allies must therefore maintain an awareness of men's tendencies toward dominating, monopolizing, or competing with others—even while we are working toward justice and equality. This does little in the way of helping women or challenging institutional structures. Allies must lose the notion that "size matters" and focus less on outcome and more on process. This will enable men to notice the incremental change emerging as part of all social justice activism.

Becoming a social justice ally is a worthy cause but it is nothing special. I have seen some men carry unproductive and exploitative behaviors into the realm of social justice work. Men who assume this work must do so out of authentic commitment and compassion. Allies must continually evaluate their intentions and focus on the collective goals of the social justice and feminist movement. I have seen first-hand how some men have become glorified and glamorized as activists, or even by sharing housework and childcare duties at home. Women do not need men to take over a movement and use it for self-serving purposes!

8. ALWAYS BELIEVE IN MEN'S CAPACITY TO CHANGE

It is important to remember that individual men are not the problem; rather, the problem is within our larger institutions. Knowing this allows us to maintain compassion and empathy for individual men caught in the system. Feminism allows men an opportunity to gain a sense of freedom: Fighting to end violence against women will result in liberation for men, too.

Sometimes men can seem resistant to change. But holding our experience of male socialization close at heart ensures that allies maintain the skills to work with some of the most guarded men. When I come across men who manifest counterproductive traits, I understand them as being somewhere on the journey and capable of change at any minute. After all, my goal as a social justice ally is to help each man move in the direction of compassion and empathy, hoping that they will continue to encounter people and experiences that will move them even further. Maintaining this sense of compassion means believing in the potential of individual men to make changes; it means believing in the capacity of larger institutions to become more equitable and accountable to our community. At times when I am challenged by the most stereotypically defensive men, I like to say to my peers, "Remember where you started. Anything is possible."

9. RECOGNIZE THE LINKS BETWEEN VIOLENCE AGAINST WOMEN AND OTHER FORMS OF INJUSTICE

Becoming a social justice ally to women means developing the skills to understand multiple forms of social injustice. The intersectionality of gender, race, sexual orientation, disability, and class is evident at every level of social justice. bell hooks reminds us in *Ain't I a Woman*, that at no point is a woman only a woman; she is a constellation of traits as a gendered, racial, sexual, and classed being. While gender has been the most salient trait in my life, I must not forget that my position as a white, heterosexual male plays a significant role in the work I do and in how others perceive me. Learning our history and locating ourselves on the privilege/oppression continuum helps ensure that we engage in social action without contributing to social oppression. I say this because I have made mistakes in this area.

When I was speaking to a group of activists, a woman asked how my work took into consideration black men's experience and relationship to women. I understood her question perfectly, but I was incapable of responding in a meaningful way. This served as a catalyst for the work I needed to do to become a multiculturally competent social justice activist.

10. PRACTICE SELF-CARE

The final step I encourage is to incorporate self-care into one's life. This is valuable with respect to ensuring that social justice allies remain committed and balanced as men. Unfortunately, I have noticed that we often only offer lip service to the notion of self-care. This is unhealthy and can interfere with the activist process. As a therapist and educator, I believe self-care is central to finding both meaning and joy in life.

One specific method I practice is called mindfulness meditation. This incorporates the skills of acceptance, nonjudgment, and present-moment orientation into my daily life. Mindfulness has been defined as a nonjudgmental awareness of the present moment. This may sound simple, but many of us struggle with slowing down and finding peace inside our self. I have found that the effort required in social justice and anti-oppression work benefits from the balancing energy of mindfulness meditation. Similar to other strategies of self-care, it has been critical for me to engage in mindfulness meditation daily and devote time to my practice.

Other social justice activists have commented on the benefits of practicing mindfulness meditation when engaging in social action. Thich Nhat Hanh, one of the pioneers of bringing Buddhism to the Western world, speaks of observing strong emotions toward others instead of acting them out. Observing one's anger or fear while witnessing or reading about acts of violence allows social justice allies to not be overwhelmed or paralyzed by anger or negative emotions. Thich Nhat Hanh further suggests that individuals can learn to understand forms of violence inside our own minds as a way of understanding how to combat violence outside the mind. He offers the simple but powerful truth, "The only antidote to hate and violence is love." As a social justice ally, I use this notion to help me generate compassion and love for men who engage in violence against women. Hate is not helpful in this process, and social justice allies who are able to move beyond this are better served as members of this movement. Although mindfulness meditation represents a method I personally choose to use to maintain compassion and energy as an ally, it is not the only method. I think it's important, though, for social justice allies to identify self-care strategies to combat cynicism and hate and cultivate love and compassion for others.

Men can help change the institutional conditions that impact the safety and lives of women and freedom of men to be authentic and compassionate beings. In sum, here's what we need to do: Increase awareness by listening and learning from women and other allies; develop the capacity to take personal risks as well as to support other allies and organizations; and believe in the capacity of all humans to end personal and collective forms of violence. Being a social justice ally is a way of gaining freedom and of expressing responsibility to our communities. Like Alice Walker said, "Activism is the rent I pay for living on this planet." Being a social justice ally to women has become the rent I pay for my privilege as a man.

Part IV

Masculinity at Work and Home

INTRODUCTION

Part IV of *Men Speak Out* contextualizes masculinity within various institutions of our culture. The phrase "Masculinity at *Work*" refers both to the literal job site and to the construction of ideas about gender. An apt—if unwieldy—title for this book section could easily be: "Masculinity at Work and Home . . . and in the Classroom, on the Playground, in the Courtroom, and the Café." In other words, no cultural location is off-limits when it comes to its impacts on men and masculinity.

The authors in this section describe both success and challenges in confronting stereotypes about masculinity that are perpetuated by institutional structures such as construction sites, the U.S. military, college, and fatherhood. These essays describe dealing with gender politics in settings that are hostile—or only slowly warming—to new ideas about men and women and gender. Reflecting on their personal experiences, these eight men discuss being sons and fathers, workers and students. They pose questions, and provide some answers, about living, working, thinking, and learning in a sexist society.

Gendered ideas about who we are, and what we are expected to accomplish, have literal costs in terms of resources, money, wealth, and leisure. The Bureau of Labor Statistics shows that well into the twenty-first century, women still do the bulk of housework and childcare. On an average day in 2011, 19 percent of men did housework—such as cleaning or doing laundry—compared with 48 percent of women. Married women with children who work full-time spend 51 minutes a day on housework while married men with children spend just 14 minutes a day on it. Men spend more time watching TV every day than women. For every 26 minutes men spend bathing or feeding a child, women contribute more than one hour of this labor.[1] Jessica Valenti points out in "The Daddy Wars" that the U.S. Census Bureau's annual report on childcare counts men's childcare as "babysitting" and "only mom's care work is considered parenting."[2] Gender-biased data collection, passive sympathizing for an overworked female partner, "helping" around the house, "babysitting" one's own children, or sharing in unpaid domestic "work only after someone else asks is not the same thing as showing initiative, rolling up the shirtsleeves, and taking care of business."[3] (And, yes, equality also includes women taking out the trash, picking up dead rodents, and fixing busted plumbing.)

And yet, pressures from a shifting economic landscape combined with changing social expectations are modulating how men experience work and home. Blue-collar men of all races lost the majority of jobs in the 2008 recession and many men saw their wages fall. "These job losses and wage cuts narrow the gender gap in pay not because women are getting ahead but rather because traditional male-dominated industries are suffering." And, as Michael Kimmel points out in *The Shriver Report*, the division of labor within the home parses out differently by race, class, and ethnicity: In every single subcategory of domestic work (such as cooking, cleaning, shopping, laundry, outdoor work, auto repair and maintenance, and bill paying):

> Black men do significantly more housework than white men. In more than one-fourth of all black families, men do more than 40 percent of the housework . . . In white families, only 16 percent of the men do that much. And blue-collar fathers, regardless of race (municipal and service workers, policemen, firefighters, maintenance workers), are twice as likely (42 percent) as those in professional, managerial, or technical jobs (20 percent) to care for their children while their wives work.[4]

Younger men today "expect to be part of a two-career couple, for financial, if not political, reasons," Kimmel reports. Some men are gradually choosing to become stay-at-home dads and primary caregivers for their children. Jeremy Adam Smith, author of *The Daddy Shift*, cautions, however, that the number of full-time dads is still relatively small and the accolades they receive are usually disproportionate to their numbers or their efforts. But these shifting trends are signs of significant hope. Tomas Moniz, co-editor of the anthology *Rad Dad*, explains that shifting demographics matter because the politics of fatherhood go beyond simply who does the parenting. When men begin reconsidering their roles within the family and in the domestic sphere, they are also "fighting the social power that men have over women and beyond *that*, challenging all of the ways that some people have power over others." It is important, Moniz writes, that we "question the social stereotypes of fathering that for so long have been used to justify"[5] gender-specific roles at home and at work.

In "Rebuilding Houses and Rethinking Gender: Construction Volunteer Work in Post-Katrina New Orleans," activist-scholar Ian Breckenridge-Jackson writes about doing construction work in New Orleans after the city was ravaged by Hurricane Katrina. Breckenridge-Jackson arrived in the Lower Ninth Ward to find foundations missing houses and personal belongings blowing through empty streets. Hurricane Katrina severely damaged or destroyed 850,000 homes and caused approximately $110 billion in physical damage. As one million volunteers made their way to the Gulf Coast to contribute to rebuilding the city, sexism and gender harassment followed. Despite the strong presence of female leadership, and feminist and queer dialogue among volunteers, post-Katrina construction sites were by no means a gender utopia, Breckenridge-Jackson writes. "Instances of sexual harassment, sexual assault and rape [took] place, and the response by leadership was at times problematic along the lines of gender and race."

From the U.S. Gulf Coast to the U.S. military, sexual harassment remains a persistent problem. Although the United States' nine-year war against Iraq officially ended in 2011, sexual harassment within the ranks of the U.S. military has not. After returning to the U.S. following a tour of duty in Iraq, Sgt. Marshall Thompson describes his shock and concern about the sexual harassment of female Army officers and enlisted military personnel that he witnessed. According to findings published in the *American Journal of Industrial Medicine*, the military environment condones sexual harassment and allows sexual assault and trauma to occur, whether intentionally or not. Twenty-eight percent of women veterans surveyed for the journal's report claimed they were raped while in the military.[6] In similar findings released by the Citadel, a public military college in South Carolina, nearly 20 percent of female cadets reported that they had been sexually assaulted since enrolling at the school.[7] The Government Accountability Office reported in 2011, that in a survey of six military bases, 82 of 583 service members had been harassed sexually during the preceding 12 months; only four people formally reported the incidents.[8]

The Christian Science Monitor reported in January 2012 that the rate of violent sexual crime has increased 64 percent since 2006 according to the U.S. Army report, which noted "rape, sexual assault, and forcible sodomy were the most frequent violent sex crimes committed in 2011. [Although] women comprise 14 percent of the Army ranks, they account for 95 percent of all sex crime victims."[9] Sexual harassment and sexual assault are distinct incidents, but they both exist on the continuum of gender/sex-based violations and warrant attention as such.[10]

Also warranting attention is the fact that the United States military has improved on its sexual assault reporting policies. Stacey Lantz, former U.S. Navy Sexual Assault Response Coordinator (SARC), explains that training, education, and reporting ability have improved since the Department of Defense changed its sexual assault policy in 2004. Victims or survivors of sexual violence now have two options: The first is known as restricted reporting by which the accuser can only discuss their case with specified personnel. With a restricted complaint, victims can receive medical and psychological support, but are prevented from filing formal charges or taking safety measures like requesting a transfer on the basis of the assault. Pursuing safety measures or formal charges requires filing an unrestricted report. This procedure broadens the number of people who may be involved with the case, requires that the identities of all parties are revealed, and enables the commanding officer to inform others beyond the SARC, victim advocate, healthcare professional, and Chaplain on a need-to-know basis.

In his essay, "Exposed in Iraq: Sexual Harassment and Hidden Rank Structure of the U.S. Army," Marshall Thompson describes what he saw and reflects on this experience. With Army Spc. Alyssa Peterson's 2003 suicide after serving in sexually pressured circumstances in Iraq, Spc. Suzanne Swift's 2007 court martial following her refusal to return to Iraq where she had been harassed by three of her commanding officers, and findings that female soldiers in combat zones are more likely to be raped by a fellow soldier than killed by enemy fire,[11] Thompson's observations take on particular urgency.

Bryan Talbot Morris's "Gender in Jakarta: Lessons on Discourse and Disparity" is about the power of language. The essay opens with a conversation between Morris and two friends over Scrabble, coffee, and clove cigarettes in an Indonesian café. Quickly, the discussion reveals to Morris how men's double standards about women and sexuality are alive and unwell. In a country with the world's largest Muslim population, Morris's superficially gender-savvy friend, John, describes his views on the politics of the veil. He liked having casual sex with a woman he met in a club, but wanted to date a woman who wears a *jilbab*, the Islamic headscarf, in effect reinforcing stereotypes of the first woman as a whore and the second as a good girl. As Morris spent more time in Indonesia, he found that John's statement was merely the start of troubling ideas he heard come from other men. "Whether listening to diplomats, expatriates, NGO [non-governmental organization] staff, friends, [or] acquaintances, the daily banter reflected a fundamental and ingrained disconnect between egalitarian discourse and the way men live our lives." This disconnect, Morris surmises, indicates although men may be publicly committed to equality, they have not yet integrated this belief. Men may be trained in gender sensitivity, Morris tells us, but it's time to talk the talk and pay attention to how speech can reinforce men's agency and women's silence.

Shifting attention to the classroom setting, Daniel Simon writes about his experience as a male student living in East Oakland and enrolled in university women's studies. "Listening, Learning, Speaking Up" begins with Simon's realization on the first day of class that he's one of only a few men in the room. "We're outnumbered," he whispers to the guy sitting to his right. A woman turns around and sneers, "What did you say?" as Simon thinks to himself, *Oh fuck. What have I gotten myself into?* As the essay unfolds, Simon confronts his moral obligation to speak up and his political responsibility to also step back and listen. In grappling with this tension, Simon reflects the growing number of men who are enrolling in courses on women's and gender studies, the growing dilemmas about what men's roles ought to be—and whether feminist theorizing is keeping up with practical reality.[12]

In regard to the classroom, there are those who prefer women's studies as a women-only space (whether women-born-women, cisgendered women, or women-identified-women). There are others who argue that academic trends in "changing departmental names from Women's Studies, or Women's and Gender Studies, to variations such as Gender Studies or Gender and Sexuality Studies constitutes a betrayal of a foundational political commitment to women's liberation."[13] It is reasonable and rational, however, that men should join in the intellectual project of deconstructing and critiquing gender expectations and stereotypes, and it is counterproductive to exclude men, or gender-variant students, through explicit or implied means.[14] And, while all of this is fine in terms of academic debate, it didn't help Simon when it came time to figuring out whether he ought to speak out or shut up in the classroom. Simon is one real-life example of Peter Alilunas's point that "Men who take Women's Studies classes often exist in a paradoxical space, the physical bearers of much that is discussed within the room while also the symbol of that which chooses not to participate."[15]

Facing his own discomfort, resistance, risks, and intermittent fear of blame, Simon describes the personal and political challenges as a man in a women's studies classroom. In doing so, Simon promotes an important conversation about men in gender and women's studies. As bell hooks argues, "Like women, men have been socialized to passively accept sexist ideology. While they need not blame themselves for accepting sexism, they must assume responsibility for eliminating it."[16]

In "A Tribute to My Father," Chris Dixon explains how shifting gender expectations in the 1970s impacted his relationship with his dad. Dixon's father was a progressive role model who was involved with men's groups that were exploring new ideas about manhood. But the elder Dixon's personality and parenting were complicated by his homophobia, a volatile temper, and his alcoholism. Dixon expresses love for his father and acknowledges his dad's simultaneous success and failure. The most sincere way of expressing my love, Dixon explains, "is by learning from [my father's] mistakes and accepting the responsibility of not repeating them."

Jeremy Adam Smith also writes about fatherhood, but from the perspective of a stay-at-home dad. Smith weaves personal narrative with national trends and data about men as primary caregivers in his essay titled "Playground Vertigo." Smith comments that while it might still seem radical today, men as full-time parents could become an accepted routine for the next generation. More men are choosing this option and we are no longer as shocked by the idea. The transformative potential for gender-neutral parenting that Smith anticipates extends beyond the home: Equally shared parenting and housekeeping will mean that the workplace and other institutions will have added pressure to respond to families' needs and realities in meaningful ways. Revising the family so that men are full and active participants in parenting may go a long way toward easing gender restrictions in caregiving and in improving the experience of parenting.[17]

"Judging Fathers: The Case for Gender-Neutral Standards" opens with Donald N.S. Unger driving north through Connecticut on the Merritt Parkway. His daughter, Rebecca, eight years old at the time, is sitting with him in the car while Harry Chapin's song, "Cat's in the Cradle," plays on the radio. As Unger talks with his daughter about his decision to be a fully engaged father and take an active role in her life, he also notes that society makes this difficult for men. For instance, it took a lawsuit to get changing tables installed in the men's restrooms along the very stretch of road he is driving on now. By the time that finally happened, his daughter was toilet trained and Unger no longer had a personal need for these facilities. However, Unger writes, it is necessary that society hold gender-neutral standards for parenting and accept men as competent, capable caregivers. Things are starting to change, but pop culture's tendency to portray men as bumbling, overgrown teenagers doesn't help, he says.

Completing this section, Michael Flood exposes the toxic myths and dangerous legal strategies of so-called men's and father's rights groups in "What's Wrong with Fathers' Rights?" According to Flood, the fathers' rights movement claims that men experience discrimination in cases of separation, divorce, and custody.[18] Flood explains that fathers' rights groups are based on "a profound denial of the systematic gender inequalities which privilege many men and disadvantage many women." Using debatable claims of gender symmetry in domestic violence, these groups actually represent an organized backlash to feminism and direct attack on women.[19] In the final analysis, fathers' rights groups give more weight to fathers' privilege for contact with their children over their children's protection from violence. Men who are going through separation or divorce certainly deserve support, Flood notes, but they're not well served by organizations that stifle men's healing process and encourage men to engage in malicious, destructive, and unproductive legal strategies. This effort to win at all costs has high costs for children, for women, and for men.

1. Bureau of Labor Statistics, "American Time Use Survey Summary," June 22, 2012. Available at: http://www.bls.gov/news.release/atus.nr0.htm (accessed June 28, 2012).
2. Jessica Valenti, "The Daddy Wars," *The Nation*, June 27, 2012. Available at: http://www.thenation.com/blog/168612/daddy-wars# (accessed June 28, 2012).
3. Shira Tarrant, *Men and Feminism*. Berkeley, CA: Seal Press, 2009, p. 141.
4. Michael Kimmel, "Has a Man's World Become a Woman's Nation?" *The Shriver Report*, 2009. Available at: http://www.shriverreport.com/awn/men.php (accessed June 28, 2012).

5. Tomas Moniz, "Introduction: The Politics of *Rad Dad*, or Parenting is about More than Pee, Poop, and Puberty," in Tomas Moniz, ed., *Rad Dad: Dispatches From the Frontiers of Fatherhood*. Portland, OR: PM Press, 2011, p. 11.

6. Anne G. Sadler, Brenda M. Booth, Brian L. Cook, and Bradley N. Doebbeling, "Factors Associated with Women's Risk of Rape in the Military Environment," *American Journal of Industrial Medicine*, vol. 43, issue 3 (March 2003): 262–273.

7. Jennifer Zahn Spieler, "Soldier's Harassment Claim Leads to Court Martial," December 3, 2006. Available at: http://womensenews.org/story/sexual-harassment/061203/soldiers-harassment-claim-leads-to-court-martial (accessed June 21, 2012).

8. "Preventing Sexual Harassment: DOD Needs Greater Leadership Commitment and an Oversight Framework." GAO-11-809, September 21, 2011. Available at: http://www.gao.gov/products/GAO-11-809 (accessed June 21, 2012).

9. Anna Mulrine, "Pentagon Report: Sexual Assault in the Military Up Dramatically," *The Christian Science Monitor*, January 19, 2012. Available at: http://www.csmonitor.com/USA/Military/2012/0119/Pentagon-report-Sexual-assault-in-the-military-up-dramatically (accessed June 21, 2012).

10. Margaret S. Stockdale and Joel T. Nader, "Situating Sexual Harassment in the Broader Context of Interpersonal Violence: Research, Theory, and Policy Implications," *Social Issues and Policy Review*, vol. 6, no. 1 (March 2012): 148–176.

11. http://invisiblewarmovie.com/.

12. Peter Alilunas, "The (In)visible People in the Room: Men in Women's Studies," *Men and Masculinities*, vol. 14, no. 2 (2011): 210–229.

13. John C. Landreau and Michael J. Murphy, "Introduction to the Special Issue—Masculinities in Women's Studies: Locations and Dislocations," *Men and Masculinities*, vol. 14, no. 2 (2011): 132–134.

14. For discussion on some of the potential problems invoked by men in women's studies, see Michael Flood, "Bringing Men Into the Light? Women's Studies and the Problem of Men," presented at *Casting New Shadows: Australian Women's Studies Association Conference*, Sydney, Australia, 31 January 31–February 2, 2001. Available at: http://www.xyonline.net/downloads/womensstudiesandmen.pdf.

15. Alilunas, "The (In)visible People in the Room," p. 210.

16. Quoted in Alilunas, "The (In)visible People in the Room," p. 226. See also, Michael Flood, "Men as Students and Teachers of Feminist Scholarship," *Men and Masculinities*, vol. 14, no. 2 (2011): 135–154.

17. Oriel Sullivan argues for a conception of change within household gender practices that is "slow and uneven, [and] in which daily practices and interactions are linked to attitudes and discourse, perhaps over generations." See Oriel Sullivan, "Changing Gender Practices Within the Household: A Theoretical Perspective," *Gender & Society*, vol. 18, no. 2 (April 2004): 207. In response to essentialist arguments that women are naturally better suited to parent children, Alexis J. Walker and Lori A. McGraw point out that while professionals may broadly agree on what children need to thrive emotionally and physically, there is no empirical evidence that these needs must either be met by a man or a woman. Alexis J. Walker and Lori A. McGraw, "Who Is Responsible for Responsible Fathering?" *Journal of Marriage and the Family*, vol. 62 (May 2000): 563–569.

18. Michael Flood focuses primarily on Australia, but the problems he identifies are directly relevant in the United States. According to Molly Dragiewicz, a criminologist and the author of *Equality with a Vengeance: Men's Rights Groups, Battered Women, and Antifeminist Backlash,* "cases in which fathers are badly treated by courts and other officials are not remotely the norm." The small percentage of divorces that end up in litigation are disproportionately those where abuse and other issues make joint custody a dubious proposition. Even when a woman can satisfactorily document her ex-husband's abuse, Dragiewicz says, "she is no more likely to receive full custody of her children than if she couldn't." See Arthur Goldwag, "Leader's Suicide Brings Attention to Men's Rights Movement," Southern Poverty Law Center, *Intelligence Report,* Issue 145 (Spring 2012). Available at: http://www.splcenter.org/get-informed/intelligence-report/browse-all-issues/2012/spring/a-war-on-women (accessed June 28, 2012).

19. The aggressively hostile misogynist strategies of so-called Men's Rights and Fathers' Rights Activists are serious enough that the Southern Poverty Law Center has included these groups in their exposés on American hate groups. See *Intelligence Report: The Year in Hate and Extremism 2011.* Montgomery, AL: Southern Poverty Law Center, Issue 145 (Spring 2012).

REBUILDING HOUSES AND RETHINKING GENDER: CONSTRUCTION VOLUNTEER WORK IN POST-KATRINA NEW ORLEANS

Ian Breckenridge-Jackson

Hurricane Katrina made landfall on August 29, 2005, and I arrived in New Orleans nine months later to assist in the rebuilding process. By that time, post-Katrina volunteerism had become a phenomenon and, within a year after the storm, one million volunteers would make their way to the Gulf Coast, leading some to label it the New Orleans Rebirth Movement (NORM). This movement was primarily made up of young, able-bodied, economically privileged, white individuals, including me. Through personal observation and interviews, I discovered that female volunteers routinely faced gender harassment, likely exacerbated by the "masculine" labor performed.

I arrived in the Lower Ninth Ward with foundations missing houses and personal belongings blowing through empty streets. Hurricane Katrina severely damaged or destroyed 850,000 homes and caused approximately $110 billion in physical damage. Katrina is easily the greatest disaster in U.S. history, but those figures tell only a small part the story. Any conceptions I had of an equitable society were shattered when I would later learn that the damage of Hurricane Katrina was foreseen and avoidable, that the hurricane itself did very little damage, and that inadequately designed and poorly maintained levees were largely to blame for 1,836 deaths. An additional 2,358 deaths are attributed to the trauma of the storm's aftermath, and over 700 people remained missing as of 2008. Of these fatalities and missing persons, the elderly and blacks were most acutely impacted. The majority of deaths occurred in New Orleans, where historically black neighborhoods bore the brunt of the human impact.

The preventable flooding caused by Hurricane Katrina exposed existing inequalities and injustices in New Orleans, a city marked by intersecting race, class, and gender inequality. Low-income blacks and the elderly largely lacked a means of leaving the city. Making this worse, the timing of the storm meant that many were running low on economic resources, waiting for the first of the month to be paid or receive social service benefits. Mayor Ray Nagin and his administration were inadequately prepared and delayed a mandatory evacuation of the city to placate business owners, despite receiving millions of dollars to plan such an evacuation. Once the storm hit, Louisiana Governor Kathleen Blanco issued a "shoot to kill" order to law enforcement in response to racist concerns about widespread looting. New Orleans police officers as well as white vigilantes slaughtered an unknown number of black men (at least 11 confirmed murders) in the chaos that followed, for which legal action would not emerge for nearly half a decade after the storm. Prisoners, disproportionately black, experienced extreme abuse and neglect during and after the storm and many were stranded in jails and prisons for indeterminate amounts of time without due process because habeas corpus was suspended. Evacuees, often referred to as "refugees" as if they were not United States citizens, were scattered across the nation, often to destinations they didn't choose and without a clear path back home. As of 2010, approximately 100,000 pre-Katrina New Orleans residents had not returned home, including 68,000 who lived below the poverty line prior to the storm. The privatization of federal assistance meant to aid displaced residents rebuild their homes delayed distribution due to bureaucratic red tape; funds were dispensed disproportionately to white applicants over black applicants; community-based funding was largely redistributed from heavily affected black neighborhoods like the Lower Ninth Ward to less affected white communities.

On the ground, I observed two types of volunteers who came to help rebuild these devastated neighborhoods. The first type were like me—lacking a critical understanding of Katrina, interested in the New Orleans nightlife, and looking for a pat on the back for "doing good work." The second type of volunteer came to New Orleans understanding the impact of interlocking systems of power both in the wake of Hurricane Katrina and in society more broadly. These activist-volunteers engaged with people in marginalized communities in a reciprocal fashion, critically evaluating their own positions of privilege while seeking to maximize the positive and mitigate the negative impacts. Despite the presence of the second type of politically astute volunteer, and despite the fact that most of the volunteers were female, gender harassment on the construction worksite was commonplace.

Post-Katrina work involved two stages of so-called masculine labor: gutting (tearing down a house to its shell) and construction (drywall, roofing, siding). Most post-Katrina volunteers—both male and female—arrived as unskilled laborers. I had no previous experience using a hammer, let alone a sledgehammer, but I learned from crew leaders, most of whom were female. They taught me how to inspect the structure of the house, use a crowbar, take down drywall, tear up flooring, remove ruined appliances and fixtures, and turn off the water, electricity, and gas.

Volunteer work is also gendered. Historically, charitable volunteer associations provided privileged women a socially appropriate space to enter the public sphere. Though the gender gap has diminished, women continue to volunteer at higher rates and contribute more hours than men, which has been connected to continuing expectations about women's greater sense of empathy and responsibility to do for others. What's more, the type of volunteer work that women engage in remains largely relegated to feminized work that adheres to conventional gender roles.

As a cisgendered man brought up in contemporary society, I have been taught since I was very young to perceive my body as a tool for carving my way through the world. Through cultural norms, media, and sports, I learned that male bodies are meant to master their environments, while female bodies exist to be visually and physically consumed by men. By the time I first was asked to grapple with these gender concepts, they were already deeply rooted within my notions of self, as they are with most men raised in a patriarchal society.

Gutting storm-ravished homes in post-Katrina New Orleans was a hybrid of "feminine" volunteerism and "masculine" manual labor. This blend enabled women to use their bodies as tools to complete work aligned with their compassion for others. Women on the jobsite instrumentally used their bodies in ways that were not geared toward male consumption. In this context, these women had the freedom to be dirty, sweaty, smelly, bloody, and to be active agents beyond merely a passive object. I don't say this to brazenly celebrate masculinity, but to highlight the dehumanization caused by the constraints of gender norms affecting both women and men.

In my experience, LGBTQ women[1] had a strong presence as post-Katrina volunteers and volunteer coordinators. Many heterosexual women rejected the constraints of demure or deferential femininity (at least temporarily) to engage in gutting, but for other women, "unfeminine work" was a deterrent to participating in this kind of physical labor. While LGBTQ women are an internally heterogeneous group, male validation generally does not retain the same influence over their choices as it does for heterosexual women, which facilitates engagement in a wider range of so-called masculine activities.

With a strong contingency of women willing to forgo male validation, it is unsurprising that feminist values informed the way in which some organizations were run. At least at particular moments in time, this was the case for the organization I initially volunteered for, the Common Ground Collective. Many of the crew leaders and a good number of mid-level managers were women. Sleeping quarters were co-ed and bathrooms were unisex, challenging socially constructed barriers across sex and gender. For those who wanted a safe space, there were designated rooms for women and LGBTQ individuals. Open conversations around issues like sexual assault and rape were not unusual. The strong presence of feminist and queer dialogue facilitated, at least to some degree, a community that sought to challenge hegemonic norms of gender and sexuality.

Despite these efforts, Common Ground was by no means a gender utopia. Instances of sexual harassment, sexual assault and rape did take place, and the response by leadership was a times problematic along the lines of gender and race. At Common Ground and at other rebuilding organizations in New Orleans, the most widespread form of sexism was harassment on the worksite. Sexual harassment is about asserting power over women in the workplace in an explicitly sexual manner, while gender harassment seeks to maintain traditional gender roles through nonsexual means. Gender harassment is commonplace in the military as women are constantly challenged as legitimate actors in such a hypermasculine workplace. Male soldiers may disproportionately scrutinize female soldiers' performance, spread gossip and rumors about female soldiers sleeping their way to the top, and challenge female competency and authority. To ask men who have been raised in a patriarchy to treat women as equals, particularly while engaging in masculine labor, is a tall order, leading to similarly widespread gender harassment in post-Katrina volunteerism.

Gender harassment was widespread in post-Katrina work. As I discovered through personal observation and volunteer interviews, nearly every woman who worked in post-Katrina New Orleans has experienced harassment. Men would generally be uncomfortable with women carrying heavy items, often offering or insisting upon taking the load. More often, if men knew that a heavy item needed to be lifted, they would preemptively restrict women's participation by doing it themselves or exclusively recruiting other men to complete the task. While others would simply comply, either to avoid conflict or due to internalized constraints, some women would push back, insisting on their capacities. While the claim that men can and women cannot lift heavy items is often justified on a problematic biological basis, other gendered aspects of gutting failed to meet even this flawed logic.

Men would often challenge women's competence on the worksite, particularly women in leadership positions. For instance, men often assumed women were ignorant about using tools, leading men to inappropriately offer unsolicited advice to women about how they should do their work. A female volunteer coordinator that I interviewed recalled how a male volunteer questioned her competence in using the most basic of tools:

> I think there's a bit of proving yourself being a woman in construction and I definitely felt that. I had one volunteer explain how to use a ruler to me, which was a little offensive because I've known how to use a ruler since I was a child.

While common for most women on gutting crews, such condescension was particularly strong for female crew leaders. Their competence was in constant question from both skilled and unskilled men, threatened by the authority of a woman placed over them in a masculine domain.

Women's participation in masculine labor compels men to assert their threatened dominance. Gendered acts such as carrying heavy objects or instructing women how to use tools allow men to feel powerful despite being surrounded by women engaging in labor improper to femininity. They are coping mechanisms employed by men to protect their threatened sense of masculine identity.

At the same time, the strong presence of women in post-Katrina volunteerism facilitated spaces in which women could vocalize their shared experiences of gender harassment and promote dialogue around such issues. I considered myself a liberal man who adhered, at least in theory, to the basic tenet of feminism that women and men are equal and should be treated equitably. Gutting provided one of those rare situations where I was working alongside women in "masculine" labor. While on the worksite, I did not consciously think to myself, "She's a woman and can't do this. I'm a man who can." However, despite my professed ideology, underlying and socially engrained scripts compelled me to take up those most masculine tasks in place of the women around me.

I was fortunate to have women surrounding me who challenged me to consciously consider how my actions were informed by hegemonic masculinity. By rendering patriarchy visible, these women's resistance indicted my underlying ideology that would otherwise have remained invisible. They gave me the gift of an improved critical reflexivity transferable to all interactions and to my internal life world.

I continue to grapple with these prejudices inherited from what bell hooks refers to as a "white supremacist capitalist patriarchy." Like culturally embedded notions of race and class, patriarchy is a thread central to the social fabric that continues to shape me. The residue of sexism stays with me. While I seek to resist, my best hope is to minimize the impacts of these noxious beliefs. In doing so, I struggle to release myself from the dehumanizing grip of being a "real man."

My struggle is not abstract. I owe it to my grandmother and my mother, who toiled and sacrificed to give me a healthy and happy childhood. I owe it to my partner, who chooses to share her life with me and loves me despite my lingering misogyny. If I have a daughter, I owe it to her to be a full parent not limited by the constraints of traditional fatherhood. I owe it to myself, someone who has been robbed of the capacity to be fully empathic and relational by paying the price of the ticket for masculinity.

All men owe this both to the women in their lives and to themselves. All people in positions of privilege are thus charged to challenge systems of power, both within and outside themselves, that oppress categories of people across supposedly meaningful differences and damage us all. There may be no final, perfect victory, but we can certainly commit to earnest resistance.

1. In this case, the Q refers to female-identified individuals who identify with a queer sexuality. This is not to erase the contributions of genderqueer individuals who also participated in post-Katrina volunteerism.

EXPOSED IN IRAQ: SEXUAL HARASSMENT AND HIDDEN RANK STRUCTURE OF THE U.S. ARMY

Marshall Thompson

When William Cohen started his job as Secretary of Defense in 1997, he made cracking down on sexual harassment in the military one of his top priorities. "We are going to make it very clear from the very top officials to the lowest in the chain of command this is not acceptable conduct," he said. With such a clear directive from Cohen and from many other military leaders, it would seem a simple matter for every disciplined, oath-bound soldier to comply. Unfortunately, it just doesn't work that way.

In May 2006, I was knee-deep in a one-year tour of duty as a military journalist in Iraq. One of my coworkers, a female sergeant, came in one morning and threw herself down in her chair without saying hello to anyone. I decided to give her some room. After all, there are plenty of good reasons for being in a bad mood in Iraq, like the constant fear of death or the balmy 130-degree weather.

About a half hour later, she couldn't stand it any longer and started venting to me about being sexually harassed the day before by a first sergeant and company commander. They had hounded her to get naked, lie across a humvee, and let them photograph her.

"I'm sorry," I said. "How did that make you feel?"

"Like a piece of crap," she replied.

I was shocked. I'd been in the military for seven years and I'd never seen people in those kinds of leadership positions treat a woman so poorly. For a long time now I've considered myself a feminist, and at that moment I considered myself an extremely pissed off feminist.

"Do you want me to talk with them?"

"No," she said.

"Do you want me to beat them up?"

She just laughed.

"I'll help you file a complaint," I said.

"No, I just want to forget about it."

I didn't want to pressure her, but I had to remind her that if she didn't make a statement, these guys would continue to make other women feel like crap. She said she understood, but the perceived cost of complaining was just too high.

"Those other girls will just have to deal with it," she said.

The next day, I left the office to cover some stories in Al Anbar province. Long hours in helicopters and convoys gave me time to reflect on how I'd become a feminist. Until I was a junior at Utah State University, I thought only women could be feminists. This all changed when one of my favorite male journalism professors wore a T-shirt to class that read, "This is what a feminist looks like." Intrigued by the idea, I tried the title on myself.

"Hello, my name is Marshall and I'm a feminist," I said aloud as soon as I was alone. It felt good. Later I found that Karen Offen, a historian specializing in feminism, defines a feminist as anyone, female or male, who protests against the institutions and ideas that promote inequalities between the sexes.

This definition appealed to me on a personal level: Since my youth, women had been some of my most respected role models, the foremost of whom was my mother's mother known simply as "Granny" to my siblings and me. Granny earned a bachelor's and master's degree in sociology during the Great Depression. When she married, she inspired her husband so much that he went back to school to get his master's in sociology. They worked together as social workers for a few short years. He died of a heart attack when my mother was eleven and my Granny never remarried. She worked full-time and raised four children. One of my earlier memories is seeing hundreds of coworkers honoring my silver-haired Granny at her retirement party. I also noticed how my father treated her. He would lean in and confer with her about the plans for the day, like a cabinet member discussing an important issue with the president.

My reverie ended as I stepped off a Black Hawk helicopter at Camp Al Asad in western Iraq. I boarded a shuttle bus that would take me to the unit I was looking for. I walked to the back and sat down behind a male lieutenant colonel, a male sergeant major, and a female sergeant. I'm a constant eavesdropper and as I stared out the window at the vast fields of dust, I listened closely to their conversation.

They were the advanced group for their National Guard unit, which would be coming to Al Asad in a few weeks. Eventually they started talking about housing. The lieutenant colonel turned to the sergeant and said, "Of course, you'll be rooming with me, just don't tell my wife."

I thought the sergeant major might stand up for his soldier and remind the commander of the sexual harassment policy.

"No, sir," said the sergeant major. "You've got it all wrong. Sgt. X is rooming with me."

The female sergeant laughed quietly and shook her head.

"You laugh," the sergeant major said. "But you know you're gonna give it up before you leave here."

I was disgusted. This was the second time in two days I'd heard of unit commanders sexually harassing their subordinates. I wanted to say something, but I was still scared. After all, maybe she enjoyed the jokes. If she were offended, it would be her responsibility to say something, not mine. Right?

I said nothing. The bus stopped, I got off, and met up with the unit I was covering. The unit commander cancelled my convoy and told me I'd have to wait a few days. Writing stories about units on the base kept me occupied, but at night, I had nothing but time to think.

Were women treated much worse in Iraq than in the United States? And if this were true, was it because the rules in Iraq were different? For instance, I would never think of pointing a loaded weapon at somebody back home, but in Iraq, that was a perfectly normal thing to do. Perhaps this shift in standards had caused some soldiers to reevaluate what they knew about sexual harassment. Out here in the desert with little to no chance of punishment, maybe it seemed okay to make objectifying and degrading comments to women. Is that what they were thinking?

Now that I was paying more attention to sexual harassment, it seemed to be popping up everywhere, and not just from superiors. In many cases, it was coming from peers.

While I was killing time before my convoy, a couple of soldiers invited me up to their motor pool to photograph their weekly basketball game. Out of eight players, only one was a female, Pvt. Y. When it came time to determine which team would play in their camouflage tops and which team would play in their brown undershirts, the players invoked a standing rule: Pvt. Y's team would play in their undershirts.

"You'll see why," one soldier said to me as he winked.

I'd met Pvt. Y a few days ago and she'd left a favorable impression. She was young and a little bit goofy with thick glasses and a boy's haircut, a skinny kid from the Midwest. When she took off her camouflage top, all the male players hooped and hollered. Her tight brown undershirt revealed that she had a larger than average chest. She blushed and almost bowed as she set her top on the ground.

"Hey, Sergeant," one of the players yelled to me. "Are you gonna get some pictures of Pvt. Y's big ol' titties bouncing around?"

"No," I said.

I didn't feel comfortable saying anything more at that point because I didn't want to embarrass Pvt. Y. However, her response to the comment was anything but embarrassed. She grabbed her breasts and shook them, an action that elicited even more cheering from the crowd.

I'm still not sure what was going on during that game. If I took what I saw at face value, I'd have to assume that Pvt. Y actually enjoyed what other women and men would consider criminally offensive. It's not completely ridiculous to assume that a woman raised in a society that puts such a high value on physical attractiveness would find sincere pleasure in the lavish attention that her body garners. I've heard this line of logic explained often by soldiers complaining about the strict sexual harassment policy in the military.

The male soldiers at the basketball game, however, were not simply complimenting their peer. It's almost comical to think they would ever use the same sort of language to describe each other's physical appearance. As if a male soldier would remove his shirt and his fellows would make catcalls and yell, "Wow, Joe, your pecs are luscious."

Pvt. Y wasn't that naïve to assume the lascivious comments were simply compliments. So why did she play along? Maybe it was a defense mechanism— an easier way to deal with the problem than filing a public report after every basketball game. But why did the female sergeant on the bus merely laugh and shake her head when her male commander made a joke about them sleeping together? Why wouldn't my coworker file a complaint against the men who had made her feel so worthless? For that matter, why hadn't I said anything when I witnessed these things happen?

The military structure requires teamwork and obedience to orders from superiors. Drill sergeants pound these ideas indelibly into the minds of every recruit. If you don't follow orders, military trainers say, people will die. So when a high-ranking person says something to you, your first response is to do exactly what they say. The last response is to question them. And when you find acceptance in a group, your first response is to cling to it. Fitting in and working as a team are necessary to survival.

It's this dynamic, however, that made former-Secretary of Defense Cohen so intent on ending the military's addiction to sexual harassment. Instead of accepting sexual harassment to retain superficial comity in the ranks, he demanded that it be eliminated.

"We're talking about men and women putting their lives on the line at some point," Cohen said in 1997. "We can't have that kind of dissension, that kind of discrimination or morale problem within the unit."

Eight years later, it seemed service members decided to ignore this command while putting their units in actual danger by allowing the sexual subjugation of women in the Armed Forces to continue. It has become such a problem that at least one female soldier publicly refused to return to Iraq.

Spc. Suzanne Swift said that during her tour in Iraq she was constantly sexually harassed by superiors, exposed to sexual banter, and coerced into a sexual relationship with her immediate supervisor. She was brave enough to file complaints, but the perpetrators received no real punishment. Because of her year of sexual degradation in Iraq, she has refused to return. For that, the U.S. military court-martialed her.

This seems like a total reversal from Cohen's zero-tolerance policy. Sadly, the military's current policies that reinforce sexual inequality and female repression go further than court-martialing. On Sept. 15, 2003, they took a life.

Originally, the military reported Alyssa Peterson's death as an "accidental discharge." But as family and local journalists dug deeper, the details of her suicide became clear.

Peterson was a devout Mormon and served as a volunteer missionary for eighteen months in the Netherlands. She was fluent in Dutch and had a gift for languages, so when she enlisted to serve her country she signed up as an Arabic interpreter. When she got to Iraq she was assigned to an interrogation unit called "the cage." The details of what went on in the cage are classified, but other female interrogators have described some of the process. Guards brought male prisoners into the cage blindfolded and then stripped them down. When the guards removed the blindfolds, the first thing the prisoners saw was a female interpreter. Superiors instructed the female interpreters to insult the prisoners' genitalia. In other cases, female interrogators wiped fake menstrual blood on prisoners, molested them, and performed strip teases. The U.S. Army has set a new low mark in sexual harassment; they turned it into a torture device.

When superiors ordered Peterson to use her sexuality as a base torture device, not only was she expected to make Iraqi men suffer, but military officers also unwittingly forced Peterson to defame the divinity of womanhood that is so core to Mormon religious beliefs. After two days in the cage, Peterson refused to continue. She changed assignments, but she didn't get over what she had done. A few weeks after leaving the cage, Peterson committed suicide.

At the time of the bus ride with Sgt. X and the basketball game with Pvt. Y, I didn't know Peterson's story and I didn't know about Swift's court martial. If I'd known then how dangerous sexual harassment could be, I'd like to think I would have done more. I don't know what happened to Sgt. X or to Pvt. Y, but I hope they're okay.

The next morning I got up hours before sunrise to catch my convoy to Camp Hit, a small outpost near the Syrian border. When I arrived at the isolated camp, I found a handful of female soldiers living and working among the male infantry soldiers and Marines. At this point, this seemed like a recipe for sexual harassment and sexual assault. I was determined to expose the problem in a story. I interviewed all five women. They each told me that nobody treated them any differently because they were women.

I started to feel optimistic. Maybe the last week was just a fluke. Maybe it wasn't all that bad. I started to look for a different angle for the story. I'd noticed that all the soldiers spoke highly of their commander, Capt. Z. This is unusual because most soldiers like to complain about their commanders. I decided to seek out this exceptional captain who, also, just happened to be a woman.

"Do you know where Capt. Z is?" I asked a passing soldier.

"Oh, yeah, she's the hot one," he said.

"Do you know where she is?"

"Just walk that way until you see a hot captain."

It didn't bother me that he said she was hot. I even laughed a bit. Out in the middle of the desert surrounded by a bunch of ugly male grunts, they had probably built this captain up to be an Aphrodite reborn. It was still an objectifying comment, but since this soldier sounded legitimately infatuated, it seemed more innocent to me at the time. Maybe it was because he was a lower rank than Capt. Z and his comment made him seem more like an adoring puppy dog than an oppressive pervert.

When I found Capt. Z, she was pretty and, more importantly, very competent. I was impressed with the efficiency with which she ran the logistics for the base. I thought to myself, "Here is one of the best and brightest of the military." I decided I might do a sidebar personality feature on her because an officer who knows her job is definitely newsworthy these days.

As a precaution, I asked Capt. Z if she felt other soldiers treated her any differently because of her sex. She said definitely not. "Great," I thought, "I've just had a bad week."

I finished up the interview and was about to ask if I could follow her around and get some photos when a male master sergeant butted in.

"Hey, Sgt. T.," the guy said to me, "you should get some photos of her with her top off."

She blushed and played it off as if it were just part of being in the Army. But I could hear her voice crackle ever so slightly with emotion. All the guys laughed as if it were some clever repartee. I didn't laugh. She didn't laugh. And I didn't dare ask her right after that comment if I could take pictures of her.

The foul minds and untamed tongues of undisciplined soldiers took something innocent and good and made it seem vulgar. They were power tripping.

I was the lowest ranking person in the immediate area and I froze, yet again. At the time, I was astounded. I thought that a captain in the U.S. Army wouldn't put up with that kind of a degrading comment. What I didn't understand at the time was that hegemonic sexism meant that anyone sexually harassing Capt. Z automatically outranked her. Sexism literally usurped the structure and discipline of the U.S. military.

I decided that day that I would no longer tolerate sexual harassment. I would speak up even if I were subordinate, even if I were poking my nose in other people's business, and even if I were afraid of embarrassing myself. I made a preemptive strike in my unit and informed everyone that if I heard anyone using the language of sexual harassment, I'd file a formal complaint myself, because it offends me personally. When men harass women with viciously sexual language, they don't only degrade the women, they degrade themselves. They demote themselves ethically and morally. But when men treat women with the honor they deserve—that *all* people deserve—then men become truly noble as well. In the end, we're all the same species and in the same military. The degradation of one degrades us all.

In 2011, Defense Secretary Leon Panetta took a stand against sexual harassment and violence in the military, stating "One sexual assault is one too many." Since my time in Iraq, service members have an option to file a confidential report. Yet the problem of sexual harassment continues. My personal stand hasn't changed the military culture of female repression in the slightest. But maybe a few men got the message that sexual harassment is unacceptable. And, still, I think speaking up may have helped a few women who felt outnumbered in a combat zone, and that's a start. After all, we feminists need to stick together.

GENDER IN JAKARTA: LESSONS ON DISCOURSE AND DISPARITY

Bryan Talbot Morris

D ays away from Christmas and sweating in the thickness of a rainless evening in central Jakarta, I sat down over coffee with two friends for what I had thought would be a casual chat. The three of us were new researchers in Indonesia, fresh from graduate school, young and excited. We met in an Indonesian language class a year earlier, and had agreed to meet up, swap stories, and compare informal notes on our experiences in a new country.

The conversation that ensued created for me a heightened awareness of the political significance of what men say when we talk about women, sexuality, and ourselves. It would not be the only experience I would have in the following year that honed my understanding about what we say, the language we use to say it, and how this reflects existing gender imbalances.

As we sat in that café, talking over Scrabble, coffee, and clove cigarettes, our conversation wove in and out of topics, from the challenges of doing research in another language, to the recently drafted Indonesian anti-pornography legislation and, ultimately, to anecdotes from our personal lives. We, three white Americans, felt perhaps a fleeting camaraderie of a shared experience that allowed us to talk freely.

John, as I'll call him, began recounting various escapades with women whom he'd encountered at bars or clubs, malls, and karaoke bars while living in Yogyakarta, a smaller city also located on the island of Java. His face conveyed obvious surprise as he commented to us, "I just didn't expect it to be like this; it has been crazy." This was John's first time in Indonesia, and while we, his audience, had spent only slightly more time in the country previously, we exchanged curious glances with each other and urged him to continue.

"There was this one woman and we, you know, hooked up. I guess I just didn't expect casual sex to be so easy here," the implication of "here" perhaps meaning "a country with the world's largest Muslim population." John went on to explain that he met an Indonesian woman in a club a couple months earlier and that they spent a couple of nights together. She became angry when he said that he did not want to be in a relationship with her. When we pressed John for details, particularly about her line of work, he immediately responded, "She wasn't a prostitute." We pressed on, but John was unwilling to seriously consider the situation further. He ended our query by saying, "She didn't ask me for money."

The three of us began joking back and forth about the woman and how exploitative sexual relationships don't necessarily require women wearing fishnet stockings, spiked heels, and working a corner sidewalk. Then, John shocked us into silence when he said, "I like the *jilbab* (Islamic head scarf). I think women who wear the *jilbab* are attractive. I want to date a woman who wears a *jilbab*. I want to date a good girl." He was dead serious.

My initial impulse was to call John an idiot. But this would have gotten us nowhere. My reaction was stifled by my shock at John's statement. Here was a man with a college diploma who was pursuing a master's degree in Southeast Asian studies; a man surrounded by development professionals and academics sensitive to global gender injustice, and particularly injustices in Indonesia. Here was a man who said, in effect, "I will sleep with whores; I want to date a good girl. Whores are useful; virgins are the marrying type." Even worse, here was a man who wasn't just reinforcing—but truly believed—that a woman who wore a headscarf did so because she was good and pious, and that the headscarf advertised this piety to the world. John thought that women who did not wear the headscarf were making a statement announcing their sexual availability. Ultimately, John thought that statement was bad. Women without headscarves could be slept with, but not married. Marriage was to be saved for the virgins, the headscarf-wearing good girls, the girls that didn't frequent the bars, clubs, and karaoke halls where he himself went looking for the bad girls.

John's remarks revealed several problematic issues. First, despite the fact that John agrees theoretically with the concept of gender equality, his comments point to the gap between what some men know they're supposed to say and what they actually believe about women. Second, John's statements indicate that the virgin–whore complex is alive and unwell. Many men have no problem sleeping with women casually and using the discourse of liberation as justification. When it comes to dating and marriage, however, many of these same men still want the virgin. Third, and slightly more complicated, is the introduction of the headscarf to the scenario: What we say about ourselves, our sexuality, and our gender does not come only from verbal cues. The headscarf speaks symbolic volumes about sexuality, yet we're not always sure what these messages are.

Ask almost any Indonesian woman if one can tell if a girl is sexually chaste or not based on the presence of a *jilbab* and most of them will laugh out loud, as if the question is ridiculous. Just because a woman wears a headscarf doesn't necessarily mean she's sexually inactive. That, at least, is the conventional wisdom in Jakarta. If he was thinking clearly, this knowledge should have complicated the picture for my friend John. But he wasn't and it didn't. According to John's confused logic, wearing the headscarf is simply a choice women make. Nothing more.

I do not share John's view of the headscarf. I don't think wearing the *jilbab* is a matter of simple choice for a woman. The *jilbab* reflects a value system that intends for women, and not men, to be covered, limited, and hidden. When young, female children are dressed in a headscarf—well before puberty—it can be a challenging, iconoclastic decision to take it off later in life. There is enormous social pressure for women—from community members, from peers, from family members—to wear the headscarf. John would perhaps be surprised to know that an Indonesian friend of ours in graduate school, who does not don a *jilbab* in the United States, wears a headscarf whenever she is in Jakarta. It's not a matter of simple choice for her: She wears the headscarf because her parents insist on it. In fact, they say, when she visits, she may hang out with whomever she wants and stay over at female friends' apartments, as long as she wears long sleeves, long pants, and a headscarf. She is in her thirties.

My point, though, is not solely about the *jilbab*. While I am questioning men's entrenched power over women as symbolically expressed through the headscarf, issues of gender and power don't just happen in far-away countries and in cultures that seem so different from our own. My intention here is to highlight how gaps between men's good intentions and what we really say are power issues, too. As Westerners we're not off the hook when it comes to critically looking at how we exert power over others. As men, we're certainly not off the hook. We can't point our finger at those "Others" (in this case, Indonesian Muslim culture that encourages and pressures women to wear headscarves). We need to examine how our own culture, with fundamentalist religious influences, continues to reinforce gender injustice and how we participate in that injustice when we open our mouths without thinking about what we're saying.

My point is that what we say about gender relations reflects an imbalance in agency, choice, and voice between men and women that is so ingrained that some of us do not recognize it when it shows up over coffee and Scrabble among friends—even when it comes out of our own mouths. I'm using my friend John as an example, but he's certainly not alone. We have been trained, after all, in gender-sensitive speak and we are unlikely to say anything that would obviously contradict our support for gender equalities.

As my year in Indonesia continued, I would find John's statement only the beginning of the troubling things I heard come from men's mouths. From diplomats, expatriates, NGO staff, friends, and acquaintances, the daily banter reflected a fundamental and ingrained disconnect between egalitarian discourse and the way men live our lives.

Approximately halfway through my research project, I was invited by the Public Affairs Officer at the U.S. Embassy to informally present findings from my research and lead a discussion over lunch about my experience in Indonesia. At the time, I was working with Jakarta's oldest women-focused non-governmental organization, an advocacy, information, and communications center. During our discussion that day, I explained how the NGO I worked with used program evaluation as a mechanism of accountability. Within the context of this specific NGO, I was discussing the difficulty organizations have in measuring their programs' impacts—for example, measuring an economic empowerment program's impact on widowed tsunami survivors—and how there are challenges in relating specific impacts from programs with the original mission and purpose of the NGO.

Because we were using women's economic empowerment to discuss impact assessment and accountability, it was no surprise that the conversation veered a bit to include development programming targeting women. During the course of this discussion, an Embassy officer made a statement both slightly off-topic and highly problematic. He said, "Well, what you've got are NGOs working from a feminist perspective. This is basically a Western ideological import. Is it suitable for the Indonesian culture?" His point was that an NGO that worked toward equality for women, and that was based loosely on feminist principles, was obviously going to have difficulty evaluating its programs' impacts because their mission was based on an ideology that was not indigenous, that was instead imported from the "West," and was therefore not easily integrated within an Indonesian sociocultural context. "How could they measure something so foreign to them to begin with?" the Embassy officer seemed to imply.

I was so angry I wanted to firebomb the room. This U.S. State Department representative had expressed an incredibly flawed, inaccurate, ethnocentric, and condescending perspective. First, he presumed that gender equality is an exclusively Western idea. Second, he assumed that if feminism were a Western import, then women in Southeast Asia would be incapable of, or resistant to, thinking they deserved equality. Third, this man's comments suggested that the Indonesian women I had been working with were not interested in changing a culture with such ingrained gender inequality.

Why would an American State Department representative dismiss progressive possibilities for Indonesian women by claiming that feminism is a Western import and therefore irrelevant? Apparently he felt comfortable ignoring the fact that the Indonesian government signed on to the United Nations' Convention on the Elimination of All Forms of Discrimination Against Women (CEDAW) in 1980. As of 2012, the United States had yet to ratify CEDAW.

Feminism in Indonesia is uniquely Indonesian. Although it may be connected with Western-based feminism, it is specific to the cultural and social needs of Indonesia. Dismissing Indonesian efforts toward human rights and equality for women under the guise of paternal cultural sensitivity is particularly troubling. Indonesian women who want gender equity do not operate on the basis of Western values. Gender equity is a status that they work toward based on their assessment that they deserve it, as does any other woman in any other country, culture, or society. To think that Indonesian feminists simply imported a Western notion, further limits the voices of these women. American women do not agree on all the goals and theories of feminism; the same is true in Indonesia. Yet there is a shared fundamental belief in both countries regarding the equal rights and treatment of women *vis-à-vis* men. Equality is not a Western import. It doesn't even exist thoroughly in the West.

So what is the link between my friend John and the representative from the U.S. Embassy? The relevance of these two stories is this: Feminism, and its profeminist actors, is a movement aimed at increasing the agency of women in a world in which there are many groups searching for movement, for agency, for increased freedom. The things we say and the language we use reflect the reality we participate in—the contradictions, the imbalances of power, the literally and symbolically structured silence of some, and the booming voices of others.

Men speak out constantly. Most disconcerting about our speech is how oblivious many of us can be about how our language reflects existing power relations. The agency men have is a fundamental benefit we reap from a social structure that allows us freedom of voice. This structure silences others in ways that are literal and symbolic. Men can speak out without realizing that what we say oftentimes reinforces the restricted agency of women to do the same. We speak out loudly without thinking about how easily our voices carry. We speak out loud in ways that reflect the breadth of our agency and unexamined power over the women around us. It happens over coffee, during luncheons and presentations, in the ways we look at and communicate with others. This essay is a reflection on the things we say.

LISTENING, LEARNING, SPEAKING UP

Daniel Simon

D ear Reader,
   If you're reading this, you may be a student enrolled in a Politics of
Gender course or a Women's Studies seminar. Right now, you might be reading
in a coffee shop, a library, or a tiny bedroom (which maybe you share with a
roommate with questionable hygiene or habits). But whether you're taking a
class or reading about masculinity and gender politics out of personal interest,
the topic is probably making you confront some ugly truths and it's not always
a comfortable process. I know that's how it is for me. I think I got the following
story straight, though I've changed the names and dates to keep things on the
safe side.
   When I was a junior in college, I enrolled in an Introduction to Women's
Studies course at Cal State East Bay to complete a requirement for my
English major. Hayward is rainy and bleak on many fall mornings and I felt
kinda blue that first day when I found a seat in a small campus classroom. I
didn't know what to expect aside from a sense that feminism would play a
central role in the class. I had only a vague concept of feminism—as I suppose
I still do—as an ideology that champions gender equality through education
and activism and strongly advocates against negative male dominance in
various forms. I got behind that concept as much as any twenty-something
guy with progressive aspirations could. But I was young and like many young
guys, I was seriously lacking in empathy and compassion. Also, like many
other guys, what little I knew about feminism I'd learned from the women in
my life: my mother, my cousins, my girlfriends. When the women's studies
professor appeared, she barely glanced at the class and proceeded to take role.
I noted that men were a slim minority of the room; there were roughly three
men and thirty women.

"We're outnumbered," I whispered to the guy sitting to my right.

"What did you say?" said a woman in front of me who turned around in her seat to face me.

"Ughmm . . . I said, we're outnumbered?" She sneered at me and looked away. *Oh fuck*, I thought to myself. *What have I gotten myself into?*

That class rests in a rather murky place in my memory, so I'm not sure exactly what I learned or exactly how I performed because I spent most of the semester in a defensive crouch like the other two male students, one of whom showed up only for exams. The professor was a brilliant and serious soul who often seemed to return to the subject of construction workers, street harassment, and catcalls. Sometimes I wondered if she lived in a neighborhood under perpetual construction by abusive meatheads who ate paint chips as children.

The professor engaged the class with statistics that became visceral by using us to represent the general population, like "There are thirty women in this room. At least ten of you have been or will be sexually assaulted in your lifetime." Or, "There are thirty women in this room. At least fifteen of you have been or will be sexually harassed in the work place in your lifetime." AIDS, rape, or abortion . . . You get the point. She left no stone unturned and forced the class to consider the recent history and consequences of how our nation had unequally treated 52 percent of its residents. My professor seemed genuinely interested in forcing/helping her female students to confront female subordination, personally and politically. And her male students? Well, we were along for a rare if somewhat-harrowing ride; I say "rare" because I think that if more men were exposed to this material, I think we'd live in a radically different country.

Our professor was relentless, and slowly some of the female students began to respond. These responses were often deeply personal, some of the women having never confronted lifetimes of feeling suppressed, compressed, repressed. There really isn't anything like watching self-awareness kicked into high gear through confrontation, and the result was that a lot of women found out that they were really angry both at men and society in the abstract, and themselves for being so slow to self-discovery. The guys were silent for the most part. We were ignored, mocked, or made the targets of discussions. Hammered into a punitive silence, we were open-eyed and slacked-jawed. My right knee ached from rubbing against the underside of the desk as my body instinctively pulled away from uncomfortable truths, put into the unfamiliar position of long-overdue political accountability.

The lectures and class discussions dented my consciousness just enough to let in a new perspective, but I was still working with abstractions, too. At the time, I lived in a really gnarly industrial section of East Oakland. The residents of my building referred to the ten-block journey to the BART station as "Walking the Gaza," because one never knew whether or not danger was lurking, random or premeditated. Walking the Gaza with my neighbor Anne one afternoon, I told her about my experiences in the class. Initially, she was amused by my very presence there, and she teased me for enrolling late and thus being forced to take the class. But after testing the waters a bit, Anne said, "Can you see where your professor is coming from?" Anne offered me her perspective on our little journey home.

When Anne walked alone to and from the BART station, she walked fast and clutched a claw of keys ready to slash at would-be assailants, real or imagined. The latter was worse actually, sometimes haunting her long after she locked her front door. She carried pepper spray in her purse even though she thought she would probably just end up blinding herself if she used it in a panic. As she described her daily experience, her face flushed and her throat tightened. Her voice became thin and then she trailed off into silence. We walked the final block fast as if we were trying to outrun the subject.

When we got home, she explained that she didn't like to think of herself as potential prey or a victim. That I could be so oblivious of her vulnerable position, and that I walked so cavalierly and so cluelessly, furthered her frustration with white male privilege. She was angry that I didn't know what it was like to walk with dread. Eventually, we segued into calmer waters, but after that day, the topic was resurrected every so often, probably when I said something that indicated I was still clueless. In terms of our friendship, I think she needed to be sure that I understood her position, as much as any guy can. Years after I left East Oakland, Anne and several tenants formed a dojo collective to learn and practice self-defense techniques. Over the phone one night, she described a scene in which the women routinely beat the hell out of the men, an emotional and physical venting of sorts. The neighborhood has gotten a lot worse because of the gang wars and "Walking the Gaza" is now equally dangerous for both male and female residents, a strange equality.

One semester, after my experience in Introduction to Women's Studies, I enrolled in another women's studies course—this time by choice and intention. I was one of seven or so men scattered among about a hundred women in a large echoing lecture hall. Our professor ran the classroom discussions as if she were a charismatic daytime talk-show host. She deftly darted up and down the rows with a wireless microphone and artfully threaded together the thoughts of her students on a wide range of issues including gender roles, power, and sex. One day, the conversation turned to grooming pubic hair and a heated argument erupted between two students in my row.

"Why the hell should I shave myself so I look like a little girl for my boyfriend?" said a redheaded female music major into the microphone. Her pale white skin burned with rage as she stared down the row just past me to the woman sitting directly to my left.

"If he wants to fuck a child, he should go fuck a child!"

The class roared. Normally reserved, she was now livid, clearly personalizing the debate. The mic was passed down the row past me to the other combatant.

"Whatever . . ." said a dark-haired female English major, "I didn't say you had to. No one said you had to. That's between you and your man." She stretched a bit before continuing, "My man likes me bare, and I'm not a fucking child! He doesn't want to fuck a child! He likes me shaved bare and 'cause I know he's more likely to spend more time down there if I'm bare, then I'll do it 'cause I like it when he goes down on me!"

The class roared again. The English major spoke often with a gutsy confidence that we all enjoyed. Well, I think most of us enjoyed it, though in this case, it clearly displeased the music major. We laughed nervously and the professor beamed. She looked around the room, trying find someone who could add to the conversation. She fixed her eyes on me.

"Well, Mr. Simon. What do you think?"

I froze. I blushed and my nose twitched. The mic was passed to me.

"I think . . . I think . . . I think women should do whatever they want to do."

The room went silent with disappointment. I looked around for help from the other guys, but I couldn't find their eyes. The mic was passed and the conversation continued on without me.

Idiot, I thought to myself. *You can do better than that.*

It's not that my answer was wrong. And I can excuse my younger self by simply admitting that I didn't know what to say or how to say it. But I did blow a good opportunity and I regret that because whether or not my perspective, or that of any guy in the room, was politically popular or intellectually deep, men have an obligation to live through that discomfort and not remain silent bystanders to the process. But we also have an obligation to listen. And for men, especially for those of us who are used to speaking up and believing our views are right (whether or not we have any actual expertise)—this can be a balancing act that can be exquisitely unnerving. Ignore the temptation to recoil. Dig in.

A TRIBUTE TO MY FATHER

Chris Dixon

My dad was different. Sure, he and I played catch and wrestled, watched sports and enjoyed *Star Wars* together. But he also talked about feelings, cooked dinner regularly, and encouraged me to play with dolls and action figures alike. He didn't even flinch when my mom began painting my toenails pink. Although I wouldn't realize it until later, my father was the first pro-feminist man to touch my life. Growing up, I knew him as a man uncomfortable with manhood. I saw him openly struggle with his own entrenched sexist and homophobic socialization. I watched him try to break down rigid gender roles, with mixed success, in his relationship with my mother. And in the process, I learned a lot about patriarchy and heterosexism, not the least of which is their frustrating resilience.

These kinds of experiences are uncommon. Most of the progressive men that I know don't have much praise for their fathers, particularly when it comes to the issue of sexism. Indeed, more than a few define their anti-sexism in deliberate opposition to their dads. Even so, I think this demonstrates how fathers are so central to our formative experiences as men around gender and sexuality. Many of us have our first run-ins with patriarchy through the older men in our lives, frequently our dads. Consciously and unconsciously, lovingly and punitively, they teach and model being male for children who are expected to identify as boys and unquestioningly accept prevailing notions of masculinity.

In order to understand how patriarchy is perpetuated, it makes sense to look first to those who most embody it—men, fathers, and sons. And yet we must also locate the unlikely chinks in its formidable armor: the sites of refusal and struggle in which men, often hesitantly, have challenged patriarchal privilege. That's why I think it's useful, perhaps crucial, to revisit our dads with both sincere compassion and unflinching criticism.

Here I'll start with my late father. I want to pay tribute to him. And I don't mean that in any kind of simple, celebratory way. Rather, this is a tribute worthy of him, one that brings together the good and the bad. In the real world, where domination and oppression intertwine with all aspects of our lives, there are no easy, uncomplicated sources of inspiration. But there are lessons. I look to my dad, then, for lessons about how to struggle against sexism and homophobia, as well as for lessons about the structures of patriarchy and heterosexism that lurked inside him and continue to lurk inside me. In his example, I find both inspiration and warning, inseparably tied.

BEGINNINGS

My dad was born in Fort Worth, Texas, in 1934, in the middle of the Great Depression. My grandmother was young, seventeen years old at the time, and she had just married my grandfather. Six months later they moved to California, where my father spent the rest of his childhood.

My dad grew up white, male, and working-class, an only child in a family constantly struggling to make ends meet. Along the way, he inherited a healthy distrust of wealth and power, largely through his own troubled father, a self-identified socialist as well as an outright racist. Tellingly, his parents gave my dad the middle name "Eugene" for Eugene Debs, the turn-of-the-century radical labor leader. And though my dad came of age during the deeply conservative 1950s, he never lost his gut sense of egalitarian ethics. Decades later as I was becoming politicized, my dad confessed that, at heart, he was forever a socialist. He was convinced that the staggering economic inequalities of our society are fundamentally wrong. I suspect that this core ethic contributed to why he accepted feminism, however imperfectly.

Poverty and hard work framed my father's young adulthood. High school offered very little, so he skimmed through while also working as a gas station attendant. After graduating, he did a stint in the army, narrowly missing the Korean War. Finding nothing redeeming about military life, my dad then entered college, worked his way through, and entered his first marriage, a union that lasted just long enough to bear four children, my half-siblings. By the 1960s my father worked for the State of California.

At first glance, my dad's story looks deceptively like a pulled-himself-up-by-his-bootstraps tale of hard-won success and class mobility. But it isn't; his opportunities and identity were clearly shaped by his access to white, male, straight privilege. Without this, he would have followed a markedly different path. To some extent, my father realized this. He wasn't oblivious to the social movements of the 1960s and 1970s or the openings that they created. My dad would later recount how the civil rights struggles forced him to clarify his values and consider his own position as a white person. Likewise, the women's liberation movement, burgeoning as he met my feminist mother in the early

1970s, challenged him to rethink his manhood and, to a limited degree, his sexuality.

INSPIRATION

My parents married in 1973, on the cusp of a major shift in gender roles and relations that would come to alter kinship, parenting, sex, work, socialization, and so much more. For sure, it was an incomplete shift, but a significant one nonetheless. I sometimes wonder how my dad took it: As the patriarchal landscape around him shook, as some of his privileges as a straight man were called into question, what did it mean to him? How did he learn to change?

One way or another my father embraced some of these shifts in roles and relations. In many ways, I grew up with and learned from a surprisingly non-traditional man. His contributions to household work, for instance, stretched far beyond occasionally barbequing hamburgers or fixing broken appliances. And contrary to the storylines on TV sitcoms, these weren't duties begrudgingly performed just because my mother asked for help. My dad consistently prepared meals, he washed his share of dishes, and when it was time to clean house, he chipped in just like the rest of us. He changed plenty of dirty diapers, cared for me when I was sick, and carted my brother and me around as my mom worked. Throughout—indeed even after my parents separated in 1994—my father was emphatically dedicated to what he called co-parenting: working together with my mother on equal terms in all parenting decisions. While American pop culture was ambivalently and belatedly coming to terms with Mr. Mom, my parents were figuring out—not always so easily—how to share chores, responsibilities, and decisions. Although seemingly inconsequential at the time, their innovations shaped how I've come to understand gender, work, and authority.

More than once, I asked my father, "Are you a feminist?" And his reply was always the same: "Yes." For him, that choice transcended our home and his relationship with my mother; it also posed a more general challenge to masculinity and men, himself included. In the late 1980s, his search for answers took my dad to the budding men's movement, a broad (and often contradictory) conglomeration of men's initiatives and organizations. His main participation was with a fairly progressive men's group, including both queers and straights, which met weekly to discuss issues like gender socialization, male role expectations, pornography, and homophobia.

This last topic was especially weighty for my dad, judging from the stories that he shared. When I was nine or ten, for example, he told me about a meeting in which pairs of men in his group had taken turns holding each other's hands while walking around the block outside. Some of them simply couldn't. Their fear of touching other men—their internalized homophobia— was too deep-rooted. But my father said that he had been able to hold hands the whole way. I saw how scared he had been, and I was proud of him.

Some years later, when I was in my early teens, my dad invited me to attend a local men's conference with him. I still vividly remember the workshops. In the morning, we joined a discussion with lesbian activist and musician, Libby Rodrick, who provided a historical overview of the feminist movement, pulling out lessons for us men to grapple with. "You all," she offered conclusively, "have a lot of work to do among yourselves." In the afternoon, we participated in a lively multigenerational "dialogue between gay and straight men." For me, still exploring my own sexuality, this was an eye-opening, exciting encounter. And our presence as a father–son duo was especially significant—for the dialogue, because we represented a tangible bridge between generations, and for me, because we momentarily moved outside the assumed heterosexuality that so often pervaded my family and my experience. As I look back, I realize that it took a lot of courage for my dad to participate.

Truth be told, though, many of the most inspirational moments with my father weren't during these major events, but throughout our daily experiences. I treasure memories of the time he explained homophobia to me or, later, our rich ongoing conversations about gender wherever we went. At the airport with him, for instance, I remember watching and talking about gender roles in greetings and goodbyes: While men were expected to be calm and collected, women were frequently tearful and openly affectionate. Of course, we couldn't, by ourselves, do away with such role limitations, but we found solace in one another as we looked and pushed at them. These were enlightening, memorable times. In them, my dad, along with my mother, taught me a way of critically eyeing the world—a way that he carried courageously into his last days.

WARNING

There was also a flipside to my dad. That is, he was far from untouched by patriarchy or heterosexism. Some of the more poignant lessons I take from him have to do with his failings. My father's shortcomings and his worst demons were inextricably linked to the workings of our social order. At best, my father determinedly pushed at the boundaries of masculinity. Yet for all of his critical self-awareness, he was still a man at times drowning in his own toxic socialization and entrenched in his privilege.

In the late-1990s, my dad finally admitted to his lifelong battle with alcoholism. I have no doubt that this struggle was tied to his larger battles with manhood itself. For most of my life he was largely dry, but he still had his moments of slurred sentimentalities as well as sheer ferocity. For him, alcohol was a coping tool. Depending on the circumstances, it was a means for male bonding, isolated withdrawal, emotional avoidance, or playful oblivion. In short, it was a copout, and a predictably masculine one at that.

Not unconnected was my father's volatile temper. In chilling detail, my mother sometimes tells horrendous stories of his most controlling, explosive states. By her accounts, his care and sensitivity were real, but they also concealed a capacity for intense rage and characteristically masculine entitlement. I definitely experienced pieces of this, but not the full brunt that my mom endured. And as she points out, even as he tried to mend and reconcile in his last years, he never took authentic responsibility.

Certainly my dad should be understood within the larger context of a society founded upon structural inequalities, like patriarchy. Single lives cannot easily bypass institutional realities. However, in some areas of his life, my father worked to challenge this context. So why the incongruity? I suspect that his failure to deal with his behavior stemmed, in part, from his difficulty reaching out and finding support. Despite his encouraging efforts with men's groups, he still relied heavily on the woman in his life—my mom—for emotional caretaking, a dynamic that many men are quick to fall back on. The gendered roles and expectations of the nuclear family—breadwinning father and nurturing mother—don't die so easily.

And while my dad generally frowned on such limited and limiting gender roles, he still sought a fixed masculinity, essential, timeless, and natural. Indeed, he was bothered by my playfulness around gender and worked to police my incursions against gender boundaries. Pink toenails when I was little may have been okay, but at fifteen, I recall his hostility while explaining to my confused younger brother that my beautifully French-braided hair perhaps signaled that I was "gay, or even transsexual." My brother didn't understand that explanation too well, and although the labels didn't bother me, the contempt was biting. From then on, I was careful to keep my more transgressive explorations of gender and sexuality safely away from my father.

Undergirding all of this was the basic fact that my dad's understanding of sexism and homophobia was regrettably shallow. He largely saw feminism as granting women rights in the public arena. He deplored individual, prejudicial, sexist acts. He saw gay rights similarly. Yet he neglected many of the patriarchal and heterosexist structures and patterns inscribed in his own heart. Consequently, his approach to the men's movement, like that of many other men, focused mainly on the obstacles and suffering among us, not the privileges that we enjoy. Sadly, he never quite grasped the whole picture.

LESSONS

My father's story has a natural conclusion. On a wintry day in December of 1999, he collapsed and died, stunning my whole family. But for me, this was less an end than a startling beginning. Since that fateful day, I've come to reflect on my dad in all of his flesh-and-blood complexity, strengthening my connection with him while also creating my own sense of closure and farewell. The process is tricky, for he was full of pointed contradictions: a pro-feminist who angrily vented upon my mother; a gender-role skeptic who nonetheless reinforced gender boundaries; an anti-sexist who failed to confront some of his most sexist patterns; a sensitive, reflective man who fled from his own feelings, long using alcohol to aid his flight. Only in recognizing these can I piece him together.

On one hand, I acknowledge his successes and the inspirational role he has played in my life. Simply put, I would not be the person that I am today without him. He helped equip me with some essential reflective tools for challenging systems of oppression. He embodied a (not entirely) different way of "being a man." And he taught me basic things: to confront my own homophobia, to contribute equally in household responsibilities, to never forget how to cry. In this sense, I carry him with me.

On the other hand, I acknowledge my dad's failings. I love him, and the most sincere way I know of expressing my love, particularly in his absence, is by learning from his mistakes and accepting the responsibility of not repeating them. As a (mostly) straight man, the son of my father, I, too, have the capacity to dwell in my rage and entitlement, to sink into avoidance and isolated withdrawal, to rely exclusively on the women in my life for my emotional caretaking. I, too, can choose to ignore my privilege. To forget any of this would be the greatest disrespect to my dad. In this sense as well, I carry him with me.

Somewhat optimistically, bell hooks recently noted in *Talking About a Revolution*, "We have for the first time a generation of men coming to adulthood who were not born into a world automatically submerged with sexist socialization that says that women are not the intellectual or work equals of men." I am of this generation of men. But for all the tremendous social shifts and major feminist successes, I, like others, haven't wholly escaped sexist or heterosexist socialization. This struggle will be a long one. I'm fortunate, though, because my father has left me with some inspiring tools and difficult lessons to help me along the way.

Thanks, Dad.

PLAYGROUND VERTIGO

Jeremy Adam Smith

The day started ordinarily enough. I came home from my office at noon. My wife Shelly went to work. I took our toddler Liko to a café for lunch and then we strollered to the playground.

From noon until 7:00 p.m. on weekdays, I'm a Mr. Mom—a term that bothers some stay-at-home dads as a knock on their masculinity. Personally, it doesn't bother me. The reader will not be surprised to hear that I'm usually the only dad I see at Liko's swim and music classes. I don't mind that, either. After a period of adjustment, I came to accept the relative isolation that goes along with my role.

But on the day in question we stepped through the playground gate into a parallel universe where the laws of gender bent and vanished (cue *Twilight Zone* theme): Liko and I found ourselves surrounded by . . . men. Three men playing with three toddlers. No women in sight.

One dad left, but another arrived. At 1:00 p.m., it was still only dads and kids. Naturally, we dads compared notes about the unprecedented situation in which we found ourselves. It emerged that one of us was a full-time stay-at-home dad but looking for a paid job; two of us had quit careers to take care of our kids, but still, out of necessity, worked part-time as freelancers; the fourth was finishing a PhD. All four of our wives worked more hours than we did.

This was the second time around for the PhD, Nick; he has a two-year-old and a seven-year-old. "There are definitely more dads on the playgrounds now than there were five years ago," Nick said.

At about 1:30, the first mom arrived with her baby. Liko and I went home for a nap. This incident raised the question: How many of us—and by "us" I mean men who are primary caregivers—are out there?

Several studies have found fathers now spend more time with their children and on housework than at any time since researchers started collecting comparable data. A 2011 census report says that one in five fathers serves as the primary caregiver to a child under fifteen—up 6 percent since 2002, which suggests a trend. And the Bureau of Labor Statistics says that about two million dads work part-time for "non-economic reasons" that include childcare, a category into which I fit. Census data also show that homes headed by single dads are the fastest-growing family type.

We need to keep these trends in perspective. It's still mostly women taking care of children, sometimes pulling double shifts as workers and mommies. When Father's Day rolls around, we stay-at-home dads are still the freaks. I'm happy to fly my freak flag, while acknowledging that for most people, the structure of the economy and society reinforces expected gender roles and limits our ability to meet the needs of our children. In her report, "One Sick Child Away From Being Fired: When Opting Out is Not an Option," University of California Hastings law professor Joan C. Williams found that only 16 percent of working-class families enjoy the luxury of having one stay-at-home parent.

Williams discovered many, many examples of blue-collar workers (mostly women, but some men) who were fired for offenses like being three minutes late because of a child's asthma attack. For many moms and dads, staying home is not an option, and a "balance" between work and family is not possible. What white-collar workers gain in flexibility, they often lose in boundaries: How many of us have spent evenings and weekends massaging PowerPoints and spreadsheets?

And yet still we fight to carve out time for our kids. "None of us at-home fathers go into it in order to be some sort of social role model," says Stephen de las Heras, thirty-eight, a digital artist who lives in Manhattan and is the primary caregiver to his four-year-old son. "We don't deserve medals. At least not for that. If anything, the correct response from people would be a completely neutral one. But we do have to put up with some shit from the less enlightened crowd, and face some additional obstacles in a mom-centric world. For that, a pat on the back once in a while can be nice, but is not required."

Exactly. In my view, dads-at-home are significant primarily to the degree they are bellwethers of a wider change in the culture, toward more flexible definitions of masculinity and femininity. Thanks to feminism—which has tried to teach us to ride the shockwave created by massive economic change—women now have more choices. So do men.

When I was born in 1970, my parents debated only whether my mom would work or stay at home. "We opted for her to stay home," says my father, Dan. "That was the question of the day. The idea that a mother could have a career and be a mom was the radical thought of the time. The option for Dad to stay home was not considered. If it was, nobody told me, and the thought never entered my head." Since then, families have changed a great deal. In

1970, men spent three hours a week on childcare. In 2000, they spent seven hours a week taking care of kids—that's a 62 percent increase from 1995. The number of stay-at-home dads has grown steadily since the mid-1990s. Men are generally spending more and more time with kids, while the time women spend on childcare remains roughly constant at around thirteen hours a week. Meanwhile, the Bureau of Labor Statistics reports that since the start of the Great Recession in 2008, men with college degrees saw their median weekly earnings drop 3 percent while the income of women with degrees grew by 4.3 percent. Today, young women's pay exceeds that of their male peers in some metropolitan areas. Thanks in part to women's growing economic power, divorce has become normal, single motherhood has become viable, same-sex couples are starting families, and many heterosexual couples are deciding not to marry even after having children together. The twenty-first-century dad can be single, queer, straight, stay-at-home . . . she can even be a "lesbian dad" who earns the money that supports her wife and children. (If you doubt me, check out blogs like Lesbiandad.net or Icallherjohn.blogspot.com.)

Families are evolving. So are men and ideas of masculinity. Conservatives (and some feminists) argue that men are by nature conquerors, breadwinners, and emotional dolts. But when Canadian sociologist Andrea Doucet studied stay-at-home dads, what constantly surprised her about these fathers "were these clear and loud male voices speaking in what scholars would call a 'language of care' or an 'ethic of care' that embraces qualities of relationality, connections, interdependence, responsiveness, and responsibility." As numerous studies are revealing, it seems that biology is not destiny. "Could it be that when men speak in a language of care," writes Doucet in her book *Do Men Mother?*, "it creates a sense of social and political vertigo?"

In caring for Liko, never have I felt more secure in my masculinity; at the same time, never have I felt less "masculine." I'm learning, slowly, to let go of the link between my self-worth and the contribution I make in the paid workforce; more and more, I measure myself against women I see as successful mothers. Does that make me effeminate? Is there a reason why I should care? I'm not replacing my wife, who is Liko's mother. For seven or so hours a day, I'm simply adopting a role that in my father's day was automatically assigned to the biological female. In caregiving I have found enormous, vertiginous freedom.

In many respects, a man out in the middle of the afternoon with his toddler, who is known to neighbors and neighborhood shop clerks and waitresses as a "Mr. Mom," is a man in drag, and queer in the most political sense of the term. That's fine with me. Yes, I've gotten criticism from relatives ("A man is supposed to support his family, and a woman is supposed to stay home"). I've also gotten sneering reactions to my blog and articles about stay-at-home daddyhood. "It's hard to believe this dude was capable of procreating," writes one blogger about me. "I'm thinking a turkey baster was involved." I know that I'm facing an uphill battle when I get back into the full-time job market. I'd be lying if I claimed that I have no doubts.

But mostly, I don't care what anybody says. When Liko and I are blasting Yo La Tengo or the Strokes or Blondie (his favorites; he has a thing for punk, new wave, and indie pop; anything that bounces, really) and I'm dancing and he's careening down the hall, arms flailing, hopping from one foot to the other, and then he runs up and hugs my leg and yells "Dada!"—life can't get any better. I helped make a new life, and that's staggering: a new human being, and a new life for me. I don't want to give him to a nanny or daycare; as much as possible, I want to take care of him and see him grow.

I'm not alone. We're seeing more and more fathers speak out about their caregiving responsibilities in blogs and books like Michael Chabon's *Manhood for Amateurs* or Joel Stein's *Man Made*. Their work, which is often very funny, helps create a culture of care and a new image of the good father. For decades, fathers have been told they're worthless, or violent, or absent. Now guys are providing positive examples, to reflect what's best in fatherhood back to men and boys. Perhaps as the process goes on, we will see more dads fight for public policies that will help them to be the fathers they want to be.

But here's the really interesting question: What impact will our choices have on the next generation? When Yale psychiatrist Kyle Pruett studied kids raised by stay-at-home dads, he found that they didn't seem to care all that much about fixed gender roles. "Gender polarization seemed a marginal, rather than central, issue for these youngsters on the threshold of their adolescence," Pruett writes. "Their equanimity concerning gender issues in their peer relations was striking because of the usual anxiety and conflict at this stage." The kids were drawn to peers who shared their views on gender roles. "None of my girlfriends want to be housewives," says one girl. "None of my guy friends want nothing to do with their kids—they think kids are cool."

And so it goes, from one generation to the next. Liko might not see "mothering" and "fathering" the way I do. If current trends continue, there could be a huge generation gap between us and our children, with many unexpected consequences. Revolutions—maybe I should say evolutions—have a way of leaving the revolutionaries behind.

JUDGING FATHERS: THE CASE FOR GENDER-NEUTRAL STANDARDS

Donald N.S. Unger

It was Sunday night and my daughter Rebecca and I were heading north on the Merritt Parkway, through Connecticut, back home to Massachusetts, after a weekend of visiting friends and family in and around New York City. Harry Chapin's song, "Cat's in the Cradle" was on the radio.

Rebecca was eight at the time, and I was in the middle of two years of teaching as a visiting professor in the English department at the University at Albany, SUNY, some 140 miles from where we lived. It was a five-hour, round-trip commute; a trip that I made about twice a week. Any time I told people where I was teaching and where I lived, they asked if—or sometimes simply assumed that—I was living in Albany half the week. It was a question that always irritated me. Would they make the same assumption about a mother with a young child?

I turned up the volume on the radio and told Rebecca to listen closely to the song. When it was over, I asked her what she thought it was about.

"That the father is sad he didn't see his son grow up?" Rebecca asked, only a little tentatively.

"That's right," I told her, proud, like any parent, that my daughter intelligently answered the question, even if I was the only one there to hear what she had to say.

Rebecca paused.

Then she said, "That's why you don't have an apartment in Albany, right? Because you don't want to be like the man in the song."

"That's right," I said again, working on keeping the emotion out of my voice, concentrating on the road ahead of me.

"I'm glad," Rebecca said.

"Me, too."

"Did you get the idea from the song?" she asked me.

"No," I told her.

That Rebecca was good at analyzing this song's lyrics made sense: I've been talking, writing, and complaining about fatherhood issues since before she was born. But I'll get to that.

It also made sense that we were having this conversation in the car; that's where a good deal of modern-day, parent–child relating seems to take place. When Rebecca was younger and my wife Cynthia was working toward tenure—both during and after two years or so that I was the stay-at-home parent—my daughter and I regularly drove that route to New York and often discussed these things. Sometimes music was the trigger; sometimes it was something more basic: like rest stop bathroom facilities.

When Rebecca was three-and-a-half—with the *pro bono* assistance of Deborah Ellis, a law professor at New York University and former legal counsel for the National Organization for Women's Legal Defense and Education Fund[1]—I got the Mobil Oil Corporation to comply with state law in Connecticut and New York and install changing tables in the men's rooms in the rest stops along Route 15, which encompasses the Wilbur Cross, the Merritt, and the Hutchinson River Parkways. Justice grinds slowly, of course; by the time this was done, my daughter was already toilet trained. Nevertheless, I take a measure of satisfaction in this accomplishment to this day, every time we make that trip and I see those changing tables.

It's worth noting that federal law offers no cause of action in such a situation. Achieving gender equity in college athletics is a federal matter—with which I have no quarrel. Whether fathers can change their children's diapers indoors while traveling, however, is a "state's rights" matter with which the federal government chooses not to trifle.

For months after the case, any time I took Rebecca into a men's bathroom, she would look around and then ask me, "Are you going to make them put a changing table in here, too?"

I would if I could and I don't think that's something I'm alone in.

Professor Ellis had a running start in taking on Mobil on my behalf: A few years earlier, her husband, also an attorney, had taken similar action against the Lord & Taylor department store chain for *their* failure to have changing tables in men's rooms.

He won, too.

It may be that the tide is beginning to turn, in terms of how we see fathers and how fathers see themselves, in how we talk about parenting, and how we represent parents in the media, in popular art, in everyday language.

As far as I'm concerned, these changes can't come fast enough; I've been waiting for them almost all my life.

When I was a teenager in the 1970s, the gender messages being broadcast were decidedly mixed. On the one hand, the feminist movement was a force to be reckoned with. Women and men who wanted change—both full civil and economic rights for women and also a more comprehensive fracturing of gender roles over all—were visible, vocal, and, in many ways, ascendant. The Equal Rights Amendment was working its way through state legislatures; many people thought it was on its inevitable way to ratification.

As a teenage boy who did babysitting in addition to mowing lawns and washing cars, these issues were directly relevant to me. There were people who were definitely happy to see a boy taking care of children. Yet, while babysitting, I still received the occasional phone call from a grandparent or friend of the family for whom I was working that clearly indicated that a male voice claiming to be the babysitter was reason for some alarm.

Now and then, I was quizzed on difficult things like the child's name, as if I might have been a slightly dim home invader who had yet to learn that it was poor form to pick up the phone, mid-rampage.

My family circumstances also made these issues more concrete than abstract. My mother was a Zionist socialist who, on graduating high school, left New York City for Israel shortly after the declaration of statehood. In part, she said in later years, she was looking for a living arrangement that dispensed with a good deal of the gendered division of labor. A few years of living on a kibbutz convinced her that Israel was not to be the home of this, then-radical, alternative. She returned to New York and took a job as a public health nurse.

My parents divorced when I was in my early teens, and my younger sister and I stayed with my father. I remember the theory that we were each to make dinner two nights per week; I don't remember clearly how cleaning chores were divided up, although I have some dim memory of charts. This system did not work smoothly or easily, but I don't believe we were undernourished. And if the house was somewhat dingy, and at times in disarray, I don't recall filth at the level of health hazard. So somehow we must have done the cooking and cleaning ourselves, with my father actively participating, as well as playing the crucial, supervisory role.

In the larger society, during the same period, while there was intense cultural and political battling going on, there was also genuine and growing support for women to take on "non-traditional" work roles, which at that time still meant almost anything outside of secretarial work, teaching elementary school, or nursing.

On the domestic front, things were beginning to change, as well—in part as a result of increased workforce participation by middle-class, white women. Intermittent glimpses of men doing housework, cooking, and taking care of children were visible, like a broadcast television station at the edge of the signal, flickering through the interference. But those changes among some men seemed at least as controversial as women moving into the workplace, if not more so.

John Irving's novel *The World According to Garp* came out in 1978, when I was in high school. The title character was a writer, a stay-at-home father, and a great cook. Sounded cool to me. But to a lot of people Garp seemed to be more wacky than admirable, more literary magic than realistic option.

John Lennon was holed up in The Dakota at this time, having essentially given up making music to bake bread and take care of his son Sean. Some people saw this as a positive model; I certainly did. But others interpreted the way that he was living his life as just another example of how he had been emasculated by Yoko Ono. There were ugly strains of misogyny and racism; she was a "Dragon Lady," in this view, who first broke up the Beatles and then broke John's spirit. How else to explain his choice to care for his son rather than continue his career? How else to explain the famous photo of Yoko, lying down, clothed in black, John curled against her, naked and fetal?

On television, there were commercials that depicted men performing domestic labor. But I am hard pressed to remember any which showed this in a positive light. For the most part, in my memory, these commercials boil down to riffs on a stereotypical exchange; the sort that we continue to see today.

Open on:

Wide shot. Suburban household. Day. An inept father is standing in the kitchen, the sink piled high with dirty dishes, something burning on the stove, a two-foot dike of detergent foam leading the way to the clothes washer, around the corner, in the laundry room.

Father (yelling to his wife, off screen): Honey, should I take the kids out of the dryer now?

Cut to:

Close up. Suburban household. Day. Wife's face as she surveys the mess, from the kitchen doorway. A mixture of amusement and disdain at his incompetence clouds her features before she moves in to displace him and restore order.

Popular culture critic Mark Crispin Miller has dubbed these sorts of scenarios examples of pseudo-feminism. A focus on male domestic incompetence gives a surface appearance of recognizing the power and authority of women. But one doesn't have to read too deeply into the subtext to see that the message is neither liberatory nor egalitarian.

What conclusion can one draw from such a scene, other than it would be sheer madness to "allow" men to continue to contribute to cooking, cleaning, and childcare? It implies a willingness on the part of men to do such work, but quickly demonstrates that we are simply not up to the task. The message seems to be, "We bow to your superior skill. Now, back to the kitchen, Honey."

What much of this suggests is that I shouldn't have been so quick to dismiss Rebecca's question about whether my behavior was cued by Harry Chapin's song. It's a song I grew up listening to. And of course—in addition to family, economics, politics, and a whole knot of other influences—books, language, advertising, television, and music *did* do a lot to shape my ideas about what kind of parent a man should or could be. How could they not have?

Today, we're at a funny moment, an interesting juncture. We may be on the cusp of fundamentally—and to my mind, positively—shifting to a much more open definition of family and of caregiving. I *hope* we are broadening what is possible—or, perhaps more accurately, what is *acceptable*—for a man to do with his life.

In the near future we may see the home open up to men in the same way that the workplace began to open up to women in the 1970s. I believe this would be a good thing, for men, for women, for children. But I would never assume that change is always easy nor that it is ever neat. We still have minefields to cross, the nature/nurture debate high on the list.

It was clear as soon as our daughter was old enough to navigate the playground that I was willing to allow her greater physical risks than was my wife. Children periodically fall down and I don't think that's always a bad thing. In many ways, it's an important learning tool, far more effective than any safety lecture that I could give.

I wasn't being callous or indifferent when I gave Rebecca a bit more freedom. I didn't walk away from her when she was attempting something new and difficult, but when she was a toddler on the playground my hand was more likely to be six inches away from her; my wife more often remained in direct contact.

I've never felt that we had any meaningful philosophical differences there. I don't complain that my wife is smothering Rebecca; my wife doesn't accuse me of neglect. But our approach to parenting is clearly different. Go to any playground in America and you'll probably see a similar parenting split, often along gender lines.

Observations of this kind lead some people to argue that male–female differences have innate, biological sources. Others ascribe differing parenting styles to nurture rather than nature. We might be more confident about being able to change our gender roles if we believe these parenting tendencies are learned through our culture rather than being hard-wired, inborn differences.

I don't have the answer. And I have no interest in picking a side.

Instead of trying to resolve the nature–nurture debate, what I want to advocate instead is respect for personal choice and individual difference. If geneticists find a variety of genes that they have been hunting for some time now—the genius gene, the criminal gene, the gay gene, the mothering gene, the super-athlete gene, the warrior gene—will this really put a smooth end to a variety of ideological and sociological debates about women, men, and parenting that have been roiling societies for generations?

It seems unlikely.

We do better to look at actions in context and judge them apart from labels, to look at what is being done, rather than who is doing it. In observing a parent on a playground then, the question becomes not "Is that child being maternally smothered or paternally neglected?" but, rather, "Does the level of attention being given to the child fall within reasonable parenting practice?"

In other words, *Is that person taking care of the child?*

Not a perfect solution. This approach loses some of the warmth and specificity of either "maternal" or "paternal" and has a slight utilitarian tinge to it.

But what I'm asking for as a fully engaged father is essentially the same thing that women have been fighting for in the professional sphere for forty years or more: a gender-neutral standard of assessment.

Judge me on whether or not I am an effective parent, not on whether or not I'm a pretty good parent *for a man.*

1. Now known as Legal Momentum.

WHAT'S WRONG WITH FATHERS' RIGHTS?

Michael Flood

Twenty years ago I joined my first anti-sexist men's group. I've had a passionate commitment to profeminism ever since, nurtured through men's anti-violence activism, Women's and Gender Studies, editing a profeminist magazine, and now pursuing a career in feminist scholarship. Men's violence against women is an obvious area for anti-sexist men's activism, as it's one of the bluntest and most brutal forms of gender inequality. I've organized campaigns in groups like Men Against Sexual Assault, run workshops in schools, helped run a national White Ribbon Campaign, designed violence prevention programs for athletes and others, and done research and writing on violence against women. But I've also been forced to critique and confront anti-feminist men in so-called men's rights and fathers' rights groups. Their efforts are having a growing influence on community understandings of, and policy responses to, gender issues.

MEN'S RIGHTS AND FATHERS' RIGHTS

Any man who publicly supports feminism will find himself up against negative stereotypes of, myths about, and hostile responses to feminism, feminists, and the men who support them. "Men's rights" and "fathers' rights" groups represent this in concentrated and toxic form.

The fathers' rights movement argues that fathers are subjected to systematic discrimination as men and fathers, in a system that is biased toward women and dominated by feminists. Fathers' rights groups overlap with men's rights groups and both represent an organized backlash to feminism. Fathers' rights and men's rights groups are the anti-feminist wing of the men's movement, a network of men's groups and organizations mobilized around gender issues.

Two experiences bring most men (and women) to the fathers' rights movement. The first is deeply painful marriage breakups and custody battles; the second is when non-custodial fathers are dissatisfied with loss of contact with their children or with regimes of child support. Fathers' rights groups are characterized by anger and blame toward ex-partners and the legal system, believing that both have deprived men of their rights to contact with their children and to be free from financial child support obligations.

LIES AND DENIAL

All this matters to profeminist men because men's rights and fathers' rights advocates and organizations are doing harm to the causes in which we believe. They are our political opponents. These anti-feminist networks are hindering progress toward gender equality, and in some cases, they're even making things go backward. Fathers' rights groups are well-organized advocates for changes in family law, and vocal opponents of feminist perspectives and achievements on interpersonal violence. And they're having some successes. I'll return to this in a moment.

I try to push feminist and profeminist perspectives in the public domain, by giving media interviews, writing op-eds, making speeches, and producing accessible information like fact sheets and articles for the lay reader. As part of this, I've critiqued the claims made by anti-feminist men's groups. I also monitor their activities and agendas, by checking on their websites and reading their literature. And sometimes, I've engaged in direct debate. I used to go to the mainstream men's movement events around Australia, large men's festivals and men's gatherings of 100 to 200 men. Committed anti-feminist men are regular participants in these. Profeminist men are a much smaller minority and anti-feminist or, at best, non-feminist notions are part and parcel of the men's liberation perspectives shared by most participants in the men's movement. More recently, I've posted comments on fathers' rights websites, and responded to others' postings on the blog of the Australian White Ribbon Campaign.

I don't think that every profeminist man has to engage in direct debate with men's rights and fathers' rights activists. But we all have to deal with anti-feminist reactions and beliefs in society in general, as well as the pernicious influence of these more organized agendas. We should know what they're saying, what's wrong with it, and have other ways of responding to the issues they claim to address.

So, what's wrong with men's rights? Above all, anti-feminist men's perspectives are based on a profound denial of the systematic gender inequalities that privilege many men and disadvantage many women. Yes, some men are disadvantaged and some women are privileged, but these have more to do with other social divisions—class, race, age, and so on—than they do with gender. Yes, there are times when individual men are harmed or cheated by individual women—we are all human, after all, but such instances do not support anti-feminist men's claim that men are the "new Jews," suffering under what they call a global "feminazi" regime. Men's and fathers' rights groups offer a bizarre and fundamentally inaccurate portrayal of feminism as anti-male and fail to see the enormous hope for and goodwill toward men which it embodies. Fathers' rights groups tell lies about the extent of women's false allegations of abuse or domestic violence. And both men's rights and fathers' rights advocates make dodgy claims of gender symmetry in domestic violence based on studies using problematic and much-criticized tools of measurement and highly selective readings of the literature.

Violence is a key area of fathers' rights activism because it's a common issue in family law proceedings. We know that the time around separation and divorce is one of the riskiest in terms of women's subjection to violence by an intimate partner or ex-partner. More widely, violence against women is a confronting example of gender inequality and thus central to struggles over the meaning and shape of contemporary gender relations. Violence is one of the most worrying areas in which men's and fathers' rights groups are having an impact.

FATHERS, VIOLENCE, AND FAMILY LAW

There are three ways in which the fathers' rights movement has had a damaging impact on the field of violence against women. These are readily apparent in Australia, and evident in the United States and elsewhere as well. First, fathers' rights groups have negatively influenced laws and policies that affect the victims and perpetrators of men's violence against women, particularly when it comes to cases of separation, divorce, and child custody.

Above all, fathers' *contact* with children has been privileged over children's *safety* from violence. In large part due to publicity efforts by fathers' rights groups, an uncritical assumption that children's contact with both parents is necessary now pervades the courts and the media. In Australia, the Family Court's new principle of the "right to contact" is overriding its principle of the right to "safety from violence." In short, family law increasingly is being guided by two mistaken beliefs: that all children see contact with both parents as in their best interests in every case, and that a violent father is better than no father at all. Greater numbers of parents who are the victims of violence are being subject to further violence and harassment by abusive ex-partners, while children are being pressured into contact with abusive or violent parents. The Court now is more likely to make interim orders for children's unsupervised contact in cases involving domestic violence or child abuse, to use hand-over arrangements rather than suspend contact until trial, and to make orders for joint residence where there is a high level of conflict between the separated parents and one parent strongly objects to shared residence.

Second, fathers' rights groups have had a negative impact on community understandings of violence against women and children. They have discredited female and child victims of violence by spreading the lie that women routinely make false accusations of child abuse to gain advantage in family law proceedings and to arbitrarily deny their ex-partners access to the children. The Australian evidence is that allegations of child abuse are rare, false allegations are rare, and false allegations are made by fathers and mothers at equal rates. In any case, allegations of child abuse rarely result in the denial of parental contact.

Fathers' rights groups also claim that women routinely make up allegations of domestic violence to gain advantage in family law cases and use protection orders for vindictive reasons rather than any real experience or fear of violence. Again, Australian research finds instead that women living with domestic violence often do not take out protection orders at all, and when they do, it is only as a last resort in the face of severe violence.

Another dimension of the fathers' rights movement's damaging impact on community perceptions is to do with men's versus women's violence. Advocates encourage the mistaken belief that domestic violence is gender-equal. I've debunked this claim in detail elsewhere, but here is a lightning-quick critique:

It's simply not true that men and women assault each other at equal rates and with equal effects. To support the claim that domestic violence is gender-symmetrical, advocates draw almost exclusively on studies using a measurement tool called the Conflict Tactics Scale (CTS). But anti-feminist advocates use CTS results only selectively. More importantly, the CTS is a very poor method for measuring domestic violence: it asks only about violent acts, ignoring their initiation, intensity, context, history, consequences, or meaning.

Let's say that I've been systematically abusing my wife over the last year. I've hit her, I've constantly put her down, I've controlled her movements, and I've forced her into sex. And once, in the midst of another of my violent attacks on her, she hit me back. My various strategies of power and control have left her physically bruised and emotionally battered. And her one act of self-defense just made me laugh. But according to the CTS, we've both committed at least one violent act. So the CTS counts us as equivalent. (Note here that, if our positions were reversed and it was my *wife* who'd been systematically abusing *me*, the CTS would still be a poor measure of the violence. It's crappy either way.)

There's a whole mountain of evidence—crime victimization surveys, police statistics, and hospital data—that domestic violence is not gender-neutral. Men do under-report, but no more than, and probably less than, women. Yes, some men are victims of domestic violence, including by female partners. And there are important contrasts in women's and men's experiences of domestic violence. When it comes to violence by partners or ex-partners, women are far more likely than men to be subjected to frequent, prolonged, and extreme violence, to sustain injuries, to be subjected to a range of controlling strategies, to fear for their lives, to be sexually assaulted, to experience post-separation violence, and to use violence only in self-defense.

There are obvious signs that the fathers' rights movement's attention to domestic violence against men is not motivated by a genuine concern for male victimization. The movement focuses on domestic violence when the great majority of the violence inflicted on men is not by female partners but by *other men*. For example, a four-year study of admissions to the Emergency Department of a Missouri hospital found that among the over 8000 men who had been assaulted and injured, only 45 men were injured by their intimate female partners or ex-partners, representing 0.55 per cent of male assault visits and 0.05 percent of all male visits. Boys and men are most at risk of physical harm from other boys and men.

In addition, the efforts of the fathers' rights movement to modify public responses to the victims and perpetrators of violence harm female and male victims of domestic violence alike. This is the third kind of impact the movement has had on interpersonal violence. The fathers' rights movement tries to erode the protections available to victims of domestic violence and to boost the rights and freedoms of alleged perpetrators. The Lone Fathers' Association and other groups argue that claims of violence or abuse should be made under oath, they should require police or hospital records as proof, and people who make allegations that are not then substantiated should be subject to criminal prosecution. They call for similar limitations to do with protection orders. Fathers' rights groups also attempt to undermine the ways in which domestic violence is treated as criminal behavior. They emphasize the need to keep the family together, call for the greater use of mediation and counseling, and reject pro-arrest policies.

These changes would represent a profound erosion of the protections and legal redress available to the victims of violence, whether female or male. This agenda betrays the fact that the concern for male victims of domestic violence often professed by fathers' rights groups is hollow. Fathers' rights groups often respond to issues of domestic and sexual violence from the point of view of the perpetrator. And they respond in the same way as actual male perpetrators: They minimize and deny the extent of this violence, blame the victim, and explain the violence as mutual or reciprocal. Fathers' rights advocates have expressed understanding or justification for men who use violence against women and children in the context of family law proceedings. And, ironically, they use men's violence to demonstrate how victimized men are by the family law system. Fathers' rights groups also attack media and community campaigns focused on men's violence against women and harass community sector and women's organizations that respond to the victims of violence.

Yes, male victims of domestic violence deserve the same support as female victims. And we don't need to pretend that they total 50 percent of victims to establish this. And we're certainly not doing them any favors by attacking the systems and services set up to support and protect them or the women who put the issue on the public agenda in the first place.

SUPPORTING FATHERS

Men who are going through a separation or divorce certainly deserve services and support. But they're not well served by fathers' rights groups. Fathers' rights groups stifle men's healing processes, constrain and harm their relations with their children, and directly compromise the wellbeing of children themselves. First, many groups offer their members identities based only in victimhood, centered on hostility toward and blame of the legal system and their ex-partners, and colored by misogynist norms. Such approaches fix men in positions of anger and hostility, rather than helping them to heal. Some groups encourage their members to engage in malicious, destructive, and unproductive legal strategies.

There is no doubt that many of the individual men in fathers' rights groups want a greater involvement in their children's lives, but these groups have done little to foster fathers' positive involvement in children's lives, whether before or after separation and divorce. The fathers' rights movement focuses on fathers' "rights" rather than the actual care of children. It prioritizes formal principles of equality over positive parenting and the wellbeing of women and children. It conflates children's welfare with parental equality, ignores actual caregiving divisions of labor, and neglects the real obstacles to shared parenting both in couple families and after separation or divorce. Many fathers' rights groups seem more concerned with re-establishing fathers' authority and control over their children's and ex-partners' lives than with actual involvement with children. They neglect the real challenges of maintaining or setting up shared parenting after divorce, arguing for one-size-fits-all approaches based on joint custody, which won't work for most families.

Fathers' rights groups also have been willing to compromise children's wellbeing. They've tried to force parental contact on children regardless of children's wishes and wellbeing, to reduce non-resident parents' obligations to financially support their children (although some aspects of current child support regimes *are* unjust), and to undermine the protections and support available to child victims of abuse and domestic violence. Through their hostile and misogynist depictions of resident mothers and their attempts to control mothers' management of finances, parenting, and contact, fathers' rights groups also have fueled interparental conflict, leading to more problems with contact and further stress for children.

BEATING THE BACKLASH

The achievements of the fathers' rights movement are already putting women, children, and even men at greater risk of violence and abuse. The fathers' rights movement has exacerbated our culture's systematic silencing and blaming of victims of violence and hampered efforts to respond effectively to the victims and perpetrators of violence. Fathers' groups have done little to encourage fathers' positive involvement in parenting, whether before or after divorce, and in some ways they've even made things worse. More generally, men's rights and fathers' rights groups are hampering progress toward gender equality or pushing it backward.

However, the new politics of fatherhood has not been entirely captured by the fathers' rights movement. There is potential to foster men's positive and non-violent involvement in parenting and families. Key resources for realizing the progressive potential of contemporary fatherhood politics include the widespread imagery of the nurturing father, community intolerance for violence against women, growing policy interest in addressing divisions of labor in child care and domestic work, and men's own investments in positive parenting.

Responses to separated fathers should be father-friendly, accountable, and oriented toward encouraging positive and ongoing involvement in their children's lives. We should be working to respond to separated fathers, not only because of the emotional and practical needs they have, and not only to encourage their ongoing and positive involvement with children, but also because doing so will lessen the recruitment of separated fathers into the fathers' rights movement. In other words, providing compassionate and con-structive services for separated fathers is important in part because it diverts them from participation in fathers' rights networks. And doing this is desirable because such networks are harmful for law and public policy, for women and children, and for separated men themselves.

At the same time, we must confront the dangerous ambitions and dis-honest claims of the men's and fathers' rights backlash. We need to directly subvert these groups' agendas, spread critiques of their false accusations, and respond in constructive and accountable ways to the fathers (and mothers) undergoing separation and divorce. We must step up efforts to engage men in positive ways, building partnerships with supportive men and men's groups and with the women's movements. All this is part of a broader profeminist effort, to build a world of gender justice.

Part V

Men and Feminism

INTRODUCTION

the problem with most movements is
that they
move alone
a house divided
—S.A. Griffin, "A House Divided"[1]

F eminism is a practice, a perspective, and a process. It involves constructing new frameworks for understanding politics and power while simultane-ously setting concrete goals for change.[2] Feminism is a theory that puts gender at the center of how we see the world. It is a social and political movement interested in improving the conditions of all people, in particular women. The question is this: If feminism is primarily concerned about the status of women, then what is—or what ought to be—men's role in this movement? Is there room in the picture for men?

The following six essays explore sexism, harassment, oppression, and equality. They investigate the intersecting impact of gender, race, nation, and sexuality. They raise questions about men's relation to the feminist movement as allies, activists, and observers. They talk about how to stand up and get involved while avoiding the pitfalls of paternalist protectionism.

Some ask whether or not feminism is a title that suits men well, even when they are committed to gender justice. These debates over terminology are nothing new (and they are not limited to men). In the United States in the 1940s and 1950s, for example, identifying as feminist

> risked evoking images of being militant, racist, a sexual prude, bourgeois, strident, or just plain selfish. Similar assumptions are still made today . . . Some men who recognize the problems of gender repression, misogyny, sexism, and the politics of domination take a stand by identifying as feminists. Others call themselves pro-feminists, feminist allies, [or] antisexist activists.[3]

Ernesto Aguilar, an anti-racist organizer who identifies as pro-feminist, explains that he does so primarily because "women have paid a tremendous price throughout history for standing in support of feminism, and men just have not done that to the [same] extent." Because we live in a patriarchy, Aguilar cautions, "men's voices oftentimes get privileged in movements, and the danger of men co-opting a struggle women have led and sacrificed so much for is very real":

> As a man of color, I have to see it in the frame of how the privileged often treat questions of privilege. For example, in the racial context, many advocate colorblindness, this parallel notion that communicates in essence we combat discrimination by treating every person's stake in a movement as equal. The problem with stating that feminism is about liberating men too, and shifting this conversation about whether someone is for or against excluding people, is that we validate a false notion: that men have an identical, practical stake in women's freedom as women, who themselves are targets every day. A white person's stake in racial justice is at its most basic starkly different than that of a person of color, and similarly a man's stake in a movement for women's liberation is different too. Men especially need to be aware of and respect that distinction.[4]

Men who are feminist allies actively support gender justice. Regardless of whether these men engage the title "feminist," the movement for gender and social justice benefits from men's participation. Because most women and men live among each other, without men's active engagement with gender justice, efforts to solve the problems are ultimately limited. If men do not take active roles in resolving the politics of housework, male violence against women, hiring and wage disparities, or gender bias in the media, then women are talking into a feminist echo chamber.

As things stand, however, there is a tendency to conflate the term "feminist" with women. Given this inclination, how we can better understand and imagine new possibilities for men and feminism? We need to do so because assuming that feminism is only a woman's problem raises serious existential questions (Can I be a guy and be a feminist?) and pragmatic questions in regard to political strategy and activism (Who will set the agenda, who will do the talking, who will make the coffee?). It's important to face these questions head on. Feminist strategy is stifled in achieving its goals of gender justice if it remains an exclusionary movement based on essentialist assumptions about who can join the movement, let alone if it is suspicious of men who do. Linking feminism with women and basing feminist knowledge production on identity is problematic, reinforcing the same dichotomies and gendered traits of masculinity that feminism claims to oppose or wants to subvert.[5]

As long as feminism *itself* gets lumped with women, and as long as we continue to suppose that women know something special *as women* and in particular as *feminist* women, then sex/gender identity as the foundation for feminist politics and theorizing remains problematic by virtue of placing women within feminism and leaving men on the outside.[6] Melding masculinity with men, and femininity with women—and femin*ism* with women only—leads to the assumption that the term "feminist men" is oxymoronic. According to this train of thought, as Michael Kimmel puts it, a feminist man is either (a) not a "real" man or (b) cannot be a real feminist.[7] These misconceptions keep intact the gender binaries that feminism sees as underscoring the very power and privilege inequities it seeks to eradicate. In writing about their perspectives on and experiences with feminism, the authors in this section direct our thinking away from these binaries. Yet at the same time that men in feminism has advantages, there is the possibility that a feminism with men will lose its focus on women.

The puzzle is this: How can we (a) make room in feminism to account for men as "our comrades in struggle,"[8] while (b) retaining a central focus on women, yet (c) avoid reinscribing the gender binaries that feminism-as-female invokes? To borrow awkwardly from Charlotte Bunch, what would it mean to feminism if we "added men and stirred"? The essays in this section consider what it looks like when men promote women's issues as strategic political allies, and when men use feminist tools for enhancing gender justice for all.

Feminism benefits from men's inclusion in several ways. First, including men as feminist allies helps break down a gender dichotomy where feminist-equals-female, and where it therefore becomes extremely strange or weird to think of a man as being a feminist. Similarly, thinking of feminist-as-female excludes genderqueer or intersex people, which is inconsistent with the principles of gender justice. There is also a practical advantage: There is strength in numbers and feminism could use more allies.[9] Third, there is an enriching effect that comes from men and women defending feminist views together. Feminist men can be unsettling to detractors and can help shift the terms of dialogue.

A fourth benefit of men participating in feminist politics is that there are times when men, because of past involvement with sexist practices and institutions, such as street harassment, gender discrimination, or violence against women, can be helpful in questioning, exposing, or critiquing these practices. Finally, including men in our conceptualization of feminism helps build a politic that is broadened by the integration of interlocking oppressions.

Because of the overlapping experience and impact of race and class, many black women—and other women of color—have been unwilling to ignore men in the community in favor of a feminism that focuses solely on women *as women*.[10] Patricia Hill Collins writes that black women expressed ambivalence about feminism during the 1960s and early 1970s less because they rejected feminism's core ideas, but rather because they hesitated "to work with white feminist groups exclusively on gender issues while neglecting issues of class and race."[11]

Feminism today exists under this hangover. Feminism has had to face its history of separatism and internal racist dynamics, a history that overlooks important strategic and ideological alliances between women and men. It is simply not true that all men are "always dominant over all women in all things"[12] at all times and places, and in all cultural contexts. Nor is it true that male domination is the only social justice issue at hand. When men reflect on experience and politics to construct feminist perspectives on gender and social justice, as they do in this section, we can more effectively respond to the challenges and demands of intersectionality. An expanded, male-inclusive feminism can help account for issues of race, class, ethnicity, sexual orientation, and gender. This facilitates alliances within and across communities. Coalition building and dialogue across differences is critical to feminist development.[13]

Another way to think of feminism as a politic that has room for men is to conceptualize feminism as a movement committed to issues of global concern, domestic improvement, access to rights, and freedom from political and personal oppression. In *The Fire This Time*, Vivien Labaton and Dawn Lundy Martin define contemporary feminism as the process of "women and men doing social justice work while using a gender lens."[14] Following Labaton and Martin's lead, feminism clearly has room for men without necessarily losing its focus on women. Current threads of feminist theory (especially those informed by postmodern and queer theory), tend to resist essentialist notions of womanhood and instead complicate what we mean by sex and gender. With this sort of feminist analysis, "masculinity" stands to be critically problematized, just as concepts of "femininity" have been. This can be done without depoliticizing concepts of subjugation, domination, or oppression by claims that sexism affects all equally.

Still, there are legitimate reasons to be cautious about men as feminists. Some, of course, fear that including men's perspectives might simply erase women from feminism, or at least diminish their central role. In *Feminism Without Women: Culture and Criticism in a "Post-Feminist" Age*, Tania Modleski argues that when men become a feminist mouthpiece, we dangerously re-contain women within a masculine universalism by "returning critical practice to a 'pre-feminist world'" in which men produce knowledge.[15] A second reason for caution is that feminism may be co-opted to focus on the ways in which men are oppressed by masculinity instead of on the physical and material manifestations of gender inequality like rape, domestic violence, and wage disparity. Third, celebrating men as feminist partners may inadvertently reinforce the idea that if men are doing something, it must be good although feminism has long recognized this troubled assumption and insisted on the legitimacy of women's perspectives and demands. Fourth, some might be suspicious that feminist men are just cashing in on the opportunity to promote their own self-interests (e.g., getting academic jobs or dates with women). As sociologist and masculinities expert Michael Messner notes, it is important that men's ongoing contributions are politicized and not relegated only to the realm of individual, personal venture.

The essays included in this section are not self-serving apologies for reactionary men's rights. They are not exposés on men as victims. They do not invoke the so-called crisis of masculinity that alarmist pundits claim is afflicting boys and men today.[16] The authors in this section, instead, consider the issues of feminism and gender justice by drawing on their personal experience and in doing so expose important political concerns.

Brandon Arber, a law student and former college athlete, recalls the derision and negative reactions from guy friends when they found out he was taking women's studies courses. Arber defines feminism as opposing rape, abuse, and discrimination against women and girls. To Arber, feminism is about improving conditions for all by erasing apathy. Raised to believe that fighting for women's rights is synonymous with fighting injustice in general, the idea that men can be feminist is, Arber claims, "Just Common Sense."

In "Why I Am Not a Feminist," Haji Shearer explains why he rejects the term. A social worker from Massachusetts, Shearer is professionally committed to improving gender equality and healthy masculinity in the black community. He suggests that "healthy manhood advocates for the equal rights and responsibilities of women and men." Shearer's essay raises important issues about race and feminism, and "how race consciousness and feminism can both converge and be at odds."[17] Yet because Shearer has good reason not to describe himself as a feminist, this prompts us to consider whether it is the feminist title or one's political intent that is the more important.

When Greg Bortnichak was in college he worked at Starbucks foaming lattes and brewing coffee. This job brought a steady stream of customers his way, a microcosm of the social universe Bortnichak was studying in school. Bortnichak explains that, for him, feminism could include many things like working to change unjust laws, or eliminating damaging media stereotypes. But in "The Starbucks Intervention," Bortnichak makes the political personal as he deals with misogynist customers, and sexist and racist co-workers.

Amit Taneja grew up in India, later moved to Canada, and now lives in the United States. A "poor, immigrant, big-boned, non-Christian, gay person-of-color," Taneja draws from a broad, transnational experience in describing his perspectives on masculinity, sexuality, identity, oppression, and power. Taneja's essay, "From Oppressor to Activist: Reflections of a Feminist Journey," concludes with a demand for action in which he challenges readers to make a personal and political commitment to social justice activism.

In "Abandoning the Barricades: or How I Became a Feminist," masculinities scholar and anti-sexism activist Michael S. Kimmel describes the origins of his gender awareness. Written in 1975, Kimmel's essay reflects back to his experience transferring from an all-male college to join the first men attending Vassar. One of the oldest women's colleges in the United States, Vassar College became coeducational in 1969. This experience transformed

Kimmel's relationship with women while providing him with new ways to deal with men. Looking back now, more than thirty-two years later, Kimmel metaphorically turns to see who is coming up behind him in the quest for gender justice. He is encouraged to see generations of young men mobilizing in support of gender equality.

Rob Okun's "Confessions of a Premature Pro-Feminist" recalls his involvement with the antiwar movement opposing U.S. involvement in Vietnam. While becoming politically active during the early 1970s, Okun sees how discrimination against women didn't just happen "out there," but also was present within seemingly progressive, activist circles. This spark of awareness drew Okun into a lifelong commitment to profeminist activism and social change. Now the Director of the Men's Resource Center for Change, based in Amherst, Massachussets, Okun writes, "despite media reports smugly belittling activism as just a phase in a young person's life," the movement for social justice is alive and well and "worth tapping into over the course of a lifetime."

Feminists include all those who identify the unequal and unjust distributions of power and resources as a problem. The inclusion of men in the feminist agenda can be strengthening for each of us, as these authors clearly show. Those who identify with feminist politics and perspectives share the perception that gender disadvantage occurs systematically, even if they lack consensus about the solutions.[18] Men's participation will require a political and ethical commitment based on recognizing "the need to eradicate the underlying cultural basis and causes of sexism and other forms of group oppression."[19] Understanding how power works in terms of gender—but also in regard to class, race, sexual orientation, nation, age, ability, religion—is central to feminist thought and action.[20] Feminism does not reject men, but the abuse of power, *per se*.

1. S.A. Griffin, "A House Divided," in *Unborn Again*. Los Angeles: Phony Lid Books, 2001. Used with permission.

2. For an overview of feminism and feminist theory, see, for example, Rory Dicker and Alison Piepmeier, eds., *Catching a Wave: Reclaiming Feminism for the 21st Century*. Boston: Northeastern University Press, 2003; Carole R. McCann and Seung-Kyung Kim, eds., *Feminist Theory Reader: Local and Global Perspectives*, second edition. New York: Routledge, 2010; Robin Morgan, ed., *Sisterhood Is Forever: The Women's Anthology for a New Millennium*. New York: Washington Square Press, 2003; and Rosemarie Putnam Tong, *Feminist Thought: A More Comprehensive Introduction*, third edition. Boulder, CO: Westview Press, 2008. For essays on men and feminism see Tom Digby, ed., *Men Doing Feminism*. New York: Routledge, 1998.

3. Shira Tarrant, *Men and Feminism*. Berkeley, CA: Seal Press, 2009, pp. 23–24.

4. Ernesto Aguilar, "Men, Feminism, Race, Movements and the Cult of Hugo Schwyzer: The F Word Interviews Ernesto Aguilar," in *People of Color Organize! Your*

Decolonial, Anti-Patriarchal, News Resource. Available at: http://www.peopleofcolor organize.com/analysis/men-feminism-race-movements-hugo-schwyzer-interview/ (accessed June 25, 2012).

5. Feminist practice has deep theoretical and historical roots in identity politics. A core aspect of feminist strategy lies in making personal experience both visible and political. However, there are potential pitfalls with this approach in regard to women, men, and experience as an epistemological foundation. I argue this point in "Stepping Out of Bounds: Feminist Men and Political Organizing," unpublished paper presented at the Western Political Science Association Annual Conference, Las Vegas, Nevada, March 9, 2007. For other discussions on feminist epistemology and feminist standpoint theory, see, for example, Sandra Harding, ed., *Feminism and Methodology.* Bloomington, IN: Indiana University Press, 1987; and Linda Alcoff and Elizabeth Potter, eds., *Feminist Epistemologies.* New York: Routledge, 1993.

6. Patrick Hopkins, "How Feminism Made a Man Out of Me," in Tom Digby, ed., *Men Doing Feminism.* New York: Routledge, 1998, p. 42. As Judith Grant writes:

> Feminism cannot simultaneously be the lens through which experiences are interpreted, and also find its grounding in those experiences. That is, the feminist interpretive lens cannot be grounded on women's point of view . . . To ground feminism in women's experiences and then to look to feminism to interpret those experiences is a tautology. To the extent that feminist standpoint theory accepts this tautology, it cannot accomplish what it sets out to do.

Stated somewhat differently, a theory cannot be tested on the same data used to build that theory. See Judith Grant, *Fundamental Feminism: Contesting the Core Concepts of Feminist Theory.* New York: Routledge, 1993, p. 101.

7. Michael S. Kimmel, "Who's Afraid of Men Doing Feminism?" in Tom Digby, ed., *Men Doing Feminism.* New York: Routledge, 1998, pp. 60–61.

8. bell hooks, *Feminist Theory*, especially Chapter 5, "Men: Comrades In Struggle." Cambridge, MA: South End Press, 2000.

9. The second, third, and fourth points are made by James P. Sterba, "Is Feminism Good for Men and Are Men Good for Feminism?" in Tom Digby, ed., *Men Doing Feminism.* New York: Routledge, 1998, p. 298.

10. Black women have challenged the implicit and overt white racism within the feminist movement. The 1977 Combahee River Collective articulated these concerns noting that material conditions prevent most black women from upsetting "both the economic and the sexual arrangements that seem to represent some stability in their lives." At the same time, black women and black men share commonly situated experiences of race and class in a capitalist, white imperialist society. See The Combahee River Collective, "A Black Feminist Statement," in Carole R. MacCann and Seung-Kyung Kim, eds., *Feminist Theory Reader: Local and Global Perspectives,* second edition. New York: Routledge, 2010, p. 106.

11. Patricia Hill Collins, "Book Review: Separate Roads to Feminism: Black, Chicana, and White Feminist Movements in America's Second Wave," *Acta Sociologica*, vol. 49 (2006): 231–232. Internal racism has troubled the American feminist movement most

obviously during the abolition/suffrage era and again during the black liberation/civil rights/women's liberation movements of the late 1960s and early 1970s. The problem hinged on white feminists' unexamined race and class-privileged assumptions that women's issues could be separated from race and class issues.

12. Judith Grant, *Fundamental Feminism: Contesting the Core Concepts of Feminist Theory*. New York: Routledge, 1993, p. 162.

13. Patricia Hill Collins, *Black Feminist Thought: Knowledge, Consciousness, and the Politics of Empowerment*. New York: Routledge, 2000, pp. 35–36. Collins's discussion pertains specifically to the development of black feminist thought. By extension, her insights are useful in considering how to create feminist politics and knowledge that is expansive enough to include men, without losing the advantages of women's self-defined knowledge.

14. Vivien Labaton and Dawn Lundy Martin, *The Fire This Time: Young Activists and the New Feminism*. New York: Random House, 2004, p. xxiii.

15. Discussed in Robyn Wiegman, "Unmaking: Men and Masculinity in Feminist Theory," in Judith Kegan Gardiner, ed., *Masculinity Studies and Feminist Theory*. New York: Columbia University Press, 2002, p. 36.

16. See Hanna Rosin, "The End of Men," *The Atlantic*, July/August 2010. Available at: http://www.theatlantic.com/magazine/archive/2010/07/the-end-of-men/8135/. For responses and counter-stories to Rosin's report of an unprecedented role reversal that has allegedly left men struggling for equality, see Ann Friedman, "It's Not the End of Men," *The American Prospect*, June 10, 2010. http://prospect.org/article/its-not-end-men-0; and Michael Kimmel, "A War Against Boys?" in Michael S. Kimmel and Michael A. Messner, eds., *Men's Lives*, ninth edition. San Francisco: Pearson, 2013, pp. 93–98.

17. Andrea G. Hunter and Sherrill L. Sellers, "Feminist Attitudes among African American Women and Men," *Gender & Society*, vol. 12, no. 1 (February 1998): 81. See also, Patricia Collins, *Black Feminist Thought*. New York: Routledge & Kegan Paul, 1991; Paula Giddings, *When and Where I Enter*. New York: Bantam, 1984; bell hooks, *Ain't I a Woman?: Black Women and Feminism*. Boston: South End Press, 1981; Gary Lemons, "A New Response to 'Angry Black (Anti)Feminists': Reclaiming Feminist Forefathers, Becoming Womanist Sons," in Tom Digby, ed., *Men Doing Feminism*. New York: Routledge, 1998.

18. Shira Tarrant, *When Sex Became Gender*. New York: Routledge, 2006, p. 32.

19. bell hooks, *Feminist Theory From Margin to Center*. Cambridge, MA: South End Press, 2000, p. 33.

20. See Gloria E. Anzaldúa and Analouise Keating, eds., *This Bridge We Call Home: Radical Visions for Transformation*. New York: Routledge, 2002; Judith Butler, *Gender Trouble: Feminism and the Subversion of Identity*. New York: Routledge, 1990; Patrick Califia, *Speaking Sex to Power: The Politics of Queer Sex*. San Francisco: Cleis Press, 2002; Cherríe L. Moraga and Gloria E. Anzaldúa, eds., *This Bridge Called My Back: Writings by Radical Women of Color*. Berkeley, CA: Third Woman Press, 2002; and Michelle Tea, ed., *Without a Net: The Female Experience of Growing Up Working Class*. Emeryville, CA: Seal Press, 2003. bell hooks, *Killing Rage: Ending Racism*. New York:

Owl Books, 1996. hooks writes that the institutionalized structure and patterns of domination negatively impacting women are repeated in all other arenas wherever particular groups of people are suppressed, oppressed, or subjugated. See also, bell hooks, *Where We Stand: Class Matters*. New York: Routledge, 2000.

IT'S JUST COMMON SENSE

Brandon Arber

Male student: What class did you just have?

Me: Women's Studies.

Male student: Oh, shit. Is that a requirement?

Me: Naw.

Male student: Are you stupid? Then why the fuck are you taking it? HaHa. I always knew you were a faggot. Isn't the class full of, like, feminists? Are you the only dude in the class?

Me: Well, I mean, I consider myself a feminist.

Male student: Mmmpff! You gotta be kidding me.

Me: Being a feminist just means I don't think girls should be raped, abused, discriminated against, or denied health services, especially if they get pregnant. What, you disagree with that?

Maybe my definition of feminism is too . . . easy. The way I was raised, however, was that fighting for women's rights was synonymous with fighting injustice in general. So saying that I am a feminist is as easy as saying I'm hoping for the best for all people, and trying to act accordingly. Some might think that this definition robs the word of its gravity, or maybe a sense of total commitment. But I'm not fighting a holy war here. I don't see political or social struggle as a zero-sum game. And my moral beliefs don't come enumerated in some rulebook, whether conservative or liberal. I aspire to more pragmatic, humanist values: caring for all people and using reason to bring about a better world. It's hard to deny that women have been screwed over. So I don't think I'm being revolutionary in saying I'm a feminist. It just makes sense.

Another male student: Whatever, man . . . I was in this Comm class last year that was, like, all girls and we were talking about how there's a male bias in the media, right? And the evidence they used for it was that Meryl Streep was obviously such a better actress than DeNiro, but DeNiro gets all this recognition and makes so much more money and shit. Fucking Meryl Streep? So most of the time I just kept my mouth shut 'cause I knew these girls were just being bitches, right, and the professor would obviously be on their side. But this time, I just said, "Hey, maybe it's not bias. Maybe it's because DeNiro is actually a better actor." The whole class just blew up at me calling me ignorant and shit. I got the dirtiest fucking looks for the rest of the semester. They couldn't even think that maybe it was their own preference that made them think there was a bias in the first place! No, I understand what you're saying. I'm not sexist, but feminists are fucking crazy.

For many guys, sitting in a room full of feminist women doesn't sound like the most comfortable way to spend an afternoon. This negative reaction to the idea of taking a women's studies class is not just a reflection of ignorance. Liberation can get very personal. Sometimes people feel alienated or personally blamed for being the oppressor. At the same time, too many activists preach to the choir, and then pat themselves on the back about how righteous and ground-breaking they are. Or they take radical action just for the shock value. But there is power in being willing to engage in confrontation, and this is important.

The problems we are fighting are systemic. They are aggregate consequences of individual decisions. What seems more widespread than overtly bad action is complacency and apathy; a refusal to engage. I think our political emphasis should be on opening eyes, not hardening hearts.

You might ask, who is this white man coming out of nowhere, claiming he's a feminist, and who then proceeds to tell me how to run my movement? Well, I don't care if I'm not welcome at first. I'm patient. I'll wait. As a college athlete, as a beneficiary of white, upper-middle-class male privilege and access, I know that feminism is still a dirty word from the locker-room to the board rooms that are still dominated by men. And it's not only because all men are pig-headed. Of course, many men are still insensitive, homophobic, sexist, or abusive. And even the best-intentioned men perpetuate oppression by the language we use and the jokes we make.

But there is also a great potential for men as allies. Many of us see ourselves as victims of prejudice by virtue of being black, Asian, Muslim, or Jewish. And, whether we know about it or not, most of us probably have had a friend, girlfriend, sister, mother, or wife who was abused or sexually assaulted at some point in her life. So it's not the goals and concerns of feminism but, rather, feminism's reputation that keeps a lot of men from dealing with the issues. Ultimately, though, we have to step up. When we need to make decisions either in our own private lives, or regarding public policy, a feminist perspective has to be a viable option. Because when it's time to dig in, we are going to want the true feminist majority behind us. The potential is there. It's just common sense.

WHY I AM NOT A FEMINIST

Haji Shearer

I am not a feminist. Applied linguistics prevents me from adopting the title. Feminist is derived from feminine, referring to the female sex. As an African-American man who supports equality for women I don't feel it's necessary, or even beneficial, for me to feminize my personhood in order to do the right thing *vis-à-vis* gender. I know men who identify as feminist, but that doesn't work for me. Even among women, the term feminist has had less acceptance in the black community than among whites. Feminism is defined in my *American Heritage Dictionary* as a doctrine that advocates or demands for women the same rights granted to men. I am all for that. I support equal rights and responsibilities for women without injecting the confusing etymology that implies being feminist is akin to being feminine or female.

There is no comparable male term in English for feminist. Masculinist doesn't work. It might be more accurate to coin a new phrase to identify men who support women's full humanity. True manhood must advocate for equal rights and responsibilities for women as a component of integrity. In fact, I consider it a short-sighted compromise for a man to identify as a feminist. Does a white person identify as black to do anti-racism work?

Men who stand up for women's equality are valuable educators within the patriarchal camp precisely because we are men. We shouldn't minimize that advantage. I need not make my feminine side primary in order to honor my mother, sister, or daughter. Because so much viciousness has been committed in the name of false manhood, some have confused the most toxic aspects of patriarchy with true manhood. That is a mistake.

We must reclaim the essence of manhood from thugs and pimps, corrupt businessmen, imperialist warmongers, and juiced up athletes. Manhood needs to be defined by its peaks, not its valleys. Healthy manhood acknowledges the inner feminine and inner masculine of each human being. Healthy manhood advocates for the equal rights and responsibilities of women and men. Healthy manhood honors the inherent value and goodness of all people.

I am a man. African-American, urban, happily heterosexual, conceived in 1961. Some of my earliest memories are of social movements. Blue Hill Avenue burning during the 1967 riots, Dr. King assassinated in 1968, being one of the first black children voluntarily bused to an almost all-white suburban school in 1969. My father was a star among his nine brothers and sisters; avoiding the drug addiction that captured his father and several siblings, he founded a successful, community-based, medical laboratory. My mother, unlike many in my neighborhood, was able to full-time parent until I, the youngest of their three children, was fully ensconced in primary school. After that she worked in the family business with my father in a position of shared authority.

As the youngest child and the only boy, I was privileged. The division of labor I most remember among my siblings was the nightly chores. My sisters took turns washing the dishes. I took out the trash. Not only did my trash duty take far less time to finish compared to washing the dishes but on top of that, I had more freedom to explore the neighborhood than my older sisters. My mother encouraged my sisters to stay in the safety of the yard while I replicated Fat Albert and the gang all around the block. And then, of course, there was the sexual double standard.

Although my mom denies it today, I recall getting the message from her, and from society at large, that it was okay for me to have sex before marriage, but it wasn't okay for my sisters. The only message I got from my dad on the subject were his late nights out.

Despite these discrepancies, as a child and young man, racial tension was always more apparent to me than gender injustice. I remember claiming to be a Black Panther as a child in the late 1960s so the white bully who was harassing me would back off. A decade later I joined an organization started by former Panther, Stokely Carmichael (who was then named Kwame Ture). The All African People Revolutionary Party (AAPRP) was open only to people of African descent and was dedicated to uniting the African continent under one socialist government. When I joined I didn't know about Carmichael's infamous remark about women as social activists. Asked in 1964 what position women in the Student Non-Violent Coordinating Committee (SNCC) could take, he reportedly answered, "Prone." Given the leadership of many women in the AAPRP, Ture's assessment of his sisters' ability had improved in the intervening decades.

Truth be told, I was not a very dedicated revolutionary. I felt like I had missed the glory days of the 1960s: the police shoot-outs, the so-called Free Love, the ubiquitous drugs. I wanted not only the chance to bask in some of that glow, but I wanted some action! When it became apparent that there were no weapons stashed in AAPRP safe houses to confront the pigs and that all these revolutionaries actually did was study books and have discussions, I boogied.

But, in what would be a reoccurring theme in my life, I was attracted to powerful women in the organization. In fact, a female friend introduced me to the group in the first place. She was a beautiful and intelligent sister and, surely, a large reason for joining was to get closer to her. (I would discover, alas, that I was not the only would-be revolutionary motivated, at least in part, by sex.) Fortunately, she and I became close friends. Although the sexual component never developed between us, it did between me and another comrade.

Both of these beautiful black women taught me about politics, history, and interpersonal relationships. Yet, I don't recall either of them ever calling themselves a feminist. And as I befriended and worked with other progressive black women, the word feminism rarely was uttered, or it was disdained as the purview of wealthy, white women. I understood that addressing the inequalities foisted on women by men in the ruling elite was not something that immediately concerned those of us in the black community. The main issue at hand was racism. The feeling was, *Let's get that worked out first and then we'll turn to gender.*

Another brake on the widespread adoption of feminist ideology in the black community is that bastion of male privilege, the church. One small example: A few years ago my wife and I co-facilitated a couples' workshop in a local church, with a dynamic female pastor assisting us. Our group started with seven heterosexual couples, but early in the program almost every man's attendance became sporadic. Only two of the men managed to complete the ten-week course. Despite the men's lackluster performance, the pastor spoke one evening about a bible verse that states a man is the head of his household.

One of the women in our couples group was having none of that. She passionately detailed the neglect and ill-treatment her man had inflicted on their family—including abandoning her that evening—and she described the extra burdens she had to bear because of his irresponsibility. How, she demanded, could he be considered the head of the household when he was too much of a punk to even attend a little couples' workshop? The pastor, usually an eloquent advocate of her position, had no convincing reply.

In my own family, my wife and I consciously try to share the roles of both head and heart of our home. Growing up amidst the gender awakening of the 1970s surely affected my ideas. As a child, I could sense the disruption in the social fabric of traditional relationships. I remember hating the fact that my father was never around. Granted, he was mostly working and he provided a decent income for the family (especially admirable considering his own primary role model for manhood/fatherhood was a drunk). But I remember as a boy thinking that I would be around for my children because it hurt me so much that my father wasn't around. That's why the most important place I practice gender equality in is within my marriage and family.

I married an independent-minded woman dedicated to exercising her full rights and accepting her full responsibilities (although like many of us, she often seems more concerned with the former rather than with the latter). Even though we are both African-Americans, I understood from the beginning of our relationship that, as a man, I hail from a more privileged group, and I was committed to trying to level the field.

After my wife, Jasmin, and I conceived our first child, I spent some years volunteering with a black-woman-led, community-based childbirth organization where my wife had started working as a midwifery apprentice and breast-feeding counselor. These women were engaged in the revolutionary act of reclaiming the birth experience from the medical industrial complex. They understood the downside of the patriarchal birth experience that became standard practice in this country after World War II. Midwifery was destroyed, women were disempowered, infants were abused, and people of color were disrespected. And even these progressive black women did not call themselves feminists. So eager were they to eschew the feminist label, they adopted the word "womanist," a term popularized by Alice Walker, to differentiate themselves from their white, middle-class, feminist sisters. With such a strong group of black, female role models distancing themselves from the feminist label while upholding the ideals of gender equality, it's little wonder I turned a cold shoulder to the term. I support the goals of feminism—equal rights of women in the home and workplace, for example—but I never related to the culture of feminism.

Eventually, I became a social worker and, because there was a void in serving this population, working with men became my specialty and one of my passions. As I began practicing family support work with fathers, I saw that men were often ignored by female social workers who were supposed to service the whole family. The need to engage men was crucial because it was obvious that much of the conflict in families came from the inability of parents to communicate. Some of this was the long-standing failure of couples to engage in truly intimate relationships. Some was due to the transformation in relationships inspired by the 1970s-era women's movement that resulted in a shifting power dynamic between family members, leaving many men confused and angry. Some men I work with are angry about a perceived loss of power in the home. It seems to them that both women and children had been empowered by changes in social policy over the last thirty years. *So guess who lost power?* they ask me rhetorically.

Initially, most of the men I counseled were African-American or Latino, working-class or lower-income. Talk with these men about Affirmative Action in the workplace and they easily understand that a systematic pattern of discrimination has prevented them from excelling in society. Therefore a pattern of favorable treatment is a reasonable remedy to correct historic wrongs resulting from slavery, Jim Crow, and institutionalized prejudice perpetuated by society's dominant group of whites. I've found some success in helping men of color accept the radical shifts in gender equality thrust upon them by equating it to Affirmation Action for relationships.

Most men can acknowledge a historical burden experienced by women. Even black or Latino men who have been excluded from the old boy network still have the ability to physically oppress women. Most honest men can acknowledge seeing or hearing of a woman being beaten, raped and/or financially exploited both in romantic relationships and in the community at large. Sometimes women very close to them were hurt in these ways. This well-established gender terrorism is akin to blacks being oppressed by whites for generations. If you acknowledge the similarities, you can see the need for similar restitution.

In discussing the legacy of slavery, some whites fall back on the old excuse, "I never owned slaves" and "I didn't benefit from slavery." In reality, though, a third-grader could draw a direct line from the resources and benefits accrued by whites during slavery to the downtrodden condition of blacks today. Likewise, as men we benefit daily from a conspiracy of male privilege and are burdened with some of the collective karma of our gender's actions. For example, I never raped anyone, but another man sexually abused my wife. As she and I became intimate, and as we worked through the healing process, some of her anger at her stepfather's depraved behavior was transferred onto me. Would it be fair for me to cry, "Hey don't associate me with him. I'm not like that. I'm different"? Possibly. But that wouldn't eliminate the association in her mind and, one way or another, we'd have to deal with that.

The more effective way to deal with it might be to accept that men have oppressed women for generations. Men consciously working to undo that oppressive history, interpersonally and socially, unleash a powerful healing force in the world. Activating this force requires men of goodwill to listen to our sisters and even abdicate some of our power to them because men have exploited our position in almost every global culture that exists. One need not be a feminist to understand that.

THE STARBUCKS INTERVENTION

Greg Bortnichak

I'm the kind of twenty-something guy you would expect to work in a coffee shop. I play guitar and cello in an experimental punk band and have some cool music downloads in my collection. I'm tall and lean, with an explosive mess of dark hair that makes me look like the love child of Edward Scissorhands and Blacula. Most people correctly guess that I'm artistic and a bit to the political left.

What they may not realize is that I am a self-defined male feminist. Being a feminist is mighty powerful stuff because staying true to ideals about equality and justice involves consciously altering the way I behave. The bottom line is that I try to reject personal acts of subjugation, and I do my best to combat the systems that enable others to be oppressive. As the saying goes, the personal is political.

My brand of feminism is all about not imposing patriarchal power on the women in my life, and hoping to set an example for the boys and men I meet.

From the time I was seven and too short to play ball with big kids, to the time I was thirteen and too sensitive to party with the cool kids, to now when I struggle with masculinist ideology, I have always felt that dominant culture only truly benefits a select few. So I do my best to reject it. I do it for me. I do it for my partner, and for every man who feels alienated by the expectations that culture places on guys who do not quite fit the "man's man" mold. I do it for anyone who feels constrained by the music videos on TV because they see both women and men reduced to sexual commodities. But the question remains, *how do I do my feminism*? And, more importantly, how am I a *male* feminist?

It's tricky. And the truth is that a lot of time I feel friction between being a man and being a feminist. Problems come up when I want more than anything to take feminist action—to act in defense of someone who is being victimized by patriarchal power—but my aid is unwelcome or inappropriate or potentially does more political harm than good.

Allow me to illustrate: I work at Starbucks. I spend roughly twenty hours each week serving coffee to strangers, sometimes as many as several hundred each day. And you better believe I see it all. Customers reveal all kinds of personal details. So do my co-workers. I put up with a lot from them: sexist and racist jokes, routine descriptions of masculinist sexploitation, flat-out ridicule for my feminist views. And at the end of the day when my feet feel like they're ready to fall off, and my entire body reeks of espresso grinds, I think back and try to make sense of it.

A customer comes in and begins telling us about this scheme he has to buy a wife. What he really wants to do is hire a housekeeper, but he thinks it's funnier if he tells us that he's wife shopping today. He complains about doing housework, saying he'd rather pay a cute, young girl twenty bucks an hour to do his chores for him rather than do them himself, or worse, get re-married to have yet another woman sit at home all day, take his money, and bitch at him when he gets home from work. He keeps saying there is nothing worse than married life, to which the guys I'm working with chuckle in agreement. The only girl working at the time, Joy, is offended. She tells the customer that marriage won't be bad at all for her husband—she will do all the housework and more (wink, wink) for her husband. For free. Joy wants to be a housewife, and she gives me a hard time for being feminist. The customer tells Joy that she's sweet but that she won't be sweet forever. He's expecting his purchased "wife" to be totally obedient and pleasant every hour of every day. Then, as an afterthought, he mentions that he has no problem getting his "non-domestic" (wink, wink) needs met elsewhere for not much more than it's going to cost him to buy this wife of his.

Later, my girlfriend, Ana, decides to come by and do some homework, keeping me company as I work. She is sitting alone in a far corner, completely engrossed in her studies. A man with slicked-back silver hair, white guy, probably in his fifties, and appearing to be quite wealthy (gold jewelry, designer golf shirt, the works) steps into line and begins staring at Ana. He makes no effort to hide this, and gets out of line to walk around behind her and get a better look. Then he gets back into line and cranes his neck to see down her shirt and up her dress. I see all of this, and I'm simultaneously disgusted and pissed off. He's such trash. I would love to call him out, or lay him out right then and there, but I risk losing my job if I'm rude to the customers. So I bite my tongue. It gets to be his turn in line and he still won't stop staring at her, not even to place his order. He's holding up the line, people behind him are starting to get flustered, and I lose it.

"What's so interesting over there, Sir? You seem to be looking very intently at something," I ask as innocently as I possibly can. "That girl in the corner," he says like he's ready to eat her. He doesn't take his eyes off Ana once. "Oh yeah, what do you think?" I'm trying now to sound as sleazy as I possibly can in an attempt

to lead him to believe that I'm going along with the shameless objectification of Ana. "I think she's a real pretty girl in that little dress of hers." He licks his ugly thin lips and makes a face that screams "pervert." I've caught him red-handed at his patriarchal bullshit, and at this point, I'm done: "Well I think she's a friend of mine, and I think she'd feel violated if she knew you were staring at her like that." I say it low and threateningly beneath my breath so as to not cause a scene. "I think she should get used to it," he replies. There is no hint of apology in his tone. It's like I'm wrong for telling him not to lech at a girl who could be his fucking granddaughter! I glare at him like I want to burn a hole in his face with my eyes and growl, "I think you need to learn a little respect." He leaves. I'm shaking.

I go to Ana and ask her if she saw what just transpired. She says no, that she was completely unaware. When I tell her what happened she is visibly upset. She thanks me for sticking up for her and waits for me to finish my shift without returning to her homework. The woman in line behind the silver-haired man approaches me before leaving and wishes me goodnight, smiling at me in a way that I could only interpret as solidarity.

That night I had nightmares about the silver-haired man. He was so ruthless in how he visually dismembered Ana that he put me in touch with a very distinct fear. No one had ever made me so mad, or provoked such a reaction from me. But was it even my place to step in on Ana's behalf? Was I being over-protective? Despite Ana's appreciation for my fast action, I still could not get this encounter out of my mind. The silver-haired man obviously saw nothing wrong with what he did. I even had a co-worker poke fun at me for bothering that "poor old man." The woman in line behind the silver-haired man was my best assurance—as iffy as it was—that speaking up was the right thing to do.

Yet I could not help but feel unsettled about how I chose to respond. After all, I don't doubt that if Ana looked up at the right time, she would have reacted more strongly and defended herself far better than I. And if Ana had been the one to terminate the encounter, perhaps she would have a stronger feeling of closure or justice. I had to wonder what it meant that I defended Ana instead of simply bringing her attention to what was happening. Did my chivalrous feminism reflect some duty I feel to protect her? And if so, does that mean that on some level I think she is incapable of protecting herself? Even worse, what if my actions actually revealed a sense of possession or ownership over Ana? And what about that burst of anger I felt? How stereotypically masculine to feel angry in light of something another man did to my girlfriend. This encounter with the silver-haired man raises so many difficult questions for me about whether pro-feminist men ought to step in to help women or instead focus our efforts on enabling women to protect themselves.

On the night of the scuffle in Starbucks, Ana happened to be wearing a gorgeous dress that was short, with a very low neckline. She has gotten upset in the past over men leering at her when she wears this dress. Sometimes I think about gently suggesting to Ana that she shelve the dress, but I don't think it's my place to say so. I do not want Ana to continue feeling violated by these tactless creeps but, at the same time, I do not want her to compromise her own sense of beauty, self-expression, and sexuality. I also don't want to be perceived as controlling or paternalistic. It is not Ana's fault that some men feel it's their right to stare crudely at young women. But still, it upsets Ana, and it happens less when she does not wear this particular dress. It is clear who is at fault. It's the voyeurs like that silver-haired man at Starbucks. But if men like that deny responsibility, and if women have the right to wear whatever they damn-well please, and if I happen to see what's going on, then shouldn't I step in and speak my mind?

I've run into a dilemma: It's true that men can deflect unwanted attention, but in doing so we risk offending or patronizing women who are capable of protecting themselves, or insulting women who like this sort of thing. I know that some women rely on the male gaze to feel attractive and some may dress in ways to get attention on purpose. Women have the right to express themselves through their clothes and demeanor in any way they see fit. But I risk sounding sexist if I advise a girl not to go to certain parts of the city looking a certain way, and I risk feeling guilty knowing someone could get hurt if I don't speak up.

The problem lies in knowing when it's okay to intervene; in knowing when to act on my personal feminist beliefs, and knowing when to hold back. Mastering this discretion is something I grapple with each day. Sometimes I get to thinking that I'm setting myself up for an unconquerable task by trying to live the life of an active male feminist. Sometimes it feels so daunting that I consider giving up. But then I remember what got me here in the first place, and it gives me hope. Feminism is something I embrace because it helps me think more clearly about who I am and how I behave as a man in this society. When I keep this in mind, I understand that I'm not about to defeat the patriarchy overnight, but that I can feel a little better knowing I'm not letting it defeat me little by little, each and every day.

FROM OPPRESSOR TO ACTIVIST: REFLECTIONS OF A FEMINIST JOURNEY

Amit Taneja

My gay friends say I'm part of the "family," but sometimes strangers call me "fag."
I was born in India, but I have been called a "sand n****r."
I became a Canadian citizen recently, but I am still called an "Indo-Canadian."
I am working on my doctorate, but I anticipate being in large debt for my education through my late forties.
I am Hindu, but I am often asked if I have found Jesus.
I am fluent in English, but it is my fourth language.
I am big boned, but I am often mistaken as fat and unhealthy.
I work legally in the U.S., but my official status according to the government is "Alien Employee."

INTRODUCTION

As a poor, immigrant, big-boned, non-Christian, gay person of color who happens to be working in a country where Others are feared, some people would say that I have a lot going against me. And they would be right. However, despite all that works against me, I still feel that I have power. Correction: A lot of power. You see, I was born with a penis and I was taught early on that this simple fact meant I was inherently superior to about half of the human population. The mere sighting of my anatomy at birth outlined my destiny in this life as being smarter, taller, faster, stronger, funnier, and in general just "better" than women. That is what I was taught.

Despite all the messages that were bored into my brain about my supposed male superiority, I have come to a place of questioning, resisting, and actively changing the tape that plays as the background music in my head. I have come to fight the sexist messages that I was raised with and, more importantly, to duck and cover from, deflect, and strike back against the thousands of similar messages that come my way on a daily basis.

I write this essay as snapshots of a life-changing journey. It is not a complete story, or even chronological for that matter. But it is a story of important markers on my path of becoming a feminist. This journey brought me from a place of unquestioned male power and privilege to experiencing oppression myself. The journey ends at my resting place as a life-long, hardcore, die-hard, to-my-last-breath, capital "F" Feminist.

SNAPSHOT #1: GET YOUR BROTHER SOME WATER

Summers in India were hot, and while little girls helped their mommies cook and clean at home after school, little boys could run around being rascals, playing cricket, and flying kites. I remember coming home one afternoon after a long day of playing marbles with the other boys. No sooner had I entered the room, than my mom asked my younger sister to get me a tall glass of water with ice. My sister resisted and complained, "Why do I have to get him water? He never gets me water when I come home!" My grandmother immediately chastised her, saying that such talk would keep her single all her life, and that she would never land a husband. (My grandmother was more right than she could have known. My sister is a lesbian and now walks around proudly wearing her "Well-Behaved Women Hardly Ever Make History" T-shirt.)

I remember this story about the water so vividly. I might have made a face at my sister while agreeing with my grandmother. Whatever my grandma said made a lot of sense to me at the time. I was brought up to believe that the man is the breadwinner, the decision maker, the provider, and the protector for his family. Women exist to serve the men and children in their lives. These notions made it seem reasonable that it was my sister's job . . . no, change that to duty . . . to bring me water.

I remember this story because of the way my sister looked at me. There was part contempt, part anger, some pain, and perhaps resignation to her fate as a woman. I don't know precisely what she was thinking, but I remember feeling guilty when she came back with a glass of water. I only took a sip (even though I was parched). Somehow I felt that I didn't deserve that glass of water just because I was a boy and she was a girl. But I knew that to question the system would be wrong. I put that event deep in my memory scrapbook, but the seeds of questioning my male privilege were planted for years to come.

SNAPSHOT #2: ISN'T 99 PERCENT GOOD ENOUGH?

Sonali Mehta* and I were good friends in high school in India. We had a fierce, but friendly, competition over who would get the top rank in math each semester. Sometimes I came out ahead, and sometimes she did. Many a teacher commented that Sonali was very gifted in math and sciences, *especially for being* *a girl.* We both tied with 96 percent on our preliminary practice tests before our provincial board exams at the end of twelfth grade. We both studied hard for our exams and the pressure was on for the final showdown. We took the exam and immediately compared notes. It seemed that Sonali and I both had the same answers to most of the questions.

Fast-forward. Two months later. We nervously opened our grade envelopes. I peeked with one eye open and saw my score was 97 percent in math. Another friend saw my grades and yelled over my shoulder, "Sonali, Amit got 97 percent. How did you do?"

All heads are turned in our direction, and I saw Sonali sitting quietly with a tear running down her cheek. Oh no! This was supposed to be a friendly competition. She couldn't have done that bad to be crying! I went over to comfort her and saw her grades lying on her desk. Her crying became louder and more noticeable. The paper read, "Math 99 percent." I was really confused at this point. She got the highest marks, but yet she was sad. I asked why she was crying, and Sonali said that she was upset because she did not get a perfect score of 100 percent. I responded by saying, "You still have the highest grade in our class!" She quietly replied, "I am a girl. I am told over and over again that I am exceptionally good at math as far as girls go. I didn't want to be just exceptionally good. I wanted to be perfect; to prove them all wrong! You wouldn't understand." Suddenly it all made sense. And from that day on, I have cringed (and always confront people) when I hear the words "especially gifted for a girl."

SNAPSHOT #3: THE OPPRESSOR BECOMES OPPRESSED

It was the beginning of my freshman year in college, and my family and I had immigrated to Canada nine months earlier. I had a Presidential Full Tuition Scholarship in Engineering and I was determined to do well in school. I wanted to build bridges because they fascinated and scared me at the same time. While I was preparing for the adjustment to living on my own, I also became fascinated and scared by feelings of attraction toward men. I was actively exploring the idea of accepting my same-sex feelings and eventually "coming out" but, at the time, I felt very unsure.

I was sitting in the dorm lounge watching television during the first week of classes when a gay character came on the sitcom. One of my floormates said how much he hated fags, and another agreed by saying that he would "beat the crap out of any fag" he met. Uh oh! Cancel the coming out. I did not need to be hated on, much less beaten for being gay. The obvious path to avoid this was to deny all feelings for men and be as straight-acting and macho as I could.

I started out small by trying to be a heterosexual man (or what I thought it meant to be a heterosexual man). At first that meant making small comments about women, their bodies, their breasts. But that didn't seem enough.

I kept thinking that "real men" would be able to see through my façade, so I had to step it up and be more macho than most men to prevent my dirty secret from emerging. I had to turn into Captain Hyper-Hetero, the imaginary superhero who safeguarded masculinity by being the manliest man possible.

I started talking more loudly in the presence of other men (while avoiding all contact with women). I kept telling others that I was looking for sexual adventures with women (okay, it was a lot more graphic than that, but I choose not to repeat or remember the details). Soon word got around about my comments, and the women in my building were avoiding me because I was an all-around sexist jerk.

The plan was working. Men thought I was a player and women didn't want to have anything to do with me. Until one day a female neighbor reached out to me, and pointed out that my comments were hurtful, demeaning, and revolting. I was treating women like "meat," and that was not going to get me anywhere. I realized that I was causing harm and fear amongst the women who lived close to me. This was not really me. I was ashamed of what I had done. I just blurted out, "I am gay, and I am trying to hide behind this mask of being super straight." I knew at that moment that I had a critical choice to make and I could not lead a life of lies. More importantly, I could now relate to what it felt like to be oppressed. It was a life-altering moment, and I found love and forgiveness from the women around me when they heard my story. We stayed up late at night, eating ice cream and sharing stories of oppression and fear, while building dreams of a future filled with confidence and hope. And we also created a list of the most eligible bachelors in our dorm, but that is another story for another time.

SNAPSHOT #4: FITTING THE GENDER BOX

After the demise of Captain Hyper-Hetero I decided to come out more publicly. Life was good and I was trying to fit in with the straight world while finding my place within the gay community. The more out I became on campus, the more I was targeted by messages of homophobia from the straight community and racism and classism from the queer community. Straight men questioned my masculinity and often made assumptions that being gay meant that I had to be effeminate. It seemed like I didn't fit in completely in either the straight world or the gay world. I was too femme for the straight boys, and not femme enough for the pretty, out, campy, white, gay crowd. Drag queens in the gay bars were relentless in making fun of my outfit, my accent, and my looks. I dressed too breeder for their liking and I was told that I needed to "gay it up a little." I was told, "Go get some Abercrombie, honey!"

I went looking for Abercrombie clothing, but I could neither fit in it nor afford it. At the same time, the straight men (and sometimes straight women) would belittle the "queeny fags" and the "butch dykes." It seemed to me that if drag queens and butch dykes did not exist, then straight people would only see the "normal gays (and lesbians)" like me, and there would be little reason for them to hate us. I was being taught the message that those who transgress gender boundaries are bad and should be looked down upon. And I bought that message for a while (until I took women's studies courses, and things changed).

I realized through these experiences that the roots of homophobia lie in sexism. People are taught to be afraid of those who defy gender norms because doing so topples the power granted to men over women. Homophobia is an offshoot of sexist ideology, and even gay and lesbian people are not immune from homophobic thinking because sexism is active and alive in our society.

SNAPSHOT #5: BOYS GO TO COLLEGE

After college, I moved from Canada to the United States to pursue graduate studies. I recently shared with an American buddy of mine that being born in India (which is a very gender-segregated society) I was exposed to numerous messages about male superiority from an early age. He thought that such thinking was "barbaric and idiotic," and he felt good knowing that we lived in a country where young children are not taught such gibberish. "Whoa, hold on a second. Is that really true?" I replied. "Are young children in the United States not taught notions of male superiority? I don't think it is a lot different here," I said. The messages about gender inequality are a lot more covert in U.S. culture, but they have the same effect.

My friend was not quite convinced so I shared with him the story of a recent visit to my partner's family in Ohio. My partner's brother has two children: a five-year-old boy named Colin and a four-year-old girl named Grace, who was asked by her parents to recite the new poem she'd been taught. In a shy tone she recited the following to us:

Boys go to college to get smarter
Girls go to Jupiter to get stupider

Grace's poem was met with a loud round of laughter from an assortment of adults including grandparents, uncles, aunts, and cousins. Everyone laughed except me. The smiling, laughter, and clapping following the performance signified to Grace that her poem was met with approval. In fact, later that night Grace offered to recite the poem again when new company arrived. It was heart-breaking and eye-opening to see that the adults in the room did not understand the significance of the message that was being taught to Grace and reinforced for everyone else.

From the time they are born, little boys and girls are taught gender-"appropriate" behaviors, dress, and hobbies. But they are also taught to dream and aspire in gendered ways. It is no coincidence that little boys want to grow up to be firefighters, police, and pilots, while girls want to be princesses who live in Barbie's Dream House. I wonder what would happen to men and women's self-esteem and career aspirations if children were taught that they could be whatever they wanted to be. I think we should all dream of the day when good-minded men, women, and those in-between make a commitment to egalitarian parenting and continually striving to create social change.

SNAPSHOT #6: THE GLASS CUBICLE: COMPLICATING GENDER

During college, I worked at a fast food restaurant for three summers. Make that three l-o-n-g summers. Nicole,* a co-worker who had worked at the chain for five years, said that she was thinking of leaving. I asked her why, and she responded that she did not see herself getting promoted anytime soon. She explained that except for one woman who worked the weekend graveyard shift, all the managers were men. Nicole said that the vast majority of the male supervisors and managers had worked at the establishment for a lot less time than her, and that she was never promoted.

Frustrated from being passed over for a promotion several times, Nicole approached the owner with her concerns. He denied there was any sexism at play, and mentioned that the men who had been promoted were "just better workers." To prove his point he called a staff meeting and asked if anyone was unhappy with promotions or had any concerns. The owner was known to be moody and petty. Although several women had privately shared their frustrations with me, no one spoke up out of fear. The owner said that since no one had anything to say, there must not be a problem. All too often, silence is taken as a form of agreement when in reality the silence is saying a lot more. Nicole was shortly moved to the evening shifts, which conflicted with her family commitments, and she quit within a month.

I share this snapshot because it had profound meaning for me. I always envisioned the glass ceiling as something that affected professional women like lawyers and MBAs. The truth is, though, that working-class women are even more prone to its effects. To this day, women still make around 81 cents on the male dollar. This wage difference is exacerbated by race. And when we consider class, (dis)abilities, nationality, and immigration status, it becomes clear that some women don't just experience the vertical push of the glass ceiling. They're getting pressed from all sides. The glass ceiling doesn't tell the whole story: Some women's lives are confined within a small glass cubicle. Feminist ideology recognizes the complexities of how oppression affects us and involves a much larger lens than only women's rights.

SNAPSHOT #7: SEXISM WITHIN THE QUEER COMMUNITY

I was hanging out with some gay male friends, when one of them stubbed his toe and let out a cry of pain. One of the other men in the group yelled "Stop being a pussy and take it like a man!" Later that evening, another queer man claimed that he was "allergic to vagina in every way possible." When I pointed out the sexist and misogynistic undertones of their comments, these men became very defensive and claimed that they had little to nothing in common with women, and they couldn't care less about women's issues. Another one responded that he could "barely tolerate the dykes at the pride marches."

Unfortunately, these comments are part of many gay men's repertoires. Some gay men deal with gender and sexuality by either acting macho, or by being a "mean girl" and hating on other "bitches." While my friends claimed their comments were made in jest and with no ill intent, these words actually have a damaging effect on their individual psyches and on the soul of the queer rights and women's rights movements.

I've struggled to explain gay men's sexist behavior. Queer people are oppressed in many ways by heteronormative society. Maybe some gay men deal with this particular powerlessness by hanging onto their male privilege. Perhaps this is also why some white queers are unwilling to acknowledge their skin privilege and the racism within the gay community.

I think it is important for social justice activists to confront sexism within the queer community and challenge misogynistic thinking. There is a grave problem within our community when some gay men claim that they can "barely tolerate" lesbian women. Only certain people with social position have the power to "tolerate" another human being. Of all people, gay men should know what it feels like to be "tolerated." Those of us who don't have social power are often taught to hope for tolerance at best. For many of us, full inclusion and acceptance are not even on the menu of options. The gender split within the queer community needs to be addressed because our internal and external struggles are connected by sexist and misogynistic ideologies. I have hope that activism from the transgender, intersex, and genderqueer community will help educate others in meaningful ways.

ACKNOWLEDGING AND RESISTING PRIVILEGE

The preceding seven snapshots portray my understanding of oppression and provide the foundation of my feminism. I want to bring this essay to a close by considering the biggest challenge in my journey to being a feminist: acknowledging and resisting privilege.

I experience oppression in a number of ways because of the intersection of my sexual orientation, race, ethnicity, national origin, class, language, and religion. As I said, I am a poor, big-boned, immigrant, gay man of color. Some days I feel the weight of the world on my shoulders. *I can't imagine what a day without oppression feels like.* Yet, still, I know that I have male privilege. The issues for me are multiple: How do I acknowledge and resist my male privilege? And why should I refuse one form of advantage when I am disenfranchised in so many others?

I've toyed with these ideas for a long time and here's what I've come up with: A common thread links all forms of oppression. It is not possible to fight just one form of oppression while neglecting others. And often we ignore how privilege and oppression are heavily mediated by class; that is, by the power and money that provide access to refuge and support, and open doors for people who are subjugated in other ways. This insight helps me reconcile my struggle between being multiply oppressed while also wanting to keep my male privilege.

I have learned that our personal decisions must reflect and support our political ideologies. We are not relieved from responsibility for politically conscientious action by claiming that our personal and political lives do not mix. Those of us who are oppressed don't have a choice. Our personal decisions are seen and treated as political, whether we want them to be or not! I cannot enter a same-sex marriage and expect that decision to be seen as politically neutral. Neither can I hold hands with my partner in public, nor try to be a foster parent without my actions having political meaning assigned to them.

The Advocate, America's largest gay and lesbian publication, recently posed the following question: "Is the gay community welcoming to people of color?" While I understand the intent of the question, I also see the implicit assumption that the gay community is white, and that white people have the power to accept (or tolerate) queer people of color. We need to problematize these assumptions and how we compartmentalize our identities. While some of our struggles may appear different on the surface, we are all connected through our intersecting identities and through the common experience of oppression.

We need to understand that there is no such as thing as completely disconnected identities. Race, class, gender, sexual orientation, age—and all other signifiers of identity—intersect in meaningful and powerful ways to shape our individual and collective experiences. We must always talk about women's rights and gay and lesbian rights while also thinking about xenophobia, classism, racism, transphobia, etc. Doing so allows us to acknowledge the existence of those of us who carry multiple burdens, but also strengthens all our movements under one collective stance. We should not worry about which oppression is worse than the other, but about the fact that all oppression is worth speaking out against. Many of us are in positions of oppressor and oppressed at the same time. This knowledge must fuel our passion for ending oppression by abdicating and resisting norms that give us privilege over others. Women's rights are the same as civil rights, which are the same as gay rights, which are the same as immigrant rights. We are all connected and only together will we be able to create lasting change.

Lastly, I want to encourage readers to make a personal and political commitment to social justice activism. I am suggesting something well beyond the realm of participating in diversity training or signing an online petition. Some people believe that acts like these absolve them of their moral responsibility to participate in further social justice activism. The typical corporate diversity training does little to make us examine our assumptions and merely gives us license to continue to exercise our power while maintaining a superficial front of understanding and tolerance. True social justice work starts with grassroots activism and extends in scope from local to national to global. We need to keep moving forward. We need to work for social justice until we reach a place where equal opportunity exists for everyone not just on paper, but also in practice.

* Pseudonyms used.

ABANDONING THE BARRICADES: OR HOW I BECAME A FEMINIST

Michael S. Kimmel

There's a well-known, probably apocryphal, story about an encounter between Henry David Thoreau and Ralph Waldo Emerson. Thoreau had been arrested and was in jail for tax resistance, and Emerson came to visit him. (I always imagined the scene as a sort of Hollywood set in which Emerson would lean against the outside of the brick building and peer through the bars on the window at his incarcerated friend.) "My friend, what are you doing in prison?" Emerson is said to have asked. "My friend, what are you doing out of prison?" replied Thoreau.

I have always thought of this story when, over the years, people have asked about the origins of my political activism for gender equality and my interest in studying men and masculinities. The question—why would I, as a man, support women's equality?—is the wrong question. To my mind, the only right question is, why doesn't every man support women's equality? After all, equality is right, just, fair, and supposedly as American as apple pie. More than that, though, gender equality is the only way for men to have the sorts of relationships we say we want to have—with women, with other men, and with our children.

But every story does have a beginning—or, more accurately, several beginnings. The narrator, always unreliable, gets to choose which of these stories is most fitting for the occasion, and it gradually becomes the master narrative, the font from which other subsequent narratives seem to flow inevitably and ineluctably.

So, when I'm asked, I often tell stories that date from graduate school: about helping to found an activist group dedicated to ending rape, about joining a men's consciousness raising group, about the founding of a national organization for pro-feminist men that would eventually become the National Organization for Men Against Sexism (NOMAS). Or I describe how I was challenged, pushed, and confronted by feminist women friends to examine my own behavior. Or the experience of encountering, for what I assumed then was the first time, women who had been battered or raped, and my decision to try to do something—anything I could—to work with men to stop.

There are, of course, other stories, earlier stories, about my gender socialization as a boy, my experiences with boy culture, sports, and the small violences we both do and are done to us to extract an uneasy conformity to norms of masculinity that we neither created nor particularly like.

During graduate school, while I seem to have been accumulating all those other stories I would rely on as pieces of an explanation, I reflected on my undergraduate experience, and how participating in an unusual historical moment—the first coeducational class at Vassar College—had affected my political development and my support of feminism. I wrote the following essay in 1975 with no particular outlet in mind, more as a way to try and begin to sort those experiences into a coherent narrative.

Vassar provided what we sociologists often refer to as "taking the role of the other." Being in such a small but visible minority afforded an angle of vision that was rare and in some ways precious: I was able to witness male predatory sexual behavior not from the point of view of the perpetrator (although there was surely plenty of that) but from the point of view of those upon whom such behavior was being launched.

This essay is the product of that initial immersion into thinking analytically, sociologically, about the political engagement I was inching toward. It was an essay written to try and map a personal trajectory toward a politics I hadn't yet quite defined.

Typically, when reading an article or essay I wrote many years before, I often wince at the sorts of glaringly dumb things I said. Yet occasionally, there is a moment, a sentence, a phrase, that sings to me still, that resonates for me today, that makes me feel some affection for the boy who wrote it.

Reading this essay now, I wince, wondering about the sophomoric formulation, the self-congratulatory posture, the self-righteousness, and the moral high ground I somehow found easier to occupy at age twenty-five than I do more than thirty-five years later. For example, I soon backed away from calling myself a "feminist" and developed a rhetoric of "pro-feminism" to try and position myself relative to the women's movement without appropriating the term.

But I also smile in recognition of the effort, and identify with the young man struggling toward something that he didn't know at the time would come to define his adult life.

Sure, there are a few sentences that are no longer true, a few where I was carried away on the wings of hyperbole. And yet there are a few that are even more true. The Denver Broncos aren't notable for holding hands in their huddles anymore—but so many other teams do!

The impulse to "turn around and see who's behind you" has, today, two meanings for me. It pushed me to look back to the rich historical legacy of men who supported gender equality. The documentary history, Against the Tide: Pro-Feminist Men in the United States, 1776–1990 *offers a collection of original statements, pamphlets, speeches, and articles so those men's actual words might continue to inspire new generations of men.*

Today, it also means that I look behind at new generations of young men who are now taking the lead in efforts to mobilize men in the support of women's equality. True, it is somewhat disconcerting to realize that my work now can be filed under the category of "history"—as the present always straddles past and future, I'm afraid

I've now begun to list towards the past. Yet there is something immensely gratifying for having been part of a rich tradition of men publicly supporting women's equality, and also for working with others to continue that legacy. I offer this essay now to that new generation of men as one small part of that history, that legacy.

I've left the text as I wrote it in 1975, changing only a few grammatical errors and inserting a line or two here or there for clarification.

I do so not because I stand behind every word I wrote more than thirty-five years ago; indeed, I would take a few things back, mute or sharpen various points, or change the language. No, I leave it the way I wrote it not because I stand behind every single word, but because I still stand with the young man who first wrote them.

In the spring of 1973, noted anthropologist Margaret Mead, speaking at Vassar College, mentioned the exciting new relationships between women and men she had been observing at Yale. She remarked that most of the male–female relationships had been re-oriented around non-sexual friendships rather than sexual involvement. In fact, she noted that many of the dormitories reminded her of enormous extended families, characterized by an inviolable incest taboo, with sexual coupling maintained only outside the dorm.

As I left the lecture, my friends commented how laughably incorrect her perceptions of Vassar were, and that, with the introduction of coeducation, the college had been transformed "from a convent into a roller derby" in which indiscriminate promiscuity was the norm. Although I had been away from Vassar for almost a year at the time, I argued that Mead was more or less accurate in her perceptions and they roughly matched my experiences at Vassar. My years there as a student were far from a sexual free-for-all; in fact, it was in that context that I first began to take sexual involvement seriously. These notes are an attempt to describe the ways in which the character of my interpersonal relationships was begun to be transformed.

AVANT LE DÉLUGE

I would be lying if I was to write that my sexual development into an American man has been even, smooth, or consistent with the value patterns that seem most common. But it would be similarly incorrect to say that I am somehow different than most men. I grew up in the same society, with the same sets of values, as everyone else.

I was raised in a comfortable, upper-middle-class suburb near New York City. Largely white and predominantly Jewish, high school was seen mostly as an uncomfortable but necessary obstacle to hurdle on the way to college. A high level of social order was maintained by the simple, omnipresent threat that any wrongdoing would immediately "go on your college record." The thought of being prevented from going to college was so powerful that most of us docilely stayed in line. In fact, among my peers, the mere fact of going to college was not nearly as important as where one was going. We were judged, and judged each other, by the academic reputations of our chosen schools. And although there was hardly a moment during my high school life when I wasn't morbidly preoccupied with women, often to the point of distraction, I knew that a "quality" education could only be obtained at a men's college.

My preoccupation with women was probably a substantial motivation to desire a single sex college. Women *were* a distraction, the finest distraction ever invented, to be sure, but a distraction nonetheless. A friend, who had gone to Dartmouth, had given me some brotherly advice: "You should have your work during the week, and your women on the weekends. Never let them overlap." Indeed, they couldn't overlap. Women were soft and cuddly weekend playthings, and weekends were a time for a rapid retreat from the intellectual world. The work-week was reserved for study to understand the world, with either the desire to make it or overthrow it (sometimes both). The last thing that was to be on our minds was serious intellectual discussion on a weekend designed for fun. That "fun" I was told early in my freshman year meant "the three Bs: booze, broads, and (foot)ball."

The better part of my first year at that all-male school was spent making many of the symbolic gestures that would demonstrate my opposition to what I saw around me. My definition of myself was a residual category, which was composed of the negation of what I observed around me. What they were, I would not be. They drank for relaxation, I advocated temperance; they enjoyed athletics, I wrote poetry; they seemed happy, I vacillated between a desperate depression and maudlin self-pity; students were oriented toward engineering and sciences, I would major in philosophy and art; they lived in fraternities, I would live in a commune (which, it strikes me now, are not so different as we once thought); they wanted to use their education to climb higher on the social ladder, I wanted to use mine to topple the ladder.

By the middle of my second year, it seemed futile to continue in an atmosphere in which I couldn't grow except in opposition. I was too well socialized, though, to abandon education altogether and drop out. I decided to transfer.

UNLEARNING THE LIES

The entire fabric of my interpersonal relationships was dramatically changed during the years I was a student at Vassar. In this section, I will try to sketch some of the ways in which my relationships with women were transformed, while the next section will deal with the new ways I found to relate to men.

The changes in my relationships with women were the result of the confluence of three factors, each in itself necessary, yet none sufficient by itself to foster that change. First, I began to deal with women in the context of a high level of intellectual discussion. Secondly, I was able to observe from a unique position the complex and subtle ways in which men relate to women, as an observer of the men from nearby men's schools and the men at Vassar, as well as a participant in the working out of my own relationships. Finally, and most importantly, all of my development must be seen in a larger social and political climate that characterized the dramatic changes that were felt throughout American society in general, and the focus of a large part of that change on the institutions of higher education. In particular, there was a sense of attempting to make one's personal relationships consistent with one's political convictions; that is, recognizing the political element in personal relationships.

When I first arrived in the fall, 1970, Vassar was in the midst of an institutional identity crisis. Having made a commitment to coeducation, the school was in the throes of a cataclysmic collective reappraisal of its intellectual and social priorities. Now that they had decided to admit men, what were they going to do with them? The college had taken a major step in defining the terms of the coeducational transition as "coequal" which meant, in essence, that neither sex would receive deferential treatment, and the college's orientation would not be ordered solely on criteria of gender.

There were, however, some substantive changes that were brought about with the coming of the men. As with many single sex colleges in difficult (or inaccessible) locations, Vassar on a weekend often appeared as it does during a summer: a campus abandoned to the lonely or excessively studious. Most women simply packed up and left for a nearby men's college committed to providing adequate cultural diversions for its residents. (Most of the more popular men's schools were also located in or near a major city, which independently generates its own cultural diversions.) In fact, until 1971, the college still chartered at least one bus to transport Vassar women to Yale for the weekend. (As I had a good female friend who had transferred to Yale that first year, I believe I hold the distinction of being the first male to ride the Yale bus.)

With the arrival of men as a permanent fixture on campus, the weekend exodus began to wane. The college began to organize weekend cultural activities, developing, for a college of its size, a remarkable number and wide range of things to do. And if Vassar women were as likely to stay around campus for the weekend, the men from the nearby schools would be sure to come to Vassar. And when they came, I found myself in the uncomfortable position of observing in operation those very values that had initially led me to go to a single sex college. This time, however, I found myself on the other side.

Friday evening dinners in my dormitory were often characterized by the obtrusive entrance of a small, but conspicuous group of men. Upon entrance, they would separate into pairs and trios, single out a table that had a number of attractive women who appeared to be unattached, and begin the long symbolic dances of seduction. Most of the women I knew reacted with a combination of indignant anger and curious fascination, coupled with an uncomfortable anxiety that they might, if approached, be unable to get rid of these men. I was, at first, embarrassed to be a man and watch the spectacle enacted by many other men, and to see the effect it was having on my friends.

I felt angry at the men and protective toward the women. How could these men, I asked, who know nothing about these women, with whom I live, expect to spend the night with them? I believed that if I wasn't going to sleep with them so indiscriminately, neither should they. I felt then as I had earlier felt with my younger sister. Her sexual involvement would develop when it was her choice to develop it, not on the momentary whim of someone trying to convince her that it was her choice. I wanted to protect her from those calculating bastards. I knew their routines too well; I had tried them myself. And neither my sister nor my friends in the dorm had to stand for that nonsense.

For a while, I was committed to subverting the blatant attempts of the "intruders." When I saw a friend being harassed, I would often walk up to her table and, pretending to be her lover, lead her away from her suitor. When masses of West Point cadets would show up, a number of men responded more systematically; once, for example, a telephone call to the dorm receptionist from "Colonel Taggart" ordered all cadets back to the West Point bus for unannounced evening maneuvers. In all, though, my self-concept was still derived negatively, relative to the men from the men's colleges.

It was an uncomfortable position. I am, after all, a man. Yet I was finding, in my own relationships, that the traditional male behavior patterns were not capable of letting me develop relationships that were satisfactory either to me or to the women with whom I was involved. There was always a residual fear that my resistance to these men's behaviors might mean I was gay, yet I was pretty sure I was heterosexual. I began to search for new ways of relating with women based on new criteria for relationships.

The classroom became the first arena of personal struggle. Quite often (since there were so few men in the entire school, and even fewer junior transfers—my graduating class of 478 included only 26 men) I was the only man in a class. But rarely, if ever, did I dominate the discussion. I was somewhat surprised—and not always delighted—to discover so many women who were as bright (if not brighter), verbal, and articulate as I was. But there was something else, far more profound. While my previous classroom experiences had been successful, they had always left me feeling isolated and alone as each man tried to outdo the other for precious grades. My classes at Vassar were not only characterized by a high level of intellectual rigor, but a warm, non-competitive atmosphere that was both stimulating and supportive.

My education had previously been a form of delayed gratification in which certain tasks, however distasteful, had to be learned for externally defined ends. At Vassar, however, I began to see something inherently gratifying and exciting in intellectual pursuits. By learning in a non-competitive atmosphere, I was unafraid to become personally committed.

This commitment was heightened greatly by the content of the courses as well as by the context. In the social sciences, we were dealing with issues of immediate consequence, and classroom discussion was often highly personal and political. Sometimes the two were fused. I believe I learned more during these discussions than at any other time.

But this, too, must be kept in perspective. My college days were at a time of great social and political unrest, which was largely, but not entirely, centered around universities. I do not agree with those critics who argue that the withdrawal from active encounters and confrontations with the symbolic agents of the war-crazed establishment was the result of the failure of the student movement to generate any meaningful changes. Rather, I think that any political movement that will be worth anything must periodically undergo serious self-examination of its own internal dynamics to make them congruent (as much as is possible) with the society one is trying to build. And Vassar women, with their long tradition of fighting in the forefront of the women's movement, were painfully aware of their position in a sexist society. Many women at Vassar were involved in the carving out of new, positive identities for themselves as women, not in relation to the occupational role of a man (like being a "lawyer's wife") but relative to themselves as women.

I felt, for myself, that in feminism was the ability to break free of arbitrarily defined modes of behavior that had been defined for me by someone else and to finally develop ways of relating that were consistent with both my personal experiences and my political philosophies.

LEARNING TO LIVE THE TRUTH

The fact that there is such a widespread women's movement in modern America implies the very obvious fact that women are not equal. And while it is not the function of this piece to develop either the characteristics of the subtle mechanisms that systematically oppress women, nor to suggest the logistics of the demystification of sex roles in a sexist society, it is useful to recall here Sally Kempton's words: In the war against sexism, "the outposts of the enemy are in our own heads."

Women are, to be sure, the victims of centuries of domination. But women, too, daily reproduce those very mental structures which have oppressed them, and in the transmission of those values with each other, victimize other women. The underlying logic of women's consciousness raising is a logic of collective struggle to unlearn the lies of their lives. It is a process of learning to unlearn, an internal battle with an enemy both without and within.

While men have collectively been the front-line army of the victimization of women, they are themselves victims of the perpetuation of those same values. The same mental structures have been internalized, in no less a profound way, deep into the inner reaches of the male unconscious. Men develop myths about both women and men that perpetuate the existing value structures. Although different in kind from the myths that women develop about themselves (but which nonetheless serve the same function of keeping them alienated from one another), male myths are no less deeply rooted and no less profound.

Some of these myths deal specifically with our relationships with women. Women, we are told, are designed biologically to be more naturally disposed toward domestic tasks. They do not experience the same passions or drives that men experience. They need not have an orgasm to enjoy sex, but men must experience orgasm. Their reactions are more likely to be emotional than logical. The list goes on and on. Most myths are designed to soothe our fragile ego from serious vulnerability in sexual encounters.

The myths we maintain about ourselves with other men are equally profound. Young boys, kissing their father goodnight, will someday (at an "appropriate" age) be told that grown men do not kiss, they shake hands. It is unnatural for men to show any physical affection for one another. (Except, of course, the more-than-male athletes, who can get away with it. I am yet to hear anyone accuse the defensive unit of the Denver Broncos, who hold hands during their huddle, of being homosexual.) It is not manly to show any type of emotion at all. Men are always rational. Men do not cry.

In short, women are reduced to whimpering mindless house servants and men to calculating emotionless rocks. And if we are going to change our relationships with women to develop non-exploitative relationships, we must simultaneously alter the ways in which we deal with other men.

My experiences with other Vassar men were fundamental to my becoming able to take the leap from the secure plateau of traditional relationships into the uncharted void of non-exploitative relationships. Although I will return to this shortly, I cannot overemphasize the positive functions of social support. It is a powerfully lonely experience to attempt the transformation of the values that have, for so long, made one whom he or she is. And it is both a relief and an impetus to continue when we discover other men involved in the same struggle.

But one reaction after taking those early steps is to turn around and see who's behind you. My steps were not individual steps, but social steps. I was determined to turn around and help those who were first struggling to take those same risks. I became a freshman counselor in my dormitory, and through that experience, found that many students were still somewhat traumatized at the thought of seeking professional help. Consequently, a number of students, Vassar's resident psychiatrist, and I organized ourselves to develop a peer-counseling program to augment the already overworked professional staff.

In my experiences as a counselor, I dealt with other men who were having difficulty in establishing healthy relationships. A number of men, who had not had any successful dating experiences in high school, had declined offers of admission to superlative men's schools to come to Vassar because they felt they could not only receive an excellent education, but could meet and date a variety of women. When, after three or four months at Vassar they were still unable to develop those relationships, they frequently turned the situation on themselves, believing themselves to be "natural" failures with women. Many men I spoke with voiced fears about their own sexuality, and a sizable number were anxious about possibly being latent homosexuals. Many men, measuring their successes quantitatively, expressed some reservations about the quality of their relationships. Nearly all of them spoke about their inability to develop meaningful friendships with men.

The atmosphere I tried to create with each of the men I met was one of empathy and support. I could not help but relate personally to so many of their fears and anxieties, and consequently was not able to ever achieve the dispassionate distance that often characterizes "professional" relationships. Nor did I seek to achieve it. I wanted instead to understand the dimensions of each man's emotions and to share with him the sense that I was able to feel, and had felt before, what he was expressing.

Rather than feeling alone in my attempts to reconstruct my relationships along more trusting lines, I began to realize how many men were struggling with similar problems and identical causes. We are never taught how to relate with one another; instead we are taught how not to relate. The rules that govern our most important activity as human beings, the formation of interpersonal relationships, do not tell us what we should do, but what we should not do. And seeing so many men in a similar position led me to the feeling that men, too, need a positive collective experience with each other to better come to terms with our individual transformations. Male consciousness raising should not be seen as the activity that men participate in because their women are involved in women's groups. On the contrary, we developed our male group as a positive response to our perception that men must become part of a collective process of redefinition of our identities within a context of mutual trust and support. This is the essential feature of consciousness raising groups. And while the overwhelming majority of the men who participated did so, at first, because of a desire to understand their relationships with women, we soon realized that we were simultaneously and irrevocably altering our relationships with each other, and, by extension, with other men.

WHERE WE ARE GOING

Men in the modern world face perhaps the most serious challenge to their traditional modes of behavior that we have ever faced. Traditional male roles are one of the single largest causes of a great deal of the anxiety, fear, confusion, and unhappiness that we experience. Not only have men become insecure about their identities at work (when so many of us are easily replaced by machines that are so much more efficient) but profoundly insecure about our identities at home. Because of our training, we are afraid to show these anxieties, for the compounding fear of being viewed as weak.

The sexual revolution, like any political revolution, has left many casualties in its wake. We have been brought up in a world of evaluations based on our performances, and our most intimate performances are also our most vulnerable. Men are not the only gender that is capable of evaluating lovers on the basis of their performance, and many men have simply dropped out of the race for fear of losing. As Stirling Moss once wrote: "There are two things no man will admit he can't do well: drive and make love."

We are afraid to relate to other men for fear that we might be secretly gay, or that they might be, or that "things" might just get out of control. It appears far more secure and far less risky to simply avoid the issue, thus cutting us off from any expression of trust between men.

It would be far too facile to throw the entire burden of this very complex problem on individual men (or individual women) and argue that if only we could clean up our personal lives, everything else would fall into place. This line of reasoning ignores a very fundamental issue: The society in which we live is maintained precisely through the perpetuation of our traditional behavior and reinforced by myths about natural predispositions.

On the other hand, it is a convenient shirking of individual responsibility to fail to confront ourselves as the microcosmic reproduction of these very social values on the individual level. We cannot afford to simply wait for the great social transformation to happen of itself, and in its wake sweep aside old modes of relating.

Instead, both levels of action are necessary. At every level, we must collectively confront the maintenance of a system based on competition instead of cooperation, profit as opposed to pleasure; a system that teaches callous manipulation of others for our own ends rather than the development of sensitive and trusting relationships as ends in themselves. But we must also be constantly in the process of transforming ourselves into the people we want to be.

This personal transformation is by no means easy. For me, it has barely begun. And that beginning has been frightening and painful. It means leaving the comfortable security of social behavior that has been well defined over the years and carefully delimited by easily discernible sets of rules, and jumping into a netherworld of non-exploitative relationships for which there are no rules. Without those rules, there is no basis for evaluation and no knowledge of the expectations of others involved. And it is very scary to be making up the rules as you go along.

It means working out the logistics of sexual demystification, in which sex is no longer maintained as a scarce commodity but a beautiful facet of human expression. It means transforming our deeply rooted definitions of behavior. For example, it involves the transformation of our definition of weakness from the inability to conceal one's emotions to the inability to express those emotions. Conversely, we must transform strength from the impermeability to pain to the ability to express whatever we feel. It means giving up standard behavior patterns (no matter how successful they are by someone else's criteria) for the discomfort of not knowing exactly where you are. It means not playing the games in which someone else has made up the rules, but taking active control of our own lives. It means abandoning the enemy's outposts in our heads, and beginning the process of dismantling the barricades that sexism has erected in our lives. It often means being very profoundly alone.

There are a number of things that I have found, that, while they don't eliminate the loneliness and the fear, nonetheless provide the grounding so I can continue. Feminist women have constantly supported me in my struggles and shared the problems and the anxieties (as well as the exhilaration) of their struggle to transform their selves and their environment.

The greatest impetus has been from other feminist men, who are similarly trying to deal with the ways in which we relate to women, to ourselves, and each other. In both structured situations (like consciousness raising groups) and informal discussions with friends, I have felt both sensitive understanding and support for my own development. The process is by no means complete. I wish that I could report to you, at this time, that I have successfully undermined all those traditional values and replaced them with new "liberated" values. But I haven't. In fact, I have barely begun a struggle that will probably last for my lifetime. And yet I am convinced, even at this early stage, that I have begun to develop qualitatively superior relationships, with both men and women, than any I have ever known. The process is still frightening and painful at times. But it isn't so lonely anymore.

If anything is clear from my personal account of my development into a male feminist, it is this: I am not an exception, who by virtue of the presence or absence of one particular component, or the existentially unique composite of a number of components, has been thrust into the void of non-traditional relationships. Rather, I am part of a growing number (and I am amazed at how rapidly it is growing) of normal, "regular guys" who have started to reclaim their lives as their own. Once taken, it is a long and difficult road to keep control of it. But we cannot give it back.

CONFESSIONS OF A PREMATURE PRO-FEMINIST

Rob Okun

I look out at the expanse of lawn before me to a sea of lighted matches held aloft, dotting the dusk sky with sparks of brightness like white caps on a rolling ocean. The Washington Monument looms large—a stoic rear guard ready for another gathering of volunteers reporting for anti-war duty on a balmy evening in the nation's capital. It is May 8, 1970. I am a sophomore at George Washington University.

From my perch in the corner of a temporary stage, I can see both the intense, bearded poet at the microphone inviting the assembled to hold up their "lights of peace" and, before me, the illuminated, outstretched arms of thousands of my brothers and sisters. Now, holding his harmonium up to the microphone, Allen Ginsberg begins playing and chanting, mixing a spiritual longing for peace among all beings with acerbic, poetic jabs at the current occupant of the White House—the architect of a brazen, disastrous Vietnam War policy—Richard Milhous Nixon. Days before, the Commander-in-Chief had announced to an increasingly divided nation that he had ordered a new assault, a bombing campaign in Cambodia. Outraged, students around the country began staging hastily planned demonstrations to protest this audacious, illegal widening of the war outside of Vietnam. On May 4, at a demonstration at Kent State University, Ohio, the National Guard shot four students dead and wounded several others. Days later, Mississippi State Troopers killed two students and wounded twelve others at Jackson State University. The war had come home.

Situated just four blocks from the White House, George Washington University was a geographically appropriate campus host for national demonstrations. I played a small part organizing the gathering on the evening of May 8, a cultural prelude to the massive demonstration scheduled for the next day. Along with hearing Ginsberg's poetry, before the night was over we also listened to Judy Collins sing "Where Have All the Flowers Gone?" and to Abbie Hoffman symbolically silencing Nixon, speaking to the nation through a giant cabinet model television placed at center stage. Before the weekend was over, a widening crack in the shaky consensus to wage war in Southeast Asia was exposed.

In the late summer of 1968 I was eighteen years old and beginning college. The 1960s had been like a wildflower growing in a New England meadow that needed minimal sun and rain to thrive. The era was rife with the light of possibility and the storms of injustice, offering me a heady mix of social conditions in which my political awareness quickly grew. It had just been a matter of time. In those days it would have taken real effort not to be aware of the anti-war and civil rights movements: News anchor Walter Cronkite brought them to our supper table every evening through the black and white portable television on the kitchen counter. Our family debated both over mom's meatloaf. The women's movement, however, was not part of the conversation. Even though a number of years had passed since Betty Friedan published her catalytic book, *The Feminine Mystique*, the ideas and activities of women's liberation had not yet intruded upon the American family's dinner hour. So when I arrived at George Washington University on a steamy August afternoon—the shocking display of Chicago Mayor Richard Daley's police brutally beating student protestors at the Democrats' presidential convention still on the front page—the women's movement was not what I saw. It would be some time before I understood women's second-class citizenship as a central component in the social-change puzzle I was beginning to try to solve.

My parents had barely said goodbye that August day in 1968 when I hopped on a bus for a view of the "Other Washington." As an alternative to the University's sugar-coated bus tour of the city's landmark monuments, radical politicos had organized a tour through areas of the city the university did not want students to see: the parts scorched and burned by angry, grief-stricken African-Americans outraged at the assassination of Martin Luther King, Jr. just four months earlier. On that bus were many students who, I would discover, shared my passion for social justice. They were the people I would come to know. Like me, they were hungry to find and shape an alternative culture.

Looking at the boarded-up buildings from the window of the bus, witnessing the rubble in front of vacant storefronts, I felt tears welling up in my eyes. "This is the 'Other Washington'—and the 'Other America,'"—I thought. My college education had begun. The bus ride I took that weekend set a course for my life.

Back on campus—in clean, white, well-appointed, Northwest Washington— I was struck by what the bus driver had asked toward the end of the tour: "It's been four months since Dr. King was murdered and the riots happened. No one in this city has yet to begin rebuilding. Why?" To my eighteen-year-old eyes the gap between whites and blacks, haves and have nots, could not have been more apparent.

My alternative orientation to university life continued the next day with a protest of the Soviet Union's recent invasion of Czechoslovakia. I accompanied a group of activists on an otherwise conventional tour of Washington, D.C.'s Embassy Row. At the Soviet Union stop, however, while a Moscow hack spouted the party line, at a prearranged signal a handful of us stood and held signs aloft decrying the invasion. Mine, if memory serves, simply read, "For Shame."

As the fall semester unfolded, only my Journalism and American Civilization classes—which sometimes referenced news of the day as text—nudged me to class. Otherwise, school was a major distraction from my education in the streets. I could feel my connections with my new tribe deepening and, as they grew stronger, I began to enlarge my definitions of friendship, of family, and of community. And it was through that loose collection of hippies, freaks, and activists that the first glimmers of my awareness of gender politics began to glow.

Decades later I recognize how uninformed I was about the politics of women's liberation, not to mention gay rights. Neither was visible to me during my years in Washington. What I did sense was a vaguely articulated question posed by an inner voice: *If I'm promoting peace over war in Vietnam, and integration over segregation for people of color, what about equality over subjugation for women?* At the time, though, I had neither the language nor the community to spark an inquiry into women's second-class citizenship. At George Washington University in 1968 women's studies classes did not yet exist and feminist newspapers like *off our backs* had not yet begun publishing. It would be four years before the first issue of *Ms.* magazine arrived on the newsstands. What I had to go on was a vague feeling something wasn't right; it was a feeling I didn't always pay attention to.

Anti-war political meetings in those years were loud, boisterous, and dominated by white males. We were a flamboyant group—men in olive army fatigue jackets, red and blue bandanas around our throats or foreheads, tie-dyed T-shirts, faded blue jeans with carefully sewn patches at the knees. Women often wore peasant blouses and long denim skirts. Our footwear was unisex: army boots in winter; moccasins, sandals, or bare feet in summer. The irony of appropriating army culture on the one hand and Native American clothing on the other was lost on us, obscured, perhaps, by our hair. Which was everywhere—long, straight, and parted down the middle; men's to their shoulders, women's at least to the middle of their backs. The wispy beards that some of us had at eighteen, grew thick and full by twenty-two. Curly-haired white guys let their hair grow out into Afros, another obvious cultural appropriation. Think Jerry Garcia meets Jimi Hendrix.

While I'm sure I didn't consciously take note of the gender makeup of our meetings, in a roomful of twenty there were usually no more than five or six women. As hip and as cool as we were, it was usually guys who spoke out—whether planning the next demonstration or organizing the trip to a Grateful Dead concert (or just the next trip). They spoke with a sense of entitlement that could only be described as white male privilege, a term not yet coined and clearly not widely understood by men. What was it that allowed me to make the connection between whites' privilege and oppression of blacks—

which we all saw clearly by then—but not men's privilege and oppression of women?

I suppose I can fall back on my eighteen-year-old naiveté, my lack of experience in how the world worked. But deep down, I knew something wasn't right. In the tiny anti-war movement office on G Street, a storefront sandwiched in between a deli and a dry cleaners, we drank coffee and Coke, smoked cigarettes and pot, separated women from men. Well, not exactly. The separation was more along the lines of women and children in one category; men in the other. As young and innocent as I appeared, I was initially steered to the women's section of our revolutionary ship of state. But since in the late 1960s our movement—unlike the *Titanic*—hadn't run aground or hit an iceberg, it was women and children last, not first. The women and the younger men made coffee, ran the mimeograph machine, hit the streets to put up posters, tried to convince other students to join the cause. Occasionally, a woman or two took the floor at a meeting and passionately and powerfully talked about an upcoming action, but this was the exception. There was a blindness among the male anti-war movement leaders, a presumption that as men they were entitled to be in charge.

Long before the photograph of Cuban revolutionary leader Ché Guevara became a famous T-shirt, it seems our movement had claimed as its own the romantic, masculine vision his portrait represented. There was little room for women's ideas, women's ways. It is no surprise that an independent women's movement would evolve alongside—and independent of—the anti-war movement. And it is no wonder that the insights of feminism would contribute so significantly to social change consciousness in subsequent decades.

As long-haired, rebellious young men moving to the pulsing drumbeat of the anti-war protest movement, many of us saw our path to adulthood diverging from the path our peers were taking in the jungles of Vietnam. I remember one spring driving on the Washington beltway in my brother's VW, seven of us packed in en route to Baltimore for a Janis Joplin and Big Brother and the Holding Company concert. We came upon a caravan of seven or eight open-backed army trucks tightly filled with soldiers in camouflage uniforms, topped with matching, flat-rimmed caps over closely shaved heads. We were keeping pace with them, us in the left lane and them in the right, heading, for the moment, in the same direction. We were all the same age yet we were taking such different roads to manhood. In those days when I saw soldiers I'd shake my head dismissively, not understanding what drew them to the military.

My friends and I were part of a movement that rejected militarism as the defining ideal of a masculine identity. We knew that anti-war activism meant we risked being seen as less than "real men" (even though a popular slogan from the period read, "Girls Say Yes to Boys Who Say No"). Sadly, we never tried to find common ground on which to meet with those who were soldiers.

But tonight, as we rode alongside the caravan, I asked myself, "Who were these soldiers?" Were they shipping out soon for Nam? What was it like to be leaving behind everything and everyone you cared about? I was riding in the front passenger seat nearest the caravan. The folks on my side of the car rolled down our windows and started flashing the peace sign at the soldiers. Miraculously, the soldiers flashed it back, a sea of hands raised high, index and middle fingers spread wide. In that moment I felt joined by our youth and our idealism, even if we lived in a parallel universe.

As we passed the lead truck, I locked eyes with a soldier who reminded me of a kid from my hometown in Massachusetts. He looked tough and unemotional. I was beginning to get an inkling about how some guys my age were playing out their passage into manhood and I understood that the smooth stock of a rifle could actually be a comfort to him. I didn't yet know what my brand of masculinity would end up looking like, but I knew it would not include sleeping with my rifle, a soldier's best friend.

Midway through the concert that night, when the darkened Baltimore hall was hazy with marijuana smoke, the image of the caravan of soldiers came back to me. I had never heard Janis Joplin sing live before and her voice that night tore "a little piece of my heart" as it scratched, cried, and caressed. She spoke to us as members of the tribe and I felt hopeful, buoyed. Somewhere in the jumble of memory and emerging adult consciousness was a young man finding his way.

I remember a gathering in the G Street movement office where we were planning a demonstration some weeks before the 1968 presidential election. We were going to hang effigies of the three major candidates—vice-president Hubert Humphrey, former vice-president Richard Nixon, and Alabama's segregationist governor, George Wallace. (Like many of my friends, I supported the candidacy of black activist, social critic, and comic Dick Gregory but I was only eighteen and, in those days, I wasn't old enough to vote.)

At the meeting I was sitting near an "older" woman in her twenties who, like me, was closely following the conversation. What distinguished her, I recall, was that frequently during the meeting she made insightful comments, offering at one point an idea about when to unveil the hanging figures for most dramatic effect. An older second-tier leader with long, dark hair and a handlebar moustache kept casting furtive glances at her while she spoke. Maybe he was interested in her but I remember feeling his expression more closely resembled the one parents shoot children when they want them to shut up. I felt vaguely upset and confused but wasn't quite sure why. It would be a long time before I'd be able to translate those feelings into words. If I had they would have been something like: *This woman is too smart to be running the mimeograph machine. She should be running the meeting.*

The light is beginning to fade as Judy Collins walks out to perform before the throng assembled that Friday evening. The stage we are on is large enough to hold about twenty people. I am in a good spot in the back corner, able to easily see the performers, speakers, and the crowd. Judy's luminescent blue eyes assess the scene as she stands for a moment acknowledging the sustained applause. Then she strikes a chord on her guitar and begins to sing. She rallies us, inspires us, enthralls us—her sweet, soaring soprano gliding overhead, its angelic vibrations a blessing. For a few moments she carries me beyond the vulnerability I am no longer able to mask, beyond the widening war I can't slow, beyond the callous government I can't awaken. And then she sings, "Where Have All the Flowers Gone?" ending with the verse that asks, "Where have all the young men have gone? . . . Gone for soldiers, everyone. When will they ever learn? When will they ever learn?"

I can no longer choke back the jangle of raw emotion I've been stuffing down. Tears begin to well up as all the pain and confusion, all the anger and despair I am feeling about the war, my country, my life, come flooding out. The very feelings that invincible young men are never supposed to show are there for all to see. The group on stage had packed in tight while Judy was performing, but now they part as she steps away from the microphone creating an aisle for her to walk through, guitar at her side. I am at the end, a longhaired manchild looking as if he'll burst into tears any second. She keeps walking and, even in my fragile state, I can tell she is headed straight for me, her wide, robin's-egg blue eyes brimming with compassion. I don't know what she did with her guitar but the next thing I remember is she gently held my face in her hands, looked at me with great tenderness, and leaned forward to plant a soft kiss on my lips. Then she was gone, taking with her much of the pain that overwhelmed me.

I have carried that memory with me all these years not just because Judy Collins kissed me, but because that moment was the beginning of a passage. It was years before I knew what the passage meant, years where I would slowly begin to live its meaning—allowing myself to be more vulnerable, allowing myself to show up more for my feelings. For a man coming of age in the last third of the twentieth century to express any feelings—besides anger—was rare.

It would take the next two decades to recognize that the tears I shed that night were not the sign of boyish weakness but were a healthy expression of being a man. During these years I began to improve my "Emotionalese," a language I long-sensed that the women in the anti-war movement office on G Street spoke fluently. Activist women seemed to know how to forge a new politics that integrated fluency in the language of emotions with a fiery passion for social justice and liberation. This was the moment defined by the feminist realization that "the personal is political." Like many men, though, I wasn't yet comfortable with the notion of integrating my inner and outer life. If more of us had, perhaps we would have worked alongside the activist organization "Another Mother for Peace." There would have been a parallel organization founded by fathers. After all, fathers—and men—are as interested in protecting their children from war as mothers and women. It may be hard to believe from today's perspective, but social conditions in the late 1960s were not yet ripe for men to say so.

The struggle women were waging to free themselves from the yoke of patriarchy became one I embraced. Not all at once, and not perfectly. But as part of the student protest movement I began to realize that women were being denied full access to power and privilege in a seemingly progressive political movement. This smoldering truth has never been extinguished. And while championing feminism became integral to my life, the embers of that support began to glow most brightly once I started working in a men's center. This work sparked a vision of gender reconciliation and of creating generations of strong, independent girls and sensitive, caring boys.

As my awareness of inequality grew, I began to see glimmers of the privilege I enjoyed. As a young, white male I felt entitled to do whatever I wanted. Even the specter of anti-Semitism didn't often intrude upon my life. The queasy feelings I had that women were marginalized had no real outlet beyond my slowly emerging consciousness. It seemed as if there was nothing I could do.

I'm certain women I knew at the time would have had reason to characterize me as sexist; perhaps a "kinder and gentler" version, but nonetheless far from a full-fledged ally. Few people outside of the burgeoning women's liberation community recognized the glaring blind spot in the vision of male leaders in the 1960s' anti-war movement. Women who exercised leadership in that movement had to do so by emulating their male counterparts, often adopting a confrontational male style. Shifts in gender roles and sharing power more equitably became noticeable during the anti-nuke movement in the mid-1970s where women exercised more leadership and had more of a voice. Nevertheless, sexism remained rampant in most progressive organizations.

My own path kept moving closer to actively engaging in gender politics, first by championing feminism and then working to redefine masculinity. During the 1980s as a proponent of feminist political art and, in the 1990s, as an advocate of male-positive, pro-feminist, gay-affirmative, anti-racist men's work, I came to discover the missing piece in my own social change puzzle. The halting voice of a timid eighteen-year-old recognizing that women in the anti-war movement were being given short shrift had matured into a man who was speaking up and speaking out. Today I direct the Men's Resource Center for Change, a progressive men's center that is seen nationally and internationally as a model for action. I take great satisfaction in the close collaborations we have developed over the years with battered women's shelters, rape crisis centers, women's newspapers, and feminist foundations. My wife and I live in an egalitarian household where my daughters proudly describe themselves as feminists and my son is an outspoken pro-feminist.

I developed my political awareness and became an activist not in isolation, but in community. My commitment was fueled by the camaraderie of kindred spirits walking block after block through late-night Washington, often beginning in the shadow of Richard Nixon's borrowed White House. My friends Buzz, Larry and Claire, Rob, Larry K, David—and their yearnings for justice and peace—kept me going. They inspired me and supported me because we shared a burning passion to change the world. The convergence of age, place, and time was nothing short of alchemy. The energy I felt coursing through me at eighteen triggered a lifetime's supply of political adrenaline—a mix of idealism, passion, practicality, and determination slowly seasoned, over the years, with patience.

My life has been shaped by being a part of 1960s history. I could feel it in 1972 when I interned at a Summerhill-inspired "free" school in Maine, sharing with young people a vision of a world without war or discrimination. The feeling was there five years later when I committed civil disobedience trying to halt construction of nuclear reactors in Seabrook, New Hampshire. And it was there in 1982 that, while serving as editor of the alternative energy/anti-nuke magazine, *New Roots*, I was arrested in front of the Soviet Consulate in New York City two days after a million people marched demanding a freeze of the nuclear arms race. Even the responsibilities of parenthood couldn't dampen a committed heart. In 1985, when my daughter was six weeks old, she rode in the back seat of the family station wagon in the middle of the night as her mother and I slipped out every block or so, painting human silhouettes on the streets of our town, symbolically representing the vaporized victims of the atomic bombs dropped on Hiroshima and Nagasaki on August 6 and 9, 1945.

Despite media reports smugly belittling activism as just a phase in a young person's life, a period before supposedly one settles down to join the daily commute toward consumerism and apathy, the spirit and heart of a movement for justice—call it the Children of Woodstock Nation, the Spirit of Seattle, the name doesn't matter—is alive and well. It's a spirit worth tapping into and returning to often over the course of a lifetime.

Part VI

Taking Action, Making Change

INTRODUCTION

M en increasingly identify as feminist whether by name or by action, or both. Journalist Elissa Strauss writes that "the rise of gay activism over the past decade has also drawn more men to the women's movement, due to the overlap of issues and objectives."[1] Then there are those men who become aware of feminist issues and gender justice activism because they had feminist mothers, date feminist women, or have other significant interaction with female feminists. Masculinities scholar Raewyn Connell comments that most men she knows support feminism because of these important personal relationships with women.[2]

Yet, the fact remains that men are frequently not engaged with feminist politics because they do not feel welcome, because they do not think the issues pertain to them, or because it simply does not occur to them to get involved. At the same time, separatist feminist groups may intentionally or inadvertently exclude men. Without men's active participation in feminist political organizing, however, three problems emerge: First, feminism without men inadvertently essentializes a political perspective while paradoxically arguing against essentialist foundations; second, a purportedly inclusive social movement risks framing itself in exclusionary terms; third, a political movement that has among its goals the equal access to the goods of society—and an equitable division of domestic work—renders itself responsible for doing the "dirty work" of fixing sociopolitical and interpersonal gender problems.

Feminism comprises both activism and knowledge construction. While these spheres inform each other, they are also qualitatively and politically distinct. Because some aspects of men's participation are more controversial than others, it is crucial to first unpack feminism: Feminism is a practice, a perspective, and a process; it includes constructing new frameworks for understanding politics and power while simultaneously setting concrete goals for change. Feminism can be both loudly political and deeply personal. The essays in this section reflect both sorts of action and change.

The question is, What are—or, what ought to be—men's roles in feminist activism and knowledge production? And do the challenges of men's participation and inclusion vary accordingly?

There are reasonable arguments for being cautious about men's participation in both knowledge production and in more applied forms of feminist political organizing. It may bother some women if men show up for a feminist rally such as SlutWalk or Take Back the Night. Some women object to men teaching in women's studies departments or running a campus women's center. The role of men in feminist leadership positions understandably remains an ongoing point of contention. But the issue of men's feminist activism is perhaps easier to deal with. By comparison, men's role in knowledge production is a far trickier proposition because this raises issues of identity, experience, and the privileging of perspectives. However, the bottom line is that when men get involved, there is the potential for achieving great success in reaching feminist goals—both personal and political. Sacchi Patel, co-founder of the online activist resource, MasculinityU.com, explains that it is important to engage men in redefining masculinity and to encourage men's equal role in issues such as ending gender violence.[3]

The six essays that complete this collection consider a variety of ways of taking action and making change. The strategies include public or private measures, analog and digital means. Each author encourages or documents the moments of epiphany by which men might find reasons to change and to become critically aware of the sorts of choices they are making in regard to sexism, masculinist behavior, and their relations with others. It is sometimes easy to blame institutions for promoting or upholding sexism, patriarchy, and kyriarchy. But as scholar Chris Pringle notes, institutions such as sports, for example, are not good or bad. Like so many institutions, "sports [per se] are not the problem; sexism is."[4] Given that we each live in relations to institutions, or derive enjoyment from them, then how can we improve the legislative process, or pop culture media, sports, or even radical politics? The authors in this section address this question.

"Men for Women's Choice" is a statement about reproductive health and choice, collectively written by a group of long-time activists in the pro-feminist men's movement. Promoting the basic premise is that all people should have the right to autonomy and bodily integrity, and that women should control their own bodies, the statement emerged in response to reactionary debate and sweeping legislation passed in states across the country—primarily by men—that deny women's access to reproductive health measures, from condoms to abortions. These issues suddenly re-emerged as contested political terrain following the 2010 elections and heated up even more in 2012.[5]

In "Living Online," Jeff Pollet writes about how the search for feminist community led him to online blogs and listservs. Pollet is aware that he is both an ally and a visitor among the online feminist community, and he writes about navigating his responsibility to both step back and listen, and to come forward and speak up. Pollet notes that anonymous blog commenting, hostile trolls, and a digital take-down culture, creates hostile, divisive space in a movement intended to foster collective action and solidarity.

"Steel-Toed Boots" is the story of Cliff Hixson, a working-class guy who grew up in the housing projects of Pittsburgh, Pennsylvania. Author Tal Peretz chronicles his friend Cliff's radical transformation from a racist skinhead to a progressive-minded student. Cliff, who wants to be a rehabilitation counselor in the inner city in order to make a positive difference in young people's lives, first crossed paths with Peretz in their college women's studies class. How does someone learn that hate and aggression are seemingly viable choices for "doing" masculinity? And what does it take to change their view?

"Good Ol' Boy: A Tale of Transformation in the Rural South" is a story of profound personal change. Author Jay Poole grew up in the southern, rural countryside. His parents were fundamentalist Christians and members of the Ku Klux Klan. In complete contrast to everything he had been taught was right, Poole realized he was gay. "Good Ol' Boy" describes his dramatic change in perspectives as he leaves behind the racist, hegemonic surroundings of his childhood to become a progressive-minded adult.

Based on his documentary, *The Bro Code: How Contemporary Culture Creates Sexist Men*, filmmaker and philosopher Thomas Keith's essay, "Breaking Down the Bro Code," describes homophobic rants, sexist quips, and alpha-male performances that are slim cover-ups for misogyny and homosocial engagement. There is epidemic date rape and sexual assault on college campuses, bro-posturing, sexist bravado, media celebration of sexist story lines and imagery, and an unwillingness by many men to examine themselves to see how their words and actions are contributing to sexism and misogyny in America, Keith explains. Yet he remains optimistic—if impatient—for the efforts of anti-sexist writers and speakers, activists, educators, and artists to impact the status quo and make a change.

The final essay in this collection, written by Chris Crass, is titled "How Can I Be Sexist? I'm an Anarchist!" A long-time anarchist and community activist, Crass confronts his surprise upon realizing his own sexist tendencies. These are subtle—almost invisible—patterns, but no less powerful than overtly sexist practices. Crass explains that history and contemporary life are full of examples of women's ideas gaining legitimacy only after men appropriate these views. This leads the public to believe that men are the primary culture producers. Crass provides clear-cut suggestions for men who are working for gender justice so that they can do so in ways that confront sexism, while avoiding the arrogance of privilege.

1. Elissa Strauss, "Do Men Belong in the Women's Movement?" *AlterNet*, February 13, 2012. Available at: http://www.alternet.org/media/153984/do_men_belong_in_the_women%27s_movement?page=entire#AlterNet (accessed June 25, 2012). See also http://bit.ly/AyGYol #AlterNet.

2. See R. W. Connell, "Long and Winding Road: An Outsider's View of U.S. Masculinity and Feminism," in Judith Kegan Gardiner, ed. *Masculinity Studies & Feminist Theory: New Directions*. New York: Columbia University Press, 2002.

3. http://www.masculinityu.com/ (accessed June 21, 2012).

4. Richard Pringle, "Sport, Strong Women, and Feminist Epiphanies," in Shira Tarrant, ed. *Men Speak Out: Views on Gender, Sex, and Power*, first edition. New York: Routledge, 2008, p. 245.

5. Michael Kimmel, Michael Kaufman, and Harry Brod. "Men for Women's Choice," *Women's Media Center Features*. March 12, 2012. Available at: http://www.womens mediacenter.com/feature/entry/men-for-womens-choice (accessed June 24, 2012); see also People for the American Way, "The GOP Takes Its War on Women to the States." Available at: http://www.pfaw.org/media-center/publications/gop-takes-its-war-women-states (accessed June 24, 2012).

MEN FOR WOMEN'S CHOICE

Like an ever-growing number of men around the world, we think that women should control their own bodies.

We hold these truths as deep moral beliefs. All humans should have the right to autonomy and bodily integrity. For women and men, this often means the same thing, but for women, it has an additional meaning: the ability to make choices regarding whether she will bear a child.

We believe that no man should be able to force a woman to bear a child she does not want. No man should be able to limit her ability to obtain safe and effective means of contraception.

We believe that the government has many important roles in our society. But the state has no place in the bedrooms of the nation.

There are those (including some who support this statement) who believe that abortion and contraception interfere with the workings of God. Men who support women's choice respect each person's right to make their own birth control and abortion choices based on their beliefs. At the same time, we share the belief that none of us has the right to limit or interfere with a woman's moral position or personal choices, nor interfere with health care providers who are assisting her right to exercise those choices.

As men with strong moral beliefs, as men for women's choice, we especially emphasize our belief that no man—no husband, no boyfriend, no judge, no doctor, no politician, and no religious leader—should have control over a woman's body. Ever.

With a wave of fresh attacks on women's rights, now is the time for us, as men, to speak out with loud and clear voices to express our profound concern. We urge men:

- to speak out in our communities, media, places of worship and halls of government in support of a woman's right to safe and effective means of contraception and abortion;
- to oppose arbitrary laws and regulations that make it difficult to obtain these medical services;
- to keep abortion out of criminal law and see it solely as a medical procedure to be utilized by a woman in consultation with her doctor;
- to support enhanced government funding and policies to ensure that women's reproductive rights are not only rights on paper, but that all women, regardless of where they live, where they work, or their financial resources, can obtain safe and effective birth control and abortion if they so choose;
- to support positive sexuality education in our schools that focuses on healthy relationships, sexual decision-making, and reproductive health (including the safe and effective use of birth control);
- to support political candidates who support these rights.

WHAT IS MEN FOR WOMEN'S CHOICE AND HOW CAN YOU MAKE A DIFFERENCE?

1. We are *not* an organization or a conventional campaign. We are part of a decentralized effort to encourage men to speak out in support of women's right to access safe and effective means of birth control and abortion.
2. We are men of all walks of life, religions, races, ethnicities, and political affiliations.
3. We encourage you to copy the statement (or download the PDF file at http://bit.ly/wb8dL5) and:
   - Circulate copies to your friends by email or in print form.
   - Post it on your website, Tumblr, Facebook, Google+, or other social media page.
   - Encourage members of your teams, clubs, organizations, unions, and associations to sign on and circulate it.
   - Use it as the text for an ad in your local paper.
   - Tweet about it.
4. We urge you to start a local campaign and:
   - Create posters, videos, music.
   - Hold breakfasts, vigils, press conferences in support of women's reproductive rights.
   - Raise money for organizations that campaign for women's reproductive rights or provide birth control and abortion services.
   - Support political candidates that support women's rights.
5. We also encourage you to speak with respect to those who disagree with you; and you should expect the same respect in return. One of the main tactics of those who want to control women's rights is to muzzle thoughtful discuss-

ion, to polarize, and to vilify and demonize those who disagree with them. We encourage men to take the moral high road, proudly holding our beliefs while respecting the right of others to hold their personal beliefs, as long as they don't force them upon others.

6. Who are we? What is Men for Women's Choice? It is us. We are you.

LIVING ONLINE

Jeff Pollet

Question: Are you a feminist?
Jay Smooth: Yeah, of course. Any argument I've heard from a man about why he's not
a feminist has always boiled down to rationalizing his own privilege and his desire
to hold on to it.
—vyou.com[1]

Not so long ago, in a world before blogs, I walked into a Women's Studies classroom for the first time. It was awkward. I wasn't quite sure what to expect, although I knew there might be some resistance to my being there. I left voicemails for the professor prior to the start of classes but they went unanswered. Since I hadn't heard back, I took a chance and showed up for class. *After all*, I thought, *I was registered for the class, and I wasn't afraid of feminists, or lesbians, or women, or anything like that.* Still, I was afraid of intruding, of getting in the way, of being somewhere I wasn't welcome—and for what might be perfectly good reasons. I walked into the class fully prepared for the possibility that I might be asked to leave. I kind of expected it and had already made my peace with that.

What actually happened was far less dramatic than any of that. That first day of class was just mildly uncomfortable—mostly for me. As I found my seat, I didn't see any friendly faces but there weren't folks scowling at me, either. I caught a few sidelong glances that I guessed were out of curiosity. The professor came in and class began like any other: handing out the syllabus, discussing the structure of the course, looking through the reading list.

But then there was a discussion. The professor noted that I had left her a voicemail asking if it was okay for a guy to take the class. She didn't really mind, she told us, but she thought that maybe some people in the class would mind, so she wanted us to all discuss it. Should we take a vote? Should there be a policy? Here was our first real class discussion: Did a man belong in a course on feminist authors?

This was academia, so it was kind of an abstract discussion. In part, we were talking about "a man." And yet, there I was, an actual man. It was pretty obvious that this wouldn't have been the first discussion of the semester had I (or some other guy) not been there. The general consensus was positive—it was good a guy was there, more guys should learn this stuff, that kind of thing. There were a few people who thought that the class should only include women, but mostly people were fine with me being there. In the end there wasn't a vote. The professor just decided to let me stay in the class, and my participation could be part of a continuing conversation if people wanted that to be a focus at all.

We never really talked about it again and I kept relatively quiet in that class. I mostly listened (though I'm sure I talked too much for some people), and what I learned most in that class was how to listen better. It was really my first experience being in a room full of women discussing anything. Sad but true. I never went out with my classmates to get a beer, even when they were kind enough to invite me, but I still got a glimpse into a feminist community. I had at least rubbed shoulders with it. And it felt good—a bunch of smart, driven women changing the status quo was a great group of people to hang out with for a few hours each week. Spending time in that community helped to start the slow process of shifting my view of the world. When I left college I missed that community quite a bit.

Fast forward. After graduation, I got my first-ever desk job, and it came with a perk: constant Internet access. That meant constant access to feminist websites and blogs. You name it, I read it. I read blogs that were to become "mainstream" feminist blogs, like *Feministing* and *Feministe!*, but I also read individuals' blogs with a feminist slant, like Kameron Hurley's *Brutal Women* and *Bitch, PhD*. I reveled in it. (You know, on my breaks.) Early on, I (kind of ignorantly) read blogs written mostly by white women feminists, but eventually I discovered sites like *Incite: Women of Color Against Violence* and *blac (k) ademic* among many others. I hadn't been a part of any feminist community since college, really, and here was a (virtual) community that was full of all types of feminists, including but not limited to young, old, queer, straight, black, white, able-bodied, disabled, women, womyn and, yes, *men*. It didn't seem like there were many men writing explicitly about feminism back then, but there were at least a few. Some men wrote for feminist blogs run by women. A few blogs sprang up that were launched by men. And where men weren't writing posts, they were commenting. It was a relief to know there were more of us out there than I'd thought. It felt like a community, I had a way to connect.

This was an Internet Win. Not only could I read what women were writing about feminism, but I could also read what men from around the world had to say in their posts and comments. And, of course this was also the Internet Fail. It turns out that many men aren't feminist but, rather, trolls. There are whole contingents of men online who are explicitly *anti*-feminist—even misogynist—and those boys are loud and proud.

Thing was, partly because online feminist communities have to deal with the douche-bag guys, there was also a seemingly endless discussion about whether or not men could be feminists at all, and whether, or to what degree, they should be allowed in online feminist spaces. It was as if the first discussion in my women's studies class was repeating itself over again, with the added damage of flame wars, trolling, anonymous anger, and banning. I didn't have quite as much caution in stepping into these feminist online communities as I did in stepping into the feminist community on my college campus. Some of this was because, by now, I had a small bit of experience in feminist circles, but it probably had more to do with the semi-anonymous nature of the feminist blogosphere. I began to be more cautious as I read what men had to say online about feminism.

While lots of feminist sites clearly encouraged men to post and comment, there was a recurring conflict centered on whether men could be feminists. That debate popped up pretty consistently. A comment thread would be moving right along and then: Bam! A commenter would be criticized because he was a man "taking up space" on a feminist blog, even if he may have been saying something which was, from his (however limited) perspective, insightful. The mistakes that even well-meaning men make while commenting on feminist blogs are numerous enough, and predictable enough, that many feminist blogs developed an FAQ/Feminist 101 section for the central purpose of educating these men. *Shakesville* has a special section of their FAQ just for the well-meaning-but-ignorant men. Titled "Helpful Hints for Dudes," it says:

> Sometimes, and rather frequently in recent weeks, privileged men (here, generally meaning straight cis men) email me asking advice on how to interact with the women in their lives. I get questions on everything from how to be a feminist husband to how to navigate intimacy with a survivor of sexual assault, and so I'm starting a new series that offers Helpful Hints to privileged men who genuinely want advice about how to be a more feminist-friendly dude.
>
> I'm starting with the most basic—and often the most problematic—interaction between men and women: The Conversation. Lots of guys want to learn more about deconstructing their privilege, but are pretty awful about obtaining that information without upsetting the women with whom they're conversing.
>
> This, then, is a very rudimentary, but also very straightforward, primer for dudes who want to communicate more effectively with female partners, friends, relatives, and colleagues during good faith conversations about feminist issues.[2]

The FAQ then lists a bunch of hints for men who are just starting out with feminist concepts such as "#3 No woman speaks for all feminists." Men who stumble into conversations and make the same mistake that a hundred others have before him can get pointed to the FAQ instead of (or in addition to) being called out as ignorant dumbasses.

But even men who are aware of these FAQs, who are attempting to tread lightly, are often shut down, even when they are sincerely trying to contribute to the conversation. On the popular feminist blog *Feministe!*, commenting on a post about "gaslighting" (the process by which abusers make their victims feel as if the abuse is imaginary by making them doubt themselves on every level), a commenter named "James" attempted to introduce another aspect of the problem. James wanted to note that he had caught *himself* gaslighting, and wanted to better understand how it perpetuates violence, and how to stop doing it. James seemed like the kind of guy who had already read the FAQs— he recognized that he may have been derailing the online conversation and explicitly asked for help from male allies, rather than take up the time of feminist women on the thread. He says:

> I'm really trying not to make this a 'what about a menz' post, but I feel like I should talk about this from an abuser's perspective. This isn't intended as an excuse. Rather, I'd like to address any male feminist allies.
>
> That's a hard label to swallow, isn't it? Abuser. But first step to recovering is admitting the problem.
>
> Me and gaslighting started with my father. My dad gaslit my mom all the time when I was growing up; though at least what was visible to me wasn't as drastic as some stories that have been told in these posts. Mostly it seemed like a joke, making ludicrous claims or obvious lies that everyone knew was false . . . [T]he patriarchy is constantly telling men that women are petty, shallow, catty, and vindictive. Women play games. Men are straightforward. Men are taught that to be any of these things at any time is simply impossible. But no one's perfect. We're all small sometimes. This creates a sort of cognitive dissonance that only gaslighting can resolve.
>
> So what's the fix here? I know what I'm going to do to try and stop it.
>
> Recognize the problem. I'm going to stop making any jokes that could possibly be gaslighting. Even if I think a 'joke' is obvious enough or silly enough to recognize and not do any harm, I'm not in a position to judge that.
>
> All men need to watch themselves for this, too. It's too easy to slip into or write off [gaslighting] as a 'joke.' You may think because you've never done anything remotely close to the horribleness in the stories in this thread that you're safe, but you're really not. It's a subtle, inching path to gaslighting.[3]

Something in the original post about gaslighting struck a chord with James, and he wanted to warn other men about how one can slide into being an abuser, which seems like an important thing to talk about. And even though James acknowledged that he didn't want to derail ("what about the menz" is shorthand for the very real tendency online for men to shift the discussion away from women), the author of the original post responded with a sarcastic correction to what James wrote, replacing "gaslighting" with "self-awareness":

> [James]: The patriarchy is constantly telling men that women are petty, shallow, catty, and vindictive. Women play games. Men are straightforward. Men are taught that to be any of these things at any time is simply impossible. But no one's perfect. We're all small sometimes. This creates a sort of cognitive dissonance that only self-awareness can resolve.

There, I fixed that for you.[4]

With a quip, the author effectively ended any conversation that James had attempted to start. What's more, this conversation-ender came from Lauren Bruce, one of the founders of *Feministe!*, a blog that is particularly feminist-guy friendly. In my opinion, Bruce is one of the best feminist writers online, but her shutdown of James is heartbreaking to me. At the same time, in a larger context, I also understand Bruce's response. It's difficult for feminist women to have an online community, a place for discussing serious issues like abuse, when men come in trying to work out their issues, as well. Not to mention what happens when ill-intentioned men show up. If blogs like *Feministe!* are meant to be spaces for women to work on feminist stuff, what *about* the men?

There were (and are) plenty of men invading feminist spaces—including those obviously anti-feminist men, but also well-meaning men, like James, above, who were ignorantly stumbling into the middle of conversations that had been going on for a long time. These men were called out and sometimes they were banned. Added to this mix are self-described radical feminists, who oversimplify this stuff, boiling it all down to the idea that men who really care about women will sit down and shut up:

> Nice men need to learn to be quiet and listen for a change instead of explaining our oppression to us and telling us how we're wrong. Genuinely nice men do not demand that we accommodate and prioritise [*sic*] their delicate feelings in our discussions. Preventing women from discussing supports male power and male power hurts women and children. Women discussing and supporting each other is crucial to women's survival—it really is ok to put our own needs first, in fact the survival of the planet and our children depends on it.[5]

And that's among the kinder versions of such thinking on the "radfem" blogs, which don't dominate the conversations online, but which are some of the most vocal. Of course, I don't totally disagree with this radfem train of thought. I just think there ought to be *some* spaces online for feminist-minded men to do good work and to find support. Maybe the contentious threads involving men, trolls, radfems, and others is part of living online. Perhaps this process goes with the territory of a feminist blog. But seeing the issue come up again and again is distracting, and sometimes really disheartening.

Mostly I feel welcome to comment on feminist sites. And the places where I'm not welcome make sense: Some places are explicitly women-only and there are reasons for this. To my mind, that's no big deal. That is one of the great things about the Internet: It's pretty big. There's plenty of room for me to be involved in other online spaces. Of course, discussions about who is a "Good Feminist" or what makes "A Good Man" continue to crop up. When an anti-choice conservative politician like Sarah Palin calls herself a feminist and reactionary men claim they deserve equal rights, these issues need to be addressed.

It gets frustrating, though. As a guy who identifies with many feminist ideals, it can be debilitating to participate in a community where sometimes my contributions are welcome—even encouraged—and in the next moment my community asks, for the millionth time, "Can men be feminists?" (This is sometimes a direct response to something I've said.) The question pops up a lot more when a feminist guy has done something uninformed/stupid/sexist/misogynist, or admits to having done something wrong in the past. And, boy, do we feminist men screw up. The thing is, feminist women screw up, too. Women even do misogynist stuff sometimes. And while they might get called out, nobody goes around fundamentally questioning whether women can be feminists after such a screw-up. It's just recognized that sometimes women make mistakes and they can improve upon their politics. But when male feminists make personal or political mistakes (and, again, we do! often!), the basic idea of men-as-feminists gets questioned. Maybe that's just how it has to be, but it's still discouraging. I recognize—and this is very important to me—that accountability is crucial to feminism's success as a social justice movement. I know that keeping women central in the movement is a core aspect of feminism. Grappling with the challenge of doing so is part of the little balsawood cross that male feminists have to bear. It's not that heavy and it's nothing like the burdens that women continue to bear.

I get that.

And yet, I find myself lamenting a lack of feminist community that I am consistently allowed to engage in. Sure, I'm privileged in various ways: As a man, as a white guy in the United States, as a cisgendered person. I understand that "my communities" (white, cisgendered) are considered the norm, and I get unearned privilege and power from all of that. I don't have a right to ask oppressed or subjugated communities to welcome me with open arms. That's how relinquishing unearned privilege works. But in some real sense, those hegemonic communities are not mine. I exist in a world that I didn't create and I quickly get booted from circles that recognize I am fighting status-quo sexism.

The moments of connection I share with other feminist men are fantastic but those moments aren't enough to entirely sustain me. Because female feminists, transgender, and genderqueer folks are sometimes skeptical of me and my (male) kind—often for good reasons—finding my place within feminist communities is challenging in ways that I'm not sure can be (or should be) overcome.

There are good reasons for feminist men to create an online community. There are feminist blogs with men in mind, some of them written by men. Among my favorites at the moment are *fem-men-ist* (http://fem-men-ist.blogspot.com/), *No, Seriously, What About Teh Menz* (https://noseriously whatabouttehmenz.wordpress.com/), and *Tranifesto* (http://tranifesto.com/). Recognizing that I should stop whining about not having enough of a community, I tried to create a group blog, *Feminist Allies* (feministallies.blogspot. com), and though it didn't last as a group project, it was a community for at least a little while. I continue to worry that there aren't enough places for feminist-minded men to gather in real life or even online. I worry that the impediments to building such a community are just too great. I'm frustrated by how this bogs down our potential activist energy and enthusiasm for social change.

There are great groups that center around anti-violence work; many of the online sites run by men with feminist roots center around violence prevention and education (*Men Can Stop Rape*, http://www.mencanstoprape.org, is a great one.) This violence-prevention work desperately needs to be done, but it can't be all that men have to offer a movement for equality. We need a strong, safe, positive environment for pro-feminist and feminist men to interact, to not only dismantle sexist structures but to help build other structures of equality. This doesn't mean that men should take over feminist spaces or clamor to be so-called leaders in existing feminist communities. And it doesn't mean that online blogs and websites created by men won't be problematic. But I think positive male feminist community is a good goal. I, at least, feel that I need it. Women who do social justice work around gender know how difficult this work can be, and many of them know the joy, and perhaps even the necessity, of existing within supportive networks.

Men doing gender-based social justice work also benefit from this support. I'm not sure what these future online communities will look like but they need to exist if men are going to continue doing feminist work. One day it would be nice to have more feminist sites that explicitly include folks of all genders—without constantly asking who's allowed to belong. If the women in my Feminist Authors class could accept a guy spending time with them before we blogged or emailed or G-chatted our way into activism, then I suspect there is still hope—online and off.

1. http://vyou.com/hiphop/27724/Are-you-a-feminist-Why-or-why-not.
2. http://www.shakesville.com/2011/02/feminism-101-helpful-hints-for-dudes.html.

3. http://www.feministe.us/blog/archives/2011/11/21/one-abuse-script-with-many-faces/#comment-411589.

4. http://www.feministe.us/blog/archives/2011/11/21/one-abuse-script-with-many-faces/#comment-411666.

5. https://apublicblogging.wordpress.com/2012/04/25/sick-of-tippy-toeing-around-nice-men-on-feminist-blogs.

STEEL-TOED BOOTS

Tal Peretz

I am finally starting to understand Cliff Hixson. Seeing him in a women's studies class is striking, even confusing: Standing nearly six feet tall, with his red beard and earlobes stretched over an inch wide, dressed in black jeans with a band T-shirt reaching over his thick, tattooed arms, Cliff looks like a cross between a boxer, a biker, and a bulldozer. It isn't his physical size that gives this impression, but something about his persona, his personality projecting into the world around him like backlighting, like a personal sound-track.

Seeing Cliff outside of class, working on a project with his steel-toed boots on a classroom table, he fits right in. He seems perfectly at home cutting out circles of paper for buttons bearing feminist slogans like *"There is an ASS in sexual harassment for a reason!"* As he talks, a big friendly grin offsets the smooth scar slashing across his left cheek. During a childhood fight, someone picked up a board with a nail and threw it at him, hitting Cliff across the face and ripping his cheek open. The scar dances as he speaks in a relaxed, sandpaper baritone.

"That was my thing—I was angry, and I expressed it through fighting. I always enjoyed fighting. I really liked it."

"I've only got into one fight at Penn State," Cliff begins, holding up his index finger for emphasis.

"A friend of mine likes to play basketball. I suck at the game, but I'm the guy who makes the teams even. I just run around the court, get the ball and miss, and everyone gets mad at me and won't give me the ball again.

"One day I go to the gym. I have on a black hoodie with an Iron Cross over my heart. The back of that jacket has a big Iron Cross on it, too. It says

'Hated and Proud.' Across the shoulders it says 'American.' On the bottom it used to say 'Skinhead.' I still have that jacket at home.

"I'm in the locker room, unlacing my boots, getting ready to play basketball, and I see this guy go by. He gives me a stutter-look, a double take. I've been in enough fights to instantly know that something is going to happen. I start tying my boots back up.

"He comes up and I'm ready. My boots are tied and I'm like, 'What's up?' He's like, 'You got a lot of interesting patches on that jacket.' And I go, 'Yeah, what's the problem?'

"Well, what do they all mean?"

"'All of them, or just one specifically?' I asked, because already I know what he's talking about. 'That Iron Cross,' I tell him, 'is a symbol of pride. It's also a symbol for Independent skateboards. It's also a symbol for . . .'

"I start being a jackass about it. He's like, 'It's not a symbol of white pride, is it?' I say, 'To who? It depends on who you're talking to. But since you're talking to me, it's none of your fucking business what it means. Do you have a problem?' And he goes, 'No, no, it's cool . . .' and he walks away.

"I take off my boots and go to play basketball. Like I said, I'm not a good player so when the guys pick teams I don't get chosen. My buddy does, though, and when I tell him I'm leaving he asks me to take his ball back to the dorms. So I'm holding his basketball, and my gym clothes, and I come out of the bottom of Rec Hall, going up the steps. I get to the top, and I have my hood pulled over my head, and I hear, 'What's up now, you racist motherfucker?'

"Just as I look up, I'm grabbed right where the Iron Cross is and hit with a hard right. I mean, this guy hit me across the face with everything he had, and I was stunned. I look up, the blurriness is going away, and he's holding out his arms going 'Whassup now? Whassup?'

"I just hit him one time, but—y'know when you're a little kid and you fantasize about hitting someone as hard as you can? It was that hit. His head snapped back. There was instant blood. He flew back maybe six steps, turned around, and took off running."

Cliff is a born storyteller. If we still valued that talent, he'd be made for life. As it is, he just got fired from his job as a janitor at the Pennsylvania State University after organizing the union workers against a supervisor known for sexual discrimination, harassment, and threatening employees. Cliff is also taking classes, studying to be a rehabilitation counselor. He wants to help kids like himself escape the effects of negative masculinity.

"The idea," he explains, "is to work with inner-city gang kids, specifically boys, and find out why they feel the need to act out their masculinity in violent ways. Because what happened with me is that after I started learning about masculinity, things started to click."

Presently, Cliff and I are working on a group project for a Men and Masculinities course, the first of its kind at Penn State. Cliff is sharing concerns about his final presentation for the class; his plan is to describe his transformation from racist skinhead to socially conscious feminist.

"I worry a little about how people will perceive me, because I still have some of that racist skinhead image. I still have all the tattoos . . . but, you know, most of them aren't really me anymore. Like this one here." Cliff rolls up his sleeve as he speaks, pointing to a tattoo that reads, "I feel the blinding rage." It's inked in red. Cliff holds out his arm so we can see the jagged lettering above the thick, black barcode and just below the black, shadowy face of a screaming man.

"I'm a little concerned," Cliff continues, "because I don't want my presentation to sound like, 'This was my life; end of story,' because my life-story is still changing."

And so Cliff's description comes out disjointedly, in convoluted bits and pieces, because it is a real, true story. Life isn't linear; it doesn't follow a neat story arc. Life doesn't often make nice, neat sense and, for Cliff, the unfolding of his life is far from over. He weaves metaphors and side-stories, takes tangents, fields questions, and gestures emphatically in the air.

Cliff's story starts in the projects of Uniontown, a poor neighborhood south of the steel city, Pittsburgh, Pennsylvania. Cliff grew up in a loving family, although there were some problems with alcoholism and violence.

"My father was always a big fighter. He told us stories about how he beat up a teacher, or beat up two guys. Those were his glory stories. I remember watching my dad beat a guy until he was a puddle of piss and blood. When the guy started begging and crying for an ambulance, my dad dragged him out into the street. The guy probably would've died out there but my mother called the paramedics. As a kid, you watch something like that and you learn that the way to deal with anger is to get satisfaction from someone else's sorrow.

"By second grade I was already such a troubled kid that they put me in a class for learning disabilities. There was only one LD class for the whole school and I was the youngest kid in the room. Not only was I still fighting, but now I was fighting fifth and sixth graders."

Hearing this, I start to see how Cliff developed that look of determination, that nonchalant aggression. Facing down boys twice your size when you're only eight years old could easily ossify through years of social pressure. I begin to wonder how Cliff managed to break down such habits.

"I don't think I would be the person I am today had it not been for Lindsey," Cliff explains, referring to his wife. They've recently married, though they've been together for eight years.

"I've taken some women's studies classes, but I never would have taken them without her. She's the one who motivated me to be something, who told me, 'You're not stupid.' Honestly, if it wasn't for that I would not be a student and I never would have gone to college. College wasn't for me. I was proud to be working class. Lindsey encouraged me to apply, to make something of myself."

Although Cliff has learned so much in college and he has swapped words for fists, he still has something of a penchant for confrontation. Cliff seems to recognize that this is left over from old habits, but he also sees this aggression as an inherent part of his personality. Since it's something he can't get rid of, he turns it to good use.

"Like, today, I'm walking from class downtown, and I see these guys standing on the corner of the street, holding a big sign that says 'Abortion Kills Children' and something about Hitler.

"I walk up to one of the guys, and I ask, 'First of all, where are you from?' The guy tells me they're from Ohio, so I ask him why they came this whole way to stand here and bother us in State College, PA. He says, 'We're here to educate people, young women at Penn State.' So I ask him 'You think you know all about abortion, huh? You've studied it? Have you ever talked to a woman about it? Maybe a woman who has had one? Are there any women here with you?'"

I listen to Cliff, nodding my head; I've noticed that there are never any women with these groups. I wonder how it is that Cliff's immediate instinct is to confront people so directly.

Cliff continues his story noting sarcastically, "I'm glad a group of guys are here telling women about their reproductive rights.

"It's just funny to me," he continues, "the way these people come around, holding these signs up. They want to show where they stand, they want everyone to know their position, but they don't want to be challenged.

"I have a very hard time passing people and letting something go. Back when I was an angry person, if something made me mad, I was in your face about it. I'd get in your face for looking at me wrong, for looking at Lindsey wrong—for anything I didn't like. I still react strongly to things, only now I'm confronting different issues like when I hear someone call someone else a fag, or when I see some guy staring at a girl's breasts."

I ask Cliff what changed, and he doesn't seem to have a clear answer. "It was a long process," he explains. He continually points to Lindsey's influence, but neither of us thinks it was just her. At some point Cliff started questioning his own identity choices, and eventually he began making or taking other paths. Lindsey helped, as did starting school, taking women's studies classes, meeting new people, and hearing new viewpoints. Ultimately, when the opportunity arose, Cliff made the decision to change himself. He tells me a few other stories that mark his way, but we both know change this radical can't be spelled out in a few stories.

Cliff backtracks to high school, when he started shaving his head and cultivating his angry image. "In high school, no one messes with a skinhead. You look at a skinhead and you know they're bad news," Cliff tells me, as if I need this reminder. By the time he moved to Chicago, standard dress included bomber jackets or black, hooded sweatshirts with patches, punk aphorisms and band names, skinhead slogans emblazoned across the shoulders in red-stitched fabric, and sometimes that Iron Cross over the heart.

"I was at this club in Chicago checking out some band, and this girl comes up to me and gets all up in my face. She starts grabbing my jacket, talking about my patches, telling me she can't stand me and stuff. I don't even know the girl!

"Now she's right in my face. She's talking and yelling, her spit hitting my face. I can feel the warmth of her breath just boiling my blood. She's grabbing at my patches, my Iron Cross, and I tell her not to touch me. She tells me her friends are waiting for me outside. When I go to leave, I see eight or nine multiracial skinheads—there's an Asian guy, a couple black guys, some white guys. They're in full skinhead gear; bombers, braces and boots, and they're just waiting for me.

"I start looking around the back of the club, off to the sides of the stage, you know, to see if there's a back way out. Then I just said, 'Fuck it' and went out the front door. I looked around, and I just start talking. I'm saying things like, 'Yeah, you guys might beat my ass, but you'll know it took all of you to do it,' and I just keep talking to them.

"Turns out, these guys were SHARPs . . ." Cliff has to pause and spell it out: Skinheads Against Racial Prejudice. They dress like skinheads so most people think they're Nazi, white-power guys, but they're almost like an anti-racist gang or something.

"If I would've run from the SHARPs waiting outside the club they would've come after me because they would've known I was alone and scared. But because I walked right up to them just started talking in their face, they thought I might have been part of a set-up.

"When they finally realized I was alone, they were too impressed with my mouth to start kicking my ass. One guy actually came up and said 'Let's go have a drink,' but I didn't drink. He said, 'No, it's on me,' but I still refused. He said, 'You've got some fuckin' balls.'

"At about that time I was just getting out of being an angry racist guy, but I still wanted to keep that skinhead image of aggression. I liked the intimidation factor. So I started calling myself a SHARP for a while.

"I realized that I wasn't as racist as I projected. Basically, I realized that I hate all kinds of people, so it must not be a special race thing."

Once Cliff told this story, I started piecing together why he wanted to hang onto his skinhead look and badass attitude: People have something to gain from adhering to a certain mindset, persona, or set of norms. Understanding why some people hang onto negative perspectives can help redirect their energy to more productive purposes. Perhaps what Cliff got from identifying as a racist skinhead was the protective image of aggression and a sense of community. Seeing the chance to maintain a similarly protective image and community, but without the dehumanizing racism and negativity, may have helped create the opportunity for Cliff to change. I asked Cliff just what he got from the skinhead identity, and he surprised me with his reply.

"I still like the image, the idea and the unity behind it all, the non-conformist attitude of it. I like the edge of it, and that's where I feel comfortable. For me it's about working-class attitude, not about race. Being a skinhead was to me about being a strong person and being true to myself.

"I remember in seventh grade, this one teacher called me to her desk on the first day of school, and I hadn't even done anything yet," Cliff tells me. She says 'I know how you are, I know what kind of student you are, and I'm not going to deal with it.' She takes me to the hall and stands there pointing at a spot on the floor saying, 'If you sit here, don't make any noise, don't cause any trouble all year, you'll pass.' So that's what I did, and I passed.

"Now I look back and wonder why I don't have an education . . . I can't read, I can't write, and I feel the effects of it now that I'm trying to get a college degree. For a while, Lindsey would actually sit down and help me, just to get a little better understanding of how I read. I'd read out loud to her, and she'd be like, 'Oh, okay, you really can't read!'"

Cliff laughs, self-effacing, and then modifies his statement: "*Well*. Can't read *well*. I've actually walked out of classes. The first day of my first women's studies class, the professor was handing out the syllabus, and different people were taking turns reading it out loud. When it got near to me, I got up and went out into the hall. I waited in the hall until it was way past me, and then went back in and sat down like nothing ever happened. I didn't want to look stupid."

Sitting across from him, watching him relate easily to the other members of our study group and hearing him discuss feminist philosophy, I find this hard to believe. First, Cliff doesn't strike me as the type to be afraid or ashamed of anything. He exudes self-confidence like an octopus leaking ink. Harder still for me to believe, though, is that Cliff would have trouble with something I consider so basic and so fundamental, like reading. It certainly isn't apparent when talking to him.

"Once I was in college and took an intro to women's studies class I really started to open my eyes to a lot of things. That's when I started to critically look at myself, what opinions I had, and why I had those opinions. I started really thinking about it and realized that I definitely had a kind of masculinity, an aggression, in me, but yet at the same time—it took looking at myself critically to realize that I wasn't really being me."

Cliff still wears his steel-toed boots, but not because he's constantly ready for a fight. And he doesn't go out of his way to look aggressive. But most significant is his simple presence in class as one of the most outspoken voices for gender equity, human rights, and progressive change.

"I don't dress like a skin anymore, although I do still have my old hoodies and jackets. Actually, the other day I put on some old cuffed-up pants and my Doc Martens because I didn't want to dirty any of my newer clothes, and Lindsey said, 'You're not going to start dressing like a skinhead again, are you?' But I'm not the old Cliff anymore. The only fight I've been in since moving here was the one at Rec Hall, carrying my friend's basketball. I'll admit it, though, I was really thinking about pounding those guys on the corner with the signs today."

Reading this piece as I'm drafting it, Cliff starts getting emotional.

"It's good, because it's true. This is stuff I talk about all the time. I'm always telling people my story. Maybe there's someone like me, early me, who might read something like this and go, 'Y'know . . .'" He trails off, imitating some earlier self, reconsidering his life choices.

Cliff has a new job working part time at a florist's shop. I think that says a lot about the changes in his views about masculinity. I find myself wondering if he seems as out of place at work as he does in our women's studies class, but then I look around and realize that he isn't out of place at all. This semester, Cliff is taking classes in feminist philosophy and rehabilitation education. And of course, his story is still going, and he's still telling it.

GOOD OL' BOY: A TALE OF TRANSFORMATION IN THE RURAL SOUTH

Jay Poole

My mother and father were in the Ku Klux Klan. Yes, you read that correctly. Both of them became members in the late-1950s as rumbles of integration grew into loud booms across the southern United States. Mom and Dad were both raised in the rural South. They were born during the Great Depression and spent their adolescence in a post-World War II environment that witnessed a resurgence of opportunities to seek the great American dream. Dad dropped out of high school during his senior year to work in a veneer plant and Mom, despite her hatred of being singled out for ridicule over what she wore, managed to graduate from high school. (Mom only had one brassiere, two skirts, two blouses, and one pair of penny loafers.)

My mother always said that she married so that she could have a bathroom—the house she lived in as a teenager had no indoor toilet, only an outhouse. Mom was bright and managed to land a job at Sears in customer service (a very appropriate job at the time for a female—it was, after all, a service position). Mom was very successful at Sears and she and my father saved up enough money to buy the house that would become my home. So, with working-class parents who held traditional southern values and who believed in the superiority of white, Christian, heterosexuals, I was bound for a journey that would take me into the throes of trying to become a "good ol' boy." I arrived, though, at a place of despair about knowing who I was and who I wanted to become.

I was born in 1962. Great social changes were beginning to occur and people like Mom and Dad were frightened at the prospect of living and raising a child in a world that was going to be so different from the one they knew. I suppose it was this fear that fueled their decision to join an organization like the KKK that promised to keep the social order of the South intact.

My early years were spent in a world dominated by a masculine power structure that emphasized the superiority of white men over all other people (and creatures, for that matter). Women's role was defined as inferior and subordinate to men. I was born with the "privilege" of being a white southern male, and with the expectation that I would follow in the footsteps of my father and his father before him to become a hard-working, productive, and respected man in the community.

What I came to recognize was that men in the rural South were, if anything, supposed to be rocks. They were supposedly invincible. It was understood that you should develop a love of sports, particularly those involving physical contact. Basically, any opportunity to beat the hell out of another guy should be your greatest desire. You must not cry when being beaten or battered on the playing field—or off it. A southern boy (particularly a rural southern boy) must love hunting. You should have your first BB gun by the time you are ten and your first rifle by the time you are thirteen.

I went on my first hunt when I was eleven years old. We spent the entire night in the woods following the hounds on the trail of several raccoons. I remember the smell of cigarettes and chewing tobacco mixed with the faintest odor of whiskey as my father, myself, and three other men tore through the underbrush on that cold November night. Hunting taught me that "real" men can conquer just about anything, and that hunting and killing are testament to the power that men possess. I noticed that most women did not hunt. My mom's role was to see that my father and I had a good meal and warm clothes before we ventured into the woods. She was supposed to be concerned about us until we came safely back home. I learned about competition as I listened to my dad and his friends talk about whose dog was best at tracking the prey and which football or basketball teams were going to win during the season. They never talked about being sad or about love. Those were sissy things and I quickly understood that these topics were off limits for men. About the only thing that resembled tender emotion were discussions about turning to Jesus in times of trouble or concern. It was in the southern Baptist Church that I learned about the power of God the father, God the son, and God the Holy Ghost—all presumably male.

Dad never went to church. It was Mom who dressed me in my Sunday best and took me to hear weekly sermons about the awesome power of the heavenly father. The preacher spoke with great passion about the fires of hell and how we were dangling over them. That's why being saved was of utmost importance. Living a good life meant that you had accepted Jesus as your Lord and Savior into your heart. The stories we studied in Sunday school emphasized the role of the man as the decision-maker and the leader of the family. Women were to support their husbands and serve as the men provided for the family. Certainly being a man was much better than being a woman; at least that seemed to be the position of my local church and community. By the time I was in my teens, I was a fundamentalist Christian and I desperately wanted to be successful in my role as a man. It was here that I encountered problems.

Some early photos in the family album caught my eye as a teenager. There I was, a two-year-old in my mom's heels with her patent leather purse draped over my arm. I was beaming! In another picture, I am standing with Mom at the kitchen counter mixing a bowl of cookie dough, again smiling from ear to ear. There were more! One of me ironing; another folding clothes; and yet another sitting with my legs crossed to one side delicately holding a kitten. What did this mean and why were these pictures in the family photo album? I certainly did not appear to be doing things that I had learned boys were supposed to do. Far from it; I was doing "girl" things.

I knew that successful boys were athletes. And I learned in school that popular boys had several girls swooning after them, proving their sexual prowess. By these terms, I was not a successful boy. My attempts to be an athlete failed miserably. I could not hit or catch a ball of any kind. I loved talking to girls, but none seemed interested in dating me and the feeling was mutual. I began to realize that I was sexually attracted to other boys, a feeling that rocked the very foundations of my identity. Boys were not supposed to like other boys, so why did I? I did not see myself as sissy . . . but, then, there were those pictures. I was supposed to be a man and, now, my definition of what that meant was completely knocked out from under me.

My upbringing taught me to despise and fear those who were sexually "perverted." I found myself in an existential crisis as I had my first sexual experience with another male. On the one hand, it felt wonderful, natural, and so right. On the other hand, it was gut-wrenching—a sin punishable by death as the preacher said many times quoting verses from the King James version of the Bible. "Queers" were sick and God forbid you were one.

My identity as a man was spiraling down a dark hole leaving me with a void in knowing who or what I was. I avoided appearing feminine at all costs for fear of being discovered. I made every attempt to cross my legs at the ankle, not the knee. I was careful about gestures I made with my hands and practically sat on them if they did "womanly" things. I tried to walk like the jocks at school. Most of all, I dreaded gym class because my lack of athletic ability was exposed to the world, diminishing my ability to pass for a "normal" guy. Later, I would come to recognize that society had made up these rules about gender by which I was so desperately trying to live. At the time, though, the ideals of masculinity and femininity seemed completely real and I thought I had to conform.

By the time I was a young adult, everything that I had been taught by my church, at school, and at home was under suspicion. I began to question those narrow-minded values that Mom and Dad worked hard to instill in me. I distanced myself from the standards by which I grew up and it was in this displacement that I began to discover who I was and who I wanted to be. I recognized the importance of social activism in the gay liberation and feminist movements in bringing attention to the inequity, prejudice, and discrimination toward women and men who express their gender and sexuality in a manner that some people find unacceptable.

As I began to associate with people outside my very insulated hometown and church, I recognized that there are many differences among people and that difference is not negative. My initial reaction was to feel anger, rejection, confusion, and disgust toward my family, church, and hometown. At some point, though, I needed to make sense of where I'd come from and where I'd arrived.

I'm not excusing bigots and homophobes for marginalizing or discriminating against others, but I recognize now that people reflect what they know. And what they know is what has been taught to them. As we are exposed to new ideas, or if we expose ourselves to new information, we may initially react with trepidation. But, if we spend some time with this new information—whether we find it in books, movies, people, or situations—we can be transformed. I have learned that informing one's self is a key to change and growth.

Our society is filled with so many beliefs and stereotypes about all sorts of people. It seems important that we each assume responsibility for taking the frightening step toward encounters with unfamiliar people, places, and experiences. Doing this can help dispel the sort of thinking that has caused so much harm and grief.

My personal journey has enabled me to recognize the importance of questioning what we believe, grappling with why we believe it, and ultimately, facing the challenging task of de-centering ourselves so that we have the opportunity to grow. Many of us sit comfortably in belief systems that are handed to us. It is in that comfortable place that prejudice, discrimination, and oppression are often born.

The questions I now ask myself focus on challenging those beliefs that are most comfortable for me. I have come to understand gender and sexuality—and race and religion—in much different ways from the way I understood them as a teenager and certainly, much differently than my parents understood them. Perhaps, as I stretch my thinking even more, the concepts I have around gender will be redefined once again. As a fifteen-year-old, I never would have believed that I would come to challenge what I learned about being masculine and feminine, straight and gay, black, White, Latino, and any number of categories that defined my position in this incredibly diverse world.

We are all students and we are all teachers and it is within the appetite of human curiosity that we begin to discover all that is around us, leading us to think, re-think, and imagine new possibilities. If my mother and father had been able to recognize the benefits of asking questions about the world of hate and fear that they came to know, perhaps they would have opened the space to embrace those who were not like them and my battle with my own identity would have not been as arduous a journey.

Chapter 40 *(handwritten)*

BREAKING DOWN
THE BRO CODE

Thomas Keith

While interviewing a prominent figure in the gender equality movement for my first film, *Generation M: Misogyny in Media and Culture*, I remember this person cautioning me about the possible blowback I would get for taking on subjects of sexism, feminism, misogyny, heteronormativity, and in general, gender. From my background in music and sports, I have a good deal of experience with guys who celebrate their sexism and homophobia through insulting and leveling language, so I wasn't particularly deterred. I have also witnessed plenty of what I call "bro behavior" from guys when they get together in packs of more than two. The homophobic rants, sexist quips, and alpha male performances are legendary among boys and young men (and sadly, among men in their 30s and beyond). They attempt to convince women, other guys, and themselves, that they are 100 percent hetero dudes who do not tolerate any feminine behaviors among their ranks. I am also someone who has a background in philosophy, so I am used to a good debate. But nothing could have prepared me for what was coming my way over the next five or so years.

The first wave of blowback came from the most obvious source: unapologetically sexist men (the D-Bro or dumbass bro). As part of promoting a film, much like promoting a book or a new EP release, you hit the road and begin to hear from fans and critics alike. So, off I went around the country. From California to New York and lots of places in between, the initial round of criticism took a sophomoric and unlettered approach with comments like:

"Well, males are dominant in every species on the planet . . . that's the way nature is, dude!"

At one particular screening, one D-Bro actually shouted:

"The penis goes inside the vagina, bro, not the other way around!"

No one knew what point he was making or what biological topography had to do with the mistreatment of women by men, but the audience groaned appropriately and we moved on. When once I rhetorically asked an audience after a screening of my film why Rockstar Games would include the rape and murder of female prostitutes as part of the player options in Grand Theft Auto, one D-Bro condescendingly cackled from the back of the auditorium, "They're prostitutes dude! . . . You can't rape a prostitute!"

In city after city, state after state, I continued hearing comments from men, and usually young men since I speak mainly at colleges and universities, that would make my head spin and cause many audience members to recoil in disgust. The comments were not terribly unlike those of Sasha Baron Cohen's movie character "Borat" who insisted to a group of feminists, "women's brain is size of squirrel brain . . ." But Borat was satire by making fun of sexist and racist imbeciles, while the comments I was receiving from young men were not meant to be satirical and certainly not meant to reflect anything other than a defense of angry sexism.

In my new film, *The Bro Code: How Contemporary Culture Creates Sexist Men*, one of the interviewees who is now a good friend of mine, Angel Acosta, offered a reality check, saying to me, "Some guys you are never going to reach. You're wasting your time with them." I don't know if he's right, but Angel raises a good point: D-Bros are not interested in a dialogue that critically examines male privilege or men's violence toward women and other men; rather, they carry a preemptive hostility toward anyone who dares challenge their privilege and the sexism that goes with it. Or at least they front like they do.

At one college, during the Q&A after a film screening, an older man challenged me about the rates of men's violence toward women by saying (again, out loud in front of hundreds of people), "I don't know where you're getting the idea that women are being sexually assaulted at the rates you claim . . . I've never seen a woman sexually assaulted." Comments like these always bring out the cynic in me where I begin to think that the only way this man could ever understand the multiple fallacies embedded in the underlying assumptions of his pseudo-argument were if he underwent a complete educational do-over. I was supposed to capitulate my position to the brute observational force of this man's lack of personal experience.

But these are the "soft targets" of sexist men. These are the same guys who worship sports, beer, and porn, and who have no intention of investigating any of their beliefs in a serious manner. These are the stereotypes that provide inspiration for those who produce beer-guzzling, frat-boy-friendly films like *Superbad*, where even the McLovin's of the world are doing everything in their computer-geek powers to get sex. These are the guys whose vernacular includes calling other guys "fag," "pussy," and "bitch" as insults to keep their bro-kingdom pure from what they view as feminized masculinity. These dudes often sport the ever-present backward baseball cap, others join fraternities, some drive big jacked-up trucks. Most do their best to make sure their voice is the loudest in the room (since they judge arguments in terms of decibel levels rather than in terms of cogent premises).

The next round of my critics were the I-Bros ("I'm not sexist, bro!") who carry an effort-laden, Bohemian cool about them, while carefully concealing their sexism. They masquerade in the guise of egalitarian, profeminist men. They are usually incapable of getting through a sentence without a sarcastic I'm-smarter-than-you chuckle. Privilege drips out of their pores as they "correct" those who dare challenge them about the club scene, or what men really want, or their take on modern women and sex. But if you listen closely, these are often the guys who victim-blame the most. If the subject under discussion is the rate of sexual assault at fraternity parties, the I-Bro is quick with a comment about consensual sex, what they call "grey rape," or "rape myth," or some chatter about both parties drinking ("dude, she and I were both fucked up!"), while maintaining a strict "I am for women's rights" exterior.

Recently, I took heat from some I-Bros when I publicly challenged lingerie parties and what was being advertised as an XXX-mas party on campus just before Winter break. These parties are designed to encourage young women to attend wearing only lingerie and high heels, and of course, the alcohol is flowing like Niagara Falls with men having a sexual investment in how much alcohol women at the party drink. The flyers strewn around campus read, "Will You Be Naughty or Nice?" In class, I noted that sexually themed college parties are some of the highest risk environments for sexual assault on women in the entire nation. An I-Bro broke me off with, "Dude, women are the ones organizing the party; they are the ones who want it [insert: sarcastic laughter]." This bro wanted me to understand that he "should not be held responsible for exploiting women who want to be exploited." He wanted to make sure culpability rested at the feet of women and not the men who are only too willing to attend the party to troll for sex.

At this same college, as part of a class I teach on the philosophy of love and sex, a group of students that included a healthy number of I-Bros resisted the idea that sexual assault on college campuses is as serious a problem as I was reporting it. These students attend a small liberal arts college where cliques are common and the students know each other fairly well. Several I-Bros in class commented that sexual assault "may" happen "occasionally" at large, public universities where fraternity members can blend into a larger campus community without notice, but that such a thing couldn't happen at a small college like theirs where "everyone knows everyone." Ironically and sadly, I returned to class the very next Tuesday to a campus buzzing over the report that a young woman from that campus had been raped the previous Saturday night at an off-campus party thrown by students from this college. Many students in my class were incredulous at the report and soon camps of students were forming over whether this woman was actually raped or whether she was creating a false report for reasons unknown. The I-Bros in class were the most skeptical of the bunch, as they reported that they knew this "girl" and that she drinks a lot and wears "skanky clothes." In essence, they were saying that if something happened, she was probably asking for it. A few other young men in class were quick, however, to call them on the assumption they were making and to point out that this blame-the-victim mentality was the very thing we were discussing in class just prior to the sexual assault over the weekend. I call this latter group of young men, along with the many women in class who were horrified by what took place at the party, "the choir." They get it.

Yet, all of this I-Bro resistance, along with the more blatant D-Bro resistance, to gender equality and anti-sexism made me ask myself, *How much of our work reaching out to young men to critically examine the way they define themselves as men is simply a case of preaching to the choir?* When you think of any revolution in human history, the people who organize the protests are those who come from groups that are being subordinated by privileged groups. Those who belong to privileged groups are rarely interested in a process of self-examination as part of an effort to bring about a meaningful sense of equality. Those who do break from the folds of the privileged herd to support the voices of the oppressed are usually met with great resistance and scorn. In making two films that examine sexism and misogyny in our culture and the media that supports this sexism, I have felt that resistance all too often.

One leveling tactic to marginalize men who support gender equality that I have experienced many times when discussing this subject with audiences is to have my sexual orientation questioned. Bros will often call out men who dare fight for gender equality as being "fags" or the faux sophisticated bros will ask in a veiled homophobic, and what they believe to be inoffensive, manner, "Are you gay?" This tactic is a bro attempt to compartmentalize men who work for gender equality. Bros who feel threatened by women who are gaining authentic equality feminize men who are working on behalf of gender equality, reinforcing and even celebrating their own explicit and unapologetic sexism. Any guy who disagrees with a bro is cut down and put in his place.

But when audiences are receptive to the message of making strides to realize gender equality, it is usually the case that the audience is composed primarily of females who know all-too-well the sexism found in bro culture. Often, the men attending film screenings and discussion panels about confronting sexism already support gender equality. The guys who most need to hear and think about these messages are nowhere to be found. Or, they sit in the back of the room with arms folded, glaring, and at the ready to break out a snide comment should they perceive an attack against their male supremacy.

This bro-resistance to the challenge of predatory behavior by some men at college parties was driven home to me when I was handling a Q&A after a screening of *The Bro Code* at a large national conference in New York City. A PhD in social psychology went after me for "not being honest" about women who attend parties dressed for sex. His point was that women are just as predatory about sex at college parties as are men, but that I was wrongly laying blame solely onto men. The audience grew uncomfortable as this man's challenge was clearly focused on a central premise of my film. I reminded him that men rape women at wildly disproportionate rates compared to the number of women who rape men, and that his comment only served to demonstrate how even well-educated men can be I-Bros.

Shortly after this confrontation, I was talking with a social-justice activist who wondered out loud whether we are really having any effect in the work we do. I get the concern. It is virtually impossible to escape the nonstop celebration of sexism in media, and bro culture feeds off of a sharply gendered world where men are king and women are depicted as sexual nitwits who (should) constantly obsess about their looks. This is one of many reasons why I oppose sexually themed parties on college campuses where some "bro-ho" or "XXX" theme is promoted. The parties reflect a media-influenced ethos of bros as virile, drunken, party gods, and women as scantily dressed vixens whose sole reason for being is to seduce and satisfy male sexual desires (and this stereotype is often sold to women as being empowering).

So, against the background of epidemic numbers of date rape and sexual assault on college campuses, bro-posturing, sexist bravado, media celebration of sexist story lines and imagery, and an unwillingness by many men to examine themselves to see how their words and actions are contributing to sexism and misogyny in America, are the efforts of anti-sexist writers and speakers, activists, educators, and artists falling on deaf ears?

I don't think so. While it is beyond doubt that many men are not going to listen to or care about the negative impact of their behavior on women, there are men who might be called "marginal bros" (M-Bros), who are reachable. These guys are often found alongside D-Bros and I-Bros, but they do not defend sexist practices and seem open to questioning the status quo.

In traveling around the country talking to groups of women and men, these M-Bros are the ones who give me the most hope. Scores of young men of this type have confided in me that they long for a serious and meaningful relationship with a woman and they realize that the bro-universe of masculine dumb-assery is not getting it done. They realize that mimicking the bros on *Jersey Shore* is a recipe for shallow, meaningless relationships that will set off problems for themselves down the line when they are ready for a relationship that has meaning. Many of them also have female friends, sisters, or other female family members who have experienced first-hand the damage of being sexually assaulted by a bro, and these men want no part of that lifestyle.

One young man stands out to me. After screening my latest film at an East Coast university, a young man asked to talk to me. With his permission, my film crew shot the exchange between us. He told me that a man raped his sister at a frat party and this violent event had torn their entire family apart. His sister had become antisocial, depressed, and suicidal; his father had become withdrawn and also suicidal; and he, himself, was carrying around a vicious rage toward frat guys in general that he realized was self-destructive, but that he didn't know what to do with that rage. Before the rape of his sister, he identified himself as a bro, a frat dude, who liked to drink and "score" with women . . . but no longer. He had actually internalized his anger toward himself as well as toward other young men of a certain type, because he viewed himself as being "one of those guys who took advantage of women" back in the day. He knew the routine: get her as fucked-up drunk as possible, and then get her to a room where you have sufficient privacy and control to do what you want to her. This former D-Bro or I-Bro was now an M-Bro who wanted to make a positive difference after finally understanding the devastating consequences of misogynist, self-serving bro-behavior.

Guys who know how bro culture works from the inside can have powerful influence on other men who might look like him, talk like him, or share a lot of the same experiences. And whether we like it or not, bros listen to other bros. As men, we are socialized to marginalize or ignore female voices, as well as the voices of men who are considered feminine in any way. This is a big part of how patriarchy establishes and maintains itself. Boys are taught that males are more important than females, which includes the view that the opinions produced by men are more important than the opinions produced by women. This means that the M-Bro is crucial in getting other men to take sexism seriously and to challenge and disrupt current models of masculine behavior. Guys who are part of greater bro culture, but who also get the dysfunction that is part of that culture, are the bridge-builders who can help to create better men. Can you imagine the impact someone like an NBA or NFL icon would have on bros if he were to call out men for their sexism and misogyny? Sadly, bro culture, which includes much of sports culture, does not support such a revolutionary alignment with gender equality, although a recent PSA created by the National Basketball Association called out boys and men for using the homophobic slur "that's so gay," which does not squarely treat the problem of sexism as a common ingredient in male sports culture, but is a good start for an organization that would not have produced a PSA of this type even ten years ago.

Anyway, I'm optimistic. I believe that like other forms of social injustice that are being challenged and disrupted today (racism, classism, ageism, homophobia), sexism's heyday will come to an end. For those of you who are out on the front line of this fight, I do not believe you are simply preaching to the choir. You are integral links in the chain that creates change, even if you are not there to see the change happen, and even if you're like me . . . impatient for that change to take place.

chapter 41

HOW CAN I BE SEXIST?
I'M AN ANARCHIST!

Chris Crass

"What do you mean I'm sexist?" I was shocked. I wasn't a tough guy jock. I didn't hate or assault women. I wasn't a bad guy. "But I'm an anarchist! How can I be sexist?" I was anxious, nervous, and my defenses were up. I believed in liberation, in fighting against capitalism and the state. There were those who defended and benefited from injustice—and then there was us, right? I was nineteen years old. It was four years after I'd gotten involved in radical politics, and my sense of the world was slipping.

My girlfriend, Nilou, held my hand and patiently explained. "I'm not saying you're an evil person, I'm saying that you're sexist and sexism happens in a lot of subtle and blatant ways. You cut me off when I'm talking. You pay more attention to what men say. The other day when I was sitting at the coffee shop with you and Mike, it was like the two of you were having a conversation and I was just there to watch. I tried to jump in and say something, but you both just looked at me and then went back to your conversation. Men in the group make eye contact with each other and act like women aren't even there."

This can't be true, I thought. Maybe it's just her deal. Maybe she's just having a hard time and we can get past this.

She continued, "For a long time I thought maybe it was just me, maybe what I had to say wasn't as useful or exciting. Maybe I needed to change my approach, maybe I was just overreacting, or that it was just in my head and I needed to get over it," she explained. "But then I saw how the same thing was happening to other women in the group, over and over again. I'm not blaming you for all of this, but you're a big part of this group and you're part of this dynamic." While I struggled to understand what she was telling me, this conversation changed my life. Fundamentally, Nilou pushed me to realize that in order to work for liberation I needed to make a lifelong commitment to feminist politics and practice against male supremacy.

So how could I better work for change? And what could I suggest to gender, class, or race-privileged guys who were also committed to positive social transformation?

More and more gender-privileged men in the anarchist movement are working to challenge male supremacy. We recognize that patriarchy exists, that we have material and psychological privileges as a result, and that sexism undermines political movements. Women, transgender, and genderqueer people have explained it repeatedly and said, "You all need to talk with each other, challenge each other, and figure out what you're going to do." We need to listen to them. However, there are also men in the movement who agree that sexism exists, but deny their personal participation in it.

Lisa Sousa, who is part of the San Francisco Independent Media Center and AK Press, told me that in recent discussions she's had in groups about sexism and gender, she's heard the following responses from men: "We are all oppressed"; "We should be talking about class"; "You are just using gender as a way to attack such and such."

These comments sound so familiar. While it is tempting to distance myself from men who say things like this, it's important that I remember that I've made those comments, too. As someone who believes in movement building and collective liberation, it's crucial for me to be honest about my experiences, mistakes, and learning process.

When I think back to that conversation with Nilou and her explanation of how sexism operates, I remember trying not to shut down, trying to listen. The word "but" repeated over and over again in my mind, followed by: "It was a misunderstanding"; "I didn't mean it that way"; "If I knew you felt that way I wouldn't have done it"; "I wasn't trying to do that"; "I would love to see you participate more"; "No one said they didn't want to hear what you had to say"; "We all believe in equality"; "I love you and would never do anything to hurt you."

Looking back ten years later, it's amazing how often that same list of "buts" comes running to mind. I'm more like those "other" men than I'd like to admit. Many of us who have been challenged on sexism get stuck in the defensiveness and frustration of not knowing what to do. Or, in the rush to solve the problem, we overlook the depth of the problem to begin with.

Nilou, who comes from a middle-class, Iranian family, spent hours talking with me about sexism. It was tremendously difficult for both of us and only in retrospect can I comprehend how courageous it was for her to do this. A clearly defined dualistic framework of good and bad shaped my politics. If it was true that I was sexist, then my previous sense of self was in question: I must have been bad. Nilou pushed me to develop a more complex framework. She helped me begin to locate myself in a complex power analysis of society in which I had material and psychological privilege as a man. I knew this was a profoundly important moment in my growth and it still felt like shit.

Two weeks later as our anarchist study group meeting came to a close, Nilou raised the concern that "sexism is happening in this group." "Oh my God," I thought, "What am I going to do?"

She listed the examples she had told me. The five other men in the room now amplified the defensive reaction that I'd had. Other women started speaking up. They had experienced these dynamics as well and they were tired of it. The men were shocked. They began listing all the reasons why claims of sexism were simply misunderstandings, miscommunications, and misperceptions. With genuine sincerity they said, "But we all want revolution."

To understand the situation we were in, I should give some background history. We were members of the United Anarchist Front. It was an activist youth group formed by political punks in Whittier, a suburb in Southern California, in the late-1980s. Focusing on animal rights, we regularly held anti-corporate protests at McDonald's and passed out literature on vegetarianism in our high school classes. (For information check out www.mcspotlight.org.) The driving force in the group was Mike Rejniak, a sixteen-year-old, working-class punk who dressed like a Catholic school student, regularly used something called the Internet, read philosophy, and was enormously popular at school in almost every clique and scene. We were heavily influenced by English anarcho-punk bands and, for the first few years, the UAF was essentially a group of teenage guys who grew up together doing politics. In 1991 the Gulf War radicalized us. We participated in mass peace marches in Los Angeles, repeatedly covered our school in anti-war chalk graffiti, passed out anti-capitalist, anti-militarist literature, argued U.S. foreign policy with teachers during classes, and faced off with the young Republicans in the debate club—and won. Through all of this we developed a visible left-anarchist pole at our high school that gave legitimacy to radical politics.

While the UAF itself comprised a handful of people, our social scene grew to a core of over forty people. Our frequent parties brought together young people from multiple high schools and colleges in the area who were mostly feminists, anarchists, progressives, and queers. By 1992, more people began working with the UAF, including April Sullivan who was the first woman in the group. We worked with other anarchist groups around Southern California and joined the Love and Rage Network that put forward a revolutionary anti-imperialist, feminist, anti-racist, anarchist politics in their monthly newspaper, a publication that we distributed at punk shows and at school. The Rodney King verdict in 1992 further galvanized us: We went to black-led, anti-police brutality marches and argued with students and teachers about the meaning of the L.A. riots. As many shook their heads saying, "They're animals" or "It's senseless violence," we argued—in classroom debates, in the school newspaper, and in flyers we handed out—that people were responding with justified rage against unemployment, poverty, police violence, and white supremacy.

Out of this momentum a few us decided it was time to bring more organization to the UAF. We started having regular meetings and invited people from our social circle to join us. Soon we had a dozen members. We divided our activities into work committees and launched a study group to help us develop our political analysis. This was a major transition because prior to this we had done our work informally over coffee or beer. The downside now was that generally two or three of us made the decisions and took all the organizational responsibility. We wanted to bring more people into the work and expand our activities. Without mentors or role models, we experimented. We were about six months into the process of building a collective when Nilou raised the issue of sexism in the group.

While people debated whether sexism existed in the group, April, who came from a white, working-class, Irish family and had been in the group for well over a year, sat me down. She, too, gave me example after example of sexist behavior. Men in the group didn't trust her to handle responsibilities, even when they were newer to the group; she wasn't looked to for information about the group, nor were her opinions asked for on political questions. People turned to my friend Mike and me for political direction, but she was usually ignored. Others joined our conversation, but when April gave examples that she had just clearly explained to me, the men denied any claims of sexism as a misunderstanding. A few minutes later, I restated the exact same examples given by April and this time the men agreed that perhaps these incidents were, in fact, sexist.

April called it out immediately and explained what was happening. Her ideas, coming from my mouth, were being taken seriously, when they were dismissed coming from her just minutes before. There it was. I still didn't want to believe that sexism was happening, but now I saw it. It felt horrible, like a kick to the stomach. Nilou and April were desperately trying to get us to agree that there was a problem. How could this be happening when I hadn't intended it to and all of us were so committed to being revolutionary? I was scared to say anything.

Two months later, I was sitting silently in a men's caucus. We didn't know what to talk about. More specifically, we were nervous, unskilled, and without experience. We had not developed an agenda or a plan to help us have a useful discussion about sexism. Nilou and April proposed that the UAF spend a day talking about sexism. It was decided that we'd start with separate, gender-based caucuses and then come back together to discuss what we'd learned.

Once we broke off into our small group of men, we awkwardly tried to talk about sexism. For the most part, though, we anxiously waited for the women to return.

The women came back into the room walking arm-in-arm, while the men stood around feeling uncomfortable. The women had come to a shared understanding of their experiences with sexism and, furthermore, explored ways that sexism within the UAF was pitting them against one another.

While the women's caucus had reached depth and honesty, it was quickly apparent that the men's caucus had barely scratched the surface. Rather than report back anything meaningful, men began questioning what the women had said, and the women were now defending the points they had made. "We need to just listen," was the most that I could contribute to the conversation.

Several people left early in tears, disillusioned, and overwhelmed.

Over the next few months an important development took place. We regularly read anarchist newspapers and zines from around the country as a lifeline to a broader movement. We began looking to other groups for examples to bring to our work. The journal *Free Society*, based in Minneapolis, devoted an entire issue to anarchist groups' experiences dealing with gender and power dynamics. We devoured the articles and this transformed how men began relating to our discussions about sexism. "It's not that we're just fucked up, these issues are coming up in groups all over the country" and "they sound exactly like what women in the UAF are saying," we said. Women used the articles to highlight what they had been telling us: "Sexism is systemic like capitalism, and it's not just about you."

It was becoming clear to me and to other men that challenging sexism was about far more than learning how to make eye contact with women and asking them what they thought during UAF meetings. Indeed, it was a political commitment to challenging a system of power that operates on the political, economic, social, cultural, and psychological levels. My lack of direct eye contact was one of a thousand subtle ways that male supremacy enforces the worldview that women's work is insignificant, marginal, or non-existent. While I wanted to just stop being sexist, I was learning that this would involve a long-term collective struggle to transform the world in which we live.

THIS STRUGGLE IS MY STRUGGLE

> I haven't the faintest notion what possible revolutionary role white heterosexual men could fulfill, since they are the very embodiment of reactionary-vested-interest-power.
>
> Robin Morgan, from the Introduction to *Sisterhood is Powerful*[1]

I have periods of hating myself, feeling guilty, and afraid. I know in my heart that I have a role in liberation struggle and that there is useful work that I can do, but still the question haunts me: "Am I just fooling myself into believing that I am more useful than problematic?"

I find Robin Morgan's quote useful to struggle with (but not to get stuck on) because I grew up believing that I was entitled to everything. I could go anywhere and do anything and wherever I went, I would be wanted and needed.

Patriarchy and heterosexism taught me, in subtle and blatant ways, that I was entitled to women's bodies, that I was entitled to take up space and express my ideas and thoughts whenever I wanted to, without consideration for others. This privilege came from growing up in a society that is indeed designed by and built for people like me.

This is a very different reality than that of most people in this society; people who are told to shut up, keep it to themselves, hide who they really are, get out of the way, and to never forget how lucky they are to be allowed here to begin with.

I think it is healthy to not assume I am always needed, to learn to share space and power, to work with others, and to realize the roles that I can and should play. What is unhealthy is how rarely gender-privileged men talk with each other about these issues and how little we support each other through the process of challenging sexism and developing a healthy male identity.

I still struggle every day to really listen to women's voices. My mind wanders quicker when a woman is speaking and my instant reaction is to take men's opinions more seriously. When I walk into a room full of activists I instantly scan the group and divide people into hierarchies of status according to how long they've been active, what groups they've been part of, what they've written and where it's been published. I position myself against them and feel the most competitive with men.

I'm not proud to say this, but I'm just being honest here. When it comes to women, I add their sexual desirability to my status hierarchy tally. I have almost never zoned out on what a man was saying because I was fantasizing about him. But I have repeatedly found myself sexually distracted while listening to women speak, women who are organizers, leaders, and visionaries. I'm all about crushes, healthy sexual desire, and a pro-sex orientation. That is not what I am talking about. This is about owning up to power, entitlement, and my own role in marginalizing women's leadership in a society that is violently misogynistic.

I wish I didn't get defensive on a regular basis, but I do. I get frustrated and shut down by conversations about how power operates between my partner and me. I get defensive about how the world interacts with us and how that influences our dynamics. I know that there are times when I say, "Alright, I'll think more about it" when really I am thinking, "Leave me alone."

Male supremacy negatively impacts how I communicate with my partners, friends, and comrades. It negatively impacts how I want, express, conceptualize, and make love. It negatively impacts how I live my life and how I organize. Male supremacy hurts men's relationship with themselves, to women and people of all genders, and to the earth. It has shaped our emotional lives so as to effectively advance a violent, militaristic, misogynistic, anti-queer, brutally competitive economic system. I am enraged by the resulting damage I see in men's lives all around me.

Patriarchy tears me up. Every person I meet bears the scars of patriarchy.

bell hooks writes that love is impossible where the will to dominate exists. I want to believe that I can genuinely love and that it is possible to forge a nonpatriarchal political practice for men—a political practice that moves men to meaningfully join with all people in a collective struggle to re-organize our society towards systemic liberation.

And in this fight we, as men, will realize that even in the face of these systems of oppression, our love, beauty, creativity, passion, dignity, and power grows. We can do this and we need to love, support, and take care of one another as we challenge, push, and encourage each other.

WE MUST WALK TO MAKE THE STRUGGLE REAL

While it's necessary to get into the hard and murky emotional issues of radical political change, there are also concrete steps men must take to challenge male supremacy. This essay is primarily focused on lessons from my own struggles in living a feminist life. However, there is a danger of emphasizing the individual over the group. I believe that organizations can also provide us with opportunities to practice our politics in a collective way that maximizes both the effectiveness of the work and the depth of learning from the process of putting theory into practice.

In the mid-1990s, the United Anarchist Front made some organizational changes. The primary move was to start a Food Not Bombs (FNB) chapter in Whittier. FNB is a network of volunteer-based economic justice, people-before-profit groups that share free food in public spaces to provide a direct service and protest homelessness and poverty. There were numerous reasons why we started a FNB group, but one was to confront sexism. We were trying to address the critique that men held all the power in the group. FNB represented an opportunity for everyone to participate in a meaningful way. There were dozens of easily identifiable roles and responsibilities for people to take on, rotate, and share. Women played leading roles in FNB, positively shifting the dynamics in the group, and yet sexism did not end as some of us had hoped. There are three key lessons that I drew from this experience.

First, some of us (across genders) were equating challenging patriarchy with making women feel comfortable in the group. While this is important, it was becoming the end goal as opposed to transforming the relationships of power. This often led to us abandoning things that created discomfort rather than struggle to figure out how to actually change them. For example, sexist dynamics persisted in our study group. But instead of finding creative ways for everyone to feel empowered in developing their political analysis, we de-emphasized the importance of having analysis and ended the study group. People continued to study politics individually, but we moved away from developing our collective analysis. We opted to maintain an unexamined peace rather than deal with the tensions.

Second, a dynamic developed amongst some of the men that detracted from our egalitarian goal. Our view was that if we believed in equality, then it should exist right now. This led men to feel guilty for having skills and experience because this reflected the patriarchal privileges that enabled us to have this know-how to begin with. Instead of sharing this knowledge with the women in the group, our reasoning was that if we were all equal, then nobody should take the hierarchical role of teaching someone else how to run the show. But we were deluding ourselves with this flawed logic. What really happened was that the historic and institutional system of male supremacy was blurred into a practice that left few possibilities for actual positive change. What's more, women's actual skills, experiences, and analyses were still overlooked and minimized and we felt a sense of despair.

Third, we didn't have an organizational frame of reference for understanding the complexities of internalized sexism and its impact on women and men. Instead, collective political challenges of the UAF were perceived as personal issues between individuals. Lacking an adequate framework led men to feel personally blamed instead of being able to hear women's critique. What we needed was a process by which all of us could begin to see ourselves as part of classes or categories of people rather than just individuals. Only then could we imagine social change, organizational change, and individual change to challenge male supremacy and develop liberatory practices.

We continued to do our work and the UAF gained momentum. We beat city hall when they tried to stop our Food Not Bombs servings. We worked against student fee hikes and for an ethnic studies program at the community college many of us attended. We brought in more new people and we continued to have fun together. However, we saw our inability to end sexism as an organizational failure rather than interpreting our ongoing commitment to challenge male supremacy as a strength to build on over the long haul. This led to conflict and divisions rather than the pursuit of collective political goals.

This experience with the UAF pushed me to recognize that we needed to go through transformations of our own while simultaneously working for revolutionary change in the world. And while this may seem ambitious, there are some things I've learned along the way that I hope can benefit others who are actively working for positive social change. To that end, below are my suggestions.

TOOLS FOR GUYS (AND OTHERS WITH PRIVILEGE) WHO ARE WORKING FOR SOCIAL CHANGE

1. Practice noticing who's in the room at social, professional, and political gatherings. How many gender privileged (biological) men? How many are

women, transgendered people, white people, and people of color? Is the majority in the room heterosexual? Are there out queers? What are people's class backgrounds? Don't assume to know people, but also work at becoming more aware by listening to what people say and talking with people one on one.

2. Count how many times you speak and keep track of how long you speak. Likewise, count how many times other people speak and keep track of how long they speak.

3. Be conscious of how often you are actively listening to what other people are saying as opposed to just waiting your turn thinking about what you'll say next. As a white guy who talks a lot, I've found it helpful to write down my thoughts and then focus on what other people are saying. Frequently others will be thinking something similar and then you can support their initiative.

4. Value other people's knowledge and experiences. White guys tend to talk among themselves and develop strong bonds that manifest in organizing. These informal support structures often help reinforce informal leadership structures as well. Asking people what they think and really listening to their answers is a core ingredient to healthy group dynamics. So practice asking more people what they think about events, ideas, actions, strategy, and vision.

5. Pay attention to how many times you put ideas out to the group you work with. Support other people by asking them to expand on their ideas and get more in-depth.

6. Think about whose work and what contributions to the group get recognized.

7. Practice recognizing more people for the work they do and try to do it more often. Offer support to other men and actively challenge competitive dynamics that men are socialized to act out with each other.

8. Be aware of how often you ask people to do something as opposed to asking other people what needs to be done. Logistics, child care, making phone calls, cooking, providing emotional support, and following up with people are often undervalued responsibilities performed by those we hold in low esteem.

9. Struggle and work with the model of group leadership that says the responsibility of leaders is to help develop more leaders, and think about what this means to you. How do you support others and what support do you need from them?

10. This includes men providing emotional and political support to other men. How can men work to be allies to each other in the struggle to develop radical models of anti-racist, class-conscious, pro-queer, feminist manhood that challenges strict binary gender roles and categories? This is also about struggling to recognize leadership roles while also redefining leadership as actively working to build power with others rather than power over others.

11. Remember that social change is a process, and that our individual transformation and individual liberation is intimately interconnected with social transformation and social liberation.

12. This list is not limited to white guys, nor is it intended to reduce all white guys into one category. This list is intended to disrupt patterns of domination that hurt our movement and hurt each other

Finally, remember that no one is free until we are all free.

1. Robin Morgan, ed., *Sisterhood Is Powerful: An Anthology of Writing from the Women's Liberation Movement.* New York: Vintage, 1970.

BIBLIOGRAPHY

Adams, Rachel and David Savran, eds. *The Masculinity Studies Reader.* Malden, MA: Blackwell Publishing, 2002.

Aguilar, Ernesto. "Men, Feminism, Race, Movements and the Cult of Hugo Schwyzer: The F Word Interviews Ernesto Aguilar," in *People of Color Organize! Your Decolonial, Anti-Patriarchal, News Resource.* Available at: http://www.peopleofcolororganize.com/analysis/men-feminism-race-movements-hugo-schwyzer-interview/.

Alcoff, Linda and Elizabeth Potter, eds. *Feminist Epistemologies.* New York: Routledge, 1993.

Alilunas, Peter. "The (In)visible People in the Room: Men in Women's Studies," *Men and Masculinities*, vol. 14, no. 2 (2011): 210–229.

Anzaldúa, Gloria E. and Analouise Keating, eds. *This Bridge We Call Home: Radical Visions for Transformation.* New York: Routledge, 2002.

Bailey, J. Michael. *The Man Who Would Be Queen: The Science of Gender-Bending and Transsexualism.* Washington, DC: Joseph Henry Press, 2003.

Barbini, Kathy, dir. *Boys and Men Healing.* Big Voice Pictures, 2011.

Belknap, Joanne. "Rape: Too Hard to Report and Too Easy to Discredit Victims," *Violence Against Women*, vol. 15, no. 1 (2010): 1335–1344.

Bird, Sharon R. "Welcome to the Men's Club: Homosociality and the Maintenance of Hegemonic Masculinity," *Gender & Society*, vol. 10, no. 2 (April 1996): 120–132.

Boykin, Keith. "No Blacks Allowed." Available at: http://www.keithboykin.com/sexuality/interracial.html.

Breines, Winifred. *The Trouble between Us: An Uneasy History of White and Black Women in the Feminist Movement.* New York: Oxford University Press, 2006.

Brod, Harry. "They're Bi Shepherds, Not Gay Cowboys: The Misframing of *Brokeback Mountain," Journal of Men's Studies*. vol. 14, no. 2 (Spring 2006): 252–253.

Bureau of Labor Statistics. "American Time Use Survey Summary." Available at:. http://www.bls.gov/news.release/atus.nr0.htm (accessed June 22, 2012).

Butler, Judith. *Gender Trouble: Feminism and the Subversion of Identity*. New York: Routledge, 1990.

Califia, Patrick. *Speaking Sex to Power: The Politics of Queer Sex*. San Francisco, CA: Cleis Press, 2002.

Cannick, Jasmyne. "Gays First, Then Illegals." Available at: http://www.advocate.com/politics/commentary/2006/04/04/gays-first-then-illegals.

Carey, Benedict. "Straight, Gay, or Lying? Bisexuality Revisited," *New York Times*. July 5, 2005.

Chabon, Michael. *Manhood for Amateurs*. New York: HarperCollins, 2009.

Chaudhry, Lakshmi. "Growing Up to Be Boys." Available at: http://www.alternet.org/story/33801.

Collins, Patricia Hill. *Black Feminist Thought: Knowledge, Consciousness, and the Politics of Empowerment*. New York: Routledge, 2000.

Collins, Patricia Hill. "Book Review: *Separate Roads to Feminism: Black, Chicana, and White Feminist Movements in America's Second Wave*," *Acta Sociologica*, vol. 49 (2006): 231–233.

Combahee River Collective. "A Black Feminist Statement," in Carole R. McCann and Seung-Kung Kim, eds., *Feminist Theory Reader: Local and Global Perspectives*. New York: Routledge, 2003.

Connell, R.W. *Gender and Power: Society, the Person and Sexual Politics*. Stanford, CA: Stanford University Press, 1987.

Connell, R.W. "Reply," *Gender & Society*, vol. 12, no. 4 (August 1998): 474–477.

Connell, R.W. *Masculinities*. Los Angeles: University of California Press, 1995; second edition reprinted 2005.

Crenshaw, Kimberlé. "Demarginalizing the Intersection of Race and Sex: A Black Feminist Critique of Antidiscrimination Doctrine, Feminist Theory, and Antiracist Politics," in Katharine T. Bartlett and Rosanne Kennedy, eds., *Feminist Legal Theory: Readings in Law and Gender*. Boulder, CO: Westview Press, 1991.

Currah, Paisley, Richard M. Juang, and Shannon Price Minter, eds. *Transgender Rights*. Minneapolis, MN: University of Minnesota Press, 2006.

David, Deborah S. and Robert Brannon, eds. *The Forty-Nine Percent Majority: The Male Sex Role*. Reading, MA: Addison-Wesley, 1976.

de la Huerta, Christian. *Coming Out Spiritually: The Next Step*. New York: Tarcher, 1999.

Demetriou, Demetrakis Z. "Connell's Concept of Hegemonic Masculinity: A Critique," *Theory and Society*, vol. 30, no. 3 (June 2001): 337–361.

Dicker, Rory and Alison Piepmeier, eds. *Catching a Wave: Reclaiming Feminism for the 21st Century*. Boston, MA: Northeastern University Press, 2003.

Digby, Tom, ed. *Men Doing Feminism*. New York: Routledge, 1998.

Dines, Gail. *Pornland: How Porn Has Hijacked Our Sexuality*. Boston, MA: Beacon Press, 2010.

Douglas, Susan J. *Enlightened Sexism: The Seductive Message that Feminism's Work is Done*. New York: Times Books, 2010.

Drummond, Murray J.N. "Asian Gay Men's Bodies," *Journal of Men's Studies*, vol. 13, no. 3 (Spring 2005): 291–300.

Eltahawy, Mona. "The Happy Muslims Who Confuse You," *Time*. Available at: http://www.time.com/time/video/player/0,32068,19402457001_18911 23,00.html.

Enloe, Cynthia. *Bananas, Beaches and Bases: Making Feminist Sense of International Politics*. Berkeley, CA: University of California Press, 2001.

Faludi, Susan. *Stiffed: The Betrayal of the American Man*. New York: Harper Perennial, 2000.

Fine, Cordelia. *Delusions of Gender: How Our Minds, Society, and Neurosexism Create Difference*. New York: W.W. Norton, 2011.

Flood, Michael. "Men as Students and Teachers of Feminist Scholarship," *Men and Masculinities*, vol. 14, no. 2 (2011): 135–154.

Flood, Michael. "Bringing Men Into the Light? Women's Studies and the Problem of Men." Available at: http://www.xyonline.net/downloads/womens studiesandmen.pdf (2012).

Friedman, Ann. "It's Not the End of Men," *The American Prospect*, June 10, 2010.

Gardiner, Judith Kegan. *Masculinity Studies and Feminist Theory*. New York: Columbia University Press, 2002.

Gellene, Denise. "Men Found to be Anorexic, Bulimic Also," *Los Angeles Times*, February 1, 2007.

Giddings, Paula. *When and Where I Enter*. New York: Bantam, 1984.

Goldwag, Arthur. "Leader's Suicide Brings Attention to Men's Rights Movement," Southern Poverty Law Center, *Intelligence Report*, Issue 145 (Spring 2012).

Grant, Judith. *Fundamental Feminism: Contesting the Core Concepts of Feminist Theory*. New York: Routledge, 1993.

Griffin, Rachel Alicia and Joshua Daniel Phillips. "Eminem's *Love the Way You Lie* and the Normalization of Men's Violence Against Women," Rebecca Ann Lind, ed. *Race/Gender/Class/Media 3.0: Considering Diversity Across Content, Audiences, and Production*. San Francisco, CA: Pearson, 2013.

Griffin, S.A. *Unborn Again*. Los Angeles, CA: Phony Lid Books, 2001.

Guttmacher Institute. "States Enact Record Number of Abortion Restrictions in 2011," January 5, 2012. Available at: http://guttmacherinstitute.com/media/inthenews/2012/01/05/endofyear.html.

Hallett, Stephanie. "Do Women Lie About Rape?" *Ms. Magazine Blog*, April

7, 2011. Available at: http://msmagazine.com/blog/blog/2011/04/07/do-women-lie-about-rape/.

Harding, Sandra, ed. *Feminism and Methodology*. Bloomington, IN: Indiana University Press, 1987.

Harding, Sandra. *Whose Science? Whose Knowledge?: Thinking From Women's Lives*. Ithaca, NY: Cornell University Press, 1991.

Hernández, Daisy and Bushra Rehman, eds. *Colonize This! Young Women of Color on Today's Feminism*. Emeryville, CA: Seal Press, 2002.

hooks, bell. *Ain't I a Woman?: Black Women and Feminism*. Boston, MA: South End Press, 1981.

hooks, bell. *Killing Rage: Ending Racism*. New York: Owl Books, 1996.

hooks, bell. *Feminist Theory: From Margin to Center*. Cambridge, MA: South End Press, 2000a.

hooks, bell. *Where We Stand: Class Matters*. New York: Routledge, 2000b.

hooks, bell. *All About Love: New Visions*. New York: Harper Paperbacks, 2001.

hooks, bell. *The Will to Change: Men, Masculinity, and Love*. New York: Atria Books, 2004.

hooks, bell. *Sisters of the Yam: Black Women and Self-Recovery*. Cambridge, MA: South End Press, 2005.

Hunter, Andrea G. and Sherrill L. Sellers. "Feminist Attitudes among African American Women and Men," *Gender & Society*, vol. 12, no. 1 (February 1998): 81–99.

Jensen, Robert. "A Call for an Open Discussion of Mass-Marketed Pornography." Available at: http://alternet.org/mediaculture/47677.

Jhally, Sut, dir. *bell hooks: Cultural Criticism and Transformation*. Northampton, MA: Media Education Foundation, 1997.

Jhally, Sut, dir. *Dreamworlds 3 (Abridged): Desire, Sex & Power in Music Video*. Northampton, MA: Media Education Foundation, 2007.

Johnson, Merri Lisa, ed. *Jane Sexes It Up: True Confessions of Feminist Desire*. New York: Four Walls Eight Windows, 2002.

Jones, Adam, ed. *Men of the Global South*. London: Zed Books, 2006.

Jones, Daniel, ed. *Bastard on the Couch: 27 Men Try Really Hard to Explain Their Feelings About Love, Loss, Fatherhood, and Freedom*. New York: Harper Paperbacks, 2005.

Kimmel, Michael S. *The History of Men: Essays on the History of American and British Masculinities*. Albany, NY: State University of New York, 2005.

Kimmel, Michael. *Guyland: The Perilous World Where Boys Become Men*. New York: Harper, 2008.

Kimmel, Michael. "Has a Man's World Become a Woman's Nation?" *The Shriver Report*, 2009.

Kimmel, Michael S. *Manhood in America: A Cultural History*. New York: Oxford University Press, third edition, 2011; originally published 2005.

Kimmel, Michael, Michael Kaufman, and Harry Brod. "Men for Women's

Choice," *Women's Media Center Features*. March 12, 2012. Available at: http://www.womensmediacenter.com/feature/entry/men-for-womens-choice.

Kimmel, Michael S. and Michael A. Messner, eds. *Men's Lives* seventh edition. San Francisco, CA: Pearson, 2007; ninth edition reprinted 2012.

Kimmel, Michael S. and Thomas E. Mosmiller, eds. *Against the Tide: Pro-Feminist Men in the United States, 1776–1990*. Boston, MA: Beacon Press, 1992.

Kitlinksi, Tomek and Pawel Leszkowicz. *Love and Democracy: Reflections on the Homosexual Question in Poland*. Krakow: Aureus, 2005.

Klein, Jessie. "Gender Is the Key to the Bullying Culture," *Women's Media Center*, March 27, 2012. Available at: http://www.womensmediacenter.com/feature/entry/gender-is-key-to-the-bullying-culture.

Knight, Michael Muhammed. *The Taqwacores*. Berkeley, CA: Soft Skull Press, 2009.

Kraemer, Kelly Rae. "Solidarity in Action: Exploring the Work of Allies in Social Movements," *Peace & Change*, vol. 32, no. 1 (January 2007): 20–38.

Labaton, Vivien and Dawn Lundy Martin. *The Fire This Time: Young Activists and the New Feminism*. New York: Random House, 2004.

Landreau John C. and Michael J. Murphy. "Introduction to the Special Issue–Masculinities in Women's Studies: Locations and Dislocations," *Men and Masculinities*, vol. 14, no. 2 (2011): 132–134.

Lonsway, Kimberly A., Joanne Arcambault, and David Lisak. "False Reports: Moving Beyond the Issue to Successfully Investigate and Prosecute Non-Stranger Sexual Assault," *The Voice*, vol. 3, no. 1 (2009): pp. 1–11.

MacKinnon, Catharine A. "Not a Moral Issue," *Yale Law & Policy Review*, 2 (1984): 321–345.

Mann, Bonnie. "How America Justifies Its War: A Modern/Postmodern Aesthetics of Masculinity and Sovereignty," *Hypatia*, vol. 21, no. 4 (Fall 2006): 147–163.

McCann, Carole R. and Seung-Kyung Kim, eds. *Feminist Theory Reader: Local and Global Perspectives*. New York: Routledge, 2003; second edition republished 2010.

McCaughey, Martha. *The Caveman Mystique: Pop-Darwinism and the Debates Over Sex, Violence, and Science*. New York: Routledge, 2007.

Milne, Carly, ed. *Naked Ambition: Women Who Are Changing Pornography*. New York: Caroll and Graf, 2005.

Miller-Young, Mireille. "Hardcore Desire," *ColorLines* (Winter 2005–2006): 31–35.

Mirandé, Alredo. *Hombres y Machos: Masculinity and Latino Culture*. Boulder, CO: Westview Press, 1997.

Moniz, Tomas, ed. *Rad Dad: Dispatches from the Frontiers of Fatherhood*. Portland, OR: PM Press, 2011.

Moraga, Cherríe L. and Gloria E. Anzaldúa, eds. *This Bridge Called My Back:*

Writings by Radical Women of Color. Berkeley, CA: Third Woman Press, 2002.

Morgan, Robin, ed. *Sisterhood Is Powerful: An Anthology of Writing from the Women's Liberation Movement*. New York: Vintage, 1970.

Morgan, Robin, ed. *Sisterhood Is Forever: The Women's Anthology for a New Millennium*. New York: Washington Square Press, 2003.

Muscio, Inga. *Rose: Love in Violent Times*. New York: Seven Stories Press, 2010.

Nagle, Jill, ed. *Whores and Other Feminists*. New York: Routledge, 1997.

Ouzgane, Lahoucine, ed. *Islamic Masculinities*. London: Zed Books, 2006.

Pascoe, C.J. *Dude, You're a Fag: Masculinity and Sexuality in High School*. Los Angeles, CA: University of California Press, 2011.

People for the American Way. "The GOP Takes Its War on Women to the States." Available at: http://www.pfaw.org/media-center/publications/gop-takes-its-war-women-states.

Phillips, Jim. "Abuse Survivors Tell of Long Road Back from Shame," *The Athens News*.

Potok, Mark and Evelyn Schlatter. "Men's Rights Movement Spreads False Claims about Women," Southern Poverty Law Center, *Intelligence Report*, Issue 145 (Spring 2012).

Pringle, Richard. "Sport, Strong Women, and Feminist Epiphanies," in Shira Tarrant, ed., *Men Speak Out: Views on Gender, Sex, and Power*, first edition. New York: Routledge, 2008, p. 245.

Quinn, Beth A. "Sexual Harassment and Masculinity: The Power and Meaning of 'Girl Watching,'" *Gender & Society*. vol. 16, no. 3 (June 2002): 386–402.

Rieger, Gerulf, Meredith L. Chivers, and J. Michael Bailey. "Sexual Arousal Patterns of Bisexual Men," *Psychological Science*, vol. 16, no. 8 (2005): 579–584.

Roscoe, Will. *Queer Spirits: A Gay Men's Myth Book*. Boston, MA: Beacon Press, 1995.

Rosin, Hanna. "The End of Men," *The Atlantic*, July/August 2010.

Rosin, Hanna. *The End of Men: And the Rise of Women*. New York: Riverhead, 2012.

Sadler, Anne G., Brenda M. Booth, Brian L. Cook, and Bradley N. Doebbeling. "Factors Associated with Women's Risk of Rape in the Military Environment," *American Journal of Industrial Medicine*, vol. 43, issue 3 (March 2003): 262–273.

Said, Edward W. *Orientalism*. New York: Vintage, 1979.

Seidler, Victor J., ed. *Young Men & Masculinities*. London: Zed Books, 2006.

Shor, Francis. "Hypermasculine Warfare: From 9/11 to the War on Iraq." Available at: http://bad.eserver.org/reviews/2005/shor.html.

Snitow, Ann, Christine Stansell, and Sharon Thompson, eds. *Powers of Desire: The Politics of Sexuality*. New York: Monthly Review Press, 1983.

Snodgrass, Jon. *For Men Against Sexism: A Book of Readings.* Albion, CA: Times Change Press, 1977.

South End Press Collective. *Talking About a Revolution: Interviews with Michael Albert, Noam Chomsky, Barbara Ehrenreich, bell hooks, Peter Kwong, Winona LaDuke, Manning Marable, Urvashi Vaid, and Howard Zinn.* Cambridge, MA: South End Press, 1998.

Spieler, Jennifer Zahn. "Soldier's Harassment Claim Leads to Court Martial," December 3, 2006. Available at: http://www.womensenews.org/article.cfm/dyn/aid/2980/context/cover.

Spurlock, Morgan, dir. *Mansome.* Paladin: 2012.

Staples, Robert. *Black Masculinity: The Black Male's Role in American Society.* San Francisco, CA: Black Scholar Press, 1982.

Stein, Joel. *Man Made.* New York: Grand Central Publishing, 2012.

Strauss, Elissa. "Do Men Belong in the Women's Movement?" *AlterNet*, February 13, 2012. http://www.alternet.org/media/153984/do_men_belong_in_the_women%27s_movement?page=entire#AlterNet.

Strossen, Nadine. *Defending Pornography: Free Speech, Sex, and the Fight for Women's Rights.* New York: New York University Press, 2000.

Sullivan, Oriel. "Changing Gender Practices Within the Household: A Theoretical Perspective," *Gender & Society*, vol. 18, no. 2 (April 2004): 207–222.

Taormino, Tristan, Constance Penley, Celine Parrenas Shimizu and Mireille Miller-Young, eds. *The Feminist Porn Book: The Politics of Producing Pleasure.* New York: The Feminist Press, 2013.

Tarrant, Shira. "Who's Accountable for the Abuse at Abu Ghraib?" *off our backs*, vol. 34, Issue 9/10 (Sept.–Oct. 2004): 15–16.

Tarrant, Shira. *When Sex Became Gender.* New York: Routledge, 2006.

Tarrant, Shira. "Stepping Out of Bounds: Feminist Men and Political Organizing," paper presented at the Western Political Science Association Annual Conference, Las Vegas, Nevada, March 9, 2007.

Tarrant, Shira. *Men and Feminism.* Berkeley, CA: Seal Press, 2009a

Tarrant, Shira. "Guy Trouble: Are Young Men Really in Crisis, or Are These Boys Done Just Being Boys?" *Bitch Magazine: Feminist Response to Popular Culture*. Issue 43 (Spring 2009b).

Tarrant, Shira. "Pornography 101: Why College Kids Need Porn Literacy Training," *AlterNet*, September 15, 2010. Available at: http://www.alternet.org/media/148129/pornography_101%3A_why_college_kids_need_porn_literacy_training?page=entire.

Tarrant, Shira. "It's a Dress, Not a Yes," in *Issues That Concern You: Date Rape*, ed. Norah Piehl. Almondsbury, Bristol, UK: Gale/Cengage, 2012.

Taylor, Verta. "Review. *The Trouble between Us*," *Gender & Society*, vol. 21, no. 1 (February 2007): 136–138.

Tea, Michelle, ed. *Without a Net: The Female Experience of Growing Up Working Class.* Emeryville, CA: Seal Press, 2003.

Tong, Rosemarie Putnam. *Feminist Thought: A More Comprehensive Introduction*, third edition. Boulder, CO: Westview Press, 2008.

Valenti, Jessica. "The Daddy Wars," *The Nation*, June 27, 2012.

Valerio, Max Wolf. *The Testosterone Files: My Hormonal and Social Transformation from Female to Male*. Emeryville, CA: Seal Press, 2006.

Vance, Carole S. *Pleasure and Danger: Exploring Female Sexuality*. London: Pandora Press, 1989.

Verloo, Mieke. "Multiple Inequalities, Intersectionality and the European Union," *European Journal of Women's Studies*, vol. 13, no. 3 (2006): 211–228.

Walker, Alexis J. and Lori A. McGraw. "Who Is Responsible for Responsible Fathering?" *Journal of Marriage and the Family*, vol. 62 (May 2000): 563–569.

Walker, Rebecca, ed. *What Makes a Man: 22 Writers Imagine the Future*. New York: Riverhead Books, 2005.

Weiss, Karen G. "Male Sexual Victimization: Examining Men's Experiences of Rape and Sexual Assault," *Men and Masculinities*, vol. 12, no. 3 (April 2010): 275–298.

Weitzer, Ronald, ed. *Sex for Sale: Prostitution, Pornography, and the Sex Industry*, second edition. New York: Routledge, 2010.

Williams, Joan C. "One Sick Child Away from Being Fired: When 'Opting Out' Is Not an Option." Available at: http://www.uchastings.edu/site_files/WLL/OneSickChildovervu.pdf.

Young, Iris Marion. *Justice and the Politics of Difference*. Princeton, NJ: Princeton University Press, 1990.

Young, Josephine Peyton. "Review. *Masculinities, Gender Relations, and Sport*," *Gender and Society*, vol. 15, no. 5 (Oct. 2001): 778–779.

INDEX

abortion 103, 291; and Men for
    Women's Choice 274, 277–9
activism: anti-rape 153–5; anti-sexist
    24–5, 26, 124, 125, 305–14; anti-war
    263–70, 307; black 39, 40, 235; gay
    273, 297–8; Muslim 54; social justice
    156–63, 224, 228, 249, 251, 297–8;
    and social media 2
Adams, Rachel 15
advertising 47–52, 90, 210
Ae Fond Kiss 56
Against the Tide 253
Aguilar, Ernesto 224
Ain't I a Woman 161
alcohol: at college parties 301, 304;
    dependence 200; and domestic
    violence 59; and sport 44, 45–6
All About Love 124, 127
All African People Revolutionary Party
    (AAPRP) 235–6
All-Polish Youth 102, 103, 104
American Journal of Industrial Medicine
    169
anarchist perspective 305–14
arousal study in men 88–9
Australia 90, 213–20
Aztec society 58, 62–3

babysitters, male 209
Bailey, J. Michael 88, 89
basketball 43–6, 288–9, 304
Bem Sex Role Inventory (BSRI) 65

biology vs. socialization 12, 30, 90–1,
    205, 211
bisexuality/biphobia 70–1, 87–93
black activism 39, 40, 235
black masculinity: in gay community 97;
    in hip-hop culture 21–7; and
    meanings of manhood 39–42
black men: domestic labor 168; gay 96,
    97, 98; murdered in post-Katrina
    chaos 176; negative stereotypes of
    24–5; perspectives on feminism
    39–42, 234–8
black women: childbirth organization
    237; and feminist movement 29, 41,
    225–6, 229, 236, 237; objectification
    of 23–4, 26, 42; pornography and
    69–70
blogs, feminist 281, 283–6
Borat 300
Boykin, Keith 96, 98
bro behavior 299–304
bullying 2, 34, 35, 116, 144

Cannick, Jasmyne 98, 100
cars 22–3
changing tables in men's rooms 298
Chapin, Harry 207, 210
Chicano/Latino masculinity and
    machismo 62–5
child abuse 117, 118, 128–34, 155, 216
childcare 167–8, 204, 205
Chivers, Meredith L. 88, 89

Christian perspectives 34, 35, 99, 236, 296–7
clothes: anti-war activists 265, 269; gay men's 246; hip-hop 22, 24, 25; *jihab* 189–90; lesbian 29; Muslim men's 55, 57; skinhead 288–9, 291; tomboy 29; women's 91, 189–90, 241–2, 302
Cohen, Sasha Baron 300
Cohen, William 181, 184
college: anti-war activists at 263–70, 307; basketball 43–6; becoming a male feminist at 252–62; bro behavior at 301–4; a gay man's experience of 245–7; men's activism to stop violence against women 153–5; men's groups against sexual violence 259–60, 289–90; sexual assaults and rape at 300, 301–4; sexual harassment of women students 256–7; women's studies 171, 193–6, 232–3, 274, 280–1, 293
college counselor 259–60
college professors 193–4, 196, 280–1
Collins, Judy 267–8
Collins, Patricia Hill 225
Combahee River Collective 31, 229n
Common Ground Collective 177–8
compassion 161, 162–3
Conflict Tactics Scale (CTS) 216
Connell, Raewyn, W. xxiv, 12, 13, 65–6
contraception 277, 278
cultural influences on sexual behavior 90–1

The Daddy Shift 168
Darkness to Light 117
dating 36, 46, 81, 106–11, 189, 259–60; gay 97, 98; lesbian 29
Delusions of Gender 12
Demetriou, Demetrakis Z. 13–14
domestic violence: and alcohol 59; fathers' rights movement and 216–18, 219; gender inequality in 216–17; prison program for 135–47
Doucet, Andrea 205
Duldung, feminist band 105

education: see college; high school
Eminem 11, 71, 107
emotional suppression 13, 65, 124, 125–6, 259, 268

Faludi, Susan 12
families: African-American 235, 236–7; evolving understanding of 205, 211; Mexican 58–62, 64; privileges of male children 235, 244; in rural South 295–7; transgender 31; women role models 182
family law in Australia 215–16
fathers: central to sons' formative experiences 197; contemporary politics of fatherhood 219; family support work with 237; murdered 39, 41–2; a progressive role model 197–202; sexual abuse by 128–34, 155; stay-at-home 168, 203–6, 207–12; supporting separated and divorced 218; violent 155, 290
fathers' rights movement 213–20
feminism: 1970s movement 208–9; and anti-war activism 265–9; black male perspective on 39–42, 234–8; black women and 29, 41, 225–6, 229, 236, 237; blogs 281, 283–6; defining 182, 232, 234, 273–4; gay man of color's perspective on 243–51; gay rights movement and 104; in Indonesia 191–2; male perspectives on 79, 199–200, 224, 225, 232–3, 239–42, 252–62, 263–70; men, benefits of including 224, 225, 226, 228; men, reasons to be cautious about including 224–5, 226–7, 274; men's activism and knowledge production 273–4; Muslim 57, 191–2; online community 280–7; pseudo 210; and racism 16, 41, 229; skinhead to male feminist transformation 288–94; terminology 223–4, 253; views on pornography 69–70, 77, 78, 85; women's studies 171, 193–6, 232–3, 274, 280–1, 293
Feminism without Women 226
feminist analysis 78
feminist masculinity 37
Feminist Porn Awards 85
Feministe! 283, 284
feminization process, male survivors of sexual assault 126
Fine, Cordelia 12
Fiorenza, Elisabeth Schüssler 14
The Fire This Time 226
Food Not Bombs (FNB) 311–12

Free Society 309

gay activism 273, 297–8
gay bars 95–6, 97
gay community: homophobia towards 102–5, 246–7; masculinity in 97, 100–1, 246; misogyny in 249; racism in 94–101, 246, 249, 250; sexism in 249
gay men: acting macho 245–6, 249; black 96, 97, 98; of color 94–101, 243–51; coming out 245, 246; in rural South 297
gay pornography 82, 83–4, 88–9
Gay Pride Parade, Warsaw 104
gay rights 100, 104, 132
gender: 1970s shift in roles 199, 208–9; of androgynous 34–8; binary view of 35; construction volunteers and disruption of traditional roles 176–9; social construction of 12, 30; stereotypes 144–5, 247–8; third 36
gender equality: an African-American man committed to 234–8; bro culture and resistance to 302–3; disconnect between discourse and reality 188–92; hampered by fathers' rights groups 219; learning from a progressive father 197–202; new generations of men mobilizing in support of 253–4
gender harassment 178
gender neutral parenting 168, 199, 203–6, 207–12
genderqueer 34–8
Generation M 299
"girlie-man effect" 91–2
glass ceiling 248
grooming products, marketing of male 47–52

Harding, Sandra xxii
Hassam, Khalil 100
headscarves (*jihab*) 189–90
healthy manhood 117–18, 234–5
Healthy Masculinity Action Project (HMAP) 117–18
Hendricks, Imam Muhsin 54–5
high school: anarchist activism in 307; avenging a sexual assault in 148–52; basketball in 43–4; bullying in 34, 35, 144; One in Four chapters in 155;

opposing prejudice in 100; a route to college 254–5; sexism in Indian 244–5; shootings 116; textbooks 103
hip-hop culture 21–7
HIV tests 83
homophobia 83, 102–5, 132, 246–7; in Church 99, 297; in communities of color 94–5, 98–9; and misogyny 103, 104, 105; in Muslim community 100; roots in sexism 247
hooks, bell 14, 37, 40, 41, 124, 127, 161, 171, 179, 202, 310
housework 167, 168, 199, 204, 209, 210
"How to Help a Sexual Assault Survivor" 154
hunting 296
Hurricane Katrina 175–80

incest 128–34, 155
India 244–5, 247
Indonesia 188–92
The Inner Circle 54
Iraq, sexual harassment in 181–7
Irving, John 209

Jewish perspective 104
jihab 189–90
johns 74–9
jokes 30, 40, 154, 183, 283
Joplin, Janis 266, 267

Kempton, Sally 258
Kimmel, Michael 12, 13, 47, 168, 225, 227–8, 252–62
Kinsey, Alfred 89
Klein, Fritz 89
Klein, Jessie 116
Knight, Michael Muhammad 55
knowledge production 273–4
Ku Klux Klan 275, 295
kyriarchy 14, 274

L.A. riots 307
Labaton, Vivien 226
Latino/Chicano masculinity and machismo 62–5
League of Polish Families 103, 104
Lennon, John 209
lesbians 29, 30, 31; of color 96, 98, 101; visibility in Poland 102, 103, 104
"Let Us Be Seen" campaign 102–5
Lone Fathers' Association 217

machismo 17; Chicano/Latino masculinity and 62–5; gay men acting 245–6, 249; sexism vs. 63

macho women 61–2

MacKinnon, Catharine 69

male identity, insecurities over 260–1

male privilege: acknowledging and resisting 249–51; in anti-war movement 265–6, 269; awarding in adolescence of 84–5; as a child 235, 244; 'nonconsensual' 37; recognizing 159–60; sexual assault of males interrupting myths of 126; steps to challenge 311–12; struggling with 309–11; tools to overcome 312–14

Male Role Belief System 137, 138, 139

Male Survivor 118

male victims of sexual assault/rape 116, 117–18, 123–7

The Man Who Would Be Queen 88

Manhood in America 12

ManKind program 137–9, 143

Marin Abused Women's Services (MAWS) 136–43

marriage 39–40, 189, 235

Martin, Dawn Lundy 226

masculine labor: in military 178; women volunteers working in 176–9

Masculinities 12, 66

masculinity: bell hooks on patriarchal 126, 127, 179; bi-sexuality a threat to ideas of 90, 92; black 21–7, 39–42, 97; challenging myths about 156–7; Chicano/Latino machismo and 62–5; critique of Euro-American models of 65–6; culture and 12, 13; evolving ideas of 205; feminist 37; in gay community 97, 100–1, 246; genderqueer escaping confines of 34–8; healthy 117–18, 234–5; Healthy Masculinity Action Project (HMAP) 117–18; hegemonic 12–15; and marketing of male grooming products 47–52; Men's Manifesto 2012 to redefine 144–7; multiple masculinities 3, 13; Muslim 53–7; "novice" 49–50; rejecting military 266–7, 268; rewards of male privilege for presenting 84–5; in rural South 296, 297; social construction of 12, 57; and sport 296, 297; violence as a central part of 41–2

masturbation 75

media: advertising 47–52, 90, 210; anarchist 309; anti-war activism 270; bisexual women in 90; celebration of sexism 303; military journalism 181–7; Muslim men in 54, 55–6; reinforcing of cultural biphobia 87–8, 92; support for "Let Us Be Seen" campaign in Poland 104–5

Men For Women's Choice 274, 277–9

men's groups xiii, 117–18, 119, 199–200, 252, 289–90; fathers' rights movement 213–20; feminist 124, 286; peer counseling 259–60; for sexual assault victims 125–6

Men's Manifesto 2012 144–7

men's movement 4, 145, 155, 199; and fathers' rights movement 213–20

The Men's Program 154

Men's Resource Center for Change 269

Mexico 58–66

military: and anti-war activism 266–7, 268; court martial 184; gender harassment in 178; sexual harassment and assault in 169–70, 181–7; suicide in 185; violence in Mexican 58–9

Miller, Mark Crispin 210

mindfulness meditation 162

Mirandé Sex Role Inventory (MSRI) 65

misogyny 24, 47, 71, 299–300; in gay community 249; and homophobia 103, 104, 105; transgender 31

Modleski, Tania 226

Moniz, Tomas 168

Monsieur Ibrahim 55–6

Morgan, Robin 309

Mormons 185

mothers 39, 42, 59, 64, 132, 144, 149, 209, 235, 295

Muscio, Inga 115

music: Duldung feminist band 105; Eminem 11, 71, 107; folk 108; Harry Chapin 207, 210; hip-hop 21–7; Janis Joplin 267; Judy Collins 267–8

Muslims 17, 53–7, 100, 188–92

National Organization for Men Against Sexism (NOMAS) xiii, 119, 252

National Organization of Men's Outreach for Rape Education (NO MORE) 153–5

New Orleans 175–80

New York Times 87
Nieves, Nestor "Tito" 144
"No Blacks Allowed" 96
non-governmental organization (NGO),
 Indonesia 191

objectification, consensual sexual 82–3
objectification of women 70, 72, 182–4,
 185–6, 240–1, 301; black women
 23–4, 26, 42; in jock culture 44, 45
One in Four program 153–5
online feminist communities 280–7;
 FAQs for men 282–3; for feminist
 men 286
online groups for prevention of violence
 286
Ono, Yoko 210

Panetta, Leon 187
parenting, gender neutral 168, 199,
 203–6, 207–12
patriarchal system 13–14, 31, 32, 37,
 124, 309–12; bell hooks on
 patriarchal masculinity 126, 127, 179;
 challenges of 311–12; and
 collaboration with capitalism 77;
 maintenance of 197, 304; oppression
 of 37–8, 40, 157
Peterson, Alyssa 185
Peyton Young, Josephine 3
pimps 75
Poland 102–5
political-personal relationships 256, 268,
 269–70
pornography 74–9, 158; feminist views
 on 69–70, 77, 78, 85; gay 82, 83–4,
 88–9; industry 76, 158; queer 80–6;
 study of men's arousal to 88–9; for
 women 83
prisoners: domestic abuse program
 135–47; in Hurricane Katrina 176
pseudo-feminism 210

queer: genderqueer 34–8; pornography
 80–6; sexism 249; theory 15
Queer People of Color Liberation
 Project 100

racism: Bible used to justify 99; and
 feminism 16, 41, 229; in gay
 community 94–101, 246, 249, 250;
 and sexism 16, 40, 41, 42, 75

racist skinhead transformation to a
 feminist 288–94
Rad Dad 168
rape/sexual assault: avenging a teenage
 girl's 148–52; childhood mythology
 of 123–4; on college campuses 300,
 301–4; false accusations of 116–17; a
 father's abuse of his son 128–34; FBI
 definition of 115–16; male responses
 to 124, 151–2; male victims of 116,
 117–18, 123–7; men's activism
 against 153–5; in military 169–70,
 187; myths and misinformation on
 116–17, 157; statistics 117, 127;
 women perpetrators of 117, 125
relationships: Affirmative Action for
 236–7; heterosexual romantic
 106–11; impact of incest on
 forming healthy 129, 131; marriage
 39–40, 189, 235; political-personal
 256, 268, 269–70; transforming male
 259–62; transforming male–female
 255–62
religious perspectives: Christian 34, 35,
 99, 236, 296–7; Jewish 104; Mormon
 185; Muslim 17, 53–7, 100, 188–92
reproductive rights 277–9, 291
Rieger, Gerulf 88, 89
Rose: Love in Violent Times 115

Sabah 56
Savran, David 15
school: *see* high school
school shootings 116
self-care strategies 162–3
sex change 30–2
sexism: in 1960s progressive
 organizations 269; in advertising
 47–8, 50–2, 210; anarchists and
 305–14; bro behavior and 299–304;
 in Church 236, 296–7; gay
 community and 249; vs. machismo
 63; media celebration of 303; and
 racism 16, 40, 41, 42, 75; resisting
 39–42; roots of homophobia in 247;
 in rural South 296; in schools 244–5;
 in times of shifting power between
 the sexes 50; towards female post-
 Katrina volunteers 178–9; in US
 military 186; women in war against
 258; in workplace 240–2, 248
sexual assault: *see* rape/sexual assault

sexual harassment xxiii, 178; of college students 256–7; in military 169–70, 181–7
Shakesville 282–3
The Shriver Report 168
Sinclair, Hamish 143
Sisters of the Yam 40
skinhead to feminist transformation 288–94
Sniffen, Chad 116–17
social justice activism 156–63, 224, 228, 249, 251, 297–8; anarchism and sexism 305–14
social media 2, 278
social movements 198–9
social workers 182, 237
socialization: biology vs. 12, 30, 90–1, 205, 211; challenging 42, 126, 127, 156–7, 199, 202
sport: alcohol and 44, 45–6; basketball 43–6, 288–9, 304; jock culture of 44, 45, 46, 304; and masculinity 296, 297
Staples, Robert 66
stay-at-home dads 168, 203–6, 207–12; 1970s 209–10
stereotypes: gender 144–5, 247–8; macho 17, 62–5; of Muslim men 17, 53, 54, 55; negative black male 24–5; racist 98
superheroes 65
Swift, Suzanne 184

Talking About a Revolution 202
The Taqwacores 55
The Testosterone Files 28
Thich Nhat Hahn 162
torture 185
traditional/hegemonic masculinity 12–15
transgender identity 28–33

United Anarchist Front (UAF) 307–8, 311
United Nations Convention on the Elimination of All Forms of Discrimination Against Women (CEDAW) 191

Valerio, Max Wolf 28

violence: as a central part of masculinity 41–2; fathers' 155, 290; a learned behavior 138–9, 142–3; male-on-male 116, 117, 118, 150–1, 217, 290, 296; military 58–9; murder 39, 41–2; online groups for prevention of 286; towards "Let Us Be Seen" photo exhibition 102, 103; women as perpetrators of 61–2, 117, 217; youth 144, 288–90
violence against women 109, 110, 142–3, 145; domestic *see* domestic violence; men working to end 156–63; Men's Manifesto 2012 to end 144–7; One in Four program 153–5; women's protection strategies 158, 195
virgin–whore complex 189
volunteering post-Katrina 175–80

Walker-Hoover, Carl Joseph 144
White Ribbon Campaign 118, 145, 147, 159, 213, 214
women: bisexual 70, 90; domestic labor 167–8, 210; in hip-hop culture 23–4, 26; listening to and learning from 151, 158, 246, 290, 291, 305–7, 308–9, 310; macho 61–2; male myths about 157, 259; mothers 39, 42, 59, 64, 132, 144, 149, 209, 235, 295; pornography for 83; preference for heterosexual male myth 92; protecting themselves from violence 158, 195; in sex industry 76, 77–8; sexual assault of men by 117, 125; violent 61–2, 117, 217; in war against sexism 258; in workplace 205, 248; *see also* black women; families; lesbians; objectification of women
women's bodies: *see* objectification of women; pornography
women's studies 171, 193–6, 232–3, 274, 280–1, 293
working class culture 64, 65, 198, 295
The World According to Garp 209

Young, Josephine Peyton 3
youth violence 144, 288–90

THE SOCIAL ISSUES
COLLECTION™

Printed and bound in the United States of America by Edwards Brothers Malloy
on sustainably sourced paper.